365
Ways to Make a Difference:
Daily Bible Readings
with

365
Ways to Make a Difference:
Daily Bible Readings
with

CANTERBURY
PRESS
Norwich

First published in 2005 by the Canterbury Press Norwich
(a publishing imprint of Hymns Ancient & Modern Limited,
a registered charity)
9–17 St Albans Place, London N1 0NX

www.scm-canterburypress.co.uk

British Library Cataloguing in Publication data

A catalogue record for this book is available
from the British Library

ISBN 1-85311-596-7/9781-85311-596-7

Typeset by Regent Typesetting, London
Printed and bound in Great Britain by
William Clowes Ltd, Beccles, Suffolk

Contents

Introduction

As the official relief and development agency for 39 Christian denominations in the UK and Ireland, Christian Aid cherishes the gospel teaching that underpins its work. This collection of daily Bible readings and reflections was originally published day by day on Christian Aid's website www.surefish.co.uk. Now these pieces have been reworked and updated to form a complete year's programme of readings.

The biblical extracts have been chosen because of their particular relevance to Christian Aid's mission to stand alongside some of the world's poorest people and for their significance on issues of social justice that are close to the hearts of those who work with us, both at home and overseas. Many of the stories and prayers come from local grassroots communities in countries where our partner organizations are working.

Each reflection contains a short extract from the Bible, some thoughts about what this might mean for the world today, a suggested action in response to the passage, and a prayer. They are indicated by the following symbols:

 Something to read from the Bible

 Something to think about

 Something practical to do

 Something to pray

The scheme can be started at any time, not just on 1 January.

The Bible quotations are from the New Revised Standard Version of the Bible, a translation that has been widely acclaimed for its scholarship, accuracy and readability. With Oxford University Press, Christian Aid has published its own edition of the NRSV, which includes an outline of the organization's work, a list of key biblical passages on different aspects of social justice, and prayers and other worship material reflecting some of that biblical teaching.

It is our hope that 365 will, like our other publications, help us to understand better that 'the Lord maintains the cause of the needy and executes justice for the poor' (Psalm 140.12).

Daleep Mukarji
Director, Christian Aid

January 1 Jesus at Nazareth

When [Jesus] came to Nazareth, where he had been brought up, he went to the synagogue on the sabbath day, as was his custom. He stood up to read, and the scroll of the prophet Isaiah was given to him. He unrolled the scroll and found the place where it was written:

'*The Spirit of the Lord is upon me, because he has anointed me to bring good news to the poor. He has sent me to proclaim release to the captives and recovery of sight to the blind, to let the oppressed go free, to proclaim the year of the Lord's favour.*'

And he rolled up the scroll, gave it back to the attendant, and sat down. The eyes of all in the synagogue were fixed on him. Then he began to say to them, 'Today this scripture has been fulfilled in your hearing.'

Luke 4.16–21

Yet another dutiful reading from the Bible. Yet another predictable visit to church. Yet another soothing prayer. Been there; done that!

Might the congregation at this service in Nazareth have thought this as they made their way to the synagogue? This sabbath day turned out to be completely different. In a brief sermon Jesus presented them with two audacious claims. First, that the promises of centuries-old scripture had found fulfilment in him. Second, that the moment of salvation for which people had longed was now! No longer was this a dutiful, predictable, soothing religious habit; it was a living encounter with God.

'This was the manifesto of Jesus Christ. It holds out hope to the hopeless.' So says Rajendra Sail, director of the Raipur Churches Development and Relief Committee, one of the partner organizations with which Christian Aid works in India. It offers evening schools to young children who have to work because their families are so poor, and campaigns for an end to child labour.

Christian Aid has compiled this book to offer a refreshing approach to the Bible – an active encounter with God instead of a duty. So, if you feel ready to spend a year reading the Bible with the world's poorest communities in mind, organize yourself now! Make a New Year resolution about how and when you will read the Bible each day, and get ready to be surprised.

Your word to guide me; your cross to save me; your life to heal me. Jesus come!

A prayer from Madhya Pradesh, India

January 2   Jesus under attack

All spoke well of [Jesus] and were amazed at the gracious words that came from his mouth . . . He said, 'Truly I tell you, no prophet is accepted in the prophet's home town. But the truth is, there were many widows in Israel in the time of Elijah, when the heaven was shut up three years and six months, and there was a severe famine over all the land; yet Elijah was sent to none of them except to a widow at Zarephath in Sidon. There were also many lepers in Israel in the time of the prophet Elisha, and none of them was cleansed except Naaman the Syrian.' When they heard this, all in the synagogue were filled with rage. They got up, drove him out of the town, and led him to the brow of the hill on which their town was built, so that they might hurl him off the cliff. But he passed through the midst of them and went on his way.

Luke 4.22–30

Whatever happened to turn an exciting church service into an attempted murder? Something horribly familiar in today's world – a refusal to accept that God is at work in ways that are bigger than we realize.

Jesus had told the Jews of his home town what they wanted to know: that God favoured them. But then he told them things they did not want to know: that God favoured others as well – Gentiles such as those who lived in Sidon and Syria. And he could prove it from the stories of their heroes, Elijah and Elisha, who were the means by which God's salvation came to 'outsiders'.

Jesus was not planning to be the patron saint of religious people; he was going to be the Saviour of the world. The Jewish congregation treated this as blasphemy. It was neither the first time nor the last that people have attempted to kill someone to defend a short-sighted religious vision.

Find out something you did not know about another religion. Visit a library, have a conversation, or type the name of a religion into an internet search engine. Hold disagreements in your peripheral vision and focus instead on where the work of God is evident.

. . . make me love the Hindus, make me love the Buddhists, make me love the Muslims, make me love the Jews, make me love the Sikhs, make me love the Christians, make me love the . . .

January 3   Jesus heals

After leaving the synagogue [Jesus] entered Simon's house. Now Simon's mother-in-law was suffering from a high fever, and they asked him about her. Then he stood over her and rebuked the fever, and it left her. Immediately she got up and began to serve them.

As the sun was setting, all those who had any who were sick with various kinds of diseases brought them to him; and he laid his hands on each of them and cured them. Demons also came out of many, shouting, 'You are the Son of God!' But he rebuked them and would not allow them to speak, because they knew that he was the Messiah.

At daybreak he departed and went into a deserted place. And the crowds were looking for him; and when they reached him, they wanted to prevent him from leaving them. But he said to them, 'I must proclaim the good news of the kingdom of God to the other cities also.'

Luke 4.38–43

Luke's account of Jesus' life reminds me of magazines that feature 'A day in the life' of someone notable to give an insight into their priorities. Jesus makes clear what the motivation of his life is: to 'proclaim the good news of the kingdom of God'. The rest of his crowded day shows how we will recognize the work of the kingdom being achieved – in health for those who are sick; in peace for those who are distressed; in strength for those who are in need.

However, there is a deep spirituality revealed in these verses too. While others hustle Jesus for activity, he seeks out quiet places in which to pray. But Simon's mother-in-law grasps something important – realizing the blessing she has received at Jesus' hands, her inclination is to pass it on by serving others.

'A day in the life of Christian Aid' would also feature serving others for the sake of God's kingdom, and it would certainly include working for health, peace and strong communities. If you have access to the internet, find out how this is achieved at www.christianaid.org.uk/aboutca/who/who.htm

Lord of endless time, I bring to you this one day in my life. May it be one of service, may it be one of prayer, and may it be one of good news. At its end, may this world be better because I have been in it, and because you have been in me. Amen.

January 4   Blessings

[Jesus] looked up at his disciples and said: 'Blessed are you who are poor, for yours is the kingdom of God. Blessed are you who are hungry now, for you will be filled. Blessed are you who weep now, for you will laugh. Blessed are you when people hate you, and when they exclude you, revile you, and defame you on account of the Son of Man. Rejoice on that day and leap for joy, for surely your reward is great in heaven; for that is what their ancestors did to the prophets.'

Luke 6.20–23

There is nothing wonderful about poverty, nor hunger, nor mourning, nor persecution. Absolutely nothing! Jesus' original hearers knew this only too well. I wonder how they reacted to his words. They would have been startled, obviously (and it is a shame that we have become so familiar with Jesus' sayings that they have lost their unsettling power). But after their shock, did the crowds dismiss Jesus' words as romantic rhetoric? Apparently not! They believed them, and they found hope in them.

There were two things about the kingdom of God that Jesus' followers grasped. First, that we have a spiritual standing which is not related to our physical conditions and which can transcend them. And second, that we have an eternal destiny which will exceed our present circumstances in every way.

I am embarrassed to write these things because throughout my life I have never experienced a single day during which I have not been readily able to eat a meal. They come with more integrity from the theologian Arnaldo Zeneto, writing from the context of one of poor communities of Nicaragua: 'To struggle, laugh and smile in the midst of aggression; to be cheerful, to hope, to love and not to be intimidated. This is the grace of God.'

Go without something non-essential today – a snack, a television programme, a visit to the pub, a newspaper. And as you notice its absence, think about what it would feel like to go without something essential.

Lord Jesus, let me be honest! I want your blessing, but I don't want to be poor. I want to be filled by you, but I don't want to go hungry. I want to rejoice to know you, but I don't want to be hated for it. Take me as I am, I pray, and make of me what you want me to be. Amen.

January 5   Turn the other cheek

[Jesus continued:] 'Love your enemies, do good to those who hate you, bless those who curse you, pray for those who abuse you. If anyone strikes you on the cheek, offer the other also; and from anyone who takes away your coat do not withhold even your shirt. Give to everyone who begs from you; and if anyone takes away your goods, do not ask for them again. Do to others as you would have them do to you. If you love those who love you, what credit is that to you? For even sinners love those who love them.'

Luke 6.27–32

Jesus talks about three ways in which humans relate.

First, there is reciprocal conduct. If a boy racer carves you up at traffic lights, you force your way angrily ahead of him. Internationally, if a country expels a dozen diplomats accusing them of being spies, you even the score by ejecting twelve of theirs. This, says Jesus, is the unacceptable way in which most of the world operates.

Second, there is empathy conduct – treating others as you wish to be treated. In personal terms this means that you resist slagging off difficult colleagues and hope that they will copy your example. In global terms it is the kind of behaviour that governs treaties in which nations agree that neither side will use nuclear weapons first. Jesus seems realistically positive about this.

But the third approach is grace conduct. If you're slapped on the cheek (an insult in Jesus' day), tolerate the indignity calmly. If an army officer demands your jacket because he is cold (a soldier's right in first-century Jerusalem) your attitude should be, 'The poor man's freezing. I wonder whether he would like my sweater as well.' This is the behaviour to which Jesus calls us. The international implications are profoundly challenging. Jesus' concept of loving enemies, which is so familiar that it seems warm and charming, is actually wild and revolutionary.

Jesus' words about those who beg are unsettling to anyone who works in a city. But people who beg for money in the streets are humans, loved by God, and we are called to exercise grace conduct. This week make a point of acknowledging them instead of brushing past, even if it is only to say, 'Sorry. No!'

Teach me your way, O Lord, that I may walk in your truth; give me an undivided heart.

Psalm 86.11

January 6   Love your enemies

[Jesus said:] 'If you do good to those who do good to you, what credit is that to you? For even sinners do the same. If you lend to those from whom you hope to receive, what credit is that to you? Even sinners lend to sinners, to receive as much again. But love your enemies, do good, and lend, expecting nothing in return. Your reward will be great, and you will be children of the Most High; for he is kind to the ungrateful and the wicked. Be merciful, just as your Father is merciful.'

Luke 6.33–36

Did Jesus know how hard it is to love your enemies? Surely yes! So why did he ask the impossible? Because he was setting us the highest challenge – to be like God.

Has God done to us what we have done to him? Absolutely not! If that were God's way he would have insulted, rejected and then ignored us long ago.

Has God dealt with us in the way we might expect? Indeed no! If God had given us the kind of salvation we might devise, it would have strings attached, conditions imposed, expectations to fulfil. We would have given up.

Instead, God's ways with us have entirely been marked by grace. He has been utterly long-suffering and more loving than anything in our imaginations. He has blessed us who have cursed him. He has been kind to us who have forgotten him. He has loved us who have hated him. He has made us his children.

'Would you like to be your heavenly Father's child in this world?' Jesus asks. 'Then go and do the same.'

Yesterday was 'Twelfth Night'. By tradition Christmas decorations come down today, the first day of Epiphany. Your home will be bare, so where the Christmas tree stood place a symbol of determination to 'be merciful'. It might be a candle, a cross, a ribbon, a collecting box, a plant – whatever reminds you of Jesus' call to live by different standards from much of the world.

Lead us from death to life; from falsehood to truth.
Lead us from despair to hope; from fear to trust.
Lead us from hate to love; from war to peace.
Let peace fill our hearts, our world, our universe. Amen.

During the Gulf War of 1990–91 this prayer was placed on a 'peace table' in Durham Cathedral

January 7 Judging others

[Jesus said:] 'Do not judge, and you will not be judged; do not condemn, and you will not be condemned. Forgive, and you will be forgiven; give, and it will be given to you. A good measure, pressed down, shaken together, running over, will be put into your lap; for the measure you give will be the measure you get back.'
He also told them a parable: 'Can a blind person guide a blind person? Will not both fall into a pit? A disciple is not above the teacher, but everyone who is fully qualified will be like the teacher. Why do you see the speck in your neighbour's eye, but do not notice the log in your own eye? Or how can you say to your neighbour, "Friend, let me take out the speck in your eye", when you yourself do not see the log in your own eye? You hypocrite, first take the log out of your own eye, and then you will see clearly to take the speck out of your neighbour's eye.'

Luke 6.37–42

First a warning: If you make judgements about others they will rebound on you because God will assess you by the same standards.

Next, a question: Why are you so preoccupied with other people's faults, rather than your own?

Finally, a command: Examine your own failings and find forgiveness. Then when you look at others it will be in a context of gratitude, and that allows you to be both accurate and merciful.

A hundred years ago Christians who were passionate about eliminating poverty distinguished between 'deserving' and 'undeserving' poor. The adjectives have changed, but it takes longer for attitudes to disappear. Are there traces in the reservations some people have about supporting work among those who live with HIV? Or projects that create opportunities for people leaving prison? Or in distinctions between 'asylum seekers' and 'economic migrants'?

Go to a mirror and look at your eyes. Remind yourself of the colour, the shape, the detail. What do others see when they look at these eyes – kindness or judgement? Ask God to show you what must be removed from your outlook in order to have a right assessment of others' needs.

Take away from our hearts, O Lord, all suspiciousness, indignation, anger and contention, and whatever is calculated to wound charity or to lessen brotherly love. Have mercy, O Lord.

Thomas à Kempis (1380–1471)

January 8   Wise and foolish builders

[Jesus said,] 'Why do you call me "Lord, Lord", and do not do what I tell you? I will show you what someone is like who comes to me, hears my words, and acts on them. That one is like a man building a house, who dug deeply and laid the foundation on rock; when a flood arose, the river burst against that house but could not shake it, because it had been well built. But the one who hears and does not act is like a man who built a house on the ground without a foundation. When the river burst against it, immediately it fell, and great was the ruin of that house.'

Luke 6.46–49

The evidence of God at work in our lives is seen not in the words we say, but in our obedience to the call of Jesus. When crises come, long-standing habits of obedience mean that our spiritual lives are prepared for difficulty – and that is where rock-solid strength can be found for all the other parts of our lives.

In May 2004 it rained very heavily in the area where Haiti borders the Dominican Republic. The earth on the hillsides gave way, sending mudslides crashing into the villages below. About 3,000 people died. Thousands of farming animals were lost and crops were washed away (bananas, corn and beans). Five schools and two health centres were destroyed

Why did Haiti flood? Should we blame God? Is it a punishment for disobedience? Hundreds of Haitians climb the hillsides every day to chop down trees for firewood to make charcoal. Such is the level of poverty that selling it is their only means of making money. But chopping down forests means that rainwater can no longer be absorbed, and it cascades down the hillsides, sweeping away everything in its path. This tragedy was not caused by God; it was caused by poverty.

Being prepared for natural disasters is one of the abilities which poor communities need in order to thrive. Find out more about how Christian Aid helps people reduce the risk of emergencies such as the one the Caribbean at www.christianaid.org.uk/world/emerresp/response3.htm

O God our refuge and strength, our help in times of trouble, have mercy on the lands where the earth has given way. Prosper those who rebuild houses, and strengthen those who rebuild hope, so that entire communities may face the future without fear. Amen.

January 9   A delicate balance

Bless the Lord, O my soul. O Lord my God, you are very great.
You are clothed with honour and majesty . . .
You make springs gush forth in the valleys;
*   they flow between the hills,*
giving drink to every wild animal;
*   the wild asses quench their thirst.*
By the streams the birds of the air have their habitation;
*   they sing among the branches.*
From your lofty abode you water the mountains;
*   the earth is satisfied with the fruit of your work.*
You cause the grass to grow for the cattle, and plants for people to use,
to bring forth food from the earth, and wine to gladden the human heart,
oil to make the face shine, and bread to strengthen the human heart.

Psalm 104.1, 10–15

The new series that begins today looks at what the Bible teaches us about the planet on which we live. The whole of this psalm rejoices in God's plan for the world – every part supporting every other part and every creature in its place. It credits to the brilliance of God what scientists call 'ecology' – humans, animals and plants in delicate balance, a single community of creation. Find the lines where the poet rejoices that one part of God's creation sustains another part.

In what detailed ways have you been dependent on the plant, animal and mineral world already today? In what ways have they been dependent on you? The splendour of God's creation is that he made it capable of supporting life in such an intricate way; the grace of it is that he also made it so beautiful.

Look out of the nearest window and take in the shapes, patterns, textures and colours that you can see. Don't stop looking until you find something beautiful that you had not noticed before.

Glory be to God for dappled things . . .
All things counter, original, spare, strange:
Whatever is fickle, freckled (who knows how?)
With swift, slow; sweet, sour; adazzle, dim;
He fathers-forth whose beauty is past change:
Praise him.

Gerard Manley Hopkins (1884–89)

January 10   Circle of life

O Lord, how manifold are your works!
In wisdom you have made them all;
    the earth is full of your creatures.
Yonder is the sea, great and wide,
   creeping things innumerable are there,
     living things both small and great.
There go the ships, and Leviathan that you formed to sport in it.
These all look to you to give them their food in due season;
when you give to them, they gather it up;
when you open your hand, they are filled with good things.
When you hide your face, they are dismayed;
when you take away their breath, they die and return to their dust.
When you send forth your spirit, they are created;
   and you renew the face of the ground.
May the glory of the Lord endure for ever; may the Lord rejoice in his works.

Psalm 104.24–31

Last week I wore new shoes to a wedding. Mistake! They gave me
a blister and I limped to the reception. However, this week some
healing process that I will never understand, but which God has
buried deep in the scheme of things, has got to work inside me to
mend the broken skin. To me, that's as good as a miracle!

   The same is true of Earth – forces that God has placed in it work slowly but
ceaselessly to heal the world. Poisons get broken down into their harmless con-
stituents in the sea. The carbon dioxide which humans breathe out is drunk in
by the world's trees and converted into the oxygen we need to survive.

   But what happens when humans invent chemicals so complex that the sea
fights a losing battle to keep pace with the poisons poured into it? Or when
humans pull down trees so fast that what is left cannot cope with the vast
quantities of harmful gas we release? Or when, as the atmosphere warms, ice
melts, the oceans rise, and lands close to sea-level in developing countries flood
catastrophically?

Use biodegradable products to wash and package everything!
They break down into harmless particles much quicker than their
equivalents. Go and check the labels in your cupboards.

Think back over the way you have travelled, cleaned and kept
warm during the last twenty-four hours. Take time to reflect on
the realities of our world and confess to God our failures.

January 11 Taking control

The Lord God took the man and put him in the garden of Eden to till it and keep it. And the Lord God commanded the man, 'You may freely eat of every tree of the garden; but of the tree of the knowledge of good and evil you shall not eat, for in the day that you eat of it you shall die.'
Then the Lord God said, 'It is not good that the man should be alone; I will make him a helper as his partner.' So out of the ground the Lord God formed every animal of the field and every bird of the air, and brought them to the man to see what he would call them; and whatever the man called every living creature, that was its name. The man gave names to all cattle, and to the birds of the air, and to every animal of the field; but for the man there was not found a helper as his partner.

Genesis 2.15–20

God's extravagant gift to humans is to give away privileges which are his by right: to name things, to impose cultivation, to maintain control. The responsibility of women and men to 'keep' God's creation is clear. These words could be interpreted in a stewardly or a selfish way. Where have you seen both happening?
Humans have often been part of God's healing process. Of hundreds of species that have become extinct in the wild over the last thirty years, humans have reintroduced eighteen to their natural habitat through breeding in captivity. It is a desperately slow process, but it works. However, damage is not a slow process. It seemed that sea otters had been hunted to extinction for their pelts until a tiny colony was found in Alaska and helped, cub by cub, back into a substantial population. Then on Good Friday 1989 the tanker *Exxon Valdez* spilled ten million gallons of oil into the sea and killed 12,000 at a stroke.

Go through the rubbish bins and sort out what can be recycled or reused – glass, paper, carrier bags. Wherever you use paper in the kitchen, bathroom or for writing on, check whether the package has a symbol which indicates that it is recycled.

The greed that damages tomorrow's world to comfort today's;
The laziness that litters tomorrow's world to ease today's;
The stupidity that pollutes tomorrow's world to convenience
    today's;
Father forgive.

January 12   Who is in charge?

The Lord your God is bringing you into a good land, a land with flowing streams, with springs and underground waters welling up in valleys and hills, a land of wheat and barley, of vines and fig trees and pomegranates, a land of olive trees and honey, a land where you may eat bread without scarcity, where you will lack nothing, a land whose stones are iron and from whose hills you may mine copper. You shall eat your fill and bless the Lord your God for the good land that he has given you.

Take care that you do not forget the Lord your God, by failing to keep his commandments, his ordinances, and his statutes, which I am commanding you today. When you have eaten your fill and have built fine houses and live in them . . . do not say to yourself, 'My power and the might of my own hand have gained me this wealth.' But remember the Lord your God, for it is he who gives you power to get wealth.

Deuteronomy 8.7–12, 17–18

After escaping slavery in Egypt the Hebrews spent forty years in the desert preparing to settle in a new land. The contrast between the oppression they had known and the luxury they were to experience was huge. Deuteronomy records God's warning – don't assume that such good fortune is yours by right!

There followed the most environmentally sensitive legislation ever made for a nation. It covered what we would call bio-diversity, protection from over-intensive cultivation or mining, and even sanitation. We will read some of these laws in days to come.

The fact is that, because we gobble up resources faster than the planet produces them, there is a genuine possibility of catastrophe. Our constant quest for cheaper energy is disastrous. This winter could we accept one degree less warmth in our homes and wear a thicker sweater? These are options for our generation. But unless we take them now, our children will have no choice at all.

Instead of consistently finding the bath water too hot and adding cold, turn the temperature at which your water is stored down to what you really need. (Incidentally, a shower uses a fraction of the water that a bath uses.)

Let all I see today be holy,
Holy taste and holy sound,
Conscious of a good Creator,
May I walk on holy ground.

January 13 The widow, the orphan, the refugee

When you reap your harvest in your field and forget a sheaf in the field, you shall not go back to get it; it shall be left for the alien, the orphan, and the widow, so that the Lord your God may bless you in all your undertakings. When you beat your olive trees, do not strip what is left; it shall be for the alien, the orphan, and the widow. When you gather the grapes of your vineyard, do not glean what is left; it shall be for the alien, the orphan, and the widow. Remember that you were a slave in the land of Egypt; therefore I am commanding you to do this.

Deuteronomy 24.19–22

Forget corn, olives and grapes – what I love is asparagus! Thousands of us do, which is why it is now readily available in our shops and supermarkets. Much of it comes from Peru, where there is big money to be made – but not by the factory workers, for whom £2.30 is a typical reward for a ten- or twelve-hour day. Meanwhile in Ica, where asparagus is grown, villagers find that their water supply has been depleted in order to irrigate the fields. The Peruvian economy needs the exports, and we want our asparagus ever cheaper – but some of the world's poorest people are subsidizing our luxury vegetables.

The principle behind the verses is that we should not be seeking every last penny of profit just because we can. There are other issues to take into account, such as the impact that our business practices have on vulnerable people. Among the Hebrews, widows, orphans and refugees (who could not rely on help from their families) were particularly vulnerable.

Recent health scares associated with over-intensive farming techniques show that the kind of blessing God has in mind as a result of honouring this command is not only a spiritual one, but a practical one.

Visit www.christianaid.org.uk/world/where/lac/perup.htm to find out more about Christian Aid's work in Peru.

Lord God, before I am exhausted from earning every last penny, filling every last second, pushing every last boundary, show me a better way.

January 14   Taking advantage

If you go into your neighbour's vineyard, you may eat your fill of grapes, as many as you wish, but you shall not put any in a container. If you go into your neighbour's standing grain, you may pluck the ears with your hand, but you shall not put a sickle to your neighbour's standing grain.

Deuteronomy 23.24–25

Yesterday's Bible passage made it clear that those who owned property or ran businesses were not to be so driven by profit that they became insensitive to the needs of the poor people in their community. The rules which governed trade were set up to benefit the poor as well as making business thrive.

Today shows the other side of the coin. People were not to take advantage of the spirit of generosity that was incorporated into the Hebrew laws by ransacking neighbouring property and claiming it was their right. There was and is a difference between taking shared pleasure in the bounty of God's provision and assuming that someone else's good fortune is there to be looted. (Why am I reminded of Homer Simpson, simultaneously despising and taking advantage of the open-handedness of Ned Flanders?)

Christian Aid is campaigning for a reform of the rules that govern international trade so that they are no longer shaped by rich countries solely to their own advantage. But that doesn't mean doing away with rules altogether. Sometimes there aren't rules where there should be. It's fairness that Christians seek, not free-for-all!

Is there anything that you have borrowed from someone and have been meaning, but failing, to return? Today's the day!

O Saviour, pour upon me thy spirit of meekness and love; annihilate the selfhood in me; be thou all my life. Guide thou my hand which trembles exceedingly upon the rock of ages.

William Blake (1757–1827)

January 15   Short-term gain

If you besiege a town for a long time, making war against it in order to take it, you must not destroy its trees by wielding an axe against them. Although you may take food from them, you must not cut them down. Are trees in the field human beings that they should come under siege from you? You may destroy only the trees that you know do not produce food; you may cut them down for use in building siege-works against the town that makes war with you, until it falls . . . You shall not muzzle an ox while it is treading out the grain.

Deuteronomy 20.19–20; 25.4

These verses seem strange companions until you realize that they are both about the dangers of short-term gain. Destroying food hastened a conquest, but laying claim to a devastated land was an empty victory. A muzzled ox could not eat the corn, which gained every last grain of profit, but did nothing to nurture the exhausted animal.

Three pictures come to mind from years gone by: Kuwaiti oil-wells set ablaze by retreating enemies; farm animals succumbing to BSE from the very food that was meant to nurture them; a swathe of rainforest the size of Israel cut down every single day in order to gain access to mineral resources. We cannot simply blame the people who cut down the trees. The UK ravaged its own forests 800 years ago. Trees get cut down not because people are destructive, but because they are poor. It is as if someone has buried a treasure-trove in their back garden. And when they hear voices saying, 'Don't you dare dig up the treasure,' they reply, 'But how do I feed my children?'

In Colombia, Christian Aid supports organizations that create alternative strategies for development, which preserve the land and the culture of the people.

Turn your television off at the set, not with the remote control. To keep the red standby light on still takes 85 per cent of the electricity that the full picture does – a short-term gain that both wastes your money and may contribute to climate change.

O God, I look forward in faith to the day when the meek shall inherit the Earth. In the meantime, I will work with determination for the day when they shall inherit the mineral rights.

January 16 Cancelling debts

Every seventh year you shall grant a remission of debts. And this is the manner of the remission: every creditor shall remit the claim that is held against a neighbour, not exacting it of a neighbour who is a member of the community, because the Lord's remission has been proclaimed. Of a foreigner you may exact it, but you must remit your claim on whatever any member of your community owes you. There will, however, be no one in need among you, because the Lord is sure to bless you in the land that the Lord your God is giving you as a possession to occupy, if only you will obey the Lord your God by diligently observing this entire commandment that I command you today.

Deuteronomy 15.1–5

There is an understanding in the Bible that inequalities between rich and poor will inevitably arise. But that is never tolerated as a permanent condition. Instead, the followers of God were to overturn again and again the structures that allowed the wealthy to stay that way at the expense of the poor. Debts were not to multiply decade upon decade until a new generation was trapped into poverty by events that took place in the days of their ancestors. Underlying all financial arrangements was the goal of a world in which there were 'no poor among you'.

The verses which suggest that foreigners could not share in this generosity make us uncomfortable until we recall how Jesus extended the concept to take in people of every race and religion. A Jewish academic quoted Deuteronomy to him and asked, 'Who is my neighbour?' Jesus responded with the story of how a 'foreign' Samaritan was a good neighbour to a man who had been mugged when fellow-Jews let him down.

The Jubilee Debt Campaign, inspired in part by these verses, works for the cancellation of debts inherited from a previous generation by our 'neighbours' in the world's poorest countries. In each decade God's people will need to address new forces which emerge to push rich and poor apart. Find out more at www.jubileedebtcampaign.org.uk or write to The Grayston Centre, 28 Charles Square, London, N1 6HT and ask for copies of their 'Drop the Debt!' flyer.

Father in heaven, forgive us our debts as we forgive those who were in debt to us, so that there may be no poor among us and so that all the world may know your blessing.

January 17   Attitudes and actions

If there is among you anyone in need, a member of your commu-nity in any of your towns within the land that the Lord your God is giving you, do not be hard-hearted or tight-fisted toward your needy neighbour. You should rather open your hand, willingly lending enough to meet the need, whatever it may be. Be careful that you do not entertain a mean thought, thinking, 'The seventh year, the year of remission, is near', and therefore view your needy neighbour with hostility and give nothing; your neighbour might cry to the Lord against you, and you would incur guilt. Give liberally and be ungrudging when you do so, for on this account the Lord your God will bless you in all your work and in all that you undertake. Since there will never cease to be some in need on the earth, I there-fore command you, 'Open your hand to the poor and needy neighbour in your land.'

Deuteronomy 15.7–11

There are two attitudes to justice: the mean-spirited kind which involves doing as little as our conscience will allow us to get away with, and the ungrudging one which simply takes joy in doing good. Why should our attitude be more like the second than the first? Because that is how God has behaved toward us.

God demands nothing of us; rather, he has very high expectations of us. For the world to prosper in the way he intends it requires that all of us have selfless attitudes and do not take advantage of others just because we can. The system has always been wide open to abuse, of course (the Hebrews could abuse the system by refusing to be generous in year seven when tackling poverty would be really costly), but how wonderful for God to assume us to be better people than we actually are.

Make a completely gratuitous gift today to someone or some cause – perhaps to someone who doesn't strictly deserve it.

May those who are poor be freed from their hunger,
may those who struggle be freed from injustice,
may those who need peace be freed from violence,
and may those of us who are comfortable be freed from our
        indifference;
so that together we may all be free to work for change.

Christian Aid/Nigel Varndell

January 18   Fairness, not favours

You shall not spread a false report. You shall not join hands with the wicked to act as a malicious witness. You shall not follow a majority in wrongdoing; when you bear witness in a lawsuit, you shall not side with the majority so as to pervert justice; nor shall you be partial to the poor in a lawsuit.

Exodus 23.1–3

There were three temptations for the ordinary Hebrew citizen when it came to the legal system: to spread damaging rumours, to keep company with crooks and then find oneself coerced into committing perjury on their behalf, and to kow-tow to influential people.

Those temptations have not gone away, but for those whose day-to-day life does not involve law courts they present themselves in different ways: spicy gossip about fellow churchgoers, compromise with the worldly standards of friends or colleagues, deference to those who might be useful to us in the future. Do you recognize those as difficulties in your own life with which you need to deal?

It would be easy not to notice the last of today's rules for living. Followers of God are not to be biased toward the powerful, but neither are they to show partiality to the poor. The world's poorest communities do not ask for favours: they ask for fairness.

Are you aware of an injustice which has taken place – either an apparent miscarriage of justice which has been reported in the media, or a local event in your school, community or workplace? Use your influence to put it right (not gossiping, compromising or toadying – just writing a letter).

Grant me, O Lord:
to know what is worth knowing,
to love what is worth loving,
to praise what delights you most,
to value what is precious in your sight,
to hate what is offensive to you.
Do not let me judge by what I see,
nor pass sentence according to what I hear,
nor be influenced by all that dazzles.
Rather may I judge rightly between things that differ,
and above all, search out and do what pleases you.

Thomas à Kempis (1380–1471)

January 19   Helping enemies

When you come upon your enemy's ox or donkey going astray, you shall bring it back.
 When you see the donkey of one who hates you lying under its burden and you would hold back from setting it free, you must help to set it free.

Exodus 23.4–5

I have just been struck all over again by how wonderful it is to be cared for by a God whose compassion extends to my unco-operative neighbour's clapped-out donkey!

Sometimes we stereotype the Old Testament as full of judgement and the New Testament as full of grace. But when Jesus told his followers to 'love your enemies and pray for those who persecute you' he was not overturning the principles of the Old Testament law; he was rediscovering and extending them. In shaping a society that cared for its powerless members, God was insistent that they should take after him – generosity and kindness being extended to all on the basis of need, regardless of personal differences or alliances.

Throughout its history Christian Aid has been committed to working wherever need is greatest. It works alongside communities regardless of their religion, nationality or ethnic group. It supports programmes that address the legacies left by conflicts – both the poverty which is the inevitable consequence of fighting, and issues of reconciliation. If old conflicts are not to reignite, people who were previously enemies need to build new communities in which they can lift themselves from poverty and develop a strong sense of their own dignity.

Distance and unfamiliarity anaesthetize us to the full horror of overseas conflicts. But the more we understand, the more we share God's concern. In the margin, write a list of places you know to be scarred by conflict, then get a globe or atlas and find out or remind yourself where they are.

Teach me, O Prince of Peace:
to see humans where once I saw soldiers,
to see people where once I saw victims,
to see creatures of God where once I saw enemies,
and to see the conflict that simmers in my own heart
as clearly as that which scars the world.

January 20   Honour and respect

You shall not pervert the justice due to your poor in their law-suits. Keep far from a false charge, and do not kill the innocent and those in the right, for I will not acquit the guilty.

You shall take no bribe, for a bribe blinds the officials, and subverts the cause of those who are in the right. You shall not oppress a resident alien; you know the heart of an alien, for you were aliens in the land of Egypt.

Exodus 23.6–9

The Dominican Republic and Haiti share a border – they are home to some of the world's poorest communities. Thousands of Haitians make their way to the Dominican Republic in the hope of finding work, but when they get there they find themselves at the bottom of the pile. Without legal rights and subject to racism, they have no access to education or health care, and life can be very harsh.

Christian Aid supports an organization called Onè Respé in Santiago. It means 'Honour' (which is what a visitor says when she knocks on the door of a house), 'Respect' (which is what the owner says to welcome her guest in). By bringing people from Haitian and Dominican communities together to study the Bible and pray it aims to increase their respect and understanding for one another, and to work co-operatively to tackle the burdens that poverty has placed upon them all. The 'little schools' of Onè Respé teach children to read and write, and give them a daily meal, regardless of whether or not they have papers that give them legal rights to stay in the Dominican Republic.

Hebrews who had experienced oppression as foreigners in Egypt could fully understand, and therefore respond to, the needs of foreigners in their community. In the same way, this project in the Dominican Republic is run by those best able to empathize with the needs of vulnerable people living among them.

Find out more about Christian Aid's work in the Dominican Republic by visiting
www.christianaid.org.uk/world/where/lac/domrepp.htm

To those who uphold justice, honour;
To those who support the cause of the innocent, respect;
To those who refuse a bribe, honour;
To those who shelter the refugee, respect;
And to the God who calls us to these things, everlasting praise.

January 21   One in seven

For six years you shall sow your land and gather in its yield; but the seventh year you shall let it rest and lie fallow, so that the poor of your people may eat; and what they leave the wild animals may eat. You shall do the same with your vineyard, and with your olive orchard.

For six days you shall do your work, but on the seventh day you shall rest, so that your ox and your donkey may have relief, and your home-born slave and the resident alien may be refreshed. Be attentive to all that I have said to you. Do not invoke the names of other gods; do not let them be heard on your lips.

Exodus 23.10–13

O God, I'm tired! I'm tired of the stream of weekdays that stretches endlessly from Boxing Day to Christmas Eve. Whatever happened to that one day of the week when the roads had no traffic and towns fell quiet? I am ashamed to say, Lord God, that I can remember resenting your day of rest because, slumped in front of Sunday afternoon TV, I was bored. Come back, boredom, I need you!

God has always been concerned that our lives should have a healthy rhythm. He offered the sabbath day and the sabbatical year, once in every seven, not because he wants us to do something awkward to please him, but as a gift that will improve our lives. They are a gift to individuals for refreshment, to the land for replenishment of minerals, and to society so that once in a while the pressure relents.

A generation ago it was possible to write off these laws as outdated in a complex industrial society. However, now that we realize the impact on the world's most vulnerable people of an endless quest for the last penny of profit, the words about allowing 'the poor of your people' to benefit from the sabbath have a new relevance.

In your diary put a special note beside one day next week (Sunday or an alternative) that you can mark as a sabbath. Organize a treat for yourself that day, and plan something which could be viewed as a treat for God.

Let sense be dumb, let flesh retire,
Speak through the earthquake, wind and fire,
O still small voice of calm.

J. G. Whittier (1807–92), from 'Dear Lord and Father of Mankind'

January 22   People should not own people

If any who are dependent on you become so impoverished that they sell themselves to you, you shall not make them serve as slaves. They shall remain with you as hired or bound labourers. They shall serve with you until the year of the jubilee. Then they and their children with them shall be free from your authority; they shall go back to their own family and return to their ancestral property. For they are my servants, whom I brought out of the land of Egypt; they shall not be sold as slaves are sold. You shall not rule over them with harshness, but shall fear your God.

Leviticus 25.39–43

Once in every seven days, a sabbath. Once in every seven years, a sabbath. So when seven lots of seven years have passed, the fiftieth year calls for something deeper and more significant. The Hebrew law instituted a Jubilee Year in which land was restored to its original owners and profit from destitute people came to a halt.

In fact, as far as we know, the legislation was never enforced. And just before the birth of Jesus, the Jewish leader Rabbi Hillel instituted new rules because creditors were reluctant to give loans which might never be repaid, and so the poor were finding it impossible to start businesses and help themselves. The result was that loans became easy to get, but debt grew out of control – a situation which is still familiar in poor communities.

One principle defiantly stands. People are not to be owned by people – they are God's own. We need reminding of that not every fifty years, but every fifty seconds.

Fifty days' time will be 13 March (unless it is a leap year)! What do you hope to have achieved by then in various areas of your life? Turn to that page now and write some thoughts in the margin to review on that day.

From my wealth and poverty, I want to live in your jubilee.
Help me to give, act and pray to share your good news:
for the poor – release from unpayable debt;
for the rich – freedom from the power of money.

Christian Aid/Rebecca Dudley

January 23 Looking forward

I consider that the sufferings of this present time are not worth comparing with the glory about to be revealed to us. For the creation waits with eager longing for the revealing of the children of God; for the creation was subjected to futility, not of its own will but by the will of the one who subjected it, in hope that the creation itself will be set free from its bondage to decay and will obtain the freedom of the glory of the children of God. We know that the whole creation has been groaning in labour pains until now; and not only the creation, but we ourselves, who have the first fruits of the Spirit, groan inwardly while we wait for adoption, the redemption of our bodies.

Romans 8.18–23

Through the sheer vivacity of its existence, the entire created order is worshipping God at this moment. Our universe was created to be free. However, the sins of humankind (who have so evidently failed to live up to the standards of God which we have been considering for the past few days) have degraded and injured the whole of creation. If a sterile lake had emotions it would be depressed by its 'futility'. If a depleted ozone layer could describe itself, it would cry of its 'bondage to decay'. If a debt-crippled land had a voice, it would be 'groaning'. All of creation is longing 'on tiptoe' for the day when the kingdom of God is perfected and this ravaged Earth renewed.

God is sovereign. His vow is that glory will replace suffering.

That day will come.

Go outside your home. Clear up some litter, rip up some weeds, and tidy up the clutter. Make the place ready to welcome God. More realistically, make it ready to welcome the humans whom he loves and in whom he dwells.

Let the heavens be glad, and let the earth rejoice;
*   let the sea roar, and all that fills it;*
*   let the field exult, and everything in it.*
Then shall all the trees of the forest sing for joy
*   before the Lord; for he is coming,*
for he is coming to judge the earth.
He will judge the world with righteousness,
*   and the peoples with his truth.*

Psalm 96.11–13

January 24   **All things new**

Then I saw a new heaven and a new earth; for the first heaven and the first earth had passed away, and the sea was no more. And I saw the holy city, the new Jerusalem, coming down out of heaven from God, prepared as a bride adorned for her husband. And I heard a loud voice from the throne saying, 'See, the home of God is among mortals. He will dwell with them as their God; they will be his peoples, and God himself will be with them; he will wipe every tear from their eyes. Death will be no more; mourning and crying and pain will be no more, for the first things have passed away.'

And the one who was seated on the throne said, 'See, I am making all things new.'

Revelation 21.1–5

Considering how big a book it is, and how very curious we are about the subject, the Bible says surprisingly little about the final destiny of humankind and the planet. But it gives thrilling glimpses, and this is one of them. Looking past the glorious (but obviously not literal) language we find assurances that:

- there is life to be lived beyond our graves;
- it will be blessed by the close presence of God;
- suffering, hunger and poverty will have no place;
- everything that is worn out on Earth, including us, will be healed.

This is a source of profound hope to those who long for the world to be better. But the message of Jesus was not that the kingdom of God was a future reality; it was that his coming had initiated the kingdom of God here and now. Our mission as Christians is to begin to create today what God will fulfil in heaven.

The Christian creed is to believe in life after death. When Christian Aid devised its Mission Statement it used those familiar words but changed one. Have a look at the 'strap-line' on the back cover of the book. What do you find yourself thinking? If you can with integrity, copy it in the margin, substituting 'I' for 'we'.

Warruburru-yung amburru-yarrijgina anubani anaaraambala-manjinyung an aarrawindi-lhangu anubuguni.

Revelation 21.26 in Nunggubuyu, a language of the Aboriginal people of Northern Australia. If you would like to pray in English alongside them, it means: 'May the glory and honour of all the nations be brought into the City of God.'

January 25   Whose Earth is it anyway?

[Christ] is the image of the invisible God, the firstborn of all creation; for in him all things in heaven and on earth were created, things visible and invisible, whether thrones or dominions or rulers or powers – all things have been created through him and for him. He himself is before all things, and in him all things hold together. He is the head of the body, the church; he is the beginning, the firstborn from the dead, so that he might come to have first place in everything. For in him all the fullness of God was pleased to dwell, and through him God was pleased to reconcile to himself all things, whether on earth or in heaven, by making peace through the blood of his cross.

Colossians 1.15–20

Christians know that this wonderful planet Earth does not belong to us; it belongs to Jesus. It was created 'through him and for him'. At the end of time there will be a renewed and perfected heaven and earth. All the created order, which Jesus won back to God through the cross, will be presented to him as his own. Then, as the Earth returns to the one for whom it was always destined, we will be held accountable for what we have done with it.

God forgive us!

And will God forgive us? Of course he will! He forgives again and again, so we are not without hope. Even now it is not too late to turn to him in repentance. But actions have consequences, even forgiven actions, and we have to live with the results of what we do to our planet.

We must know this. Our children must know this. Our neighbours must know this. Our leaders must know this. In this generation time is not on our side. Let it be clear. This is the last ditch. This is where we turn and fight.

We are at the end of a series. If it has stirred you to a new concern about the state of the environment or its poorest people, tell someone powerful what you would like to see done. You can write to the President of the United States at The White House, 1600 Pennsylvania Avenue NW, Washington, DC 20500, USA, or email: president@whitehouse.gov

To a planet that yearns for you;
to a people that needs you;
to a world that is yours:
Come Lord Jesus!

January 26 The widow's oil

Now the wife of a member of the company of prophets cried to Elisha, 'Your servant my husband is dead; and you know that your servant feared the Lord, but a creditor has come to take my two children as slaves.' Elisha said to her, 'What shall I do for you? Tell me, what do you have in the house?' She answered, 'Your servant has nothing in the house, except a jar of oil.' He said, 'Go out-side, borrow vessels from all your neighbours, empty vessels and not just a few. Then go in, and shut the door behind you and your children, and start pouring . . .' They kept bringing vessels to her, and she kept pouring. When the vessels were full, she said to her son, 'Bring me another vessel.' But he said to her, 'There are no more.' Then the oil stopped flowing. She came and told the man of God, and he said, 'Go, sell the oil and pay your debts.'

2 Kings 4.1–7

A single mother fears for the future of her hungry children, who may be taken away as slaves because of debts that she cannot pay. There are powerful contemporary echoes. In countries of the developing world where health and education budgets have been slashed to pay debts to foreign banks and governments, it is women who bear the load most heavily. It is they who provide care in hospitals where there are no staff; they who walk miles for ante-natal care when clinics are closed; they who agonize over cutting the number of meals their children have every day.

But the message of the story is that God starts with what seems very little to transform situations. Halfway through, this stops being a story about despair and starts being about resourcefulness, sharing, energy, neighbourliness, hope. All these are present in the developing world today. God's miracle will be seen again when those who are crushed by debt are given the opportunity to let these qualities flow.

Christian Aid is part of a campaign for the unpayable debts of the world's poorest countries to be cancelled. To read about the difference the campaign has already made, visit www.christianaid.org.uk/campaign/debt/debt.htm

My heart goes out this day, Lord God, to all women who fear for the health and future of their children. Wherever in the world someone is tempted to despair, may your mercy flow like rich, life-giving oil. Amen.

January 27 Naboth's vineyard

Naboth the Jezreelite had a vineyard in Jezreel, beside the palace of King Ahab of Samaria. And Ahab said to Naboth, 'Give me your vineyard, so that I may have it for a vegetable garden, because it is near my house; I will give you a better vineyard for it; or, if it seems good to you, I will give you its value in money.'
But Naboth said to Ahab, 'The Lord forbid that I should give you my ancestral inheritance.' Ahab went home resentful and sullen because of what Naboth the Jezreelite had said to him; for he had said, 'I will not give you my ancestral inheritance.' He lay down on his bed, turned away his face, and would not eat.

His wife Jezebel came to him and said, 'Why are you so depressed that you will not eat?' He said to her, 'Because I spoke to Naboth . . . but he answered, "I will not give you my vineyard."' His wife Jezebel said to him, 'Do you now govern Israel? Get up, eat some food, and be cheerful; I will get you the vineyard of Naboth the Jezreelite.'

1 Kings 21.1–7

Ahab's request seems reasonable until you understand that, under Hebrew law, land was not a commodity that could be bought and sold. It belonged to the Lord. It was to be treated with the utmost respect. Naboth would have seen himself as God's tenant. Sell it to a king? 'The Lord forbid it!' He did indeed!

Ahab was a Hebrew too, but his wife wasn't. Baal was worshipped in the Canaanite culture from which she came. Under her law the monarch was absolute.

Two cultures were about to clash over a stark question: Is it possible to wield massive economic might and still exercise it in a way that benefits the citizens on whose life it has such an impact? It is a question that echoes down the centuries of warrior kings, of empires governed by European countries, and of the transnational corporations of our generation.

A recent addition to the list of foods that have been fairly traded is wine from the vineyards of Chile or South Africa. You can get more details from Traidcraft Wines by telephoning 0191 491 0591.

May everything that has breath – large and small, weak and strong, humble and powerful – bring their worship to the God of justice in lives that are obedient to him. Amen.

January 28   Enduring tragedy

[Jezebel] wrote letters in Ahab's name and sealed them with his seal; she sent the letters to the elders and the nobles who lived with Naboth in his city. She wrote in the letters, 'Proclaim a fast, and seat Naboth at the head of the assembly; seat two scoundrels opposite him, and have them bring a charge against him, saying, "You have cursed God and the king." Then take him out, and stone him to death.' The men of his city, the elders and the nobles who lived in his city, did as Jezebel had sent word to them ...

As soon as Jezebel heard that Naboth had been stoned and was dead, Jezebel said to Ahab, 'Go, take possession of the vineyard of Naboth the Jezreelite, which he refused to give you for money; for Naboth is not alive, but dead.'

1 Kings 21.8–11, 15

A terrible tragedy – the murder of an innocent and industrious man by the very government whose responsibility it was to protect its people. All it took was one murmured lie and a crowd too scared to resist. It is a story repeated endlessly through history.

In Burma the State Peace and Development Council (the military government) are accused of inflicting torture and forced labour on the Karenni people and other ethnic minorities. Hundreds of thousands have been forced to flee their homes. Tu Lar Paw is one of them. Four of her seven children died during the persecution, and she was forced to leave her job as a science teacher and risk the treacherous journey to the border of Thailand. There the Burmese Border Consortium, a Christian Aid partner, helps to create self-governing bodies to manage the village-style refugee camps that are home to thousands like Tu Lar Paw. Unlike Naboth she has survived the persecution. She became head teacher of the school for refugee children, and was elected to the key post of chair of the Karenni Refugee Committee.

Find out more about Christian Aid's work in Burma by visiting www.christianaid.org.uk/world/where/asia/burmap.htm

Lord, hear the cries of those who are far from their homes and long for the day when they can return. In your tender mercy, speed the day. Amen.

January 29   Judgement

The word of the Lord came to Elijah the Tishbite, saying: Go down to meet King Ahab of Israel, who rules in Samaria; he is now in the vineyard of Naboth, where he has gone to take possession. You shall say to him, 'Thus says the Lord: Have you killed, and also taken possession?' You shall say to him, 'Thus says the Lord: In the place where dogs licked up the blood of Naboth, dogs will also lick up your blood' . . .

When Ahab heard those words, he tore his clothes and put sackcloth over his bare flesh; he fasted, lay in the sackcloth, and went about dejectedly. Then the word of the Lord came to Elijah the Tishbite: 'Have you seen how Ahab has humbled himself before me? Because he has humbled himself before me, I will not bring the disaster in his days; but in his son's days I will bring the disaster on his house.'

1 Kings 21.17–19, 27–29

Elijah, later recognized to be the great prophet of the Israelites, was Ahab's nemesis. The king called him 'my old enemy'. His chilling words of judgement referred not just to the death of an innocent man, but to Ahab's entire regime, which had allowed poor people to be abused as a means of maintaining power and creating a palace of shameful luxury. The king's repentance, shallow though it seems, was apparently genuine. Three years of peace followed, but when the end came for Ahab and Jezebel both suffered a predictably grizzly death. And the name of Naboth, standing for all who had died or disappeared under their rule, was shouted by the conquering army.

And all this agony over a vineyard! Whatever you next drink, toast the memory of countless thousands like Naboth who have lost land or life at the hands of those who have kept themselves in power by ruthless means. It is a sombre toast, but drink with joy that judgement will surely come.

Bless your people, Lord,
who have walked too long this night of pain.
Too many women mourn the loss of their sons,
and all the Earth is turned into another Calvary.
With your Spirit, Lord, we cry for peace.
With your Spirit, we struggle to be free.

A prayer from the Philippines, on behalf of the mothers of peasant farmers killed as they petitioned for land reform

January 30   David and Bathsheba

In the spring of the year, the time when kings go out to battle, David sent Joab with his officers and all Israel with him; they ravaged the Ammonites, and besieged Rabbah. But David remained at Jerusalem.

It happened, late one afternoon, when David rose from his couch and was walking about on the roof of the king's house, that he saw from the roof a woman bathing; the woman was very beautiful. David sent someone to inquire about the woman. It was reported, 'This is Bathsheba daughter of Eliam, the wife of Uriah the Hittite.' So David sent messengers to get her, and she came to him, and he lay with her. (Now she was purifying herself after her period.) Then she returned to her house. The woman conceived; and she sent and told David, 'I am pregnant.'

2 Samuel 11.1–5

Can you do whatever you want just because you are the king? The story we read over the past three days made it clear that God's answer is no. The story of Elijah and Naboth showed that God's standards should be central to public ethics. The story of David and Bathsheba demonstrates that the same is true of private morality.

From the start, Bathsheba is seen as the victim, not the guilty one. David should not have been idling in his palace; he should have been at war. Bathsheba was married to Uriah, a man whose name meant 'the God of the Jews is my light', so even though he was a foreigner he seems to have known better than David.

It is all too easy to see how temptation began. Over the next few days we will see how it grew into a catastrophe that blighted several generations. That is what infidelity can sometimes do. It would be good to take stock of your own life as you read the story, because temptations are easiest to overcome when they first occur, not when they get a grip.

Make life easier for yourself today by making temptation more difficult. Throw things out, erase files from the computer, tell someone to stop contacting you, ask someone to help you be strong. Do whatever it takes!

O God who promised to be the strength of weak people:
at the swiftest moment of choice,
at the toughest moment of temptation,
at the best moment of opportunity,
don't let me fail you. Amen.

January 31 A righteous man

David sent word to Joab, 'Send me Uriah the Hittite.' And Joab sent Uriah to David. When Uriah came to him, David asked how Joab and the people fared, and how the war was going. Then David said to Uriah, 'Go down to your house, and wash your feet.' Uriah went out of the king's house, and there followed him a present from the king. But Uriah slept at the entrance of the king's house with all the servants of his lord, and did not go down to his house. When they told David, 'Uriah did not go down to his house', David said to Uriah, 'You have just come from a journey. Why did you not go down to your house?' Uriah said to David, 'The ark and Israel and Judah remain in booths; and my lord Joab and the servants of my lord are camping in the open field; shall I then go to my house, to eat and to drink, and to lie with my wife? As you live, and as your soul lives, I will not do such a thing.'

2 Samuel 11.6–11

David was in a mess. Bathsheba was pregnant and it would soon become obvious that she had committed adultery. He could doubtless brazen it out, but for Bathsheba it might mean execution. So David attempted a cover-up. He ordered her husband home from the war on the pretext of needing to be briefed. He assumed that, after six months of all-male company, Uriah would find Bathsheba irresistible. When her baby was born, people would remember his leave with a smirk. (I presume you have already guessed what 'wash your feet' was a Hebrew euphemism for!)

David's deviousness was foiled by straightforward goodness. It was a religious festival and the army was marking it with a period of celibacy. Uriah considered himself a soldier, even off-duty. To make sure he was not tempted by his wife's 'come-to-bed smile', he wouldn't even meet her. Not even when David pumped him full of alcohol! David would have to think of something better than that. Or something worse!

It takes a huge amount of energy to maintain a lie. Is there anything in your life which could be made less complex simply by telling the truth? Weigh it up!

Lead me in your truth, and teach me,
for you are the God of my salvation;
for you I wait all day long.

Psalm 25.5

February 1   State murder

David wrote a letter to Joab, and sent it by the hand of Uriah. In the letter he wrote, 'Set Uriah in the forefront of the hardest fighting, and then draw back from him, so that he may be struck down and die.' As Joab was besieging the city, he assigned Uriah to the place where he knew there were valiant warriors. The men of the city came out and fought with Joab; and some of the servants of David among the people fell. Uriah the Hittite was killed as well . . .

David said to the messenger, 'Thus you shall say to Joab, "Do not let this matter trouble you, for the sword devours now one and now another; press your attack on the city, and overthrow it." And encourage him.'

When the wife of Uriah heard that her husband was dead, she made lamentation for him. When the mourning was over, David sent and brought her to his house, and she became his wife, and bore him a son. But the thing that David had done displeased the Lord.

2 Samuel 11.14–17, 25–27

David's misdemeanour was escalating into a crisis. He was the father of Bathsheba's child. He had attempted to cover this up by creating the circumstances in which people would assume that Uriah (her husband) was the father, but it had not worked. Rather than face up to the consequences of what he had done, he arranged for Uriah's death. With only Joab (the army commander, whom he trusted) aware of the truth, David thought that he had got away with murder – literally. But he was wrong. It is not possible to hide such things from God.

When Philip, Duke of Edinburgh, went to Jerusalem in 1995 he visited *Yad Vashem*, the memorial of the holocaust in which millions of Jews suffered at the hands of the Nazis in the 1940s. He wrote memorably in the visitors' book: 'God brings everything we do to judgement.' To whom would you like to say those words today? Shut your eyes and imagine yourself saying it to them. Then address the words to yourself – do they sound like an encouragement or a warning?

Lord, we pray for those all over the world who are mistakenly accused and unjustly convicted, and for those who are imprisoned, tortured and killed for their beliefs. Amen.

The prayer of a Chinese Christian following the massacre in Tiananmen Square on 3 June 1989

February 2 Condemnation

The Lord sent Nathan to David. He came to him, and said to him, 'There were two men in a certain city, the one rich and the other poor. The rich man had very many flocks and herds; but the poor man had nothing but one little ewe lamb, which he had bought. He brought it up, and it grew up with him and with his children; it used to eat of his meagre fare, and drink from his cup, and lie in his bosom, and it was like a daughter to him. Now there came a traveller to the rich man, and he was loath to take one of his own flock or herd to prepare for the wayfarer who had come to him, but he took the poor man's lamb, and prepared that for the guest who had come to him.' Then David's anger was greatly kindled against the man. He said to Nathan, 'As the Lord lives, the man who has done this deserves to die; he shall restore the lamb fourfold, because he did this thing, and because he had no pity.'

Nathan said to David, 'You are the man!'

2 Samuel 12.1–7

David had seven wives before he stole someone else's. What is it that brings someone so powerful to the point at which he or she says, 'I have done wrong'? In a world in which presidents can inflict great suffering in order to cling on to power, this is a vital question. But it is equally pertinent in relation to our personal morality. Sometimes the last person to realize that I can no longer defend what I have done is me.

Nathan took David back to his youth – days of stories, shepherding and pets. His tale was so naive that it went straight to the king's heart. If, in those youthful and relatively innocent days, David could have foreseen how his life would develop, what might he have done differently?

Think back to the days when you were youthful and relatively innocent – idealistic too, perhaps! Would that 'you' tell the present-day 'you' to change anything?

Lord God, protect all who risk their freedom to draw attention to evil. Prosper all who use godly means to end the rule of those who abuse their power. And work in the hearts of those who have done much that is corrupt so that they recognize the need to repent. Amen.

February 3   David repents

Nathan said to David, . . . 'Thus says the Lord, the God of Israel: I anointed you king over Israel, and I rescued you from the hand of Saul; I gave you your master's house, and your master's wives into your bosom, and gave you the house of Israel and of Judah; and if that had been too little, I would have added as much more. Why have you despised the word of the Lord, to do what is evil in his sight? You have struck down Uriah the Hittite with the sword, and have taken his wife to be your wife, and have killed him with the sword of the Ammonites. Now therefore the sword shall never depart from your house, for you have despised me . . .' David said to Nathan, 'I have sinned against the Lord.' Nathan said to David, 'Now the Lord has put away your sin; you shall not die.'

2 *Samuel 12.7–10, 13*

The cover-up through which David tried to evade the conse-quences of adultery and murder lasted for months. Nathan must have skewered David for hours when he laid the truth bare. But when David admitted his sin, God's forgiveness was instant. The contrast could not be more plain. Nathan tells David that God has forgiven him in no-nonsense monosyllables.

Saying 'Sorry' may start to lose its value now that a computer can make an automated voice apologize that a train is late, or a politician can apologize to a nation for wrongs committed decades ago. But in the eyes of God, sincere and simple repentance will always be followed by complete and life-changing forgiveness. That is God's nature.

If you have an apology to make, start with God. (That's the easy bit!) Now test its sincerity by apologizing to the person you have wronged. (That's the tricky bit!)

These are the words David wrote as the full impact of what he had done wrong sunk in. If you recognize anything in them which matches your own feelings, say them to God, whose forgiveness will be as absolute as it was for David:

Have mercy on me, O God, according to your unfailing love.
Wash away all my iniquity and cleanse me from my sin.
Create in me a pure heart, O God,
and renew a steadfast spirit within me.
Restore to me the joy of your salvation.

Psalm 51.1–2, 10, 12

February 4   Actions have consequences

[Nathan said to David,] 'Because by this deed you have utterly scorned the Lord, the child that is born to you shall die.' Then Nathan went to his house.

The Lord struck the child that Uriah's wife bore to David, and it became very ill. David therefore pleaded with God for the child; David fasted, and went in and lay all night on the ground. The elders of his house stood beside him, urging him to rise from the ground; but he would not, nor did he eat food with them. On the seventh day the child died. And the servants of David were afraid to tell him that the child was dead; for they said, 'While the child was still alive, we spoke to him, and he did not listen to us; how then can we tell him the child is dead? He may do himself some harm.'

2 Samuel 12.14–18

The aftermath of David's adultery with Bathsheba continued to unfold as a terrible tragedy. He had done wrong. He had tried to make sure he wasn't found out by doing something even worse. Genuinely remorseful, he had repented. And he had been forgiven.

End of story? Yes and no! God's forgiveness was total and unconditional. But actions have consequences. Even forgiven actions have consequences. For the rest of his life, David's relationships with his family brought him misery. Much of it can be traced to the jealousies that he introduced into the household by his own unfaithfulness. And some of it, like the tragic death of the baby we read of here, brought him face to face with the fact that not even a king can tell God what to do.

The work of putting right the relationships with the people we have damaged remains a responsibility, even after God has forgiven us.

The North American writer Paul Boese said: 'Forgiveness does not change the past, but it does enlarge the future.' Would your life be improved by letting go of something that has been gnawing at you? What would it take?

God in heaven, you have helped my life grow like a tree. Now something has happened. Satan, like a bird, has carried in one twig of his own choosing after another. Before I knew it he had built a dwelling place and was living in it. Tonight, my Father, I am throwing out both the bird and the nest.

A prayer from Nigeria

February 5   Restoration

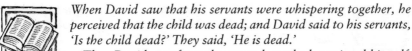

When David saw that his servants were whispering together, he perceived that the child was dead; and David said to his servants, 'Is the child dead?' They said, 'He is dead.'

Then David rose from the ground, washed, anointed himself, and changed his clothes. He went into the house of the Lord, and worshipped; he then went to his own house; and when he asked, they set food before him and he ate. Then his servants said to him, 'What is this thing that you have done? You fasted and wept for the child while it was alive; but when the child died, you rose and ate food.' He said, 'While the child was still alive, I fasted and wept; for I said, "Who knows? The Lord may be gracious to me, and the child may live." But now he is dead; why should I fast? Can I bring him back again? I shall go to him, but he will not return to me.'

Then David consoled his wife Bathsheba, and went to her, and lay with her; and she bore a son, and he named him Solomon. The Lord loved him, and sent a message by the prophet Nathan; so he named him Jedidiah, because of the Lord.

2 Samuel 12.19–25

When we read about David yesterday, he was distraught at the death of his baby. By the end of today's reading, his life has turned a positive corner. What did he do to stop punishing himself?

- He washed and changed.
- He had something to eat.
- He talked about it with someone who had shared the anguish.
- He had sex.
- He affirmed that God loved him (it is what the name 'Jedidiah' means).

Often when Christians are depressed they look for spiritual ways of addressing it. Important as those ways are, David's experience reminds us that there are some very practical things we can do as well.

I should imagine that at least one of those five practical things would improve your life today, no matter whether you are in a time of melancholy or high spirits. Whichever you choose, thank God that he has put it in our world as a source of healing.

I do not know, O God, what there is in store for me. Only let me have your grace to live with your blessing.

The prayer of a Tamil Christian awaiting repatriation to India

February 6   Nehemiah learns of the poor

[Nehemiah wrote:] Now there was a great outcry of the people and of their wives against their Jewish kin. For . . . there were those who said, 'We are having to borrow money on our fields and vineyards to pay the king's tax. Now our flesh is the same as that of our kindred; our children are the same as their children; and yet we are forcing our sons and daughters to be slaves, and some of our daughters have been ravished; we are powerless, and our fields and vineyards now belong to others.'

I was very angry when I heard their outcry and these complaints. After thinking it over, I brought charges against the nobles and the officials.

Nehemiah 5.1, 4–7

450 years before Jesus was born, Nehemiah's people had been set free from captivity by the Babylonians. They were returning home poor, but elated. But their joy was turning to misery. The wealthy Israelites had been seduced by the ways of the Babylonians, and when people fell into debt, they were taking them into slavery. It was even worse than before. The poor were slaves again – this time not to their enemies but to their own countrymen.

But Nehemiah was an exception! He was one of those people who do well no matter what the circumstances are. Even in Babylon his captors had noticed his talent and, although he spent the exile as a servant like everyone else, he had been servant to the king. When they returned home, he was a natural choice as their leader. But rich and successful though he was, he put himself on the side of the poor and argued their case. His was the first campaign to cancel unpayable debt.

At the end of the last century the Jubilee Debt Campaign generated a potential $100 billion that could be put toward education and health instead of repaying debt in the world's poorest countries. But the pressure on governments to keep their promises did not stop when the new century began. If you would like to investigate the facts and figures in some depth, visit www.christianaid.org.uk/indepth/debt.htm

Throughout history, world leaders who use their influence to put themselves on the side of the poor have been the exception, not the rule. Pray for people with a passion for justice to be elected, and for their ambitions not to be compromised when they achieve power.

February 7   Freed from debt

[Nehemiah said to the nobles,] 'You are all taking interest from your own people.' And I called a great assembly to deal with them . . . They were silent, and could not find a word to say. So I said, 'The thing that you are doing is not good. Should you not walk in the fear of our God, to prevent the taunts of the nations our enemies? Moreover I and my brothers and my servants are lending them money and grain. Let us stop this taking of interest. Restore to them, this very day, their fields, their vineyards, their olive orchards, and their houses, and the interest on money, grain, wine, and oil that you have been exacting from them.' Then they said, 'We will restore everything and demand nothing more from them. We will do as you say.'

Nehemiah 5.7–12

This is how the first campaign to cancel unpayable debt came to an end. It was a success, diverting money from debt repayments into agricultural projects. In our time, the Jubilee Debt Campaign has brought together campaigners in the northern and southern hemispheres as never before. In the UK alone 250,000 postcards were sent to the British government.

But something far more significant has happened. Samuel Waiswa's three children started school. He lives in Uganda, and his own schooling came to a premature end when fees were introduced. But because of debt cancellation, the government has been able to reintroduce free primary education, and Samuel's children go to school in their smart purple uniforms. They are taught not just in the shade of a mango tree, but in the new brick classrooms of Naisanga Primary School. 'I want them to be doctors or teachers', Samuel says.

Debt cancellation has made a great difference to Uganda. But all that has been gained is under threat from a civil war in the north of the country in which children have become the most vulnerable casualties. Find out the latest information about Christian Aid's work in Uganda at www.christianaid.org.uk/world/where/eagl/ugandap.htm

Loving God, we pray for the children of Uganda and give thanks for the schooling and health care available to them as a result of debt cancellation. We remember children in other countries who continue to suffer because of debt. May we who have access to education and medicine never take them for granted until they are shared by every human you have created. Amen.

February 8   I acted differently

[Nehemiah wrote:] The people did as they had promised. Moreover, from the time that I was appointed to be their governor in the land of Judah, from the twentieth year to the thirty-second year of King Artaxerxes, twelve years, neither I nor my brothers ate the food allowance of the governor. The former governors who were before me laid heavy burdens on the people, and took food and wine from them, besides forty shekels of silver. Even their servants lorded it over the people. But I did not do so, because of the fear of God.

Nehemiah 5.13–15

I have known the last sentence of today's Bible passage almost all my life. I barely recognize it because when I learnt it by heart in Sunday school this translation of the Bible had not yet been made. The version I learnt was: 'I acted differently because I honoured God.'

It has had more impact on me than any other Bible verse. It sums up for me the entire point of being a Christian! If faith is going to have any meaning, it must make a noticeable difference to the way we behave. Remembering that verse at key moments has both stopped me doing things and prompted me to take action. It once flashed into my head just as I had passed the concrete 'honesty box' of an unattended car park on the south coast of England without putting in any money. (Unfortunately it didn't stop me reversing into the pillar and denting my bumper when I attempted to put it right without the effort of getting out of the car!)

For Nehemiah, faith in God made a difference to his government's policies. But it also made a difference to his personal morality, because he waived his right as a governor to accumulate a personal fortune by taxing people. He believed he was made a leader of the people in order to serve them, not to benefit personally.

If you want to take the risk that it might make you a better person, learn that life-changing verse by heart: 'I acted differently because I honoured God. Nehemiah 5.15.'

Lord God, there are a hundred ways in which I want the world to be different. But I know that the change has to begin with me. May the love I have for you prompt me to act differently – again and again and again. Amen.

February 9   Why is God silent?

Why, O Lord, do you stand far off?
    Why do you hide yourself in times of trouble?
In arrogance the wicked persecute the poor –
    let them be caught in the schemes they have devised.
For the wicked boast of the desires of their heart,
  those greedy for gain curse and renounce the Lord.
In the pride of their countenance the wicked say, 'God will not seek it out';
  all their thoughts are, 'There is no God.'
Their ways prosper at all times;
  your judgements are on high, out of their sight;
  as for their foes, they scoff at them.
They think in their heart, 'We shall not be moved;
  throughout all generations we shall not meet adversity.'

Psalm 10.1–6

There are two questions here, one of which we know the answer to, and one which we don't. The first is, 'How do powerful people get away with exploiting poor people?' The second is, 'Why doesn't our all-powerful God stop it?'

The first answer is: the poor are 'persecuted' because poor countries are not able to set their own priorities when it comes to trade. In Ghana, for instance, tomato farmers struggle to sell their produce because there has been a flood of cheap tomatoes from Europe. But the government of Ghana isn't allowed to help its tomato growers. As a condition for aid from the developed world, Ghana is forced to open up its market, no matter what the cost is to the poorest citizens. Who created such unfair rules? The rich countries, of course, full of people who 'boast about the desires of their heart'.

As for the second question, generations of believers have asked why God does not intervene on behalf of suffering people. Surely it is not because he has failed to; it must be because he has decided not to. Like the writers of the Bible, we wrestle with this. Perhaps God has entrusted the task of changing what is wrong to his followers.

Find out more about the rules that govern world trade from *Trade Justice: A Campaign Handbook*, which can be obtained free of charge by telephoning 08700 787788. Alternatively you can view it at
www.christianaid.org.uk/campaign/trade/handbook/index.htm

Lord God, when you choose to be silent, give me grace to speak words that are worthy of you. Amen.

February 10   What the wicked say

*[The mouths of the wicked] are filled with cursing
and deceit and oppression;
    under their tongues are mischief and iniquity.
They sit in ambush in the villages;
    in hiding places they murder the innocent.*
*Their eyes stealthily watch for the helpless;
    they lurk in secret like a lion in its covert;
they lurk that they may seize the poor;
    they seize the poor and drag them off in their net.
They stoop, they crouch,
    and the helpless fall by their might.
They think in their heart, 'God has forgotten,
    he has hidden his face, he will never see it.'*

Psalm 10.7–11

This description of people whose actions destroy the poor seems such a cartoon that it is hard to relate to. But one feature is very familiar – the process happens out of sight. There are 'hiding places' in which these things can happen without our consciences being disturbed. Much of the damage that is done to poor communities is hidden too.

- We buy cheap food; farmers in poor countries cannot afford for their children to learn to read.
- We drive cars wastefully; low-lying countries flood.
- Our pension schemes hold shares in pharmaceutical companies; people die of curable diseases in Africa.

All these are connected, but the connection is out of sight. Self-interested people keep the connections hidden. Well-meaning people simply do not see them. They are not hidden from God, no matter how much people hope he has forgotten. You and I know about the connections. So what shall we do about it?

Christian Aid helps people challenge 'hidden' injustice through its campaigns. If you want to know how to draw injustice to the attention of key people, telephone 020 7523 2225 or visit www.christianaid.org.uk/campaign/joinus.htm, and join the huge group of people who regularly take simple actions to highlight injustice.

*From all that is dangerous, seen and unseen, good Lord protect me;
About all that is unfair, seen and unseen, good Lord challenge me;
Against all that is evil, seen and unseen, good Lord rouse me,
So that your kingdom may never be forgotten.*

February 11   Do not forget the oppressed

Rise up, O Lord;
O God, lift up your hand; do not forget the oppressed.
Why do the wicked renounce God,
     and say in their hearts, 'You will not call us to account'?
But you do see! Indeed you note trouble and grief,
  that you may take it into your hands;
the helpless commit themselves to you;
  you have been the helper of the orphan.
Break the arm of the wicked and evildoers;
  seek out their wickedness until you find none.
The Lord is king for ever and ever;
  the nations shall perish from his land.
O Lord, you will hear the desire of the meek;
  you will strengthen their heart, you will incline your ear
to do justice for the orphan and the oppressed,
  so that those from earth may strike terror no more.

Psalm 10.12–18

What strikes me most about this psalm is its selflessness. Many people ask the question, 'Why is there suffering in the world?' but actually mean, 'Why am I having to suffer?' This, however, is a plea from a comfortable setting on behalf of poor people. It could be Christian Aid's own prayer. There are four things in it which are familiar to many who pray for social justice:

* An acknowledgement that we need to pray because God can do things that we cannot do: 'Rise up!'
* A moment of doubt, because the wicked seem to get away with it.
* An expression of faith that when we pray for God to 'take the weak into his hands' we are asking something that he already longs to do.
* Confidence that creation's final destiny is for God to take control 'for ever and ever'.

God's 'hand' is mentioned twice. Draw round your own hand on a piece of paper and on it write, 'Do not forget the oppressed.' If you have a Bible on your shelf, slip it inside, so that you will come across it from time to time as a prayer to God. Or a reminder to you!

Look at your own hand for a moment or two. What do you imagine when you read of God lifting his hand against evil? What do you imagine when you read of God cradling in his hand those with 'trouble and grief'?

February 12   The Lord loves justice

> In the Lord I take refuge; how can you say to me,
>   'Flee like a bird to the mountains;
> for look, the wicked bend the bow,
>   they have fitted their arrow to the string,
>   to shoot in the dark at the upright in heart.
> If the foundations are destroyed, what can the righteous do?'
> The Lord is in his holy temple; the Lord's throne is in heaven.
>   His eyes behold, his gaze examines humankind.
> The Lord tests the righteous and the wicked,
>   and his soul hates the lover of violence.
> On the wicked he will rain coals of fire and sulphur;
>   a scorching wind shall be the portion of their cup.
> For the Lord is righteous; he loves righteous deeds;
>   the upright shall behold his face.

Psalm 11.1–7

OK, the world is in a mess! Its moral standards are lousy, people go hungry, and not a day goes by without violence. So what are we going to do?

Option one: Create a purer-than-pure Church in which we only meet Christians, watch nothing but TV evangelists, burn unwholesome books, and write to each other from nuclear bunkers using pens with Bible texts on. That's 'fleeing to the mountains'.

Option two: Meet power with power by preparing ourselves for war against tyrants and oppressors, confident that we have a righteous cause and God on our side. That's 'securing the foundations' with our modern equivalents of bows and arrows.

Option three: Take refuge in God. Trust that from heaven he knows what is happening and is God not only of 'the righteous' but also of 'the wicked'. Ally ourselves with his will and his ways by doing only 'righteous deeds' while fully engaging with the world.

Work out where the psalm writer placed himself – in the ghetto, in the warplane, or doing his best in the muddle. What changes would be needed in your life to stand in the same place?

Lead us not into imitation, but deliver us from evil.

Prayer of the East Asia Christian Youth Consultation Council

February 13   A minority of one

Help, O Lord, for there is no longer anyone who is godly;
*   the faithful have disappeared from humankind.*
They utter lies to each other;
*   with flattering lips and a double heart they speak.*
May the Lord cut off all flattering lips,
* the tongue that makes great boasts,*
those who say, 'With our tongues we will prevail;
* our lips are our own – who is our master?'*

Psalm 12.1–3

This is a prayer for anyone who has ever been in a minority of one. It is for the worker who realizes that her colleagues are saying different things to her face and behind her back. It is for the teenager who can't seem to find the words to say which would make him acceptable to the school's in-crowd. It is for the person trapped in the unbearable loneliness of living with a family who have stopped talking to each other and started talking at each other.

And the prayer is concise: 'Help!'

The writer knows what to do. He takes his loneliness and frustration to God. He knows that we have a God whose words are always true (even when they are harsh), whose words always have integrity (although we may not always want to hear what they say), and whose words have authority (enduring long after human tongues go silent).

It is true that 'our lips are our own'. We are the only people who can decide what we say. And we can use words to isolate humans from each other. But they will never be able to separate us from God.

Think back to the last thing that you really regret saying. Next, think back to the last thing that you are genuinely glad that you said. Which is most recent? Do either of them leave you with unfinished business? Make a point of saying something today which diminishes the total amount of loneliness in the world.

Dear God, be good to me.
The sea is so wide, and my boat is so small.

Traditional prayer of fishermen in Brittany, France

February 14   God will rise up

'Because the poor are despoiled, because the needy groan,
I will now rise up,' says the Lord;
'I will place them in the safety for which they long.'
The promises of the Lord are promises that are pure,
silver refined in a furnace on the ground, purified seven times.
You, O Lord, will protect us;
you will guard us from this generation for ever.
On every side the wicked prowl,
as vileness is exalted among humankind.

Psalm 12.5–8

The first part of this psalm, which we read yesterday, featured words being used to wound or to gain advantage. But this part of the psalm draws attention to different kinds of words altogether.

The first is the unambiguous 'groan' of the oppressed. Such heartfelt cries to God always receive his undivided attention. What makes a king who is sitting on a throne surrounded by his court 'rise up'? Maybe anger, maybe determination, maybe impatience – all of those must be felt deeply by God when he sees the man-made conditions which 'despoil' the poor.

The second is the uttered 'promise' of the Lord. It is a pure promise that hasn't been made casually. The image of a crucible in which the promise is refined like precious metal speaks of the painful cost of bringing those who are wronged into a place of safety. The life and death of Jesus show us just how costly that salvation can be.

The wicked have not stopped 'prowling'. Don't make a promise lightly to rise up alongside God as his messenger.

Suppose the next few words you utter were going to be the most important words you say this year. What would you say, and to whom would you say it? (OK! We all know it's Valentine's Day. But don't let that completely unbalance your thinking!) Choose what you say or write for the rest of the day carefully, so that the words are really worthwhile.

May the words of my mouth and the meditation of my heart be
acceptable to you, O Lord, my rock and my redeemer.

Psalm 19.14

February 15   Children sing praise

O Lord, our Sovereign,
  how majestic is your name in all the earth!
You have set your glory above the heavens.
  Out of the mouths of babes and infants
  you have founded a bulwark because of your foes,
to silence the enemy and the avenger.
When I look at your heavens, the work of your fingers,
  the moon and the stars that you have established;
what are human beings that you are mindful of them,
  mortals that you care for them?

Psalm 8.1–4

Three thousand years ago a poet looked up at the night sky above Jerusalem and was staggered by the size of the sky, and the brilliance and abundance of the stars. A modern astronomer turns the radio telescope toward the void and attempts to take in vast numbers and unimaginable distances of which the composer of this psalm could never have dreamed.

Whether the scale of the cosmos strengthens a belief in God or does the opposite, there is someone thinking even more powerful thoughts than the poet or the scientist, and that is a baby. A child doesn't attempt to account for God, nor describe him, deny him, or limit him. A child just wonders. Nobody (not even God's worst enemy) would tell a child that he is stupid to be in awe of what is just a random scientific accident in the great elemental soup. Instead, a child is encouraged to marvel.

Infant one; atheist nil.

And God's attitude to all this? Perhaps a bit more childish amazement would be good for us all from time to time.

Day or night, take a good, long look out of the window and up to the sky. White, blue, grey, black or, if you are lucky, a spectrum of winter sunset colours. Drink it all in!

May none of God's wonderful works keep silence, night or morning. Bright stars, high mountains, the depths of the seas, sources of rushing rivers: may all these break into song as we sing to Father, Son and Holy Spirit. May all the angels in the heavens reply: Amen, Amen, Amen. Power, praise, honour, eternal glory to God, the only giver of grace. Amen, Amen, Amen.

Third-century anonymous hymn

February 16   Human worth

You have made [human beings] a little lower than God,
and crowned them with glory and honour.
You have given them dominion over the works of your hands;
you have put all things under their feet,
all sheep and oxen, and also the beasts of the field,
the birds of the air, and the fish of the sea,
whatever passes along the paths of the seas.
O Lord, our Sovereign, how majestic is your name in all the earth!

Psalm 8.5–9

With great power comes great responsibility. Some words of Nelson Mandela: 'Our deepest fear is not that we are inadequate. Our deepest fear is that we are powerful beyond measure. It is our light, not our darkness, that most frightens us.'

In East India, Christian Aid supports a partner organization called Gram Vikas, whose objective is to help villages take responsibility for their own environment. The project started as a programme for clean water so that village ponds do not have to be used for drinking, washing and cleaning clothes. But subsequently Gram Vikas has established a way of allowing families to work together to make decisions. They contribute labour and a small amount of money, and out of it come results that benefit the whole village – toilets, bathing rooms and schemes to irrigate land for farming. Five thousand villages in Orissa have been helped in this way.

When human beings are able to work in community for the good of the land and the good of each other, we get a glimpse of why God has such a trust in our 'glory and honour'. But we also become aware of how often we fail the trust that has been placed in us.

Find out more about Christian Aid's work in India at www.christianaid.org.uk/world/where/asia/indiap.htm

O burning mountain, O chosen sun,
O perfect moon, O fathomless well,
O unattainable height, O clearness beyond measure,
O wisdom without strength, O mercy without limit,
O strength beyond resistance, O crown of all majesty,
The humblest you created sings your praise.

Mechtilde of Magdeburg (c. 1220–80)

February 17   Rich generosity

We want you to know, brothers and sisters, about the grace of God that has been granted to the churches of Macedonia; for during a severe ordeal of affliction, their abundant joy and their extreme poverty have overflowed in a wealth of generosity on their part. For, as I can testify, they voluntarily gave according to their means, and even beyond their means, begging us earnestly for the privilege of sharing in this ministry to the saints.

2 Corinthians 8.1–4

The birth of the Church in the twenty years after Jesus' resurrection coincided with a massive famine. In particular the citizens of Jerusalem were in great distress. It was the first time that the rapidly growing Church had to deal with the question: 'As Christians are we responsible for people we do not know, in places we will never visit, when we discover that they are in need?' The answer was an unequivocal 'Yes.' The only question was how to help in a way that was effective.

The solution that the leaders of the Church chose was to ask Christians in the towns that were thriving to give money. It was to be taken to places where the famine was severe and invested in projects that would provide for those who were suffering. So the letters that Paul wrote were fundraising letters. It seems obvious now, but this was the first use of the principles that inspire Christian Aid to ask churches in relatively wealthy countries to give money. The fact that the New Testament was compiled shortly after this means that giving has always been at the heart of practical Christianity.

In the first years of the twenty-first century a famine as devastating as the one in Jerusalem threatened parts of Africa – seven countries in the south and Ethiopia in the north-east. The poorest communities, especially in Malawi and Zimbabwe, still struggle to maintain a regular supply of food. Unlike the Christians to whom Paul wrote, we can see the need with our own eyes. Find out about the 'severe ordeal of affliction' of our generation at www.christianaid.org.uk/world/where/safrica/safrica.htm

I saw a child today, Lord, who will not die tonight, harried into hunger's grave. He was bright and full of life because his father had a job and feeds him. But somewhere, everywhere, 10,000 life-lamps will go out, and not be lit again tomorrow. Lord, teach me my sin. Amen.

Prayer of an African Christian

February 18   The grace of giving

[The churches of Macedonia] gave themselves first to the Lord and, by the will of God, to us, so that we might urge Titus that, as he had already made a beginning, so he should also complete this generous undertaking among you. Now as you excel in everything – in faith, in speech, in knowledge, in utmost eagerness, and in our love for you – so we want you to excel also in this generous undertaking.

2 Corinthians 8.5–7

The people of Jerusalem were enduring a desperate famine. The churches in Macedonia had collected money. Titus had agreed to become the courier, so he had visited Macedonia to receive their gift and was planning to visit Corinth so that he could add the money they were collecting to the kitty.

Paul had not really expected the churches in Macedonia to be involved. They themselves were so poor that he did not even target them in the appeal. But they were so moved by the stories they heard from Jerusalem that they had begged to participate. In fact, they gave more than the wealthy Christians in Corinth to whom Paul wrote these words.

It is difficult to tell what went wrong in Corinth. They were exemplary in their trust in God and their knowledge of what it means to be a Christian. But their eagerness to serve the Lord had not been matched by a willingness to be generous to poor people. The Macedonians had got it right almost by accident. By wholeheartedly giving themselves to the Lord they had become like him – passionately generous.

Empty the contents of your wallet or purse on to your lap – money, cards, papers and photos tucked away in the compartments. What do the contents say about . . .

- what you enjoy;
- the relationships that are important to you;
- the things you value most deeply;
- your Christian faith?

May your bounty teach me greatness of heart.
May your magnificence stop me being mean.
Seeing you a prodigal and open-handed giver,
let me give unstintingly like a king's son,
like God's own.

Helder Camara (1909–99)

February 19   Jesus became poor

I do not [ask you to give to the poor] as a command, but I am testing the genuineness of your love against the earnestness of others. For you know the generous act of our Lord Jesus Christ, that though he was rich, yet for your sakes he became poor, so that by his poverty you might become rich.

2 Corinthians 8.8–9

Why should Christians give money? Because it makes them like Jesus.

We have a God who chose to show the full extent of what it means to live a worthwhile life by emptying himself of the unimaginable riches of heaven and being born on Earth with nothing. He did not do it with a self-serving motive; he did it with a completely gratuitous generosity so that everything and everyone else in creation would benefit.

I enjoy thinking of God's love towards us as gratuitous because it's such a great-sounding word, and usually it only gets used in connection with pornography: 'Did you see the film on Channel 5 last night? Uggh, it made me shudder! Completely gratuitous, over-the-top, and just pandering to people's most basic needs.' It takes on a new meaning when it describes God: 'Did you read in 2 Corinthians about God's love for us? Aaah, it makes me shudder! Completely gratuitous, over-the-top, and pandering to people's most basic needs.'

Genuinely generous giving by God inspires genuinely generous giving to those in need.

Think back over the past two months and make a mental list of things you have been given. Start with Christmas, and enjoy people's generosity to you all over again. What has come since then? A birthday, a tax rebate, a surprise, a round of applause, a seat on a crowded bus, a kiss? What about natural gifts – spring bulbs, a sunset, a baby?

Thou who wast rich beyond all splendour,
All for love's sake becamest poor;
Thrones for a manger didst surrender,
Sapphire-paved courts for stable floor.
Thou who art love beyond all telling,
Saviour and King, we worship thee.
Emmanuel within us dwelling,
Make us what thou wouldst have us be.

Frank Houghton (1894–1972)

February 20   Plenty and need

It is appropriate for you who began last year not only to do something, but even to desire to do something – now finish doing it, so that your eagerness may be matched by completing it according to your means. For if the eagerness is there, the gift is acceptable according to what one has – not according to what one does not have. I do not mean that there should be relief for others and pressure on you, but it is a question of a fair balance between your present abundance and their need, so that their abundance may be for your need, in order that there may be a fair balance. As it is written:
'The one who had much did not have too much,
and the one who had little did not have too little.'

2 Corinthians 8.10–15

In 1820 the richest 20 percent of the world's population received three times as much as the poorest 20 percent. By 1870 it had grown to seven times as much. By 1913 it was eleven times. In 1960 it had risen to a scandalous thirty times. In 1990 it was sixty times. Twelve years later, in 2002, the richest received 114 times as much as the poorest.

It is in the context of these figures from the *United Nations Human Development Report* (2002) that we read in 2 Corinthians that 'it is a question of a fair balance'. Paul's intention was not that giving should cause a different group of people to find themselves in hardship. Rather, it was that there should be ever-increasing equality. That is the condition to which God still wants the world to aspire.

Those of us who agonize that we do not have the personal resources to make a substantial difference should not feel that we have failed. Paul points out that the key is 'eagerness'. If our hearts are set on being part of God's solution, we will find joy in giving an amount that is appropriate to our own means.

Find out what has happened to the divide between rich and poor nations since 2002 by visiting
http://hdr.undp.org/reports/global/2004/pdf/hdr04_HDI.pdf
You will find both good and bad news.

Generous God, give us open minds to understand your will for the world;
give us open hearts to draw us together toward equality;
give us open hands so that we may eagerly give to those in need;
until all the world rejoices to know your plenty. Amen.

February 21 Accountability

Thanks be to God who put in the heart of Titus the same eager-ness for you that I myself have. For he not only accepted our appeal, but since he is more eager than ever, he is going to you of his own accord. With him we are sending the brother who is famous among all the churches for his proclaiming the good news; and not only that, but he has also been appointed by the churches to travel with us while we are administering this generous undertaking for the glory of the Lord himself and to show our goodwill. We intend that no one should blame us about this generous gift that we are administering, for we intend to do what is right not only in the Lord's sight but also in the sight of others.

2 Corinthians 8.16–21

At first sight these verses look like details of someone's travel arrangements. The Christians at Corinth were to expect a visit from Titus and another person whom they did not know, but who is given a reference by Paul as being famous for his integrity in dealing with money (Luke is a good guess). The cash they had collected for famine-stricken Jerusalem was to be given to them.

At second sight it is clear that an important principle was being established. Giving had to be done in such a way that every penny went to the needy people, and none found its way into the pockets of the fundraisers. Two honourable people were involved to reduce the risk of fraud by one of them. It was not enough to say, 'God knows that we are being honest.' It was also important that there was complete accountability. That is a need which has not gone away.

Christian Aid publishes accounts of precisely what it has done with the money it has been given. The law insists that charities do so. But as a Christian organization it also does so in order to handle large amounts of money in a godly way. Find the details at www.christianaid.org.uk/aboutca/annrev/funding.htm

Lord Jesus Christ,
so that I may spend money only on what is valuable,
teach me to want only what is good;
so that I may treat God in a rich way,
teach me to treat riches in a godly way;
so that I may cling tightly to God,
teach me to cling lightly to what I own,
until my soul is content in you. Amen.

February 22 God loves a cheerful giver

The one who sows sparingly will also reap sparingly, and the one who sows bountifully will also reap bountifully. Each of you must give as you have made up your mind, not reluctantly or under compulsion, for God loves a cheerful giver. God is able to provide you with every blessing in abundance, so that by always having enough of everything, you may share abundantly in every good work. As it is written,

'He scatters abroad, he gives to the poor; his righteousness endures for ever.'

He who supplies seed to the sower and bread for food will supply and multiply your seed for sowing and increase the harvest of your righteousness. You will be enriched in every way for your great generosity, which will produce thanksgiving to God through us.

2 Corinthians 9.6–11

Generous people are blessed by God. There is nothing mysterious about that. It is not meant to imply a 'give-now-and-win-the-jackpot-later' lottery. It is simply the truth! People who have a bountiful heart for God and his world find themselves giving bountifully. They love doing it. God loves them doing it. The people who benefit from the money love it. Everyone, absolutely everyone, is blessed by joyful generosity.

In the original Greek version of these verses the word for cheerful is *hilarion*. It is easy to see which modern English word comes from that. The literal translation should be, 'God loves a hilarious giver.' It gives me a vision of the 300,000 people who collect for Christian Aid Week every year rolling with uproarious laughter as they wobble from door to door delivering the famous red envelopes.

The sense that giving to the work of the kingdom of God should be a cheerful matter gives heart to all those who raise money by marathon running, abseiling, baking cakes, holding coffee mornings, selling books and being sponsored for all kinds of eccentric activities! To stretch your imagination (or your legs) about enjoyable ways to take part in the serious business of raising money for the world's poorest communities, visit www.christianaid.org.uk/give/otherway/funevent.htm

Lord God, who walked this earth in Jesus, bless the feet of all who bring good news for the poor – those who travel to dangerous places, those who run on muddy paths to raise money, and those who walk the streets asking others to give.
Step alongside them every pace of the way, we pray. Amen.

February 23   Made rich to be generous

The rendering of this ministry [of giving] not only supplies the needs of the saints but also overflows with many thanksgivings to God. Through the testing of this ministry you glorify God by your obedience to the confession of the gospel of Christ and by the generosity of your sharing with them and with all others, while they long for you and pray for you because of the surpassing grace of God that he has given you. Thanks be to God for his indescribable gift!

Corinthians 9.12–15

A pig and a hen were walking past a church. On the noticeboard, an accusing finger pointed at the passers-by, asking the question: 'What will you do for the world's poorest people?'

'I know what we could do,' clucked the hen to the pig. 'We could team up and lay on a bacon-and-egg supper to raise money!'

'It's all right for you to suggest that,' grumbled the pig. 'For you that would be a gift; for me it would be a sacrifice!'

Something impish in me wants to compare Jesus to the pig and me to the hen. I can't explain exactly what it is about God's nature that tempts me to make such an inappropriate comparison. It's indescribable!

Make a list with three columns. In the left column write the names of organizations to which you give through a scheme of regular giving. In the middle column write others to which you have sometimes given when you notice that a collection is being made. On the right-hand side list organizations which have received a gift from you once in the past. When you see them laid out before you in this way, are there any that should move to another column, or new ones that you should consider adding? Take action!

When shall these longings be sufficed that stir my spirit night
    and day?
When shall I see my country lay her homage at the feet of Christ?
Of all I have, O Saviour sweet, all gifts, all skill, all thoughts of
    mine,
A living garland I entwine, and offer at thy lotus feet.

Indian hymn-writer Narayam Vaman Tilak (1862–1919)

February 24 Regular giving

Now concerning the collection for the saints: you should follow the directions I gave to the churches of Galatia. On the first day of every week, each of you is to put aside and save whatever extra you earn, so that collections need not be taken when I come. And when I arrive, I will send any whom you approve with letters to take your gift to Jerusalem.

1 Corinthians 16.1–3

The easiest way to persuade people to give money to a worthy cause is to artificially create an intense emotional atmosphere, press people to empty their wallets while their feelings are out of control, and then bank the money before they change their minds. That is the opposite of the approach that the Bible urges us to take when we respond to hunger or poverty. When Paul was exhorting the Christians at Corinth to give money to ease the plight of those in Jerusalem it was with these calm words:

- *Giving should be regular.* In Corinth the Christians put aside an amount each Sunday rather than scrambling money together when the collecting box appeared. It was an early forerunner of the direct debit that allows us to give in an organized and tax-efficient way today.
- *Giving should involve everyone.* But the amount should be in proportion to what an individual earns. Less prosperous people could take part in this act of Christian service, but not in a way that oppressed them.
- *Giving should have dignity and integrity.* Paul makes giving to the poor seem devoted but humdrum. Perhaps that is how it should be.

A leaflet called 'Giving to Christian Aid' is available to explain some of the ways of giving money to the world's poorest communities that are regular and orderly. Paul would be astonished by the technology but would recognize the principle! It is available from any of the addresses at the back of the book. Alternatively telephone 0845 7000 300 and enquire about regular giving.

Yours, O Lord, is the greatness and the power and the glory and the majesty and the splendour, for everything in heaven and earth is yours. Wealth and honour come from you; you are the ruler of all things. Now, our God, we give you thanks, and praise your glorious name. Everything comes from you, and we have given you only what comes from your hand.

From 1 Chronicles 29.11–14

February 25   Tithes

Set apart a tithe of all the yield of your seed that is brought in yearly from the field. In the presence of the Lord your God, in the place that he will choose as a dwelling for his name, you shall eat the tithe of your grain, your wine, and your oil, as well as the firstlings of your herd and flock, so that you may learn to fear the Lord your God always . . . eat there in the presence of the Lord your God, you and your household rejoicing together.

Deuteronomy 14.22–23, 26

From these verses in the Old Testament comes the Christian tradition that the appropriate amount of one's income to set aside for the work of the kingdom of God is one tenth ('a tithe'). The concept that a set amount of what we earn must be given away is sometimes scorned as unacceptably legalistic. And yet nothing could sound less legalistic than the process described here. It sounds more like a party!

Perhaps the principle that should inspire us is not the amount, but the fact that giving needs to be done joyfully and in a way that somehow personally involves us, rather than as a grudging duty. Other references to tithes in the 'rule books' of the Old Testament make it clear that farmers should not pick out the shabbiest tenth to give, because what was given became holy – set apart and dedicated to God. Only the best would do!

A waste? Surely not! This was a way of turning money into worship.

Gather together some friends who share your devotion to God. Have a meal. Say grace with real meaning. Talk about God and his world. Drink a toast to the just and hunger-free world we long for. Enjoy each other's company. And enjoy the fact that what you are doing is in God's presence and pleasing to him.

You, Lord, who gives food to all flesh,
who feeds the young ravens that cry up to you,
and has nourished us from our youth up:
fill our hearts with goodness and gladness
and establish our hearts with your grace. Amen.

Grace spoken by Launcelot Andrewes, Bishop of Southwark
(1555–1626)

February 26   Remembering the poor

 As for the Levites resident in your towns, do not neglect them, because they have no allotment or inheritance with you.

Every third year you shall bring out the full tithe of your produce for that year, and store it within your towns; the Levites, because they have no allotment or inheritance with you, as well as the resident aliens, the orphans, and the widows in your towns, may come and eat their fill so that the Lord your God may bless you in all the work that you undertake.

Deuteronomy 14.27–29

 These verses form part of the instructions for how the Hebrews were to give a proportion of their income to God. Sometimes the offering was used as an act of worship, eaten or sacrificed. However, once every three years it was to be given to groups whose circumstances meant that they had an unequal share in the resources of the nation:

- *Levites* – a tribe that had no territory of its own, but was responsible for maintaining the religious and administrative life of the community.
- *Resident aliens* – those who had no rights because they were not Hebrews, but who lived among them and were at their mercy.
- *Orphans* – children who starved if no one took responsibility for them.
- *Widows* – those who were too old to work, but had no other means of being supported.

Of course, some of what the tithe paid for in Hebrew society is now paid for by our taxes. Does that mean that tithes no longer have any relevance? Originally a tithe was only the beginning of what was to be allocated to God's work in the world. On top of the statutory tenth, an individual's 'freewill offering' was an opportunity to give an unspecified amount out of sheer gratitude for what God had done in the past year. C. S. Lewis wrote: 'I do not believe one can settle how much we ought to give. I am afraid the only safe rule is to give more than we can spare.'

 In these very different days of churches, taxes and social services, which groups of people are the equivalents of Levites, aliens, orphans and widows? Work it out and respond!

 Show me, Lord God, how much to give and who to give it to, so that my resources may become your opportunities. Amen.

February 27   Corruption

Now the sons of Eli were scoundrels; they had no regard for the Lord or for the duties of the priests to the people. When anyone offered sacrifice, the priest's servant would come, while the meat was boiling, with a three-pronged fork in his hand, and he would thrust it into the pan, or kettle, or cauldron, or pot; all that the fork brought up the priest would take for himself. This is what they did at Shiloh to all the Israelites who came there . . . Thus the sin of the young men was very great in the sight of the Lord; for they treated the offerings of the Lord with contempt.

1 Samuel 2.12–14, 17

This is one of the most curious of all the daily Bible readings. The system of giving tithes in the Old Testament was open to abuse and not all priests were trustworthy in dealing with the funds. This is the story of two brothers who were corrupt priests. We happen to know their names – Phinehas and Hophni.

As priests, their material needs should have been met by the generosity of God's people. However, the brothers were not content to risk the vagaries of people's giving. Instead they insisted on conducting their 'lucky dip' of the best of the Hebrews' offerings so that the first and best of what was given to God went to them. They were the original unscrupulous, Rolex-wearing, Porsche-driving tele-evangelists. You will be delighted to hear that they both came to sticky ends!

This all sounds vaguely comical today, but so long as large sums of money are given to God's work by faithful worshippers, there will always be corrupt people seeking to gain personally from it. Sadly, part of Christian Aid's work is to ensure that money that is given to address human need cannot be hijacked because of human greed.

Christian Aid's partners in developing countries have strong opinions about how to ensure that the money released by debt relief will be used to reduce poverty and not be wasted. They advocate the creation of national debt relief committees in each country to oversee the funds, and an end to conditions demanded by the International Monetary Fund in return for loans. Read their reasons in-depth at www.christianaid.org.uk/indepth/9906corr/corrupt.htm

Holy God, confound the efforts of all who seek to benefit from the suffering of others. Let honesty and aid go hand in hand until there is no more need. Amen.

February 28 and 29   Give secretly

[Jesus said,] 'Beware of practising your piety before others in order to be seen by them; for then you have no reward from your Father in heaven.

'So whenever you give alms, do not sound a trumpet before you, as the hypocrites do in the synagogues and in the streets, so that they may be praised by others. Truly I tell you, they have received their reward. But when you give alms, do not let your left hand know what your right hand is doing, so that your alms may be done in secret; and your Father who sees in secret will reward you.'

Matthew 6.1–4

Here are three images that are very familiar in the twenty-first century:

- A business using the donation of a huge (literally) cheque as a photo opportunity to draw attention to itself.
- A businessman giving a large sum to a political party, apparently for benevolent reasons, when secret negotiations have won him policy changes that will advance his own interests.
- A donor giving time or money to a charity in exchange for which a building, such as a theatre or gallery, is named after her.

Jesus' teaching rips up the value of any of these. Giving can be seen as an investment which repays one in praise from others, reciprocal benefits, or being remembered by posterity. But do not imagine that God is impressed by any of these reasons.

It is just as well that charities rarely concern themselves with what motivates their donors! But for we who give it is good to look occasionally at the hidden life of our hearts.

Secretly do good today. Nothing spectacular! Enrich someone's life (family, friend or stranger) and never tell anyone what you have done.

Let my eyes be fully open,
so that I may see the world as you see it;
let my hands be fully open,
so that all you have given me may be shared;
let my heart be fully open,
so that I may love in the way that Jesus loved;
and so may every part of me be changed into your likeness. Amen.

March 1   Pray unostentatiously

*[Jesus said,] 'Whenever you pray, do not be like the hypocrites;
for they love to stand and pray in the synagogues and at the street
corners, so that they may be seen by others. Truly I tell you, they
have received their reward. But whenever you pray, go into your
room, shut the door and pray to your Father who is in secret; and
your Father who sees in secret will reward you.*
   *'When you are praying, do not heap up empty phrases as the Gentiles do; for
they think that they will be heard because of their many words. Do not be like
them, for your Father knows what you need before you ask him.'*

Matthew 6.5–8

Our society is not one given to praying on street corners.
Occasionally I pass someone in the street who is speaking ani-
matedly to the invisible air in front of them. I assume them to be
praying, only to find that they are using a hands-free mobile
phone.

Jesus, though, was addressing a society that was far more inclined to make a
show of its religious practices. The Pharisees in particular were preoccupied
with doing the things that God had told them to do – keeping the laws, observing the rituals, paying the tithes, and so on. Not for one moment did Jesus
criticize them for doing these things. However, there were some for whom the
need to be seen doing these things, and thus win the approval of their friends,
had become more important than their inner relationship with God. And Jesus
scorned that.

As far as God is concerned, saying clever words of prayer does nothing to
impress him. But saying honest words of prayer is of great importance. Being
seen in church once, twice or a hundred times a week is irrelevant. But a discipline of constant prayer from the heart is of true, life-changing value.

A Prayer Diary is available from Christian Aid. It allows people
to pray daily from the quiet of their rooms for the world's poorest people and the work that Christian Aid does in partnership
with them. To receive a free copy every four months, telephone
020 7523 2248.

*My soul is waiting for you, Lord Jesus;
Are you not my life-giving food, Lord Jesus?
You are the one who nourishes my soul, Lord Jesus;
You give radiance to my words, Lord Jesus.*

*From Khadidhe Athmavu Ninna, a Christian bhajan (traditional
Indian chant)*

March 2 Our Father in heaven

[Jesus said,] 'Pray then in this way:
Our Father in heaven,
  hallowed be your name.
  Your kingdom come.
  Your will be done, on earth as it is in heaven.'

Matthew 6.9–10

These are the first few lines of the Lord's Prayer. Jesus taught them not primarily as words to be repeated, but as guidelines to help us know what to pray. Familiarity means that we have ceased to be astonished by the audacity of its opening. We are praying, brazenly, for the planet on which we live to become like heaven.

- Heaven is a place where God is 'hallowed' – treated as absolutely holy and set apart because of his sheer goodness and greatness. We ask God to make that true of earth.
- Heaven is a place where God's kingdom has already come, bringing total justice and unthreatened peace. We ask God to make that true of earth.
- Heaven is a place where God's will is done without question. And earth?

Today's suggestion for something to do is actually something not to do! It comes from the offices of the Community Movement of Matagalpa, a Christian Aid partner in Nicaragua that develops agricultural projects in a country where coffee farming has been devastated by a worldwide recession:

- Don't say, 'Father' if you don't behave like a son each day.
- Don't say, 'Our' if you only ever think of yourself.
- Don't say, 'As it is in heaven' if you only ever think of earthly matters.
- Don't say, 'Hallowed be your name' if you don't honour that name.
- Don't say, 'Your kingdom come' if you are weighed down with material goods.
- Don't say, 'Your will be done' if you won't accept the hard times.
- Don't say, 'Our daily bread' if you have no concern for the hungry or the homeless.
- Don't say, 'Forgive us our sins' if you remain angry with your brothers.
- Don't say, 'Lead us not into temptation' if you intend to continue sinning.
- Don't say, 'Deliver us from evil' if you won't make a stand against injustice.
- Don't say, 'Amen' without considering the words of your prayer.

Repeat the words of the Bible passage as your prayer. But first, stop and reflect, because in response to them you are destined to become a collaborator, not a spectator.

March 3   Give us this day

'Give us this day our daily bread.'

Matthew 6.11

In an ancient legend, Saint Benedict, riding from chapel one Sunday, met a peasant. 'You've got an easy job,' said the peasant. 'Why don't I become a man of prayer like you, then I could ride on horseback?'

'What makes you think praying is easy?' responded the monk. 'If you can say the Lord's Prayer just once without your attention wandering from the holy God, I'll give you the horse!'

The astonished peasant leapt at the opportunity. 'Our Father, who art in heaven, hallowed be thy name, thy kingdom come, thy . . .' Suddenly he stopped and looked up at Benedict. 'Will you give me the saddle as well?'

Greedy people have trouble praying. Hungry people can't stop themselves praying. Here at the heart of the Lord's Prayer we ask God to provide for our needs. But the way Jesus has taught us to pray does not allow us to be acquisitive, because it insists that we make ourselves dependent on God for only the basic needs of that day, every day.

One of the countries that regularly endures the threat of hunger is Ethiopia. The reason it faces famine again and again is not principally rain failure, but chronic poverty, lack of investment in infrastructure (such as rural roads and health care), lack of employment opportunities, and debt. When it comes to responding to a country's needs there is a tension between emergency help for people who need bread today and investment in the long-term recovery of the country. Tragic television images stir people to give because it is easy to see that helpless people need bread. But who will stay faithful to Ethiopia when the cameras are not there, creating the conditions in which the people can work and pray for their daily bread as dignified people, not beg for it in a crisis? Look up www.christianaid.org.uk/world/where/eagl/ethiopp.htm if you are in doubt about the answer.

Father God, give me today – 3 March – all that I need. And give me also a chance to break free from the relentless burden of wanting more than I need. Amen.

March 4 Forgive us our debts

'Forgive us our debts, as we also have forgiven our debtors.'
Matthew 6.12

These words come at the very heart of the Lord's Prayer. However, they are more familiar in the translation that asks God to forgive us 'sins' or 'trespasses'. In the original Greek version, though, the word 'debts' is used. Did Jesus have in mind the metaphorical debt of the way we have wronged other people, or literal financial debts? Or both?

It is certainly true that debt was a fact of life for Jesus' first listeners. Thirty years after his death, Jewish revolutionaries set fire to the house of the high priest Ananias in order to destroy the money-lenders' bonds and make it impossible for them to pursue debts. It may be that, as on so many other occasions, Jesus was relating faith to ordinary life. However, the release from debt for which we are encouraged to pray has conditions attached. We can only expect to find forgiveness in the measure that we ourselves have forgiven other people.

As well as being a powerful prayer that has sustained Christians for 2,000 years, the Lord's Prayer teaches us that the presence of daily bread and the absence of debt are two signs of God's kingdom having come. Speed the day!

The pressure on governments to cancel the unpayable debts of poor countries needs to continue, so that what has been promised delivers results from which the poorest people in the world will benefit. The World Bank runs the current debt relief process. The retirement of James Wolfensohn in 2005 meant a change of its president. Write to explain that a new process is needed in order to deliver more debt cancellation quickly and thus help poor countries meet internationally agreed poverty-reduction targets. Address your letter to the President, The World Bank, 1818 H Street NW, Washington DC 20433, USA.

So that financial systems may no longer burden the poorest;
so that our trade may no longer deny a fair wage;
so that debt may no longer trap nations in poverty;
God's kingdom come,
God's will be done,
on earth as it is in heaven. Amen.

March 5   Lead us not into temptation

'Do not bring us to the time of trial,
    but rescue us from the evil one.'
[Jesus continued,] 'For if you forgive others their trespasses, your
heavenly Father will also forgive you; but if you do not forgive
others, neither will your Father forgive your trespasses.'

Matthew 6.13–15

These words come from the Lord's Prayer, but they are not the
familiar words that are said in church services. That version
stresses our need for spiritual protection: 'Lead us not into
temptation.' It acknowledges that we are individuals who need to
be strong enough to find the capacity to do good. However, the
version that Matthew originally wrote down is a much more practical plea for
help in the face of physical danger. Its meaning is closer to 'Do not put us to the
ultimate test.'

Later in Matthew's Gospel, Jesus warned of a time when his followers would
face persecution because of their faith. There would be times when great evil
would need to be resisted, and the temptation to allow love for Christ to grow
cold would be great because the alternative is too costly. In places where the
worst a Christian faces is to be mocked in the media, it is easy to forget that the
plea to be spared from making the ultimate sacrifice of one's life under an evil
regime is very real to many of our fellow believers.

In the calendar of the Church's year we are in Lent. Many people
mark it by denying themselves something trivial but enjoyable –
chocolate or television for instance. So for them, 'Lead us not
into temptation' is asking God to keep their hands off the sweet
box or the remote control. It seems a far cry from the desperation
of Christians who are living in terror of the 'time of trial'. Could you mark the
days between now and Easter by spending a moment of every day remembering
those who genuinely long to be delivered from evil?

O Lord we beseech thee to deliver us from the fear of the
unknown future; from fear of failure; from fear of poverty; from
fear of bereavement; from fear of loneliness; from fear of sickness
and pain; from fear of age; and from fear of death. Help us, O
Father, by thy grace to love and fear only thee, and fill our hearts
with cheerful courage and loving trust in thee.

A prayer of the Nigerian Christian Akanu Ibaim

March 6   Fasting

[Jesus said,] 'Whenever you fast, do not look dismal, like the hypocrites, for they disfigure their faces so as to show others that they are fasting. Truly I tell you, they have received their reward. But when you fast, put oil on your head and wash your face, so that your fasting may be seen not by others but by your Father who is in secret; and your Father who sees in secret will reward you.'

Matthew 6.16–18

I was talking recently to a friend who is a Muslim. I wanted to know how her family organized their lives during Ramadan, the month of the Muslim year during which a strict fast is observed between sunrise and sunset. 'Do poor people resent having to fast?' I asked. Her answer took me by surprise. 'It is those with least who value Ramadan most,' she told me, 'because during the fast rich people know what it feels like to be poor.' Suddenly Ramadan seemed so valuable that I wondered whether I should start observing it! Christians do not have a direct equivalent, but Lent is the closest it gets. The period before Easter has traditionally been marked by self-discipline and denying oneself casual luxuries. If you don't count the Sundays, it lasts forty days – the same as the length of time during which Jesus fasted in the wilderness in what is now southern Israel.

I grew up with the attitude that this kind of self-denial is unnecessary, because that behaviour should be a feature of Christian life every day. In fact, to my shame, I remember as a teenager lecturing a schoolfriend who had given up chocolate for Lent about how unhelpful such superstitions were.

I won't make that mistake this year!

Make a decision about how you can spend the days between now and Easter in a way that reminds you regularly that many people in the world are going hungry. The method can be your secret. Will you pray? Will you read? Will you give? Will you fast?

Almighty God,
whose Son Jesus Christ fasted forty days in the wilderness,
and was tempted as we are, yet without sin:
give us grace to discipline ourselves in obedience to your Spirit;
and, as you know our weakness,
so may we know your power to save.

From the Collect for the first Sunday in Lent

March 7   Treasure in heaven

[Jesus said,] 'Do not store up for yourselves treasures on earth, where moth and rust consume and where thieves break in and steal, but store up for yourselves treasures in heaven, where neither moth nor rust consumes and where thieves do not break in and steal. For where your treasure is, there your heart will be also.'

Matthew 6.19–21

Saint Augustine became a bishop in North Africa in the fourth century. He wrote about bringing a crop of apples from his orchard into the store room. Tired from his efforts, he dumped them on the floor. A friend chided him: 'Don't leave them there. All your hard work will be wasted. The rats will get them or they will go bad. Get them up off the earth and on to that high shelf!'

Augustine used that illustration when he wrote about these words of Jesus. The incident helped him realize that he only had one life, just as he only had one crop of apples. He could not live part of his life 'on the earth' and part 'on the high shelf'. The 'earth' activities that involved money, food and sex had to match the 'high' activities of prayer and Christian devotion. There was a choice to be made. Either the whole effort and output of his life was going to be lived in a way that was worthy of heaven, or he was going to take his chances with the rat and the rot.

When everything you undertake comes with the motive, 'I do this for you, Lord', then your ordinary life, with its relentless round of mundane duties, takes on an eternal quality. That is the beginning of preparing your heart for heaven.

Think of five things you will do today: a chore, a piece of work, a conversation you expect to have, something that will entertain you, and something you will eat (even if it is only an apple)! For each of the five things, ask yourself what difference it will make if you preface it by saying, 'I do this for you, Lord.' At the end of the day look back at the way these things were done, and look forward to the time to come when heaven will be a reality.

O God, you have made us for yourself, and our hearts are restless until they find their rest in you.

Augustine, Bishop of Hippo (modern Tunisia), 354–430

March 8   God and wealth

[Jesus said,] 'The eye is the lamp of the body. So, if your eye is healthy, your whole body will be full of light; but if your eye is unhealthy, your whole body will be full of darkness. If then the light in you is darkness, how great is the darkness!

'No one can serve two masters; for a slave will either hate the one and love the other, or be devoted to the one and despise the other. You cannot serve God and wealth.'

Matthew 6.22–24

These verses suggest that there is a frightening line of connection: what you see you will desire; what you desire you will become devoted to; what you are devoted to you will live for; what you live for will eventually control you.

As far as Jesus was concerned, single-mindedness is vital to ensure that a person is sure of his footing in a world that requires us to tread our way through shadowy compromises. Just as the easiest way for a smoker to give up her craving for cigarettes is never to start, Jesus recommends that we don't even take a first glance at a materialistic lifestyle. That way we will never have to battle to reconcile two rival claims on our devotion.

Long ago, when a king converted to Christianity and ordered his knights to be baptized, many of them held their right arms out of the water. As they were immersed in the water, every part of them was baptized except the hand in which they held their weapon. When the crisis came, they could kill and maim without having to feel constrained by Christian morality.

I sometimes wonder whether it would have been easier if I had held my wallet out of the water on the day I was baptized. Then I could justify behaving from time to time as if all of me belongs to God except what belongs to me!

What are you absolutely single-minded about – people, sports teams, possessions, hobbies, ideologies? Make a list in the margin of the book. Then ask yourself where your relationship with God fits in relation to the other passions of your life.

O Lord, baptize our hearts into a sense of the needs and conditions of all.

George Fox, founder of the Society of Friends (Quakers),
1624–1755

March 9   Do not worry!

[Jesus said,] 'Do not worry about your life, what you will eat or what you will drink, or about your body, what you will wear. Is not life more than food, and the body more than clothing? Look at the birds of the air; they neither sow nor reap nor gather into barns, and yet your heavenly Father feeds them. Are you not of more value than they? And can any of you by worrying add a single hour to your span of life? And why do you worry about clothing? Consider the lilies of the field, how they grow; they neither toil nor spin, yet I tell you, even Solomon in all his glory was not clothed like one of these.'

Matthew 6.25–29

My typical Friday night's worry list: Is all this convenience food doing me any good? If I wear a tie to this party, will everyone else be in jeans? If I comb my hair forward, will the bald patch look smaller?

Actually, I'm ashamed to tell you this because I have a neighbour who also has worries about her food, clothes and body: Can I make one packet of sausages stretch to feed all five of us? Why must my children be teased at school because I can't afford the uniform? Is someone with my skin colour safe in this area?

Jesus points out that worrying is a luxury. People in genuine need know that they can't afford to waste their energy on worrying; they need to put all their strength into surviving. But let's face facts – everyone who thinks hard or feels deeply will have occasions when they worry. Faith doesn't remove all cause for worry, but it does offer a way of dealing with it.

Which set of worries is closer to your own? There are millions in the world who worry with good reason about basic needs. If you know you have more food than you need in the cupboard and clothes you never wear in the wardrobe, ask God to show you a proper use for them.

As the rain hides the stars, and as the autumn mist hides the hills, so the dark happenings of my lot hide the shining of thy face from me. Yet if I may hold thy hand in the darkness it is enough since I know that, though I may stumble in my going, thou dost not fall.

Anonymous, tenth-century Celtic prayer

March 10   Seek the kingdom of God

[Jesus said,] 'If God so clothes the grass of the field, which is alive today and tomorrow is thrown into the oven, will he not much more clothe you – you of little faith? Therefore do not worry, saying, "What will we eat?" or "What will we drink?" or "What will we wear?" For it is the Gentiles who strive for all these things; and indeed your heavenly Father knows that you need all these things. But strive first for the kingdom of God and his righteousness, and all these things will be given to you as well. So do not worry about tomorrow, for tomorrow will bring worries of its own. Today's trouble is enough for today.'

Matthew 6.30–34

Jesus gives us five reasons why we don't need to worry. Five! Count them!

- God has proved that his care extends to every aspect of creation, so imagine how much he loves humans, the pinnacle of all he has made.
- God knows precisely what every individual needs.
- Christians shouldn't be preoccupied with the same things as the rest of the world.
- If the justice of the kingdom of God dominates the actions of Christians, everyone's needs will be provided for.
- Besides, worry only gives you two days' trouble for the price of one!

To be honest, I find more challenge than consolation in Jesus' five reasons. Now that's worrying!

This series about 'A cheerful giver' has extended the meaning of giving beyond what any of us might have expected. According to the Bible, praying, doing without, forgiving, sharing and secretly doing good are all aspects of giving. God sees giving not as something special, but as an integral part of a fulfilled and healthy life.

But of all the varied action points, the one that has been conspicuously missing is: 'Write a cheque.' So before we begin a new series and the chance is lost, today's suggested action is to give money to work that builds the kingdom of God in his world. Only you can decide to whom to send your gift. (But if you ever happen to need the address of Christian Aid, you only need to turn to the back of the book!)

O Lord, give me an undivided heart, to revere your name.
Then I will give thanks to you, O Lord my God, with my whole heart;
and I will glorify your name for ever.

Psalm 86.11–12

March 11   Twelve disciples

Jesus called the twelve together and gave them power and authority over all demons and to cure diseases, and he sent them out to proclaim the kingdom of God and to heal. He said to them, 'Take nothing for your journey, no staff, nor bag, nor bread, nor money – not even an extra tunic. Whatever house you enter, stay there, and leave from there. Wherever they do not welcome you, as you are leaving that town shake the dust off your feet as a testimony against them.' They departed and went through the villages, bringing the good news and curing diseases everywhere.

Luke 9.1–6

Jesus' disciples were beginning a mission that would eventually encompass the whole world. The most surprising thing about it is how very unprepared they were. Their grasp of Jesus' significance was limited (days previously they had been asking each other, 'Who on earth is he?'). They were expected to do much, but say little.

They were to take nothing that would add convenience to their circumstances, let alone luxury. They were to carry no money, but earn what they needed. They were to pack no spare clothes, but make do with what they were wearing. They were to hold lightly to possessions, giving as freely as they received, and relying on the goodness of the Earth and its inhabitants.

All we know of their message is that they were to announce the kingdom of God. Their instructions were to drive out the forces of evil, to heal the suffering of humankind, and to declare, 'God is doing something new in Jesus; come and take a look!' That would not be a bad mission statement for any of the agencies that seek, in the name of Jesus, to be good news for poor people.

Where is your mission field? Your family, your workplace, the ends of the Earth? Think about the message you are conveying about the new thing God is doing through Jesus in what you say and do, in your response to suffering, and the simplicity of your life.

Our Lord Jesus sends you out in the power and strength of the Holy Spirit to be his faithful witnesses to your family, to your neighbourhood, to your country, and to the ends of the earth.

These words are said to new Christians at the close of a confirmation service in Iran. Turn them over in your mind and consider how you respond.

March 12   Jesus feeds five thousand

The day was drawing to a close, and the twelve came to [Jesus] and said, 'Send the crowd away, so that they may go into the surrounding villages and countryside, to lodge and get provisions; for we are here in a deserted place.' But he said to them, 'You give them something to eat.' They said, 'We have no more than five loaves and two fish – unless we are to go and buy food for all these people.' For there were about five thousand men. And he said to his disciples, 'Make them sit down in groups of about fifty each.' They did so and made them all sit down. And taking the five loaves and the two fish, he looked up to heaven, and blessed and broke them, and gave them to the disciples to set before the crowd. And all ate and were filled. What was left over was gathered up, twelve baskets of broken pieces.

Luke 9.12–17

If he so chose, God could easily end the suffering of a world in which there are millions who do not have enough to eat. Believers and doubters alike find themselves asking, 'Why does God do nothing?' Jesus' response is as straightforward today as it was 2,000 years ago: 'You give them something to eat.' Jesus risked trusting that the disciples had faith to respond to the problem they saw.

The risk paid off. Is it still paying off? In the UK and Ireland there are fewer and fewer active Christians, while the world has more and more need. But there is hope to be found in the twist at the end of the story. Twelve baskets full of food came back to refresh the twelve who had been serving others. Church statistics echo that. It is the churches that are committed to local and world mission that are growing. As the Church feeds the world, it is itself fed.

Make a point of sharing food. Pass around crisps or grapes, be part of a communion service, or invite someone for a meal. However you do it, register that God calls us to generosity as his ambassadors in the world.

Lord, I do so much want to be like you.
Like you I want to feed human beings
with love and with bread.
I want to bring hope and faith to the world
even if the world crushes me.

A prayer from Cameroon

March 13   Peter's discovery

Once when Jesus was praying alone, with only the disciples near him, he asked them, 'Who do the crowds say that I am?' They answered, 'John the Baptist; but others, Elijah; and still others, that one of the ancient prophets has arisen.' He said to them, 'But who do you say that I am?'
Peter answered, 'The Messiah of God.'
He sternly ordered and commanded them not to tell anyone, saying, 'The Son of Man must undergo great suffering, and be rejected by the elders, chief priests, and scribes, and be killed, and on the third day be raised.'

Luke 9.18–22

A bewildered friend of mine asked me whether there was one belief that unites all Christians. This was the best I could do:

- There is a God.
- In some unique but unfathomably complex way God touched the Earth twenty centuries ago in Jesus.
- That matters, personally and globally!

I can already hear the howls of protest that this either says too little or too much. Just as he did to Peter, Jesus turns to us with the all-important question: 'Who do you say that I am?' Peter's answer stressed the human nature of Jesus – the Messiah was the warrior who would free the Jews. Jesus' response stressed his divine nature – the Son of Man was a heavenly figure destined to bring judgement. But the idea that God's plan for Jesus would take him through humiliation before glory defied stereotyping. It still does!

Allow Jesus to pose the question: 'Who do you say that I am?' Don't settle for an easy response. The first answer that Sunday school children learn is, 'Jesus is the Son of God.' A child's faith is wonderful and literal, but it would be good to dwell on that in a maturer way. In what way is Jesus' relationship with God like and unlike a son? And what of Jesus' other names: Emmanuel (God is with us), Lord, Teacher, Christ (the same as Messiah) and Saviour. What are the personal implications of knowing Jesus by these names?

As the sun in all its brightness, as the snow in all its whiteness;
As the lightning, as the thunder, as the sky at night in wonder;
As the ocean in its deepness, as the mountain in its steepness;
As the hurricane in power, as the beauty of the flower;
As the rich, life-giving blood – utterly, supremely God.

March 14   Take up your cross and follow

[Jesus] said to them all, 'If any want to become my followers, let them deny themselves and take up their cross daily and follow me. For those who want to save their life will lose it, and those who lose their life for my sake will save it. What does it profit them if they gain the whole world, but lose or forfeit themselves? Those who are ashamed of me and of my words, of them the Son of Man will be ashamed when he comes in his glory and the glory of the Father and of the holy angels.'

Luke 9.23–27

A person who took up his cross in first-century Jerusalem was on a one-way journey. He was heading for execution. He wouldn't be back.

Jesus insisted that those who followed him did so without compromise. If faith in him was worth living with, then it also had to be worth dying for. I wonder how the disciples reacted to this? They had only gone with him in the first place because they wanted to see where he lived; one year on he was asking whether they were prepared to sacrifice their own lives for the mission. To die rather than forsake Jesus is a reality faced by millions of Christians worldwide. But Jesus also had in mind metaphorical deaths that are part of his followers' day-to-day discipleship:

- Following him means the death of a selfish love of oneself. 'Denying yourself' means far more than giving up chocolate during Lent; it means putting the needs of others at the heart of your life's ambition.
- It means the death of a craving for possessions (wanting to 'gain the whole world').
- It means the death of desire for praise. The contempt in which Christians are held is not something for believers to be 'ashamed' of.

Following Christ with a noose around your neck means getting used to living each day as if it were your last. What would you do today if you knew you were going to meet God tomorrow?

Servant Christ, help us to follow you unto the cross,
to recognize the true way of life in your death,
to see our hope in your self-spending love,
to die to all within us not born of your love.
Servant Christ, help us to follow you.

From 'A Litany of the Disciples of Christ the Servant', a prayer cycle from Bangalore, India.

March 15   Let the children come to me

People were bringing even infants to [Jesus] that he might touch them. When the disciples saw it, they sternly ordered them not to do it. But Jesus called for them and said, 'Let the little children come to me, and do not stop them; for it is to such as these that the kingdom of God belongs. Truly I tell you, whoever does not receive the kingdom of God as a little child will never enter it.'

Luke 18.15–17

What do children teach us about what God wants of us? That the only meaningful way to approach God is a state of complete helplessness. If you don't feed a baby, she starves because she cannot do anything for herself. It is when we acknowledge that we can do nothing whatever to impress God that we are in the baby-like state in which he can save us from ourselves.

There is no point in saying, 'I go to church', or 'I'm doing good', or 'I've said a prayer of conversion', expecting that those things qualify us for heaven. The only route to heaven is to say, 'There is no way at all I can manage this. Help me!' And then God's love can work the miracle. To achieve anything in eternal terms we need to go back to the state we were in when we had achieved nothing. We must become like we were when we were moments old. In fact, more than that – we must be *born* again.

In Ethiopia the arrival of twins is often the last straw for poor families. In the slums of Addis Ababa two helpless children can break a family, and the result used to be that Ethiopian twins had only one chance in three of reaching their first birthday. Christian Aid supports the Ethiopian Gemini Trust, which provides food, health care and education for twin children. The result is that, over twenty years, the chances of twins thriving have multiplied fivefold.

Global Gang is Christian Aid's website to help children discover what life is like for those of their age the world over. Ethiopia is one of many countries explored at www.globalgang.org.uk/reallife

Motherly God,
in whose arms are held all who cry out to you:
teach me to open my heart, my home,
even when I have little to give,
to make room for all your children
and give them space to grow.

Janet Morley/Hannah Ward/Jennifer Wild/Christian Aid

March 16 A rich ruler

A certain ruler asked [Jesus], 'Good Teacher, what must I do to inherit eternal life?' Jesus said to him, 'Why do you call me good? No one is good but God alone. You know the commandments: "You shall not commit adultery; you shall not murder; you shall not steal; you shall not bear false witness; honour your father and mother."' He replied, 'I have kept all these since my youth.' When Jesus heard this, he said to him, 'There is still one thing lacking. Sell all that you own and distribute the money to the poor, and you will have treasure in heaven; then come, follow me.' But when he heard this, he became sad; for he was very rich.

Luke 18.18–23

The ruler got more than he bargained for. He anticipated the usual Middle Eastern exchange of flattering compliments when he began, 'Good teacher.' But Jesus would have none of it. He anticipated that his claim to have kept all the commandments would be greeted with congratulations. But Jesus would have none of it. He anticipated that his question about being sure of eternal life would get a straightforward answer. It did, but by the time it came (in tomorrow's reading) he had already left.

We can't help but share the ruler's discomfort. Surely Jesus cannot mean that we too have to sell everything and give it to the poor? Was the ruler a unique case, or is poverty the only way to please God?

Luke's original readers would have made an assumption as soon as they heard that the man was both a ruler and rich. It went without saying that a landowner who was both those things had achieved it by defrauding poor people. His admirable religious life was not matched by integrity in his working life. Jesus' message was that the only meaningful way to obey the commandments was with practical acts that achieve justice, not with a facade of piety.

Look back at what you have been praying about recently – either for people or events. What would happen if, just this once, you did something practical instead of saying a prayer? Justice instead of piety. Action instead of sympathy. Try it, and see whether deed becomes a prayer anyway.

Take hold of me, Lord Jesus, willing or unwilling, full or empty, rich or poor, pious or piteous, and don't let go of me until I have followed you into eternal life. Amen.

March 17   Easier for a camel than a rich man!

Jesus looked at [the rich ruler] and said, 'How hard it is for those who have wealth to enter the kingdom of God! Indeed, it is easier for a camel to go through the eye of a needle than for someone who is rich to enter the kingdom of God.'

Those who heard it said, 'Then who can be saved?' He replied, 'What is impossible for mortals is possible for God.'

Then Peter said, 'Look, we have left our homes and followed you.' And he said to them, 'Truly I tell you, there is no one who has left house or wife or brothers or parents or children, for the sake of the kingdom of God, who will not get back very much more in this age, and in the age to come eternal life.'

Luke 18.24–30

Three or four times I have heard a sermon explaining that there was a small gate in the walls of Jerusalem called 'Eye of a Needle' through which a camel could just squeeze if it was unburdened of its baggage and sank to its knees. It is an appealing image! The only problem is that it isn't true. It was invented in the eleventh century by a dodgy Greek clergyman called Theophylact. He obviously struggled with the implications of Jesus' words as much as we do.

Why do preachers preserve his ingenious fiction? Well, if your congregation knows that you have travelled from a nice house in a nice car to preach in a nice suit, you have a good reason to soft-pedal Jesus' criticism of wealth. The point of Jesus' joke ('Did you hear the one about the camel?') is not that it is difficult but just, just possible for a rich person to get into heaven; what he meant is that it is impossible. Totally and absolutely impossible. It is hopeless for a person even to try. For a rich man or woman to enter the kingdom of God would take a miracle . . .

The same kind of miracle that raised Jesus from the dead.

Are you aware of Jesus' more uncompromising demands being soft-pedalled? Are you aware of it happening in your own life? Consider why it is happening.

From the cowardice that dare not face new truth;
from the laziness that is contented with half truth;
from the arrogance that thinks it knows all truth;
Good Lord, deliver me.

A prayer from Kenya

March 18   Zacchaeus

A man was [in Jericho] named Zacchaeus; he was a chief tax-collector and was rich. He was trying to see who Jesus was, but on account of the crowd he could not, because he was short in stature. So he ran ahead and climbed a sycomore tree to see him, because he was going to pass that way. When Jesus came to the place, he looked up and said to him, 'Zacchaeus, hurry and come down; for I must stay at your house today.'

So he hurried down and was happy to welcome him.

All who saw it began to grumble and said, 'He has gone to be the guest of one who is a sinner.' Zacchaeus stood there and said to the Lord, 'Look, half of my possessions, Lord, I will give to the poor; and if I have defrauded anyone of anything, I will pay back four times as much.' Then Jesus said to him, 'Today salvation has come to this house.'

Luke 19.1–10

I can't remember when I first heard this story of a short man and a transformed life. It was certainly over 30 years ago. I should imagine I have read it a hundred times. But today a completely new question slapped me round the head . . .

Who was the short one – Zacchaeus or Jesus?

Unsettled, I looked up the Greek text from which our New Testament was translated. Like this English version, it is ambiguous. I know how I want to visualize Jesus – tall, heroic, visually compelling. But there is, of course, no reason at all why he should not have been squat, bald, and with 'no beauty or majesty to attract us to him' as Isaiah puts it. All those qualities are part of the image of God in a human being as well.

Go and have a look in a mirror. What do you see? Black, white or any glorious shade of human skin; male or female; able-bodied or disabled; young or old or on the journey from one to the other; healthy or sick; wrinkled or smooth; coming alive or dying. Do you like what you see? Whatever you are looking at, in all its beauty and ugliness, is delightful to God.

Jesus Christ:
God's thought in a man's brain,
God's love in a man's heart,
God's pain in a man's body,
I worship.

Margaret Cropper (1886–1980)

March 19   Washing feet

During supper Jesus, knowing that the Father had given all things into his hands, and that he had come from God and was going to God, got up from the table, took off his outer robe, and tied a towel around himself. Then he poured water into a basin and began to wash the disciples' feet and to wipe them with the towel that was tied around him. He came to Simon Peter, who said to him, 'Lord, are you going to wash my feet?' Jesus answered, 'You do not know now what I am doing, but later you will understand.' Peter said to him, 'You will never wash my feet.' Jesus answered, 'Unless I wash you, you have no share with me.' Simon Peter said to him, 'Lord, not my feet only but also my hands and my head!'

John 13.2–9

Jesus shows us what authentic Christian action looks like. It looks like menial service. God strips off and becomes completely humble. By doing so he ensures that from now onward no service will ever be trivial again. Every act of compassion is raised to a Christlike status.

But for those who seek to take the servant's role of washing feet, the stripping off is vital. To humble ourselves involves taking off anything that keeps us at a distance from our fellow humans when we seek to serve them. To attempt to be a servant to the world's poorest communities, but at the same time cling on to status, privilege, control or the need to be appreciated, invalidates any attempt to be like Jesus.

Ram Chramreun lost his foot when he stepped on a landmine on Nam Sap mountain, Cambodia. He was a government soldier during a terrible civil war. Now he clears mines in Kompong Thom for the Mines Advisory Group, which works in partnership with Church World Service. At a time when most amputees were begging on the streets, they gave him a job making Cambodia safe to farm again, which he has seized courageously. However, the landscape is still littered with landmines that are the legacy of many years of war. Read about how Christian Aid supports work to clear mines and educate children about what to do if they find one, at
www.christian-aid.org.uk/world/where/asia/cambodip.htm

How beautiful on the mountains are the feet of those who bring good news, who proclaim peace, who bring good tidings, who proclaim salvation, saying, 'Your God reigns!'

Isaiah 52.7

March 20 Being a servant

After he had washed their feet, had put on his robe, and had returned to the table, [Jesus said to his disciples], 'Do you know what I have done to you? You call me Teacher and Lord – and you are right, for that is what I am. So if I, your Lord and Teacher, have washed your feet, you also ought to wash one another's feet. For I have set you an example, that you also should do as I have done to you. Very truly, I tell you, servants are not greater than their master, nor are messengers greater than the one who sent them. If you know these things, you are blessed if you do them.'

John 13.12–17

In the ancient world humility was despised as a sign of weakness. But in the kingdom of God the way to the top is by stooping down in service.

Some churches in South India mark the day before Good Friday with an equivalent of Jesus' footwashing. Each member of the congregation touches the shoe of the next person, and then brushes his own forehead with the dust. The person whose shoe has been touched then raises him to his feet and blesses him with the words of the prayer below.

Some churches in Uganda clean the rubbish from their neighbourhood. Using the prayer, 'May God clean my heart as I clean my town', they regard this as both a personal spiritual discipline and an act of mission.

Historically, British monarchs marked the day by washing the feet of destitute people with their own hands, before giving them clothes and food. James II was the last king to do it in 1688. This symbol of humility in leadership has been replaced by distributing ceremonial money to representatives of charities during a church service . . . Hmm!

There is no shortage of chores that need to be done that, while not humiliating, are not particularly pleasant – toilets to be cleaned, litter to be cleared, dirt to be scrubbed. What service, unnoticed or unannounced, would make someone's life easier?

O Lord, forgive the sins of your servants. May we banish from our minds all disunion and strife; may our souls be cleansed from all hatred and malice toward others; and may we receive the fellowship of the holy meal in oneness of mind and peace with one another.

A prayer of the Church of South India

March 21   Imitating Jesus' humility

If then there is any encouragement in Christ, any consolation from love, any sharing in the Spirit, any compassion and sympathy, make my joy complete: be of the same mind, having the same love, being in full accord and of one mind. Do nothing from selfish ambition or conceit, but in humility regard others as better than yourselves. Let each of you look not to your own interests, but to the interests of others.

Philippians 2.1–4

'For goodness sake pull yourselves together! What's got into you? Does all that Jesus has done mean nothing to you? Why, oh why, are you doing this?' The church at Philippi was obviously doing something wrong to wring this plea from Paul. What on Earth can it have been? 'Please, please, please . . . stop fighting among yourselves!'

Only a united Church could be useful in the world. Achieving it was going to be a matter of three things – working to find agreement ('same mind'), relationships that honour people ('same love'), and seeking shared objectives ('full accord'). None of these things are easy, but Jesus' life ought to be an inspiration to us as we seek them. His death on Good Friday was the ultimate expression of putting others' interests first.

All hands together to change the world;
All hands together to till the land;
All hands together to pull up weeds;
All hands together to share our joy.

This is from a song from Bambamarca, a community in Peru. It is precisely the right prayer for the unity of a rural community. Its spirit is right for Christians in the UK and Ireland too, but the details are wrong. If you were to rewrite the song for the church or neighbourhood of which you are part, how would you complete the lines?

All hands together to . . .
All hands together to . . .
All hands together to . . .
All hands together to share our joy.

The poor of the world are thirsty for justice and for peace,
their journey is unending till hate and oppression cease.
The Lord of heaven is thirsty for justice and for peace;
his battle is unending till hate and oppression cease.

A song from the pastoral team of Bambamarca, Peru

March 22   Obedient to death on a cross

Let the same mind be in you that was in Christ Jesus,
who, though he was in the form of God,
    did not regard equality with God as something to be exploited,
but emptied himself, taking the form of a slave,
    being born in human likeness.
And being found in human form,
he humbled himself and became obedient to the point of death –
    even death on a cross.

Philippians 2.5–8

The church at Philippi was on a mission to find unity, and Paul knew that the only way to do it would be for each individual member to stop thinking of himself or herself as worth more than the others. When the temptation strikes, he tells them (and us), think of what Jesus has done and emulate that.

He goes on to quote from a hymn to Jesus, reminding them how, step by step, he submitted to humiliation. He was equal in every way to the Almighty God. However, he freely waived every glory that his divinity deserved. He became human. Not merely human, but the least free and most oppressed kind of human – a slave. And although it seems impossible that he could give more, he then submitted to the most shameful death imaginable – execution by crucifixion.

This, says Paul, is what Christ chose to do on your behalf. So why do you find it so difficult to let someone else have the last word, or get their way, or have first choice?

In front of whom do you find it hardest to be humble, gracious, a servant? Imagine a three-way conversation between you, Jesus, and him or her. Embarrassing or enlightening?

Lord Christ you remain, unseen, at our side,
present like a poor man who washes the feet of his friends.
And we who follow in your footsteps,
we are here,
waiting for you to suggest signs of sharing
to make us into servants of your gospel.

Brother Roger of Taizé

March 23   Exalted to the highest place

Therefore God also highly exalted [Jesus]
    and gave him the name that is above every name,
so that at the name of Jesus every knee should bend,
in heaven and on earth and under the earth,
    and every tongue should confess that Jesus Christ is Lord,
to the glory of God the Father.

Philippians 2.9–11

This is the second part of an ancient hymn. The first half describes the journey Jesus took from glory to disgrace. Now we see what God has done in response – given him the highest honour and authority over all creation. It is the destiny of all humankind that (willingly or not) every man, woman and child will one day acknowledge Jesus' greatness and their debt to him. Depending on the love an individual has for Jesus, that is a prospect which seems either wonderful or dreadful.

Paul quoted the hymn to the Christians of Philippi to remind them of the majesty of the risen Jesus Christ, of course, but he had a more practical purpose as well. He was urging them to create a church in which disunity, infighting and personal ambition were dead. He had a vision for a community in which every day was an Easter of encouragement, compassion and joy – living now the values that will come naturally when we kneel before the glorious Jesus.

Kneeling is totally out of fashion. Even in the most traditional churches the usual position that people adopt to pray is either sitting, standing, or a strange posture that is only comfortable if you are about to shampoo your hair. So do something today that your grandparents may have done every day – find a quiet place and kneel down in order to say the prayer below.

All hail the power of Jesus' name! Let angels prostrate fall;
bring forth the royal diadem
    and crown him, crown him, crown him Lord of all.
O, that with every tribe and tongue we at his feet may fall,
lift high the universal song
    and crown him, crown him, crown him Lord of all.

Edward Perronet (1726–92)

March 24   Shine like stars

My beloved, just as you have always obeyed me, not only in my presence, but much more now in my absence, work out your own salvation with fear and trembling; for it is God who is at work in you, enabling you both to will and to work for his good pleasure.
Do all things without murmuring and arguing, so that you may be blameless and innocent, children of God without blemish in the midst of a crooked and perverse generation, in which you shine like stars in the world. It is by your holding fast to the word of life that I can boast on the day of Christ that I did not run in vain or labour in vain.

Philippians 2.12–16

'Working out' has gained a meaning that Paul (who wrote these words) could never have anticipated. Of all the things that would have bewildered him about today's society, the sight of a dozen sweaty people pounding on exercise bikes, but not actually going anywhere, would seem more bizarre than most. However, he might approve of the metaphor that we should 'work out' our salvation – keeping the salvation that God has freely given us in good shape by exercising all the qualities that Christians are supposed to display. Athletes know, when they cross the finishing line as champions, that they did not 'run in vain' on the machines or 'labour in vain' with the weights. In the same way, Christians can be assured that when they meet Jesus face to face they will delight to know that the struggle to do what is right was worth everything it cost.

What does it mean in practice for Christians to 'keep fit' spiritually? It means behaving in such a way that they stand out from the rest of society. It means that their standards are so high that people notice and appreciate them for being different. The examples Paul gives are simple things like avoiding cynical murmuring and keeping innocent of perverse habits. Just as stars in the night sky attract attention as bright dots of hope, so should Jesus' followers in a dreary world.

Some exercise? . . . Oh well, it was just a thought!

Lord God, take my flabby standards, my unfit attitudes, and my unfulfilled intentions. Train me to do better, so that I can please you. Until I'm fit to be a star, make me determined not to be an also-ran. Amen.

March 25   Raised like Jesus

What then are we to say? Should we continue in sin in order that grace may abound? By no means! How can we who died to sin go on living in it? Do you not know that all of us who have been baptized into Christ Jesus were baptized into his death? Therefore we have been buried with him by baptism into death, so that, just as Christ was raised from the dead by the glory of the Father, so we too might walk in newness of life.

Romans 6.1–4

Here's a bright idea! Let me try it out on you!

We have a God who is loving and merciful when we have done things wrong. Yes! In fact, there is nothing that God enjoys more than forgiving our sins. Yes! Right then! Let's sin as often as we possibly can, so that God will enjoy being loving and merciful even more.

Ten out of ten for ingenuity; nought out of ten for theology. Someone in the church at Rome had evidently tried that one out on Paul, agog at the prospect of orgies on a Saturday night followed by forgiveness on a Sunday morning. Hard luck, mate!

Baptism is a symbol of drowning. When a person goes under the water it is a sign that the old life of sin (whether that involved wild orgies or mild gossip) is dead for ever. When he or she emerges it is like a resurrection to a new and faultless life. Obviously we let God down from time to time as we live that new and faultless life. But that is no excuse for failing to try to live the way God intends.

Recall baptisms that you have attended – your own (whether or not you can remember it), an occasion when you were a godparent, or others for which you were in the congregation. Are there promises you made that you have been lax in keeping? Are there happy memories to rejoice in? Are there prayers that need to be said?

Servant Christ, help us to follow you deep into the waters of baptism; to link our lives with all those who grieve about the unjust way of our human life; to break free from the chains of past wrongs; to become fit to face your coming new age; to be renewed by your Spirit.

A prayer from 'A Litany of the Disciples of Christ the Servant', India

March 26   Death defeated

If we have been united with [Jesus] in a death like his, we will certainly be united with him in a resurrection like his. We know that our old self was crucified with him so that the body of sin might be destroyed, and we might no longer be enslaved to sin. For whoever has died is freed from sin. But if we have died with Christ, we believe that we will also live with him. We know that Christ, being raised from the dead, will never die again; death no longer has dominion over him. The death he died, he died to sin, once for all; but the life he lives, he lives to God.

Romans 6.5–10

An old proverb has been around since long before Paul wrote this letter: 'Death pays all debts'. A dead person cannot be a slave any longer, or be in debt any longer, or be punished any longer, or sin any longer. It would be an enviable condition were it not for the obvious disadvantages! But here is a way of having all the benefits, while staying alive: become united with Jesus Christ.

Paul's rather complicated theological argument goes like this. Christians are more than merely followers of Jesus; they are united with him. So in a sense, because he died you have 'died' too. And therefore you can rejoice in the fact that because he has been raised from death for ever, you too will rise from death and live for ever with God. No more slavery; no more debt; no more punishment; no more sin. The logical consequence of this is to live as if those things are true.

The symbol of this life, death and resurrection with Jesus is baptism. It is a sign of living, drowning and emerging into a new life. So baptized people have a responsibility to live in the righteous way that Jesus lived.

Christian Aid produces beautiful cards to give to people when they are baptized. They show Cambodian children dancing under the water from a hydrant. Inside there is a greeting, an explanation of what Christians believe about baptism, and some information about the work Christian Aid does in the interests of Cambodian children. They cost £5.99 (€9.50) for a pack of six (which might be useful for a church minister to keep in stock).

To order them, telephone 08700 787788.

From sin to forgiveness;
From slavery to freedom;
From death to life.
Alleluia!

March 27   Alive to God

You also must consider yourselves dead to sin and alive to God in Christ Jesus. Therefore, do not let sin exercise dominion in your mortal bodies, to make you obey their passions. No longer present your members to sin as instruments of wickedness, but present yourselves to God as those who have been brought from death to life, and present your members to God as instruments of righteousness. For sin will have no dominion over you, since you are not under law but under grace.

Romans 6.11–14

These words follow a complex argument by Paul about why Christians are like Jesus. They are united with him. So there is a sense in which they have died and come alive again, like him. The consequence is that they should behave in the same way that he did – obedient to God. It is going to have implications for the future, for Christians will have life after death. But it has implications for the present too, for Christians are called to lead a good and just life before death as well.

John Bangonluri is a pastor and the leader of Kaleo Baptist Women's Development Project, one of Christian Aid's partner organizations in Ghana. It is a project that gives small loans to women so that they can start income-generating schemes, such as buying shea nuts in bulk so that they can be processed into a butter which is used to make soap. He writes: 'People need spiritual help, but they need practical help too. Just like Jesus . . . the best thing you can do is to bring hope. You have to address the poverty first and then be in a position to help people spiritually. God makes a way where there is no way. "I believe in life before death", like the Christian Aid motto says.'

The Christian Aid 'motto' appears almost everywhere that the organization is referred to – on books and leaflets, on collecting envelopes, and at the foot of the website
www.christianaid.org.uk
Have a good look at it and think about its implications. Is it a belief that Christian Aid's secular and Christian supporters can unite to support?

Giver of good gifts, we are waiting for you.
And the sick are waiting for medicine.
O Jesus, you have swallowed death
and every kind of disease
and will make us whole again.

From 'Jesus of the Deep Forest', a prayer from Ghana by Christina Afua Gyan

March 28   Complacency condemned

Hear this word, you cows of Bashan who are on Mount Samaria,
who oppress the poor, who crush the needy,
who say to their husbands, 'Bring something to drink!'
The Lord God has sworn by his holiness:
The time is surely coming upon you,
when they shall take you away with hooks, even the last of you with
fishhooks . . .
Bring your sacrifices every morning, your tithes every three days;
bring a thank-offering of leavened bread,
and proclaim freewill offerings, publish them;
for so you love to do, O people of Israel! says the Lord God.

Amos 4.1–2, 4–5

Frankly, this is a disgrace! No one deserves to be called 'fat cow', especially respectable women who are happily married and regularly attend worship. And foreseeing violence just creates a climate of fear. What foul-mouthed creature is dragging this kind of language into the book?

Oh, it's God!

The extreme caricature serves to remind us how ferociously God loathes the sight of people luxuriating in wealth accumulated by keeping others in poverty. No amount of religious observance, even sacrifices and money offerings, compensate for thinking that it is acceptable for poor people to subsidize the extravagance of rich people. Amos, a farmer catapulted into the role of prophet 800 years before Jesus, returns to this theme often. He doesn't mince his words!

Over two billion people earn less for an entire day's work than the cost of a take-away cappuccino. Are you polite when you should be passionate?

Stop for a cup of fairly traded coffee. While you drink it, pray for those who have earned a fair wage to bring it to you. And for those who are not so fortunate.

Lord Jesus, teach me when to shout and when to whisper; when to oppose and when to tolerate; when to be angry and when to encourage calm. And so may my ways become ever more like your ways. Amen.

March 29   Seek God and live

Thus says the Lord to the house of Israel:
Seek me and live; but do not seek Bethel,
and do not enter into Gilgal or cross over to Beersheba;
for Gilgal shall surely go into exile,
    and Bethel shall come to nothing.
Seek the Lord and live . . .
Ah, you that turn justice to wormwood, and bring righteousness to the ground!
The one who made the Pleiades and Orion,
    and turns deep darkness into the morning, and darkens the day into night,
who calls for the waters of the sea,
    and pours them out on the surface of the earth,
the Lord is his name.

Amos 5.4–8

For centuries the people of Israel had travelled to traditional sanctuaries in order to worship the Lord – to Bethel, Gilgal, Beersheba. But God warned his people through Amos that if they went there expecting to find his blessing they would search for it in vain. Worship there had gone stale. Why? Because worship, even exhilarating worship, cannot be maintained for long if it takes place in a context where injustice goes unchallenged. Past blessings and strong traditions are no substitute for vital praise accompanied by selfless lives.

So, is the situation hopeless? Certainly not! Don't seek out a better sermon or a finer choir or a more beautiful building, says God. Seek me!

Seeking the creator of the universe can revive an old church, or establish a new church, or bring spiritual life to a person in the very chair in which you are sitting. But it won't happen where 'justice' and 'righteousness' have been laid low.

Make a list of the churches that you have attended as far back as you can remember. It may be one or many (or perhaps none). For each one, recall what was or is good about their worship, their relationships, their pursuit of justice. As you do so, memories of what was lacking in them are bound to flood in, but swat them away. Be thankful instead for the people and activities there which genuinely 'seek God'.

It is not far to go for thou art near;
it is not far to go for thou art here.
And not by travelling, Lord, come to thee,
but by the way of love. And we love thee.

Amy Carmichael (1868–1951)

March 30   Seek good, not evil

[You] hate the one who reproves in the gate, and abhor the one
*   who speaks the truth.*
Therefore, because you trample on the poor and take from them
*   levies of grain,*
*   you have built houses of hewn stone,*
*   but you shall not live in them;*
you have planted pleasant vineyards, but you shall not drink their wine.
For I know how many are your transgressions, and how great are your sins –
you who afflict the righteous, who take a bribe,
*   and push aside the needy in the gate.*
Therefore the prudent will keep silent in such a time; for it is an evil time.
Seek good and not evil, that you may live
and so the Lord, the God of hosts, will be with you, just as you have said.
Hate evil and love good, and establish justice in the gate;
it may be that the Lord, the God of hosts,
*   will be gracious to the remnant of Joseph.*

Amos 5.10–15

There are four accusations here of immoral behaviour. Can you
find them?

- Suppressing the freedom to express opposition.
- Requiring compulsory 'gifts' of grain on top of the proper rent.
- Taking advantage of strength to ignore the needs of the poor.
- Knowing all this happens, but doing nothing about it.

'The gate' was the assembly point of a town which acted as a civil court, a stock
exchange, a council chamber and a forum. The settings have changed, but the
accusations seem not to have done. Am I alone in finding that dispiriting?

Based in the Democratic Republic of Congo, Héritiers de la
Justice (Inheritors of Justice) trains people to write, broadcast
and campaign on peace and justice issues. It gives assistance to
victims of human rights violations, teaching them their rights and
giving them a voice, and mediates in conflicts. Christian Aid
supports its work. Find out more at www.heritiers.org (click in the top right
corner to read it in English).

God of hosts, may those who can speak not be voiceless, may
those who can write not be wordless, may those who can walk
not be motionless, until we have all learnt to love what is good.
Amen.

March 31 Let justice roll on

I hate, I despise your festivals, and I take no delight in your
  solemn assemblies.
Even though you offer me your burnt offerings and grain
offerings,
  I will not accept them;
and the offerings of well-being of your fatted animals I will not look upon.
Take away from me the noise of your songs;
  I will not listen to the melody of your harps.
But let justice roll down like waters,
  and righteousness like an ever-flowing stream.

Amos 5.21–24

A down-and-out was sitting on the step of a church, weeping. To his astonishment, Jesus came walking along the street, and sat down beside him. 'Why are you crying?' Jesus asked.

'They won't let me in,' he said.

'I know how you feel,' sighed Jesus, 'I haven't been able to get in there myself for years.'

Amos' words are harsh (in fact, threatening) for this age of rediscovery of excellence in worship. With thousands of teenagers attracted to church by worship led by high-quality bands, and the sales of CDs by Delirious? and POD selling huge quantities in secular shops as well as to Christians, this is a time to rejoice not to criticize.

Well, maybe! When he was composing, J. S. Bach used to write 'To the glory of God' at the top of every sheet of the manuscript lest anyone should doubt his motivation. Perhaps today's Christian musicians should write on their amps and microphones: 'To the glory of God and to bring justice to those he loves.'

Everyone has a favourite piece of worship music, whether it is *St Matthew's Passion* or *The Soul Survivor Songbook*. On a scrap of paper write: 'Let justice roll down like waters and righteousness like an everflowing stream.' Slip it inside the cover of the CD case so that next time you play it you are reminded of Amos' message.

May the peoples praise you, O God;
  may all the peoples praise you.
May the nations be glad and sing for joy,
for you rule the peoples justly and guide the nations of the earth.

Psalm 67.3–4 (NIV)

April 1   Ripe for judgement

This is what the Lord God showed me – a basket of summer fruit. He said, 'Amos, what do you see?' And I said, 'A basket of summer fruit.' Then the Lord said to me: 'The end has come upon my people Israel; I will never again pass them by. The songs of the temple shall become wailings in that day,' says the Lord God; 'the dead bodies shall be many, cast out in every place. Be silent!' Hear this, you that trample on the needy and bring to ruin the poor of the land, saying, 'When will the new moon be over so that we may sell grain; and the sabbath, so that we may offer wheat for sale? We will make the ephah small and the shekel great, and practise deceit with false balances, buying the poor for silver and the needy for a pair of sandals, and selling the sweepings of the wheat.'

Amos 8.1–6

God cracks a joke here. It's not exactly a belly-laugh, but in the original language (Hebrew) it's a pun. In the market place God draws Amos' attention to a stall of summer fruit, then declares: 'Israel has been sentenced to summary execution.'

What had provoked God to such anger? Dishonesty in trade. The ephah was a vessel used to measure out corn for a shopper. The shekel was used to weigh out the silver with which he paid for it. By making the ephah small and the shekel great, the crooked trader was selling less than he promised for more than he agreed. The poorest people, who had no land of their own and were dependent on buying wheat, lost out. In today's international trading system, the scales are still dishonestly unbalanced against the poorest.

The badge of the Trade Justice Movement, a set of unbalanced scales, is inspired by these verses. Its campaign is for rules of trade that work in favour of the poorest countries, are monitored, are decided democratically, are enforced, and cover the activities of large transnational companies as well as governments. Buy a badge by calling 01252 669628, and wear it with pride.

Shut your eyes and imagine a huge pair of old-fashioned scales. In the pan on the left, picture representatives of the world's rich countries. It dramatically outweighs the pan on the right, in which are representatives of poor countries. As a prayer, imagine the scales moving until the two sides are balanced.

April 2　Powerful opponents

Then Amaziah, the priest of Bethel, sent to King Jeroboam of Israel, saying, 'Amos has conspired against you in the very centre of the house of Israel; the land is not able to bear all his words. For thus Amos has said, "Jeroboam shall die by the sword, and Israel must go into exile away from his land."'

And Amaziah said to Amos, 'O seer, go, flee away to the land of Judah, earn your bread there, and prophesy there; but never again prophesy at Bethel, for it is the king's sanctuary, and it is a temple of the kingdom.'

Then Amos answered Amaziah, 'I am no prophet, but a prophet's son; but I am a herdsman, and a dresser of sycamore trees, and the Lord took me from following the flock, and the Lord said to me, "Go, prophesy to my people Israel." Now therefore hear the word of the Lord . . .'

Amos 7.10–16

Like many who have spoken out in God's name against injustice, Amos had an opponent. Amaziah was a court priest and his job was to take official government policy and reassure the people that it had divine approval. He did everything possible, even if it was underhand, to stop Amos 'meddling in politics' by speaking out for the poor. But whose name are we familiar with twenty-eight centuries later? The amateur who had nothing powerful on his side except for a righteous cause and God's call.

To eradicate poverty will involve Christians and their friends in every part of the world facing up to powerful systems. Are you ready to follow Amos' example?

If tradition has been followed, the Chancellor of the Exchequer has recently set the budget for the UK. Write a letter that explains your concern for the world's poorest communities, and asks him to remember their needs as he manages the budget during the next twelve months. The address is 11 Downing Street, London, SW1A 2AA. In Ireland the budget is usually set in December, but there are still good reasons to write to the Minister for Finance at Government Buildings, Upper Merrion Street, Dublin 2.

To those who rule and lead us on the Earth you, sovereign Master, have given their authority . . . Lord, make their counsels conform to what is good and pleasing to you, that using reverently, peacefully and gently the power you have given them, they may find favour with you.

Clement of Rome (c. 35–100)

April 3   I am the gate

[Jesus said], 'I am the gate for the sheep. All who came before me are thieves and bandits; but the sheep did not listen to them. I am the gate. Whoever enters by me will be saved, and will come in and go out and find pasture. The thief comes only to steal and kill and destroy. I came that they may have life, and have it abundantly.

'I am the good shepherd. The good shepherd lays down his life for the sheep. The hired hand, who is not the shepherd and does not own the sheep, sees the wolf coming and leaves the sheep and runs away – and the wolf snatches them and scatters them. The hired hand runs away because a hired hand does not care for the sheep.'

John 10.7–13

Picture sheep grazing on a hillside 2,000 years ago. In the valley is a pen with its walls made from a horseshoe of rocks. It is evening, so the sheep have been led into the fold through its narrow entrance. The shepherd is lying across the entrance. He is asleep, but trained to wake at any moment should a sheep nudge his body to try to escape, or a wild animal or thief attempt to climb across him to find supper.

The shepherd is a real human gate. He is 'laying down his life for the sheep' in a literal sense. This is a marvellous picture of both the security and the freedom of those who put their trust in Christ. For those whom life has cramped and confined, he is the exit to the liberty of the pastures – out of oppression into freedom. For those whom life has frightened and bruised, he is the entrance into the security of the fold – out of loneliness into protective love.

The religious fraud offers this for money and is useless when the crisis arises. Jesus offers this for love and stays with us no matter what it costs him.

When you lie in bed this evening, think back to these verses and the shepherd laying down his life as a guardian. Picture in your imagination those who need you as a shepherd.

O Gate of my life, lead me out to find freedom. O Gate of my life, lead me in to find security. And watch over my going out and coming in until I meet you face to face. Amen.

April 4   I am the good shepherd

[Jesus said,] 'I am the good shepherd. I know my own and my own know me, just as the Father knows me and I know the Father. And I lay down my life for the sheep. I have other sheep that do not belong to this fold. I must bring them also, and they will listen to my voice. So there will be one flock, one shepherd. For this reason the Father loves me, because I lay down my life in order to take it up again. No one takes it from me, but I lay it down of my own accord. I have power to lay it down, and I have power to take it up again.'

John 10.14–18

Sheep can be obstinate creatures. But a good shepherd loves them no less because of that. He identifies them individually (to the astonishment of many town-dwellers whose closest encounter with a sheep is a kebab). And he is known by them individually (a challenge to those who only want sheep to be intimate once they come in sweater format).

But such a relationship is never exclusive. Jesus' original Jewish hearers must have assumed that they alone were God's people. But Jesus speaks of 'other sheep' who would come from Gentile communities to swell the Church. Such words challenge any Christian group today that assumes it can draw boundaries to prescribe who is part of the good shepherd's flock and who isn't. Jesus is answerable to no one but God himself. As he has proved, not even death can tell him what to do. When you realize who is beside you in the great multitude that meets Jesus in heaven, prepare to feel sheepish!

Look round the room for signs of wool – in clothes, in the carpet, in fabrics. If you have time, find a ball of wool. Take a few strands in your fingers, and think about the other hands through which they have passed on their way to you. All strangers to you; all known to and loved by God. He has every strand numbered. And every human named!

The king of love my shepherd is, whose goodness faileth never;
I nothing lack if I am his and he is mine for ever.
And so through all the length of days your goodness faileth never;
Good Shepherd may I sing thy praise within thy house for ever!

H. W. Baker (1821–77)

April 5   Anointed

[At dinner,] Mary took a pound of costly perfume made of pure nard, anointed Jesus' feet, and wiped them with her hair. The house was filled with the fragrance of the perfume. But Judas Iscariot, one of his disciples (the one who was about to betray him), said, 'Why was this perfume not sold for three hundred denarii and the money given to the poor?' (He said this not because he cared about the poor, but because he was a thief; he kept the common purse and used to steal what was put into it.) Jesus said, 'Leave her alone. She bought it so that she might keep it for the day of my burial. You always have the poor with you, but you do not always have me.'

John 12.1–8

Usually, respectable women kept their hair covered. Usually, a slave performed the messy task of refreshing a traveller. Usually, oil was used to anoint the head, not the feet. Usually, a spoonful was enough, not a cascade.

Nothing was usual about this dinner party. Mary had the chance to do something you and I can never do – come next to Jesus and lavish tenderness on him. Would I do something similar if Jesus came to my home? I hope I would, but I suspect that a touch of Judas in me would hold me back. Now that Jesus is not with us on Earth, how can we express the same devotion? As Jesus pointed out, although we no longer have him here, the conditions that make poor people poor have not gone away. So there is still an opportunity to make an over-the-top gesture in honour of the God we worship.

Mary had bought the perfume for Jesus' burial. It would never have been needed. It was as the women headed for his tomb to anoint Jesus' dead body that news of his resurrection stopped them in their tracks. It is almost as if some intuition prompted Mary to make premature use of the perfume while it could be valued by the living. She obviously believed in life before death.

Find something with a gorgeous smell, and spend a few moments enjoying it. Let your thoughts drift upward to the risen Jesus and outward to the poor communities for whom he has such a concern.

Take my love; my Lord, I pour
at your feet its treasure store.

Frances Ridley Havergal (1836–79), from the hymn 'Take my life'

April 6   Confronting death

Now a certain man was ill, Lazarus of Bethany, the village of Mary and her sister Martha ... The sisters sent a message to Jesus, 'Lord, he whom you love is ill.' But when Jesus heard it, he said, 'This illness does not lead to death; rather it is for God's glory, so that the Son of God may be glorified through it.' Accordingly, though Jesus loved Martha and her sister and Lazarus, after having heard that Lazarus was ill, he stayed two days longer in the place where he was.

Then after this he said to the disciples, 'Let us go to Judea again.' The disciples said to him, 'Rabbi, the Jews were just now trying to stone you, and are you going there again?' Jesus answered, 'Are there not twelve hours of daylight? Those who walk during the day do not stumble, because they see the light of this world.'

John 11.1, 3–9

Lazarus' reality: death is lying in wait, frightening him because nothing in human imagination can prepare us for what is involved in crossing its colourless border.

Mary and Martha's reality: crying out to Jesus in desperation and, for agonizing days, receiving no reply.

The disciples' reality: if Jesus decides to go and help Lazarus, the death threats they have just escaped might prove fatal this time.

Jesus' reality: the times are in God's hands. If God has ordained 'twelve hours of daylight' then we can trust him not to reduce them on a whim to eleven. So Jesus is confident that Lazarus will not die prematurely, the sisters' prayer will not go unanswered, and the disciples will be kept safe on their journey. In fact, he is so confident in God that he waits two days until he knows the time is right.

At the crucifixion of Jesus we see these realities come to a head – death, unanswered prayer, fear. But the story of Lazarus gives us hope that all these things can be transformed into 'God's glory'. God's reality is love.

Remember those whom you miss. It won't do you any harm to be honest about the death, the unanswered prayer, or the fear. But also have in mind that those things are history now. The reality that stays with you is the love.

Lord God, with all my heart I want to see beyond death to the glory. When I am walking around in darkness, don't let me stumble. Amen.

April 7 The resurrection and the life

Lazarus had already been in the tomb four days . . . When Martha heard that Jesus was coming, she went and met him, while Mary stayed at home. Martha said to Jesus, 'Lord, if you had been here, my brother would not have died. But even now I know that God will give you whatever you ask of him.' Jesus said to her, 'Your brother will rise again.' Martha said to him, 'I know that he will rise again in the resurrection on the last day.' Jesus said to her, 'I am the resurrection and the life. Those who believe in me, even though they die, will live, and everyone who lives and believes in me will never die. Do you believe this?' She said to him, 'Yes, Lord, I believe that you are the Messiah, the Son of God, the one coming into the world.'

John 11.17, 20–27

By the time Jesus arrives in Martha's neighbourhood, she has gone beyond shock and grief at her brother's death. She is angry. She scolds Jesus: 'You should have been here.' But her faith did not die with her brother, because she continues: 'But I know that you can do something even now.' The presence of Jesus has the potential to put a hopeless situation in a different light.

Honest, resolute, refusing to despair – these are the characteristics of Martha that allow Jesus to make an extraordinary revelation. Resurrection is at hand. It is not just something for the future; it is already here, there and everywhere that Jesus is. He has given the life that goes through and beyond death – the life of the eternal ages for the creatures of time.

Believing this allies a person to Jesus. Believers set themselves on the path that Jesus has trod. It is a path that inevitably leads through suffering and death. But it is also the path of resurrection and life. Jesus is typically incisive with his question: 'Do you believe this?'

Many people have a vague hope that death is not the end. Many Christians believe that they will live with Jesus after they die. Few live now as if their eternal life has already begun. What difference would it make to your daily decisions if you lived with that as a reality?

Lord God of life, even in the face of anger, disappointment and sadness, help me to live what I believe. Amen.

April 8   Raised from the dead

[Jesus said], 'Where have you laid [Lazarus]?' They said to him, 'Lord, come and see.' Jesus began to weep . . .

Then Jesus, again greatly disturbed, came to the tomb. It was a cave, and a stone was lying against it. Jesus said, 'Take away the stone.' Martha, the sister of the dead man, said to him, 'Lord, already there is a stench because he has been dead four days.' Jesus said to her, 'Did I not tell you that if you believed, you would see the glory of God?' So they took away the stone. And Jesus looked upward and said, 'Father, I thank you for having heard me. I knew that you always hear me, but I have said this for the sake of the crowd standing here, so that they may believe that you sent me.' When he had said this, he cried with a loud voice, 'Lazarus, come out!' The dead man came out, his hands and feet bound with strips of cloth, and his face wrapped in a cloth.

John 11.34–35, 38–44

How bizarre! When Jesus was told that Lazarus was critically ill, he did nothing for two days. When the news arrived that Lazarus was dead, Jesus was unmoved. But now, four days after the tragedy emerged, Jesus weeps. Why now? Perhaps because Jesus knows the enormity of what he is about to do – drag Lazarus back from the perfection of Paradise to the pain and injustice of human life.

If the Easter hope of resurrection is true, then the power of death to frighten, trap or depress us is transformed. From the jubilant viewpoint of heaven, our life on earth will seem to have been a pale, fleeting thing. No wonder Jesus was 'greatly disturbed' at calling Lazarus back. The miracle gave a glimpse of 'the glory of God'. But it is as nothing compared with the glory that is the destiny of us all.

Eat an egg! In every place where Christ has been worshipped, eggs have been associated with life coming from death. They have been decorated. Their shells have been hung from trees. They have been encrusted with jewels and given as presents. They have been made from chocolate and gobbled. Even if it is only in your lunchtime sandwich, register as you eat it that heaven is your destination.

'We are an Easter people, and "Alleluia" is our song.'

Augustine, Bishop of Hippo (modern Tunisia), 354–430

April 9   Triumph

 The great crowd that had come to the festival heard that Jesus was coming to Jerusalem. So they took branches of palm trees and went out to meet him, shouting, 'Hosanna! Blessed is the one who comes in the name of the Lord – the King of Israel!' Jesus found a young donkey and sat on it; as it is written: 'Do not be afraid, daughter of Zion. Look, your king is coming, sitting on a donkey's colt!'

John 12.12–16

 All four Gospels tell the story of Jesus' entry into Jerusalem. But only one mentions palm leaves. This is curious, since for centuries we have called the day on which Christians remember these events 'Palm Sunday'. Matthew, Mark and Luke mention olive trees and cloaks being thrown under the donkey's feet, but not palms. It is not surprising, since Jerusalem is far too cold for palm trees. Perhaps the ones that John mentions had been brought up from the desert as packaging for the dates on sale in the market.

So why did the Gospel writers emphasize cloaks instead? Because throwing your cloak under someone's feet was a symbolic recognition that the person was your king. 2 Kings 9 tells us that is how Jehu accepted the throne of Israel. It was an act of submission at a political rally – your only cloak beneath your only leader.

Tongue firmly in cheek, I have a suggestion! Since the cloaks are so important, let's change the name of Palm Sunday to 'Overcoat Sunday'. Instead of waving palms, we will all throw our overcoats on the church floor for others to walk over. It will be a powerful symbol of humble submission to our fellow-believers.

Hmm! I wonder how quickly the day would become 'Second-best Overcoat Sunday'! Or, 'Jumble Sale Overcoat Sunday'!

 On a piece of paper write: 'Hosanna! Jesus the King!' Stuff it in the pocket of your overcoat to discover at some future date. As you do, ask yourself what it means to accept Jesus as king in your life. What is the real equivalent of putting your cloak under his donkey?

 He is the one for whom women lay down their cloths on the path, and pour sweet-smelling oil on his feet. They run to and fro amid shouts of praise before him: It is true – Jesus is Chief!

From 'Jesus of the Deep Forest', a prayer from Ghana by Christina Afua Gyan

April 10 Planting a seed

[Jesus told his disciples,] 'The hour has come for the Son of Man to be glorified. Very truly, I tell you, unless a grain of wheat falls into the earth and dies, it remains just a single grain; but if it dies, it bears much fruit. Those who love their life lose it, and those who hate their life in this world will keep it for eternal life. Whoever serves me must follow me, and where I am, there will my servant be also. Whoever serves me, the Father will honour.'

John 12.23–26

People rarely left Jesus with their expectations straightforwardly fulfilled. Jesus spells out the cost of being drawn to him. The seed would have to die in order for the greater fruit tree to grow (clearly a reference to Jesus' own death and resurrection). Those who follow him find a way of life which is the opposite of what they might expect. People who 'love their life' and seek self-fulfilment will discover that is the way to lose it. They will be like a seed – perfectly formed but never planted. The true way into life, says Jesus, is the apparently suicidal decision to throw your life away on to him.

The twentieth-century Indian evangelist Sundar Singh took the life of a sadhu – a penniless and wandering pilgrim. He wrote: 'The real value of ease cannot be appreciated without having known pain, nor of sweetness without having tasted bitterness, nor of good without having seen evil, nor even of life without having passed through death.'

Plant something! Think about how strange it would seem to someone who did not understand it that throwing a seed into the damp earth is a way to create a living and beautiful plant. For many herbs, now is an ideal planting time, indoors or outdoors. (If circumstances make today's action an unrealistic one, plant an idea instead!)

'It is a thing most wonderful,
almost too wonderful to be,
that God's own Son should come from heaven,
and die to save someone like me.'

William Walsham How (1823–97)

April 11   Trust in the light

Jesus said to [his disciples], 'The light is with you for a little longer. Walk while you have the light, so that the darkness may not overtake you. If you walk in the darkness, you do not know where you are going. While you have the light, believe in the light, so that you may become children of light.'

John 12.35–36

Patricia St John's novel *Star of Light* is set in Morocco. Hamid is a street kid and he visits a project for homeless boys run by an English nurse. While she is out of the room he steals something, then waits for her outside in the darkness and rain. The nurse brings out a lamp to help them on their journey through the night. She invites Hamid to come under her cloak so that they both walk in the light. But he won't! He prefers to shuffle against the wall, slipping around in the mud, out of the light's range. Finally, he misses his step and he falls. The nurse brings the lamp over to him to check that he is all right and the truth becomes clear. Splattered all over him are the remains of what he stole. Two eggs.

The nurse takes him home, cleans him up and bandages his knees, saying: 'Hamid, you fell and hurt yourself because you wouldn't walk in the light. You were afraid of it because you'd stolen my eggs. You couldn't walk with me in the light because you'd done wrong . . . I'm going to forgive you – but promise you won't steal from my house again.'

It is easy to understand the allure of darkness. The world needs Christians to re-establish how attractive goodness can be.

Christian Aid supports several projects for children who live on the streets. One of its partner organizations is Passage House, working with girls in Recife, Brazil. Its founder Ana Vasconcelos writes: 'When I began working with the girls they used to tell me the streets were the passage to hell because only people like them live there – street children, prostitutes, people who take drugs. So I asked them to help me build a space that would be a passage to heaven.' Find out more about Christian Aid's work in Brazil at www.christianaid.org.uk/world/where/lac/brazilp.htm

In the streets of Morocco,
For the girls of Recife,
On our estates and in our cities,
Wherever children play,
Lord Jesus, let there be light.

April 12   The way, the truth and the life

[Jesus said], 'Do not let your hearts be troubled. Believe in God, believe also in me. In my Father's house there are many dwelling-places. If it were not so, would I have told you that I go to prepare a place for you? And if I go and prepare a place for you, I will come again and will take you to myself, so that where I am, there you may be also. And you know the way to the place where I am going.' Thomas said to him, 'Lord, we do not know where you are going. How can we know the way?' Jesus said to him, 'I am the way, and the truth, and the life. No one comes to the Father except through me.'*

John 14.1–6

Of the many songs that irritate me, one stands out. I loathe Frank Sinatra singing: 'I did it my way.' Only one person could say those words with integrity, and that is Jesus. But he would never say them. If he swayed up to the microphone, slightly the worse for wear, on karaoke night at Matthew the tax-collector's, he would sing: 'I did it God's way.'

In this generation we no longer feel secure about trusting people on whom we once relied – doctors, pension providers, politicians. We are encouraged to trust our own judgement as to the best way to go. But Jesus didn't say, as doctors do, 'I will make the way as pain-free as I can.' He didn't say, as pension providers do, 'I will prepare you for the way.' He didn't even say, as politicians do, 'Choose me to lead you on the way.' He said, 'I *am* the way – the true way, the living way.'

These are not just words of reassurance about our resurrection to heaven; they are about how to live between now and then.

Look back on your major decisions of the last few years. In retro-spect, would you say of them 'I did it my way' or 'I did it God's way'? Does what you have learnt of God at these turning points help you trust him for the unknown future?

Lead us, heavenly Father, lead us,
o'er the world's tempestuous sea;
guard us, guide us, keep us, feed us,
for we have no help but thee;
yet possessing every blessing
if our God our Father be.

James Edmeston (1791–1867)

April 13   Gethsemane

[Jesus] went out with his disciples across the Kidron valley to a place where there was a garden, which he and his disciples entered. Now Judas, who betrayed him, also knew the place, because Jesus often met there with his disciples. So Judas brought a detachment of soldiers together with police from the chief priests and the Pharisees, and they came there with lanterns and torches and weapons. Then Jesus, knowing all that was to happen to him, came forward and asked them, 'Whom are you looking for?' They answered, 'Jesus of Nazareth.' Jesus replied, 'I am he.' Judas, who betrayed him, was standing with them. When Jesus said to them, 'I am he', they stepped back and fell to the ground.

John 18.1–9

All four Gospel writers tell us about Jesus' arrest in the garden. But some of the events that the others tell us about are missing from John's account. Jesus does not agonize over the events to come, no exhausted disciples fall asleep, and there is no kiss of betrayal from Judas. All these suggest events unfolding out of control. Instead, John writes of authorities pursuing Jesus until *he* catches them. He knows what is going to happen, he goes out to meet his captors and clearly identifies himself.

This is a version of Jesus' arrest for us to appreciate in the light of what we know about his resurrection. The event is in the hands of the God who turns all things, even evil situations, to his purposes. Even the names reveal what the Gospel writers want us to understand. Gethsemane means 'the olive oil press' and speaks to us of Jesus crushed and poured out. But John does not mention the name. Instead he locates the story near the Kidron valley, which was known as 'the valley of God's judgement'. It is here that the very attempt by Jesus' enemies to eject him from their lives serves to help him become their Saviour.

What has happened to you today that has been out of your control? Events affected by the weather, transport, the needs of family and friends, unexpected interventions by strangers? Reflect on them, bearing in mind that we have a God who turns all things, even negative occurrences, to his purposes.

Lord, I am not yet ready for you to have your way with me – but I am willing to be made willing.

Teresa of Avila (1515–82)

April 14   Pilate

Pilate took Jesus and had him flogged. And the soldiers wove a crown of thorns and put it on his head, and they dressed him in a purple robe. They kept coming up to him, saying, 'Hail, King of the Jews!' and striking him on the face. Pilate went out again and said to them, 'Look, I am bringing him out to you to let you know that I find no case against him.' So Jesus came out, wearing the crown of thorns and the purple robe. Pilate said to them, 'Here is the man!' When the chief priests and the police saw him, they shouted, 'Crucify him! Crucify him!' Pilate said to them, 'Take him yourselves and crucify him; I find no case against him.' The Jews answered him, 'We have a law, and according to that law he ought to die because he has claimed to be the Son of God.'

John 19.1–7

- For those who grasp their prison bars helplessly so that we may walk free – a thought.
- For those who rot in the dark so that we may walk in the sun – a thought.
- For those whose ribs have been broken so that we may breathe our fill – a thought.
- For those whose back has been broken so that we may walk erect – a thought.
- For those whose faces have been slapped so that we may walk in fear of no hand – a thought.
- For those whose mouths have been gagged so that we may speak out – a thought.
- For those whose pride lies in rags on the slabs of their jails so that we may proudly walk – a thought.
- For those whose wives live in anguish so that our wives may live happy – a thought.
- For those whose country is in chains so that our country may be free – a thought.
- And for their jailers and torturers – a thought, the saddest of all, for they are the most maimed, and for them the day of reckoning is bound to come.

Salvador da Madariaga, Amnesty International

Amnesty International's website is www.amnesty.org. Look it up, or contact them at 1 Easton Street, London, WC1X 0DW. Does it move you to the same pity and action as the last, terrible hours of Jesus' life?

Jesus, you were unjustly condemned by Pontius Pilate: strengthen our brothers and sisters who are suffering injustice and persecution.

A prayer from Botswana

April 15 Burial

Joseph of Arimathea, who was a disciple of Jesus, though a secret one because of his fear of the Jews, asked Pilate to let him take away the body of Jesus. Pilate gave him permission; so he came and removed his body. Nicodemus, who had at first come to Jesus by night, also came, bringing a mixture of myrrh and aloes, weighing about a hundred pounds. They took the body of Jesus and wrapped it with the spices in linen cloths, according to the burial custom of the Jews. Now there was a garden in the place where he was crucified, and in the garden there was a new tomb in which no one had ever been laid. And so, because it was the Jewish day of Preparation, and the tomb was nearby, they laid Jesus there.

John 19.38–42

The agony of the execution was over. It was in public that Jesus endured the nails, the wrenching and the pain. The gross indignity of the abuse was over. It was in public that Jesus took the derision, the ridicule and the venom. The humiliation of failure was over. It was in public that Jesus went through the questioning, the hopelessness and the despair.

In Jesus' words, 'It is finished', are relief, disappointment, release – and also a sense of accomplishment. The death that has brought salvation to humankind took place amidst clamour, crowds, belligerence and tumult.

But it was all alone, in darkness and silence, that he rose from the dead.

Seek out privacy today. Find a place where there is darkness and silence. And there, in secret like Joseph and Nicodemus, tell Jesus what his death and resurrection mean to you.

How fair and lovely is the hope which the Lord gave to the dead when he laid down beside them. Rise up and come forth and sing praise to him who has raised you from destruction.

Liturgy of the Orthodox Syrian Church

April 16   Peter sees Jesus alive

Early on the first day of the week, while it was still dark, Mary Magdalene came to the tomb and saw that the stone had been removed from the tomb. So she ran and went to Simon Peter and the other disciple, the one whom Jesus loved, and said to them, 'They have taken the Lord out of the tomb, and we do not know where they have laid him.' Then Peter and the other disciple set out and went toward the tomb. The two were running together, but the other disciple outran Peter and reached the tomb first. He bent down to look in and saw the linen wrappings lying there, but he did not go in. Then Simon Peter came, following him, and went into the tomb. He saw the linen wrappings lying there, and the cloth that had been on Jesus' head, not lying with the linen wrappings but rolled up in a place by itself. Then the other disciple, who reached the tomb first, also went in, and he saw and believed.

John 20.1–8

There are three different reactions here to seeing the empty tomb of a deeply loved friend.

- Mary was up early (a sleepless night, perhaps). It was highly unusual for the governor to release the corpse of a man executed for treason. Her first thought was that fanatics had defied Pilate's ruling and dumped the body in the criminals' grave pit under cover of darkness.
- Peter, making up in boldness what he lacked in fitness, charged into the tomb. Luke's account of these events tells us that his reaction was to wonder what in heaven's name was going on.
- The other disciple, encouraged by Peter, entered more cautiously. But it is he for whom the phenomenal truth first sinks in: 'My God! He is risen.'

Do any of those reactions find an echo in yours?

The feel of Easter Day is increasingly like any other day, with shops and services barely acknowledging that Christians are rejoicing. So no matter what day it actually happens to be, create your own alternative Easter Day in a way that includes a message to God and a celebratory treat for yourself!

When we are all despairing, when the world is full of grief, when we see no way ahead and hope has gone away – roll back the stone!

Janet Morley/Christian Aid

April 17 Mary

As [Mary] wept, she bent over to look into the tomb; and she saw two angels in white, sitting where the body of Jesus had been lying, one at the head and the other at the feet. They said to her, 'Woman, why are you weeping?' She said to them, 'They have taken away my Lord, and I do not know where they have laid him.' When she had said this, she turned around and saw Jesus standing there, but she did not know that it was Jesus. Jesus said to her, 'Woman, why are you weeping? Whom are you looking for?' Supposing him to be the gardener, she said to him, 'Sir, if you have carried him away, tell me where you have laid him, and I will take him away.' Jesus said to her, 'Mary!' She turned and said to him in Hebrew, 'Rabbouni!' (which means Teacher). Jesus said to her, 'Do not hold on to me, because I have not yet ascended to the Father. But go to my brothers and say to them, "I am ascending to my Father and your Father, to my God and your God."' Mary Magdalene went and announced to the disciples, 'I have seen the Lord'.

John 20.11–18

Jesus' first resurrection appearance was to a forgiven sinner, to someone in a state of distress, to a woman whose evidence would (in that culture) not be believed. Creation may have come with a Big Bang, but resurrection certainly didn't. It came with the whisper of a name and a message of good news.

Disasters happen in 'big bang' style – their devastation is broadcast to the world on television. Recovery happens in 'resurrection' style – quietly, and out of sight. Christian Aid responds to natural catastrophes though the Disasters Emergency Committee, a coalition of agencies who work together to appeal to the public for help. But true resurrection is the unspectacular work of those who stay to support the rebuilding of communities long after the cameras have gone.

After the initial outpouring of compassion when we hear of a natural disaster, our memories are sometimes short. Recall the tsunami that shocked the world on Boxing Day 2004. How much do you know about what has happened since? A good starting point is to visit www.christianaid.org.uk/seasia/index.htm and follow the links.

God of the springtime bulbs and the lengthening days,
we look to you for new life;
bring Easter to all this weary world.

April 18   Thomas

Thomas (who was called the Twin), one of the twelve, was not with them when Jesus came. So the other disciples told him, 'We have seen the Lord.' But he said to them, 'Unless I see the mark of the nails in his hands, and put my finger in the mark of the nails and my hand in his side, I will not believe.'

A week later his disciples were again in the house, and Thomas was with them. Although the doors were shut, Jesus came and stood among them and said, 'Peace be with you.' Then he said to Thomas, 'Put your finger here and see my hands. Reach out your hand and put it in my side. Do not doubt but believe.' Thomas answered him, 'My Lord and my God!'

Jesus said to him, 'Have you believed because you have seen me? Blessed are those who have not seen and yet have come to believe.'

John 20.24–29

This is a story in which, because doubts are honestly expressed, deeper faith follows. There are two ways of seeing Thomas – either as a man of integrity who refused to say he believed when he could not believe, or as a stubborn man who refused to accept the testimony of his ten closest friends. Whichever is true, every demand he made was met graciously by Jesus.

But Jesus went on to make it clear that proof is a privilege, not a right. Real blessing comes to those who, like the Christians of the twenty-first century, have believed because of the testimony of others. That is, after all, why John wrote his Gospel. For this sceptical age, 'seeing is believing'. But the Christian faith is that believing leads to seeing.

Incidentally, I wonder what Thomas' twin made of his or her brother's faith!

Set aside some time today to be honest to God. Be as straightforward as Thomas. Don't ask for proof or faith, but do ask for help.

Lord, I believe; help my unbelief.

Mark 9.24

April 19 Good news beside a lake

Simon Peter said to [the disciples], 'I am going fishing.' They said to him, 'We will go with you.' They went out and got into the boat, but that night they caught nothing.

Just after daybreak, Jesus stood on the beach; but the disciples did not know that it was Jesus. Jesus said to them, 'Children, you have no fish, have you?' They answered him, 'No.' He said to them, 'Cast the net to the right side of the boat, and you will find some.' So they cast it, and now they were not able to haul it in because there were so many fish. That disciple whom Jesus loved said to Peter, 'It is the Lord!' When Simon Peter heard that it was the Lord, he put on some clothes, for he was naked, and jumped into the sea. But the other disciples came in the boat, dragging the net full of fish.

John 21.3–8

If you had travelled with Jesus for three exhilarating years, witnessed his death and then been astonished by encountering him in a resurrected body, why would you go back to your old job? In thousands of poor coastal communities around the world the answer is obvious. If you don't catch fish you can't feed your family. With fish stocks depleting worldwide, this story has a resonance for many organizations that Christian Aid supports. In the Philippines, for instance, it works with Mindoro Assistance for Human Advancement through Linkages. It campaigns to preserve the livelihood of fishing communities under threat from multinational companies that want to mine for nickel on the islands without sufficient regard to the impact on the sea and those who make their living from it.

All the fishermen's skill, resources and hard work produced an empty net. It took an encounter with the risen Jesus to make a difference. There are many organizations like Christian Aid which bring together the skills of poor people and the resources of rich people in order to make the world better. But do you believe that prayer to the risen Jesus is transforming?

Find out more about Christian Aid's work in the Philippines at www.christianaid.org.uk/world/where/asia/philippp.htm

Pray for all those whose livelihood is dependent upon decisions taken by powerful people whom they never meet in lands that they will never visit. Ask that together they may be able to achieve justice.

April 20   Feed my sheep

When they had finished breakfast, Jesus said to Simon Peter, 'Simon son of John, do you love me more than these?' He said to him, 'Yes, Lord; you know that I love you.' Jesus said to him, 'Feed my lambs.' A second time he said to him, 'Simon son of John, do you love me?' He said to him, 'Yes, Lord; you know that I love you.' Jesus said to him, 'Tend my sheep.' He said to him the third time, 'Simon son of John, do you love me?' Peter felt hurt because he said to him the third time, 'Do you love me?' And he said to him, 'Lord, you know everything; you know that I love you.' Jesus said to him, 'Feed my sheep.'

John 21.15–17

Three flunked opportunities to stand up for his Lord before the cock crowed. Three painful opportunities to affirm his love for Jesus publicly after breakfast. Three demanding calls to serve God's people and make the process of repentance complete. A complicated month for Peter!

Serving Jesus by 'feeding his sheep' (and surely feeding has a literal meaning as well as a metaphorical one) is the business of his followers. Why? Not out of guilt; not in order to draw attention to oneself; not in anticipation of a reward. For Peter and for each of us it is something that proceeds naturally from love of the Lord. Where there is a genuine love for Jesus, other things follow as naturally as a sheep follows a shepherd. Let love, and love alone, be the motive that stirs us to seek peace and justice.

This will take time, so only read on if you can spare it. In your imagination, step into Peter's shoes (or rather his bare feet) as he splashes through the water and onto the beach. Smell the fish as they grill. Taste the bread. Then feel the breeze coming off the sea as you walk with Jesus, apart from the others. Tell him the things you want him to know about you – even though he knows them already. Listen to his replies. Let him give you challenges about a world which still needs to be fed.

Give us, Lord Jesus, a vision of our world as your love would make it; a world where the weak are protected, and none go hungry or poor; and give us the inspiration and courage to build it. Amen.

April 21   My enemies are defeated

I will give thanks to the Lord with my whole heart;
  I will tell of all your wonderful deeds.
I will be glad and exult in you;
  I will sing praise to your name, O Most High.
When my enemies turned back,
they stumbled and perished before you.
For you have maintained my just cause;
  you have sat on the throne giving righteous judgement.
You have rebuked the nations, you have destroyed the wicked;
  you have blotted out their name for ever and ever.
The enemies have vanished in everlasting ruins;
  their cities you have rooted out; the very memory of them has perished.

Psalm 9.1–6

Justice! The air is thick with the clamour for it. Justice in international disputes, in gender issues, in trade rules. Justice for prisoners of conscience, for animals, for asylum-seekers. Sometimes the sum total of justice in the world seems to grow; sometimes to shrink. And sometimes the worst atrocities of all are committed in the name of 'justice'. It is as though humankind, even when its intentions are best, cannot distance itself enough to see with the objective eyes that are needed. The writer of the psalm is able to rejoice in justice solely because he has taken his appeal to a higher tribunal.

He has presented his petition to the Good Lawyer who is ready to 'maintain the just cause' of the ill-treated. The trial is heard before 'the throne' of the Judge who never adjourns. In that context the writer can look back to great tyrannies that have come to an end and seemingly intractable evils that have passed into memory. Looking in a historical context, so can we. Looking with the eyes of faith, we can trust 'the Most High' to do again what he has done before.

We live in dangerous times. There are plenty of people who are prepared to use the name of God to justify actions that pursue a personal or political agenda. A killer can become a 'martyr'; an atrocity can become a 'holy war'. Listen to a news broadcast today and, as you hear the stories of people seeking justice, picture their case being put before the Perfect Judge, and see whether it changes your perspective.

Lord of lords, in places where I can bring about justice, grant me the integrity to act for you. In places where I can do little, grant me the confidence to trust in you. Amen.

April 22   God governs with justice

The Lord sits enthroned for ever,
    he has established his throne for judgement.
He judges the world with righteousness;
    he judges the peoples with equity.
The Lord is a stronghold for the oppressed,
  a stronghold in times of trouble.
And those who know your name put their trust in you,
  for you, O Lord, have not forsaken those who seek you.

Psalm 9.7–10

One word in this psalm seems more important than all the others. It is the word 'for ever'. Tyrants and criminals rise and fall, but the Christian faith is that God will have the final say. For people who are oppressed, the fact that God knows and rightly assesses all that is going on is, in itself, a 'stronghold'. Beyond time it will be more than that; it will bring restitution.

Christians (particularly in rich countries) have tended to avoid talking about the 'Day of Judgement' because it implies threat. If we talked instead about the 'Day of Justice' we would pray for that moment to come as urgently as Christians do in poor countries. Jesus the Judge holds no fear for those who long for the world to be rid of evil, hunger and poverty. The closing words of the Bible are their heartfelt prayer: 'Come, Lord Jesus!'

We are 111 days into the year. How is it going? Look ahead in your diary to something that will be really bad news – either for personal reasons, or because it is an event of international significance that will fill parts of the world with dread. In the space for that day write 'Come, Lord Jesus'. When the day arrives let it remind you that God's justice is a stronghold for that day, but an unassailable certainty for the future.

Thy kingdom come, O God! Thy rule, O Christ begin!
Break with thine iron rod the tyrannies of sin!
In war-torn lands afar thick darkness broodeth yet:
Arise, O Morning Star! Arise, and never set!

Lewis Hensley (1824–1905)

April 23 Be gracious to me, Lord

Sing praises to the Lord, who dwells in Zion.
  Declare his deeds among the peoples.
For he who avenges blood is mindful of them;
  he does not forget the cry of the afflicted.
Be gracious to me, O Lord.
See what I suffer from those who hate me;
  you are the one who lifts me up from the gates of death,
so that I may recount all your praises,
  and, in the gates of daughter Zion, rejoice in your deliverance.
The nations have sunk in the pit that they made;
  in the net that they hid has their own foot been caught.
The Lord has made himself known, he has executed judgement;
  the wicked are snared in the work of their own hands.

Psalm 9.11–16

William Laud, Archbishop of Canterbury, was led out to execution in January 1645. He had dealt severely with anyone who opposed the Church of England, particularly its dress and dignity. But his real 'crime' was to attempt to establish a regular salary for clergy by reclaiming land that Henry VIII had seized from the Church, which gave him enemies among rich landowners. He was seventy-two when he was beheaded in the Tower of London, but he looked so composed that his opponents spread rumours that he was wearing make-up. He preached a sermon on these verses from the scaffold. To worship a God who 'does not forget the cry of the afflicted' gave him such serenity that his last words were, 'Lord, I am coming as quickly as I can.'

The psalm is realistic in that, after looking back to a God who has rescued in the past, and up to a God in whose justice we can have confidence, troubles still keep gathering like storm clouds. To have confidence in such times that those who perpetrate injustice are only creating trouble for themselves is remarkable indeed.

Bring to mind people who are facing death today. Some are comfortable and surrounded by those who love them. Others are fearful and among strangers, and imagine that no one is thinking of them – mistakenly!

As thou wast before at my life's beginning,
be thou so again at my journey's end.

An ancient Scottish prayer

April 24   The hope of the afflicted

The wicked shall depart to Sheol,
  all the nations that forget God.
For the needy shall not always be forgotten,
  nor the hope of the poor perish for ever.
Rise up, O Lord! Do not let mortals prevail;
let the nations be judged before you.
Put them in fear, O Lord;
  let the nations know that they are only human.

Psalm 9.17–20

The writers of the psalms had no concept of heaven – at least not in the sense in which we understand it. The destiny of those who died was Sheol, a shadowy place of spirits. God was present there, but it was never described as a place of joy. To depart there prematurely would be a punishment indeed, a place where those who had forgotten God and forgotten the weak would themselves be forgotten.

So behind this part of the psalm is a question that thousands of people ask nervously: 'Do I matter enough to be remembered?' And the answer is that ours is a God who is incapable of forgetting. Even the poor and the sick, so often overlooked by those who have a high opinion of themselves, are deeply etched in his memory.

In South Africa, Happiness is determined to be remembered. She has not yet found the courage to tell her young daughter that she is HIV-positive. So she is making a box of memories for her – objects from important moments of her life that will tell her story should she become too ill to do so herself. Christian Aid's partner organization Wola Nani works with thousands of people who have HIV/AIDS, providing home nursing, education and care for those who have been orphaned. Because so many millions of people have AIDS it becomes hard to remember that each one is a loved individual. God remembers – but that is not an excuse for us to be forgetful.

Responding to HIV/AIDS is one of Christian Aid's priorities. To find out more about their work, visit
www.christianaid.org.uk/world/hivaids.htm

Come close in your mercy, O Lord, to remember:
the sick, in need of courage,
the bereaved, in need of consolation,
the carers, in need of strength.
And Lord, may we who are so easily distracted never forget.
Amen.

April 25 The Lord is my shepherd

The Lord is my shepherd, I shall not want.
  He makes me lie down in green pastures;
he leads me beside still waters; he restores my soul.
He leads me in right paths for his name's sake.

Psalm 23.1–3

This is the best-known and best-loved psalm. It echoes feelings that every human has – the need for a place in which striving ceases, doing good is effortless, and peace is real. It touches people because its words are simple and its images universal. In South America the sheep become llamas; in the Himalayas they are yaks; in parts of Africa they are goats. And even Londoners who only come close to a sheep when they are at a barbecue find a spot in their imagination where the serene image of being in the care of a good shepherd speaks to them! What does it tell us about God?

- That he is thinking ahead about what we need, even though we may not realize we need it.
- That he can be trusted, because his intention is not to harm us, but to nurture us.
- That there is refreshment to be found in God for those whose spirit, emotions or dignity have been battered.
- That there are just and good ways of behaving that are natural for a Christian, and those 'paths' are the ones along which the shepherd will lead willing sheep.

Don't fight any of these things!

In the village of Mbayenne in Senegal, Fatma Dieng is doing her best to be a good shepherd in one of the poorest countries in the world. She received credit from Christian Aid's partner organization the Africa Network for Integrated Development. They have also given her veterinary training, which helps keep the sheep healthy as she fattens them up to sell at a profit. But like many countries in Africa, Senegal is vulnerable when rains are poor, and life is a struggle for both shepherds and sheep. Find out more about Christian Aid's work in Senegal at www.christianaid.org.uk/world/where/wca/senegalp.htm

Wherever he may guide me, no want shall turn me back;
My Shepherd is beside me, and nothing can I lack.
His wisdom ever waketh, his sight is never dim;
He knows the way he taketh and I will walk with him.

Anna Waring (1823–1910), from the hymn 'In heavenly love abiding'

April 26 Goodness and love will follow me

Even though I walk through the darkest valley, I fear no evil;
for you are with me; your rod and your staff – they comfort me.
You prepare a table before me in the presence of my enemies;
you anoint my head with oil; my cup overflows.
Surely goodness and mercy shall follow me all the days of my life,
and I shall dwell in the house of the Lord my whole life long.

Psalm 23.4–6

The beginning of the psalm, 'The Lord is my shepherd', was a vision of green fields and idyllic lakes. It would be easy to dismiss it as escapist. But in these verses the person who wrote the psalm acknowledges that life is not always blissful. There are 'dark valleys' and 'enemies'. Is the gentle shepherd any use when the going gets tough? Oh yes! He carries a club for defence, and wields a staff so that the sheep can be prodded in the right direction when coaxing is not enough.

The metaphor then changes and the Lord is no longer a shepherd but a party-giver. And what a host! There is a buffet that those who have been making your life miserable can only drool over, the beer is overflowing the glasses, and there are beauticians on hand to make sure you look and feel great. What a contrast to the rural serenity; this is a nightclubber's dream!

Which appeals more – the tranquillity or the revelry? In either case, this is the place in which you want to stay your whole life long. In fact, for eternity! Both are places where genuine goodness and endless mercy can be found. Pursuing those is genuinely satisfying in a way that a day in the countryside or a night in a club never could be.

Plan a trip in the country or a night on the town, depending on which part of the psalm has awoken your imagination. No matter which you choose, think in advance about what the issues of goodness and mercy are in those settings. What does it mean to have moral integrity as a follower of the good shepherd or a guest of the welcoming host in those places?

Good shepherd of the sheep,
I ask to know protection and direction during dark days.
Great host of the partygoers,
I ask to be taught goodness and mercy during glittering nights.
Amen.

April 27   The glory of God

Ascribe to the Lord, O heavenly beings, ascribe to the Lord
  glory and strength.
Ascribe to the Lord the glory of his name; worship the Lord in
  holy splendour.
The voice of the Lord is over the waters;
the God of glory thunders, the Lord over mighty waters.
The voice of the Lord is powerful; the voice of the Lord is full of majesty.
The voice of the Lord breaks the cedars;
  the Lord breaks the cedars of Lebanon.
He makes Lebanon skip like a calf, and Sirion like a young wild ox.

Psalm 29.1–6

The worshippers are in the temple going about their religious observances. They sing of God's glory and strength; they praise God for his holy splendour. Very nice! But, oh boy, there is a shock about to come. Gale warning! Force ten God approaching!

When the storm strikes they interpret it as 'the voice of the Lord'. The noise is terrifying; trees snap like matchsticks; whole countries seem to be thrown into the air like leaping animals. This is our God too – not just loving and peaceful, but wild and exhilarating, untamed and rampaging. How can we possibly worship a God like that? Because not only is he so mighty that we ought to be frightened; he is so good that we can be completely confident. That power is always and only going to be used for righteous purposes.

Over what or whom do you have power? Children perhaps, or employees. Plans or timings. Land or animals. Your own destiny. Think about how you use that power – always for good?

All you powerful things praise the Lord:
Niagara Falls and Pacific Ocean, tiger and tyrannosaurus,
Killer whale and golden eagle, forces of gravity and pull of the
  tide,
Forked lightning and shout of the throng;
Praise and magnify the one who created you.

All you weak things praise the Lord:
Sparkle of light and breath of the breeze, scuttling ant and wriggling tadpole,
Tear in the eye and hair on the head, soft feathers and gentle sighs,
Scent of the rose and whisper of prayer;
Praise and magnify the one who created you.

April 28   The peace giver

The voice of the Lord flashes forth flames of fire.
The voice of the Lord shakes the wilderness;
the Lord shakes the wilderness of Kadesh.
The voice of the Lord causes the oaks to whirl, and strips the
*   forest bare;*
and in his temple all say, 'Glory!'
The Lord sits enthroned over the flood; the Lord sits enthroned as king for ever.
May the Lord give strength to his people!
May the Lord bless his people with peace!

Psalm 29.7–11

In October 1998, Hurricane Mitch dumped a year's rain on Central America in 48 hours. The power of the storm was terrifying – the most devastating for two centuries. It brought down millions of trees, allowing mudslides to cascade down the slopes and wreak devastation. Roads, bridges and villages were swept away. Ten thousand people died and 2.5 million became temporarily dependent on emergency aid.

It must have been a thunderstorm of this kind that shook the writer of the psalm into composing these words. It rolled in from the sea, then ripped south along the coast down into the desert of Kadesh, leaving destruction behind it.

His first thought was how awesome God is. The storm is mighty; the creator of the storm even more so. It is surely a mark of religious restraint that the word which sprang from him was 'Glory!' rather than . . . well, I hardly like to say!

His second thought was to realize that, in the middle of that devastation, terrible suffering must be taking place. The last two lines of the psalm are a whisper of prayer for people who have been made destitute.

Honduras was the hardest hit by Hurricane Mitch. After all these years, Christian Aid's partner organizations are still working there to rebuild the country. The University Women's Collective is one of eight organizations with whom Christian Aid works to rehabilitate agricultural work, to be better prepared for natural disasters, and to be advocates for women's rights. Find out more at www.christianaid.org.uk/world/where/lac/hondurap.htm

From the comfort of this chair, surrounded by friends, my heart goes out to those who have lost everything and everyone in the devastation of a storm. God of all power, give those who have begun their lives anew strength and determination. Amen.

April 29   God healed me

I will extol you, O Lord, for you have drawn me up,
and did not let my foes rejoice over me.
O Lord my God, I cried to you for help, and you have healed me.
O Lord, you brought up my soul from Sheol,
restored me to life from among those gone down to the Pit.
Sing praises to the Lord, O you his faithful ones,
and give thanks to his holy name.
For his anger is but for a moment; his favour is for a lifetime.
Weeping may linger for the night, but joy comes with the morning.

Psalm 30.1–5

The first line suggests a bucket being dragged out of a well at the end of a rope. Out of the dark into the light; out of the stink into fresh air; out of fear into rescue. Sheol was the shadowy, restless place of the dead which was the closest the Hebrews came to a concept of an afterlife. The poet had clearly recovered from an illness or depression that took him to death's door.

The final line is one of the Bible's glorious jewels of hope. How you respond to it depends on your circumstances. It is easier to look back at a tear-filled night and rejoice that God brought you through it than to look ahead to a joy-filled morning from the depths of suffering. The writer Frances Anderson put it like this: 'God (but only God!) can transform evil into good, so that in retrospect (but only in retrospect!) it is seen actually to have been good, without diminishing in the least the awful actuality of the evil it was at the time.'

The great theologian Jürgen Moltmann writes: 'God weeps with us so that we may one day laugh with him.' Write the words out on a postcard and put them in a place where you will stumble across them at a time when you need to be reminded that they are true.

Grant, O God, that amidst all the discouragements, difficulties, dangers, distress and darkness of this mortal life, I may depend upon your mercy and on this build my hopes, as on a sure foundation. Let your infinite mercy in Christ Jesus deliver me from despair, both now and at the hour of my death.

Thomas Wilson (1663–1755)

April 30 Mourning into dancing

As for me, I said in my prosperity, 'I shall never be moved.'
By your favour, O Lord, you had established me as a strong
*   mountain;*
you hid your face; I was dismayed.
To you, O Lord, I cried, and to the Lord I made supplication:
'What profit is there in my death, if I go down to the Pit?
Will the dust praise you? Will it tell of your faithfulness?
Hear, O Lord, and be gracious to me!
O Lord, be my helper!'
You have turned my mourning into dancing
you have taken off my sackcloth and clothed me with joy,
so that my soul may praise you and not be silent.
O Lord my God, I will give thanks to you for ever.

Psalm 30.6–12

This morning there was an email spam in my inbox that was headed: 'Guaranteed – your investment doubled in 30 days.' I can't share the vital details of this sure-fire financial scheme with you because I deleted it without reading it. It was a lie.

There are two other lies that we all (including the writer of the psalm) are tempted by from time to time. The first gets heard when things are going well. It says that real talent always gets to the top and real Christians get all the blessings they ask for. 'I shall never be moved' is a lie. The second gets heard when things go wrong. It says that God was never there at all, or not interested. 'You hid your face' is a lie. Finding his way between those lies, the poet is able to tell God straight truths. 'I deserve better than this' is his honest howl. And in return God gives a straight answer: circumstances change and thanks overflow.

Are you aware in your own life of personal circumstances colouring the way you view God? What has been unchanging across the years? What do you cling on to in honesty?

Thank you, Almighty Lord,
for destroying the bows and deadly weapons of our enemies.
Those who, with greed, freely fed fat, living off the fat of the land,
*   are hungry again.*
Those they pushed off the nation's farm hunger no more;
they enjoy your peace and harmony.
Blessed be your name, Almighty Lord.

Patrick Sesay, Makeni Christian Council, Sierra Leone, published in
Friends Again, *CTE, a collection of prayers following the end of civil war*

May 1   I take refuge in the Lord

In you, O Lord, I seek refuge;
do not let me ever be put to shame;
in your righteousness deliver me.
Incline your ear to me; rescue me speedily.
Be a rock of refuge for me, a strong fortress to save me.
You are indeed my rock and my fortress;
for your name's sake lead me and guide me,
take me out of the net that is hidden for me,
for you are my refuge.
Into your hand I commit my spirit;
you have redeemed me, O Lord, faithful God.

Psalm 31.1–5

By the time of Jesus, the words, 'Into your hand I commit my spirit' had become the bedtime prayer of the Jewish people. It is the perfect prayer of simple trust. It can sustain people through all kinds of situations in which they surrender themselves to things that are beyond their control. It is suitable for the everyday surrender of sleep, but also suitable for the ultimate surrender of death. Those words were on the lips of Jesus as he faced his last great unknown. And the same prayer strengthened Stephen, the first person to die rather than deny his Christian faith.

Why can God be trusted for occasions in which our destiny is out of our own hands? Because he is completely just ('righteous'), and in time or beyond time will see that no injustice can prevail. Because while our sense of hearing is suspended or finished, his 'ear' is never closed. Because he has a track record of being a 'fortress', with whom we have survived perilous times in the past. Let those words be in your mind not only as you turn to sleep, but also before an operation, as a plane lifts off, when confronted with danger, or on any occasion when you are at the mercy of events beyond your control.

Among the objects that are next to your bed – a light, a book, a clock, a drink – place a card with the words, 'Into your hand I commit my spirit'. Make it the last thing you look at tonight before you sleep. Or every night.

Save us, Lord, while waking, and guard us while sleeping; that awake we may watch with Christ, and asleep we may rest in peace.

From the late-night service of Compline

May 2   Have mercy in my distress

You hate those who pay regard to worthless idols,
*   but I trust in the Lord.*
I will exult and rejoice in your steadfast love,
*   because you have seen my affliction;*
*   you have taken heed of my adversities,*
and have not delivered me into the hand of the enemy;
*   you have set my feet in a broad place.*
Be gracious to me, O Lord, for I am in distress;
*   my eye wastes away from grief, my soul and body also.*
For my life is spent with sorrow, and my years with sighing;
my strength fails because of my misery, and my bones waste away.

Psalm 31.6–10

Something about this psalm reminds me of my own prayers. In yesterday's opening verses the mood was full of trust. Today the pain is back and the mood is grim. Tomorrow's verses rejoice in God's healing. But there will be more hardship before the song ends. In that respect it is realistic about the way we live. Problems rarely resolve themselves neatly.

We can choose between putting our trust in God or in 'worthless idols'. We know from experience that trust in God involves struggling on in his company. That is not so appealing as the short-cuts we are tempted by – gambling our way out of financial difficulties, using the occult to ease the grief of bereavement, or finding an escape from sorrow in a bottle, a fridge or an illegal drug. Choosing those options only delivers our destiny into the whim of someone else. The godly road through these problems is a tough one, but at least it is a 'broad place', in the fresh air, where you can see things clearly and make decisions openly.

Go out into a 'broad place' – somewhere in the open air. If you are in a tower block, try the roof. If you are in a house, go into the garden. If you are at work, take a break and go into the street. Take some deep breaths and appreciate that, with God beside you, you are not a captive to anything worthless. If it is dark or pouring with rain, so much the better. That is, after all, more appropriate to the mood of the psalm.

No astrologers. No drugs. No mediums. No gambles. No escapism. OK Lord, it's you and me together! I've no idea how I'm going to get out of this mess. Don't let me down now! Amen.

May 3 My time in God's hands

I am the scorn of all my adversaries, a horror to my neighbours,
an object of dread to my acquaintances; those who see me in the
   street flee from me.
I have passed out of mind like one who is dead;
   I have become like a broken vessel.
For I hear the whispering of many – terror all around! –
as they scheme together against me, as they plot to take my life.
But I trust in you, O Lord; I say, 'You are my God.'
My times are in your hand; deliver me from the hand of my enemies and
   persecutors.
Let your face shine upon your servant; save me in your steadfast love.

Psalm 31.11–16

The psalm writer is terribly depressed. He feels completely inadequate, he is convinced that people are avoiding him, thinks his
friends have written him off, and that his enemies are whispering
damaging things about him. Poor man! Someone who can't
summon the courage to go out because there is 'terror all around'
is seriously unwell.

A man or woman in those circumstances today can find help in ways that
were unavailable to the poet. Medication can control the 'terror' so that a person can begin to address the causes of the depression. Therapy can allow a
person to understand its cause and move on. But it would a mistake to lose sight
of the source of healing that the poet came to rely on – his confidence that God
could be trusted. Trends in modern medicine encourage treatment that recog-
nizes the whole of a person – physical, emotional and spiritual. In that respect
the psalms still have much to teach us. The prayer of hope, 'You are my God
. . . deliver me!' will never lose its power as a way to seek healing.

We can put our trust confidently in God because he has seen both
the remote past and the distant future. So 'my times' are in the
securest context when they are in 'God's hands'. As far as you
can, picture what you foresee yourself doing in one hour's time;
in twelve hours; at this time tomorrow; a month ahead; a year
ahead. Register your desire to have God watching and helping with 'his face
shining' on those activities, no matter what the circumstances.

Lord, look down on me in my infirmities and help me to bear
them patiently.

Francis of Assisi (1182–1226)

May 4   Silence the wicked

Do not let me be put to shame, O Lord, for I call on you;
let the wicked be put to shame;
*   let them go dumbfounded to Sheol.*
Let the lying lips be stilled
that speak insolently against the righteous
*   with pride and contempt.*
O how abundant is your goodness that you have laid up for those who fear you,
and accomplished for those who take refuge in you, in the sight of everyone!
In the shelter of your presence you hide them from human plots;
you hold them safe under your shelter from contentious tongues.

Psalm 31.17–20

It can take an extraordinary amount of courage to stand up against 'wickedness' and 'lying lips'. The poet confidently declares that God will protect righteous people from 'human plots'. This sounds unrealistically optimistic until you remember the personal cost to him of doing what was just – agonies of isolation and fear that have been spelled out over the past three days. To recognize God's goodness in that context is remarkable.

Marina Montoya is a spokeswoman for the community of Cacarica in a remote part of Colombia. The community is Afro-Colombian, a poor and marginalized minority group. Driven off their land by armed groups in 1997, two years later many of the families bravely decided to return home, supported by Christian Aid partners working in the region. Marina says: 'Land is our life – without it, we are nobody. We risk threats, slander and even massacre. But this is our land and it has been for the past 500 years. My faith gives me strength in the struggle. I have to be firm in my beliefs about rights, justice and freedom. As it says in our community anthem: "With truth, freedom and justice we can build peace".'

Thousands of Colombian civilians are killed every year, caught in a conflict that involves guerillas, paramilitaries and the state. Christian Aid works with thirteen partner organizations in Colombia to build a just society where human rights are guaranteed. Read about this work at
www.christianaid.org.uk/world/where/lac/colombip.htm

Do not underestimate how dangerous it is for millions of indi-
viduals to do what is right in the face of powerful people who are
doing what is wrong. 'Marina' herself has asked that we use a
pseudonym when describing her work. Pray that she will be 'held
safe under God's shelter', and pray the same for all who today are
risking their lives in a righteous cause.

May 5   Finding help in the city

Blessed be the Lord, for he has wondrously shown his steadfast
*   love to me*
when I was beset as a city under siege.
I had said in my alarm, 'I am driven far from your sight.'
But you heard my supplications when I cried out to you for help.
Love the Lord, all you his saints.
The Lord preserves the faithful, but abundantly repays the one
*   who acts haughtily.*
Be strong, and let your heart take courage, all you who wait for the Lord.

Psalm 31.21–24

Cities in the Bible are almost always places of security. People worked their fields outside the city, but retreated inside the walls if danger threatened. But they were squalid places – no streets, just spaces between houses, unpaved and full of rubbish. A swamp in winter and stinking in summer. Children were especially at risk.

However, the Bible has a resolutely positive image of what a city could be. Very often, as in this psalm, a city is a place where love can be found, and people can find courage to do good. The final image in the Bible is of a city in which God lives with his people. It is the very opposite of ancient city life – there are broad, paved streets, no crime, no wild dogs, light everywhere and fulfilled living. This gives us a glimpse of what heaven will be. But it also gives Christians a map of what God intends for the millions who live in the world's cities today.

What is the first image that comes to mind when you picture Belfast? Glasgow? Dublin? Manchester? London? Cardiff? A positive image of culture? A stereotypical image of tourism? A negative image of need? Or perhaps you have no concept at all of what some of those cities are like! Register that for millions of people they are home, and pray for them.

God of all, I pray for the needs hidden behind the glamour of the world's cities: for young people whose excitement in life has turned bitter too soon, for those who seek a home but can only find a place to sleep, for those who are taken advantage of by their fellow humans – and for their abusers, for the hardworking, respectable people rushing through their lives at great speed, never asking themselves why they have chosen to live this way. God of all, have mercy on our cities. Amen.

May 6   Forgiven!

Happy are those whose transgression is forgiven,
   whose sin is covered.
Happy are those to whom the Lord imputes no iniquity,
and in whose spirit there is no deceit.
While I kept silence, my body wasted away through my
   groaning all day long.
For day and night your hand was heavy upon me;
my strength was dried up as by the heat of summer.

Psalm 32.1–4

In 1990 a historic conference took place in the town of Rustenberg, South Africa. It was the first meeting in three decades between the white-led Dutch Reformed Church and the black-led churches that had suffered because of their opposition to apartheid. In an extraordinary act of repentance, the leaders of the Dutch Reformed Church formally declared apartheid to be a sin. Professor Pieter Potgieter confessed the guilt of the church in the injustice caused in the name of racial separateness. After he had spoken, Archbishop Desmond Tutu responded in front of an audience that was deeply moved and emotional, saying, 'God has brought us to this moment and I just want to say to you: I cannot, when someone says, "Forgive me", say, "I do not".'

There is indeed a glorious happiness in knowing that something is forgiven. It requires more than just a formula of words, more than going through the paces of an apology; it comes with a sincere recognition that what was once an intractable problem between two human beings is a problem no longer. And it requires that release to be recognized genuinely by both parties. Why do we rarely feel that exhilarating blessing of forgiveness? Because we say sorry cheaply, while continuing to hold grudges. Even in front of God we confess things without any heartfelt sorrow for them. We don't really need the psalm to tell us what to do: we know!

Is there anything that leaves you 'dried up' because you cannot let go of the resentment? You have within you the ability to let go of it, and simply decide that it is not going to matter any more. But only you can make that decision – you may prefer to cling on to it because 'wasting away' is easier than letting go.

Lord, you return gladly and lovingly to lift up the one who offends you. But I do not turn to raise up and honour the one who angers me. O God have mercy upon me.

St John of the Cross (1542–91)

May 7   You are my hiding place

I acknowledged my sin to you, and I did not hide my iniquity;
I said, 'I will confess my transgressions to the Lord',
and you forgave the guilt of my sin.
Therefore let all who are faithful offer prayer to you;
at a time of distress, the rush of mighty waters
shall not reach them.
You are a hiding-place for me; you preserve me from trouble;
you surround me with glad cries of deliverance.

Psalm 32.5–7

Samuel Johnson, the great eighteenth-century writer, was plunged into a profound grief by the death of his wife. During her last days he made her promises that he would make his peace with God, seek forgiveness, and reform his life. Afflicted with nightmares and overwhelmed with sadness, he wrote in his diary on the day before Easter 1761:

'Since the communion of last Easter I have led a life so dissipated and useless, and my terrors and perplexities have so much increased, that I am under a great depression and discouragement. Yet I purpose to present myself before God tomorrow, with humble hope that he will not break this bruised reed.'

Where is your 'hiding place'? Where can you go that you know to be a pressure-free place? Somewhere where the phone is switched off to all but those you wish to talk to; where the people around you will build you up, not drag you down? It might be a holiday destination, a journey, a specific time of day, perhaps just a particular chair or bed in your home. Either in your imagination or for real, take yourself to a hiding place where you can be alone with God. Confess, release, enjoy!

O Lord our heavenly Father, almighty and most merciful God, in whose hands are life and death, who castest down and raiseth up, look with mercy on the affliction of thy unworthy servant, turn away thine anger from me, and speak peace to my troubled soul ... Release me from my sorrow, fill me with just hopes, true faith, and holy consolations, and enable me to do my duty in that state of life to which thou hast been pleased to call me, without disturbance from fruitless grief, or tumultuous imaginations; that in all my thoughts, words and actions I may glorify thy holy name, and finally obtain ... everlasting joy and felicity, through our Lord Jesus Christ. Amen.

Samuel Johnson (1709–84)

May 8 Be glad!

I will instruct you and teach you the way you should go;
  I will counsel you with my eye upon you.
Do not be like a horse or a mule, without understanding,
  whose temper must be curbed with bit and bridle,
  else it will not stay near you.
Many are the torments of the wicked,
  but steadfast love surrounds those who trust in the Lord.
Be glad in the Lord and rejoice, O righteous,
  and shout for joy, all you upright in heart.

Psalm 32.8–11

Twenty centuries have passed since the final books of the Bible were written. Their instructions were precisely appropriate for their own age. But 2,000 years have generated two million new moral dilemmas. Every advance in technology creates a new set of questions about 'the way you should go' – both personally as a Christian and corporately as a world. How are we to know what is right and wrong in all the areas that the Bible never mentions?

Here is God's promise of guidance for those who want to be 'upright in heart'. But it involves a choice. A mule can only become obedient by coercion with a 'bit and bridle'. A close friend can tell from one glance of someone's eye what she is telling him to do. So which of those relationships would you like to have with God? 'Staying near to him' in prayer, study and fellowship leads to a relationship of steadfast love in which finding out the right thing to do and obeying it is a pleasure. One day every human will meet God face to face and be made to conform with his ways. For some, that process will seem like being a stubborn mule, broken into obedience. But for those who have already caught God's eye, there will be 'shouts of joy'.

Make a list of some recent developments in technology, and think about what personal moral questions they pose. To start the list – the internet, mobile phones, credit cards, fast food.

God be in my head, and in my understanding;
God be in my eyes, and in my looking;
God be in my mouth, and in my speaking;
God be in my heart, and in my thinking;
God be at my end, and at my departing.

From the eleventh-century Sarum Missal

May 9 The poor

When Jesus saw the crowds, he went up the mountain; and after he sat down, his disciples came to him. Then he began to speak, and taught them, saying: 'Blessed are the poor in spirit, for theirs is the kingdom of heaven.'

Matthew 5.1–3

This is the beginning of a most bizarre award ceremony. The best English equivalent of 'blessed' is 'Congratulations!' The prizes, however, go to people who are usually passed by when rewards are given. They are all groups of suffering people. Jesus is not glorifying suffering, but congratulating people because they are in the process of waking up to the truth about themselves, even if it is painful.

First, Jesus honours people who realize that they are bereft of answers to the world's most intractable questions. They are people who want to be part of a perfect, heavenly kingdom, but haven't got a clue how they can earn their place. Be happy, says Jesus, because it is at the very moment that you realize that you can do nothing to take you to heaven that God steps in and does all it takes. It is the people who are striving and straining to buy their way in by being good who are missing the point. Those who know they cannot earn God's approval and turn instead to begging for it are the ones who will inherit the kingdom.

When Luke wrote his Gospel he recorded Jesus' words in a slightly different way. His version simply says, 'Blessed are the poor.' In the Old Testament the poor and the pious were often spoken of in the same breath. Those who were hungry and oppressed set their hope on God – they had nowhere else to go. The decline of churches in rich countries and the explosion of faith in poor countries suggest that this may still be true.

Christian Aid Week is the second week of May, so signs of it are everywhere – posters, television adverts, and red collecting envelopes. Whenever you see the name Christian Aid this week register that, as well as having needs with which we are able to help, the poorest people in the world have insights that we urgently need to learn.

May God the provider, without whom we have nothing,
bless the poor by providing for their true needs,
and bless the rich by revealing their true needs,
so that poor and rich alike may inherit the kingdom of God.

May 10   Those who mourn

[Jesus said,] 'Blessed are those who mourn,
for they will be comforted.'

Matthew 5.4

This is one of those Bible verses which have become so familiar that we don't notice that Jesus meant it to take our breath away. 'God intends that at your times of deepest sadness you will find happiness.' What an extraordinary thing to say!

But notice what Jesus doesn't say. He doesn't say, 'You will be OK if you are bereaved because you will get over it.' Rather, he says that at moments of deep distress it is possible to feel the closeness of God, who was also made desolate 'with grief at the death of his Son Jesus, in ways that other people could never realize. Those who have never been brought to their lowest point by losing everything they hold dear have a theoretical understanding of what it can mean to know God's mercy. But there are some people who have gone through bereavement and speak of God's profound comfort and consolation, made real in the love and support of Christian friends. It is their witness which makes us able to trust this saying.

Some people suggest that the verse means, 'Blessed are those who mourn about how sinful they have been because they will know the joy of forgiveness.' Well, that is true as well! But I can't help feeling that Jesus meant something more personal and profound than that. Don't you agree?

Read a newspaper or listen to a broadcast, paying particular attention to news of people who have died. Some will be obituaries, but some will be large-scale tragedies involving many people. Register that the cold print or emotionless voice that delivers the news disguises terrible grief among people who have lost friends and family. Stand alongside them in their distress, and ask God to send people to them through whom genuine comfort may come. Ask yourself whether you also might have a role to play as a comforter in someone's need.

God of all comfort, defender of the helpless,
who grieves alongside widows and orphans and friends,
heal the brokenhearted and console the desolate.
Do not hide in silence from those who mourn,
but visit them with hope and healing,
so that in you they may find an unexpected blessing,
and know that peace which the world cannot give. Amen.

May 11 The meek

[Jesus said,] 'Blessed are the meek, for they will inherit the earth.'
Matthew 5.5

'The meek shall inherit the earth, but not the mineral rights.'

That is a quotation from John Paul Getty, one of the wealthiest people of the twentieth century. Very droll; probably true; and it leaves us wondering what Jesus meant! Was it an idealistic but impossible dream? Was it a call for Christians to lead a life of humility no matter what the consequences? Or was it a metaphor for a spiritual blessing that we must not take literally?

When we are utterly dependent on God, characteristics emerge in us that contrast dramatically with the world's attitude to success. One of those is without doubt a gentle and humble spirit toward others. Those who have taken possession of God's Earth by tyranny need to remember that he is sovereign and he alone controls its destiny. Those meek enough to acknowledge that receive his: 'Congratulations!'

In Brazil, the Movimento Sem Terra tries to gain rights for landless families by supporting the struggle for land reform. In one of the world's most unequal countries, it seeks to make a real difference in the struggle of the country's poorest people for land and rights. By organizing people into co-operatives, training and advising them, it has so far enabled 250,000 families to inherit and transform what is legally theirs – idle land. But standing up for the rights of the poor can be a dangerous mission. In the past ten years over 1,000 Brazilians have been killed in violent opposition to campaigns for reform. But there is an ever-increasing solidarity in communities that have grown strong through working and living together.

Christian Aid supports and funds the work of the Movimento Sem Terra. You will read the story of a family whose lives have been transformed by MST on 23 June. In the meantime, visit their website at www.mstbrazil.org to find out more.

No sound as yet of hope's first footsteps.
Glue your ear to the ground. Hold your breath!
The Master is on his way.
Most likely he will not get here when things are going well;
but in bad times when the going is unsure and painful.

Some words of Dom Helder Camara (1909–99), Archbishop of Recife, Brazil.
Allow them to lead you into gentle and humble prayer.

May 12   Those who hunger for justice

[Jesus said,] 'Blessed are those who hunger and thirst for right-eousness, for they will be filled.'

Matthew 5.6

When the Bible talks about justice (or righteousness – in the original language the two words are the same) there are three aspects. First of all, there is justice between earth and heaven – and the Bible uses legal language to describe the way the work of Jesus has changed the relationship between God and his world to declare his people 'not guilty' for ever. Second, there is justice between God and humans – a moral justice that calls each person to a life of goodness, the conduct that we know pleases God. And third, there is justice between human and human – a social justice that demands liberation from oppression, civil rights, fair law courts, and business dealings in which the poor are not taken advantage of.

If you live in one of the world's poorest communities, this saying of Jesus is about all the things you haven't got. The absence of justice is a desperation that gnaws as painfully as hunger itself. To these people, Jesus' words are full of hope.

If you live in relative comfort, this saying of Jesus is a call to stand alongside those who cannot take justice for granted. For those of us in this position, a hunger for justice comes not out of desperation, but as a choice. To us, Jesus' words are full of challenge – and the promise that opposing injustice will be genuinely satisfying.

'Hunger for Justice' is the final track of the CD *Out of the Blue* by singer–songwriter Martin John Nicholls, who works for Christian Aid co-ordinating their work in part of south-west England. It is inspired by meeting courageous and determined women in Ghana. To buy it for £12 plus postage and packing, visit www.martinjohnnicholls.co.uk

More than land, more than wealth, more than even life itself,
more than anything else I hunger for justice.
Day to day, north to south, it's hell to pay, it's hand to mouth,
more than anything else I hunger for justice.
Empires fall, powers fail, we shall see the light prevail,
more than anything else I hunger for justice.
Give me strength, give me hope, give me what I need to cope,
more than anything else I hunger for justice.

Martin John Nicholls, from 'Hunger for Justice'

May 13   The merciful

[Jesus said,] 'Blessed are the merciful, for they will receive mercy.'
Matthew 5.7

In July 1993 gunmen attacked St James' Church, Cape Town, killing eleven people and injuring fifty. It was a low point in the struggle against apartheid in South Africa, and the shock of it was reported around the world. But the response of Bishop Frank Retief could not have been predicted. 'It seemed to us as if the whole country was hating the killers,' he said. 'Someone had to pray for them. So we did.' Face to face with the murderers at the Truth and Reconciliation Commission five years later, forgiveness was asked for and received. Dawie Ackerman, whose wife died in the attack, said, 'When those young men asked for forgiveness, I felt they were sincere. It brought release.'

There is nothing easy about mercy. It requires people to dig into their souls and fight their natural desire to get even or restore their wounded pride. When mercy is genuinely offered it cures and helps and heals. However, the relief it brings is almost invariably felt by the one who gives as well as the one who receives. Those who have experienced this (and perhaps only those) know what Jesus said about mercy to be true.

Dawie Ackerman went on, 'It has brought closure . . . My wish for those young men is that they use their new-found freedom to seek the ultimate freedom, which is a freedom granted by God – freedom from sin.'

Read more about the work and impact of the South African Truth and Reconciliation Commission at its website, www.doj.gov.za/trc

Goodness is stronger than evil;
love is stronger than hate;
light is stronger than darkness;
life is stronger than death;
victory is ours through him who loved us.

Let these words of Archbishop Desmond Tutu lead you into prayer, and allow you to examine whether there are outstanding difficulties in relationships of your own in which progress could be made if the words of Jesus about being merciful became a reality.

May 14   The pure in heart

[Jesus said,] 'Blessed are the pure in heart, for they will see God.'
Matthew 5.8

In the Holy Land chapels have been built at the sites of the major events of Jesus' life. Beautifully designed and sensitive to their environment, they use colour, shape and symbols in ways that give another dimension to the way Christians reflect on the life of Jesus. One of them is at the summit of the hill that has tradition-ally been associated with the Sermon on the Mount. It is an octagonal building, full of light, with large windows in each wall giving spectacular views over Galilee. On each wall is carved one of the beatitudes – the sayings of Jesus about the way of true happiness.

As I walked into the chapel some years ago the sun was cascading in and a vivid shaft, falling directly on the words, 'Blessed are the pure in heart, for they will see God', made them seem to leap straight from the wall and into my con-science. I stood, paralyzed for a moment, profoundly convicted about the jokes that make me laugh, the thoughts that distract me, and the difference between the life that people see me live and the life going on inside my head. No wonder we find it difficult to understand God, or even to focus on him – only those who are utterly sincere could bear the dazzling vision that evaporates hypocrisy and deceit. It is not the purely religious who are clear-sighted about God; it is those who are inwardly pure.

Today we are in Christian Aid Week. It is one week of the year during which the sincerity of our desire to please God becomes transparent. This week, when we are challenged to work, pray and give for God's world, a light shines straight into our hearts. It makes it clear whether our service of God is grudging and laboured, or the natural outpouring of love for a world that needs the justice which is the hallmark of God's nature. Take a moment to think through what you are doing during this busiest week of the year, and ask yourself whether you can 'see God' in your actions and attitudes.

Enough of the slush; I want to be snow again! Enough of the ash; I want to be coal again! Enough of the compromise that keeps you hidden from me. Lord God, make me pure in heart! Amen.

May 15 The peacemakers

[Jesus said,] 'Blessed are the peacemakers, for they will be called children of God.'

Matthew 5.9

'I was born and brought up in war. I feel I have an obligation to contribute to a peaceful Sudan, to enable our children to enjoy freedom and peace.' Awut Deng works for the New Sudan Council of Churches, an organization that Christian Aid partners. She works from Kenya as an advocate for women who have been forced to flee from inter-ethnic violence in southern Sudan and take refuge many miles from their homes. 'Even though we may enjoy a better lifestyle somewhere else, it's not like being at home, sitting under a tree in southern Sudan and watching children play in peace. We are born in exile; we long to go home.'

Awut organizes mini-conferences where people can talk together and encourages communities to work towards a peaceful resolution of their differences. There have been successes. The Wunlit Peace Covenant brought an end to eight years of conflict between the Dinka and Nuer tribes, meaning that they can move about more freely, share pastures for rearing animals, and intermarry. And a peace deal between the government of Sudan and the main southern rebel movement, the Sudan People's Liberation Movement, was signed in January 2005. It brought hope of an end to the civil war in some (but not all) of Sudan.

'I know I take many risks, but I am committed to ensuring that our people live in harmony. I take it as a responsibility. There's a lost generation of children, especially girls, who were unable to go to school in a hostile environment. They lacked the kind of peaceful environment that enables a child to develop mentally and physically. We appreciate Christian Aid's support and we would like it to continue because we haven't yet reached the end of the road.' Awut Deng's work has been recognized internationally. There is no doubt at all that we can call her 'a child of God'.

To understand more about war and peace in Sudan, visit www.christianaid.org.uk/world/where/eagl/sudanp.htm

Until those who create terror set their hearts on justice;
Until those who fight over resources set their hearts on sharing;
Until those who are divided by religion set their hearts on peace;
Until the people return to their homes knowing their future is
*   secure,*
My heart cries out to you, O God, for the people of Sudan.

May 16   The persecuted

*[Jesus said,] 'Blessed are those who are persecuted for righteous-
ness' sake, for theirs is the kingdom of heaven.*

*'Blessed are you when people revile you and persecute you and
utter all kinds of evil against you falsely on my account. Rejoice
and be glad, for your reward is great in heaven, for in the same
way they persecuted the prophets who were before you.'*

Matthew 5.10–12

This final accolade in Jesus' extraordinary 'award ceremony'
brings us down to Earth. It is a reminder that those who seek
justice have set out on a course that may put them at odds with
powerful forces in the world. Those who take up the cause of the
oppressed in Jesus' name are heading down a route that may well
involve suffering and insult. Does Jesus say to them, 'Grit your teeth and suffer
this in silence'? No he doesn't! He says, 'In those desperate moments, rejoice!'

There is a remarkable moment in the story of the disciples following Jesus'
resurrection. Flogged by the authorities and ordered not to speak of him, they
go away 'rejoicing because they had been counted worthy of suffering disgrace
for the Name' (Acts 5:41). To identify with Jesus is to identify with one who
was crucified. When we see his hands stretched out lovingly toward us, we
cannot help but notice that they are scarred by the nails of Calvary. His invitation is not to a life of ease, but to a life of fulfilment.

Christian Aid Week is over. About 300,000 collectors have been
walking the streets in the name of Jesus asking people to give
money to the world's poorest communities. I'll stake my life that
some got abused on a doorstep, nipped by a dog, or caught in a
downpour. They have done it in order to stand alongside people
in Christian Aid's partner organizations who have been to prison, dodged
bombs, or been beaten up by hired hoodlums because that is the cost of
striving for righteousness. Whatever else you have to do in the next ten minutes,
put it down for a few seconds and bring to mind those who, in the name of
Jesus, have had to face miserable circumstances this month.

*Dear Jesus, as a hen covers her chicks with her wings to keep
them safe, do thou this dark night protect us under thy golden
wings. Amen.*

A prayer from India

May 17   Salt of the Earth

[Jesus said,] 'You are the salt of the earth; but if salt has lost its taste, how can its saltiness be restored? It is no longer good for anything, but is thrown out and trampled under foot.'

Matthew 5.13

Let these ideas circle round your head for a while: salt preserving a side of gammon . . . salt sprinkled on plump chips, hot from the fryer . . . a resolute grimace as salt goes into a wound . . . salt that has got damp and clogs up the cruet no matter how hard you shake . . . the gritting lorry sprinkling salt on the road as the temperatures plummet one winter night . . . 'You are salt,' says Jesus.

The principal use of salt in Jesus' day was as a preservative. It was used for flavouring and healing as well, and new born babies were rubbed with salt before being wrapped in swaddling clothes. But what Jesus had in mind was that his people were to preserve what is good in human nature, combating and preventing corruption. On this occasion Jesus is not calling for revolutionaries, but instead he sees the good influence of his followers seeping unnoticed through the structures of society and changing them for good. Being his witnesses just by being there!

Where is this kind of saltiness needed? In the health services, in industry, in financial institutions, in schools, in retail, in nightclubs, in computer techno-logy, in sport, in television. Wherever people work and play, Christians can improve the quality of the society they are part of by consciously modelling Jesus' values. (There is, of course, the horrible possibility that Christians lose their concentration and come to represent all that is judgemental, joyless and unfriendly about religion . . . brrr! . . . I can feel the temperatures plummeting already!)

Treat yourself to something deliciously salty today – some luxury crisps or nuts or bacon. (OK, I know you've got to be careful with your diet! Make sure you don't do anything harmful, but do something that prompts you to think about what 'flavour' you give to the places where you live and work. And enjoy yourself.)

Lord God,
I want to be recognized as salt among the people with whom I
live and work –
the kind that makes people lick their lips,
not the kind that people want to spit out.
May the places I go be better because I am there. Amen.

May 18   Light of the world

[Jesus said,] 'You are the light of the world. A city built on a hill cannot be hidden. No one after lighting a lamp puts it under the bushel basket, but on the lampstand, and it gives light to all in the house. In the same way, let your light shine before others, so that they may see your good works and give glory to your Father in heaven.'

Matthew 5.14–16

Night! No street lights; no headlights; no cats' eyes (in fact they won't be invented for twenty centuries). The sunlight has gone; the moonlight is hidden; the torchlight is flickering – not a good time to be travelling! It is in this context that a city on a hill, with lights shining from the windows of its houses, guides a fearful traveller to safety.

Let the wisdom of Christian ethical standards blaze out nationally and globally, says Jesus, giving a sense of direction to a society that is increasingly losing its confidence in the certainties of right and wrong.

Dark corners! A small lamp full of olive oil with a trimmed wick. Is it going to make any difference? 'How far that little candle throws his beams! So shines a good deed in a naughty world.' (Not quoted from Jesus, I have to confess, but from Portia in Shakespeare's *The Merchant of Venice*.)

Let individual and small-scale acts of goodness by each Christian be a commonplace part of life, says Jesus, in households, in streets, in communities. If, as a Christian, you want to be a person who makes life better, make sure you express that in ways that other people can see. Not so that they realize you are a good person, but so that they realize you serve a good God!

The huge Make Poverty History campaign of 2005 was 'a city on a hill'. An individual Christian rattling a collecting box for Christian Aid is 'a candle on a lampstand'. Loud and insistent, or quiet and undemonstrative – both are vital in making God's love known. Investigate the first responses to this year's Christian Aid Week activities, big and small, at www.christianaid.org.uk/news/index.htm

Blessed and holy three, glorious Trinity –
wisdom, love, might,
Boundless as ocean's tide, rolling in fullest pride,
Through the world far and wide,
Let there be light!

John Marriott (1780–1825), from the hymn
'Thou whose almighty word'

May 19   No other gods

Moses convened all Israel, and said to them:

Hear, O Israel, the statutes and ordinances that I am address-ing to you today; you shall learn them and observe them diligently. The Lord our God made a covenant with us at Horeb. Not with our ancestors did the Lord make this covenant, but with us, who are all of us here alive today. The Lord spoke with you face to face at the mountain, out of the fire . . .

And he said: I am the Lord your God, who brought you out of the land of Egypt, out of the house of slavery; you shall have no other gods before me.

Deuteronomy 5.1–4, 6–7

Well over 3,000 years have passed since the ten commandments were chiselled on stone and declared to the Hebrews to be the correct response to everything God had done for them. Every subsequent generation of those who worship God has treated them as laws that were exceptional and timeless (even if reciting them came easier than obeying them)!

But even when Moses spelled them out they were already timeless. He talks about the occasion on Mount Horeb when the laws were first given. His hear-ers were too young to remember that day, but Moses still says that the covenant (or contract) that God made then was 'not with our ancestors . . . but with us'. God's dealings with his people never were and never will be out of date.

However, with their talk of donkeys, slaves and sabbaths, it is not straight-forward to reinterpret the commandments for this generation. So for each of the next ten days there will be a question to help us reflect on how the ten commandments might have been expressed if they were written yesterday.

This is the first of ten questions to consider. Scribble a few thoughts in the margin each day.

God said: You shall have no other god to set against me. In this age of celebrities and stars, what does it mean to treat as god one who is not God?

Take, Lord, and receive all my liberty, my memory, my under-standing, and my entire will, all that I have and possess. Thou hast given it to me. To thee, O Lord, I return it. All is thine, dispose of it wholly according to thy will. Give me thy love and grace, for this is sufficient for me.

Ignatius of Loyola (1491–1556)

May 20   No idols

You shall not make for yourself an idol, whether in the form of anything that is in heaven above, or that is on the earth beneath, or that is in the water under the earth. You shall not bow down to them or worship them; for I the Lord your God am a jealous God, punishing children for the iniquity of parents, to the third and fourth generation of those who reject me, but showing steadfast love to the thousandth generation of those who love me and keep my commandments.

Deuteronomy 5.8–10

Scientists developed a computer into which they managed, over hundreds of years, to feed the sum total of knowledge. Bloated with pride at their achievement, they asked it the ultimate question: 'Is there a god who demands our worship?' There was a whirr inside the computer and these words appeared on the screen: 'There is now!'

God forbids any attempt to limit him by trying to capture his image in a static form. He cannot be defined by metal, wood, or stone – he is the creator of metal, wood and stone. He is not a thought or an ideology – he is the one through whom all thoughts and ideologies are possible. And, for that matter, he is not he – so great is he beyond all mortal concepts of gender or language. No matter what we have understood God to be, God is bigger, higher, richer, other.

And yet, remarkably, God has brought into being something which he himself has described as being 'in my image'. It is the living, human male and female – creative, capable of emotion, and independent to make choices. Ironically it is these three wonderful freedoms that enable humans to make God less than God in their lives.

Another question about the twenty-first century, and another chance to write some thoughts in the margin.

God commanded: You shall not manufacture an image and then treat it with the honour that is due to me. In this age of merchandising and advertising, what might it mean to treat an object as having more worth than the true God?

You are the great God – the one who is in heaven.
You are the creator of life, you make the regions above.
You are the hunter who hunts for souls.
You are the leader who goes before us.

A prayer from Africa, translated from Xhosa

May 21   Do not misuse God's name

You shall not make wrongful use of the name of the LORD your God, for the LORD will not acquit anyone who misuses his name.

Deuteronomy 5.11

The name of God used in this commandment is the holy 'covenant' name by which the Hebrews revered him. The closest we can get to spelling it in English is YHWH. (Try pronouncing it Yahweh.) When that name is translated in our Bibles it is spelt in capitals. (Apart from today, this book has used a more conventional capitalization.)

But the use of capitals does not fully convey the powerful impact the name had and has on the Jewish people. It is regarded as so holy that it is not even to be pronounced. When the scriptures are read in a synagogue that word is not spoken aloud – an alternative name of God is substituted. What a contrast with the way we have become used to the name of God being tossed around for emphasis, in frustration, in anger, or just to make a joke funnier.

However, there are more immediately dangerous ways in which God's name can be wrongly used. When his name is invoked to justify war, racist domination, the amassing of riches, or a terrorist attack we begin to understand why 'the Lord will not acquit'.

Another question to wrestle with: You shall not take in vain the name of the LORD your God. In this age of political correctness, what does it mean to treat the name of the LORD with a godly correctness?

Praise the LORD.
Praise, O servants of the LORD, praise the name of the LORD.
Let the name of the LORD be praised,
both now and for evermore.
From the rising of the sun to the place where it sets,
the name of the LORD is to be praised.

Psalm 113.1–3

May 22   Keep the sabbath

Observe the sabbath day and keep it holy, as the Lord your God commanded you. For six days you shall labour and do all your work. But the seventh day is a sabbath to the Lord your God; you shall not do any work – you, or your son or your daughter, or your male or female slave, or your ox or your donkey, or any of your livestock, or the resident alien in your towns, so that your male and female slave may rest as well as you. Remember that you were a slave in the land of Egypt, and the Lord your God brought you out from there with a mighty hand and an outstretched arm; therefore the Lord your God commanded you to keep the sabbath day.

Deuteronomy 5.12–15

Led by Moses, the Hebrews had escaped from bondage in Egypt. There work had meant slavery – no rest, no day off, no care, just the misery of having one's life used as a commodity to achieve wealth for someone else. Now that they were free from oppression, the Jews were commanded never to forget what they had been through, and never to replicate it when they became the employers rather than the enslaved. So there was to be a sabbath – one day in seven which was different. The people rested, the land rested, the livestock rested. There was space for worship, space for reflecting on life, and space for administering care to others.

Wherever workers are employed in conditions that show no care for their well-being; wherever the land is treated with chemicals that accelerate short-term productivity but turn it sterile; wherever animals are driven to exhaustion – in all these places God calls for a sabbath. Not merely a day's rest, but a change of practices which acknowledges that true respect for human life is connected at the deepest level to a true respect for its Creator.

Look ahead to your next rest day – whether it is a Sunday or another day. Flick ahead in this book and put a cross in the corner of the relevant page. Then turn today's commandment over in your mind. God says: Remember to keep the sabbath day holy. What does that mean in an age that is proudly active 24/7?

Lord God, save us from the unremitting drudgery of weekdays stretching from Boxing Day to Christmas Eve. All creation looks to you for rest. Amen.

May 23 Honour your parents

Honour your father and your mother, as the Lord your God commanded you, so that your days may be long and that it may go well with you in the land that the Lord your God is giving you.

Deuteronomy 5.16

In the New Testament, Paul points out that this commandment is the only one that has a promise attached. The promise of a long and flourishing life is dependent on how a society cares for its elderly. The logic is that the young watch how the generation above them care for the vulnerable, and learn from that how to care for the elderly in years to come. But if the young see the generation which works treating their income selfishly and leaving those whose earning days are over with no provision, they will do the same.

In a society with a welfare state we take it for granted that the elderly are provided for when they become frail. But not so for the Israelites when the ten commandments were given, and not so in Tajikistan where years of civil war have led to the collapse of the economy and fifty per cent of the workforce are jobless. The elderly are particularly vulnerable since there is little state support, and those who have no children to 'honour' them do not have access to basic services. In Tajikistan, Christian Aid is expanding its work and now partners ten organizations. One of them is Odamiyat, which cares for elderly pensioners and provides them with packs of food, soap and other household necessities.

Another practical question to turn over in your mind: 'Honouring your father and mother' has a personal and a community aspect. In an age when we have given responsibility for looking after the elderly to the welfare state, what is God asking of you with regard to your own family, and with regard to a generation that is living longer than ever before?

May the right hand of the Lord keep us ever in old age,
and the grace of Christ continually defend us from the enemy.
O Lord, direct our hearts in the way of peace;
through Jesus Christ our Lord. Amen.

Aedalwald, from the ninth-century Book of Cerne

May 24 Do not murder

You shall not murder.

Deuteronomy 5.17

This is the shortest of the 365 daily Bible readings. It seems the most straightforward. Life is given by God and is to be treated as sacred. Human life is precious simply because it is human life. In the plans of God for humankind it may never be used as a commodity, or a means to an end, or expendable in a cause.

However, great complexity has been added by the medical advances of recent decades. Moses could not have conceived of a world in which it was possible to research into groups of human cells in the days after conception. Nor of a world in which life could be sustained by technology beyond the span that the body's organs could support unaided. Actions which lead to death are sometimes taken in order that suffering should decrease, either for an individual or for a generation to come. Are the four stark words of our reading any help in those situations?

In fact, four words were never sufficient. Subsequent chapters of Deuteronomy qualified them with scores of detailed laws. There were laws about going to war that distinguished between just causes and murderous cruelty. There were laws that prevented 'convenient' executions. There were laws that recognized the right to meaningful life, even if it was costly, for those who were disabled or frail. Today's debates about the rights of life and death are more perplexing, but there never has been a time when the issues were uncomplicated.

The conjoined twin whose death would offer a chance of life to a sibling. The profoundly disabled person who seeks the ruling of a law court to facilitate a painless death. The embryo whose brief existence is crucial to research that might ease suffering for others. The innocent person whose death in war as 'collateral damage' is the cost of ridding the world of an evil. As you think through what the commandment means for the twenty-first century, add to this list of cases where we need God's help to know what is right and what is wrong.

The list you have made is disturbing in itself as an intellectual exercise. But each word you have written represents thousands of people, known by name and loved by God, for whom it is a terrible reality. Take time to hold them in the presence of the God of both life and death.

May 25 Do not commit adultery

You shall not commit adultery.

Deuteronomy 5.18

In the seventeenth century Robert Barker and Martin Lucas, the king's printers, were taken to the Court of the Star Chamber by the Archbishop of Canterbury, William Laud, and fined £3,000. Their crime had been printing and publishing an edition of 1,000 copies of the Bible in which a word had mistakenly been omitted from this commandment. It was the word 'not'!

I am not quite sure why I felt the need to begin this reflection with a laugh. I'm not embarrassed to write about sex, I don't think the subject is trivial, and I don't think God has changed his mind. But there is something about this commandment that touches us in a place where we are scared of being hurt. Everyone knows someone whose life has been damaged by adultery. The hurt is plain in those who have been deceived or left or infected with disease, but Tamasin Day-Lewis, producer of a Channel 4 documentary series on adultery, went further by declaring, 'I haven't yet been able to find a happy adulterer.'

Jesus, when he was commenting on this commandment, was more insistent than Moses – even 'adultery in the imagination' was sinful. And yet when a woman was dragged before him about to be executed because of adultery, he refused to condemn her. Instead he insisted, 'Go and sin no more.' Sexual infidelity is sin – but in the goodness of God it can sometimes be worked through, repented of, and forgiven.

What does it mean not to commit adultery in an age when so many choose to live together unmarried? What is a correct approach to sex for teenagers now that they no longer marry at eleven or twelve, as they did in Bible times? Now that adultery is no longer illegal in this country, what should be our attitude to countries where it carries severe punishment? Does our desire as Christians to be inclusive of all sorts of people mean that we will never say, 'You should not do that'? Tough questions to wrestle with during these weeks when we work out the meaning of the ten commandments for today.

On those who find temptation great, mercy Lord;
On those who have been wounded by adultery, mercy Lord;
On those who seek forgiveness, mercy Lord;
On all of us who want sex to be a rich joy in our lives, mercy
Lord. Amen.

May 26   Do not steal

Neither shall you steal.
Deuteronomy 5.19

Bautistina de Jesús Reyes Reyes, administrator of a 'fair trade' community shop in Honduras run by COMAL (the Alternative Community Marketing Network, a partner organization of Christian Aid) says: 'Jesus came to serve us, so we want to follow his example and serve others. We hope to form a coffee co-operative, so we can sell coffee at a better price and the intermediaries will not rob those who produce it. Here the big exploit the medium, the medium exploit the poor, and the poor exploit those who are even poorer than them. We want to help them out of this situation.'

Jim Wallis, founder of the radical Sojourners Community in Washington, USA, writes in *Call to Conversion*: 'The question to be asked is not "What should we give to the poor?" but, "When will we stop taking from the poor?" The poor are not our problem; we are their problem.'

Well . . . let's skip over this commandment quickly because it's quite obvious that Christian people would never steal.

Isn't it?

Each day of this series has featured a question that forces the commandments out of their historical bunker into the realities of this century. So today's is: How do we hear God's command in this day and age, while the selfish actions of the rich countries casually damage the lives of those who live in poverty?

What you do in response to these thoughts might start with returning to your workplace things that have drifted into your home. It might influence the way you deal with your taxes in this month-old financial year. But don't forget the really major issues of trade, the environment and rights on a global scale.

As an individual I have disguised dishonesty as good fortune;
forgive me, O God.
As a community we have disguised selfishness as protecting our
neighbourhood;
forgive us, O God.
As rich nations we have disguised injustice as safeguarding our interests;
teach us not to steal, O God. Amen.

May 27 Do not lie

Neither shall you bear false witness against your neighbour.
Deuteronomy 5.20

Sir Robert Armstrong, Britain's most senior civil servant, was in the witness stand in the Supreme Court in Sydney. It was 1986, and the case related to the publication of *Spycatcher*, a book that the UK government wanted to ban because it revealed things about MI5 which they believed were better kept secret. Buckling under the cross-examination he admitted, '[My letter] contains a misleading impression, not a lie. I was being economical with the truth.' The newspapers thought he had invented a new euphemism which seemed perfectly to describe how powerful organizations manage the way information is released so as to put themselves in the best possible light. But in fact he was quoting the politician Edmund Burke, who had coined the phrase 200 years earlier. There is nothing new about convincing yourself that a well-intentioned lie is actually the truth!

This commandment was both for public life and private relationships. It was there to protect the Hebrews from being slandered or wrongly accused in court. But it was also there to make it clear that before a God who stands for absolute truth, deceiving someone with a lie is simply wrong.

Here is another question to turn over in your mind about the meaning of the commandments today. God said: You shall not give false evidence. The end of the twentieth century gave us two new names for two old phenomena. One was 'the spin doctor'; the other was 'the truth and reconciliation commission'. Have either of them changed the way we value what is true? And do they show up anything we need to confess in our own words and ways?

Grant, O God, that we your followers may:
seek the truth,
hear the truth,
learn the truth,
love the truth,
tell the truth,
hold the truth,
and defend the truth to the death;
for it is by the truth that we will be saved from the power of the evil one,
and from the death of the soul.

Jan Huss (1372–1415)

May 28   Do not covet

Neither shall you covet your neighbour's wife.
Neither shall you desire your neighbour's house, or field, or male or female slave, or ox, or donkey, or anything that belongs to your neighbour.

Deuteronomy 5.21

I've had a credit card for nearly twenty years. I first became aware of that shiny little plastic seducer when I saw an advert with the strapline: 'Take the waiting out of wanting.' I had mine by return of post.

In complete contrast, a colleague took me by surprise last month. He made a trip to Kenya to visit a church organization that strengthens the Masai people both economically and spiritually. On the Sunday he was invited to preach and (unwisely as it turns out) attempted a joke. The translator stumbled when it came to the punchline that referred to how untidy he is. 'There is no word for untidy in the language,' he explained. Most Masai don't own enough possessions to give the word a meaning.

We have an economy which succeeds entirely because people desire things they have not got. Creating in our minds the thought, 'I need that', when the truth is that 'I want that', fuels the system. In the face of such powerful interests, it will be a brave man or woman who decides, 'I am content with what I've already got.' But that is what the commandment asks of us. Expects of us!

This is the last of the ten commandments and the ten questions which reflect on what they mean in the twenty-first century. For the first time I have noticed that there is something significant about the order in which they are put, and I wonder whether there is meant to be a scale of values that reveals something about God's design for human life. From first to tenth they refer to: God, society, family, life, sex, property. If that is the Bible's order, in what order do you feel that this generation values those things? Write a number beside each and dwell on what that might teach us.

Creator God, I confess:
that sharing is not so appealing as owning;
that waiting is not so easy as spending;
that needing is not so motivating as wanting.
God of endless giving, teach me to be content. Amen.

May 29   Keep and teach these laws

Hear, O Israel: The Lord is our God, the Lord alone. You shall love the Lord your God with all your heart, and with all your soul, and with all your might. Keep these words that I am commanding you today in your heart. Recite them to your children and talk about them when you are at home and when you are away, when you lie down and when you rise. Bind them as a sign on your hand, fix them as an emblem on your forehead, and write them on the doorposts of your house and on your gates.

Deuteronomy 6.4–9

A friend of Mark Twain's announced that he was about to fulfil a lifetime's ambition to travel to the Holy Land, climb Mount Sinai, and recite the ten commandments. Twain pointed out that there was an alternative – cheaper, less dangerous, and a far better ambition. That was to stay at home and obey them!

Is there a reason why we, as individuals or a nation, should still find appropriate ways to obey the ten commandments after all these centuries? In this paragraph that follows them lies the only reason that makes any sense. It is all a matter of love. The Lord wants us to be obedient, so those who truly love him obey him. Simple as that! It involves 'heart' (in Hebrew it means our mind), 'soul' (our emotions) and 'strength' (the willpower to do it when we would rather not), so it is a tough love.

In later years orthodox Jewish people followed these verses literally by tying the words of the Law to themselves in little leather boxes called phylacteries, and nailing them next to their front doors in cases called *mezuzahs*. Being so literal doesn't suit us, but displaying your allegiance to God publicly like that is just the equivalent of displaying a designer's logo on your clothes.

Without looking back, can you remember what all ten commandments are about? Test yourself by scribbling them in the margin. If you can't, put it right by learning them now. If you are struggling, write them out and put them on the doorpost. If you read them enough times as you leave the house, they will stick!

Lord God, obeying you sounds harsh; loving you sounds easy. But I don't do either very well. Change my heart; coax my soul; grant me strength. Make of me the best person I could be. Amen.

May 30   The coming of the Spirit

When the day of Pentecost had come, [Jesus' followers] were all together in one place. And suddenly from heaven there came a sound like the rush of a violent wind, and it filled the entire house where they were sitting. Divided tongues, as of fire, appeared among them, and a tongue rested on each of them. All of them were filled with the Holy Spirit and began to speak in other languages, as the Spirit gave them ability.

Acts 2.1–4

No one expected God to do something quite like this! In the Old Testament, God blessed individual people with the Spirit of God to equip them for particular tasks at particular times. But the coming of the Spirit at Pentecost (originally a kind of Jewish harvest festival) was unprecedented, and had an impact on all those who followed Jesus. It has subsequently changed for ever the way Christians experience God.

Even Luke, who researched and wrote this account, seems to be struggling for words to describe what was seen and heard. And for those to whom it was happening, all the words they knew in their own languages were inadequate. They could only be sure of three things:

- the Holy Spirit was responsible;
- it brought them together as Christians;
- they found themselves concerned with places in the world they had never visited.

Pentecost is the third great festival of the Christian faith. It's the only one of the Christian festivals that hasn't been hijacked off us! There's no tat in the shops and there's no overpackaged chocolate. So forget Christmas and Easter – Pentecost is the day for Christians to be glad. So (whether this year's Pentecost is past or yet to come) declare today as your own alternative Pentecost, and celebrate. Give yourself a treat! Do something spontaneous and wonderful. Do something childish. Do something so splendid for someone you love that they wonder what on Earth has come over you. And why not, because the Spirit of God is unpredictable and refuses to be restrained when love, joy and peace are let loose.

Be not lax in celebrating;
Be not lazy in the festive service of God;
Be ablaze with enthusiasm.
Let us be an alive, burning offering before the altar of God!

Hildegard of Bingen (1098–1179)

May 31   Languages of the world

There were devout Jews from every nation under heaven living in Jerusalem. And at [the sound of Jesus' followers speaking] the crowd gathered and was bewildered, because each one heard them speaking in the native language of each. Amazed and astonished, they asked, 'Are not all these who are speaking Galileans? And how is it that we hear, each of us, in our own native language? . . . in our own languages we hear them speaking about God's deeds of power.' All were amazed and perplexed, saying to one another, 'What does this mean?' But others sneered and said, 'They are filled with new wine.'

Acts 2.5–8, 11–13

Language unites and language divides. It can thrill people to 'God's deeds of power' or it can be used to sneer. In Sri Lanka it matters a great deal what language you speak, because twenty years of civil war not only wasted the potential of a beautiful country, but divided those who speak Tamil from those who speak Sinhala or English.

Ranjit da Silva is the founder of Gami Seva Sevana, an organization supported by Christian Aid. On its farm, some of Sri Lanka's poorest families are learning how organic principles can dramatically improve the yield of their land and increase their income. But at the end of every working day staff and visitors gather to worship in all three languages and also in silence because, as Ranjit says, 'Silence is silence in every language and equally in every religion.' Their act of worship brings Christians together with all the other faith groups represented in Sri Lanka to acknowledge that God is the God of 'every nation under heaven'. And so they pray to the 'Holy, holy, holy God'. In Tamil: '*Parisuththa, parisuththa, parisuththa devane*'. In Sinhalese: '*Athisudde, athisudde, athisudde deu piye*'.

In how many languages do you know the name of God? Make a point of speaking today to someone whose native language is not the same as your own, and as you do so be aware that they are known and loved by God.

*Even as the water falls on dry tea leaves
and brings out their flavour,
so may your Spirit fall on us and renew us
so that we may bring refreshment and joy to others.*

A prayer from Sri Lanka

June 1 The last days

Peter, standing with the eleven, raised his voice and addressed them, 'Men of Judea and all who live in Jerusalem, let this be known to you, and listen to what I say. Indeed, these are not drunk, as you suppose, for it is only nine o'clock in the morning. No, this is what was spoken through the prophet Joel: "In the last days it will be, God declares, that I will pour out my Spirit upon all flesh, and your sons and your daughters shall prophesy, and your young men shall see visions, and your old men shall dream dreams. Even upon my slaves, both men and women, in those days I will pour out my Spirit; and they shall prophesy."'

Acts 2.14–18

Six centuries or more before Jesus, the prophet Joel wrote his book at a time of environmental catastrophe. He looked ahead to what he called 'the Day of the Lord' – the moment when, in the supreme goodness and timing of God, things come to a head. It was to be the moment when the Holy Spirit would be cascaded powerfully on the world to make a profound change to the way God relates to his people. Peter recognized in that prophecy the events that he was experiencing at Pentecost.

What kinds of profound change? In the life of Jesus and the coming of the Spirit huge barriers had been broken down:

- The Holy Spirit had been given to 'all flesh' and every race – not only Jews but also Gentiles.
- In a society that valued women little, daughters would prophesy and their words would be taken as seriously as men.
- The generation gap would lose its power to divide, because young and old alike would be equipped to do God's work.
- Employers would find themselves working side by side with their slaves in the mission to make the good news of Jesus known.

As fast as the Holy Spirit breaks down the barricades of race, gender, age and status, humans do everything they can to rebuild them. Can you identify something that is happening locally or internationally at the moment which could be seen as part of the Holy Spirit's work, inside or outside the Church, to make people one in each of those four categories?

The hatred which divides nation from nation, race from race, class from class: Father forgive.

Written on the altar of Coventry Cathedral

June 2 The day of the Lord

[Peter continued to quote from Joel:] 'I will show portents in the heaven above and signs on the earth below, blood, and fire, and smoky mist. The sun shall be turned to darkness and the moon to blood, before the coming of the Lord's great and glorious day. Then everyone who calls on the name of the Lord shall be saved.'

Acts 2.19–21

These are the words that the prophet Joel used in anticipation of 'the day of the Lord' when the Holy Spirit would be poured out on all people, and Peter quoted them at the first Pentecost. Joel was fearful of this day. He thought it was going to be dreadful and terrifying. But we understand these verses in a way Joel could never have anticipated.

The death of Jesus, which the Gospels tell us was marked with earthquake and eclipse, has been transformed by resurrection. The departure of Jesus, which left his followers alternately doubting and determined, has been transformed by the coming of the Holy Spirit. And on the day the Spirit was poured out in that room in Jerusalem, the little local mission of Jesus exploded worldwide. The fulfilment of Joel's words had far exceeded anyone's expectations, and the results have shaken heaven and Earth. The Holy Spirit has brought the very heart of God to the very heart of a human. Nothing in all creation can prise them apart. In fact, calling on the name of the Lord is excessive. A murmur would do!

Gather up everything in your life that depresses like darkness, confuses like mist, or hurts like fire. Take a walk in your mind with all these things bundled up in your arms – past the crucifixion, stumbling into the resurrection, unsettled by the ascension, astonished by the coming of the Spirit. And then call upon the name of the Lord.

Holy Spirit, mighty wind of God,
inhabit our darkness,
brood over our abyss
and speak to our chaos,
that we may breathe with your life
and share your creation in the power of Jesus Christ. Amen.

Janet Morley/Christian Aid

June 3 God has raised Jesus

[Peter continued:] 'You that are Israelites, listen to what I have to say: Jesus of Nazareth, a man attested to you by God with deeds of power, wonders, and signs that God did through him among you, as you yourselves know – this man, handed over to you according to the definite plan and foreknowledge of God, you crucified and killed by the hands of those outside the law. But God raised him up, having freed him from death, because it was impossible for him to be held in its power.'

Acts 2.22–24

A crowd had gathered, fascinated by the extraordinary events that took place when the Holy Spirit was first given to the Christian Church. Peter was determined that they should understand their significance. It wasn't fire or wind that was responsible for what they saw, and it certainly wasn't alcohol. Behind all these phenomena, and responsible for all the excitement, was Jesus.

Peter did something that few preachers today do. He explained, step by step, the compelling reasons why Jesus should be worshipped. Jesus of Nazareth was a man (all his hearers could agree on that). He was responsible for wonders (among the crowd were people who had seen inexplicable things with their own eyes). God himself planned Jesus' ministry from ancient times (Peter would later read parts of the Old Testament that seemed to prove his point). He had died (beyond question). But now he has passed through death to a resurrected life (an astounding claim, but in the light of all they had witnessed, the only explanation that made sense).

Four hundred years later Augustine, a bishop in Africa, remained convinced. About these incidents he wrote: 'You didn't long stay with us, Lord, and yet you never did leave us. You ascended from before our eyes, and we turned back grieving, only to find you in our hearts.'

Stop and take stock of why and whether you have come to accept Jesus as someone to follow and worship – not the feelings or the habits, but the evidence.

You called, you cried, you shattered my deafness. You sparkled, you blazed, you drove away my blindness. You shed your fragrance, and I drew in my breath, and I pant for you. I tasted and now I hunger and thirst. You touched me, and now I burn with longing for your peace.

Augustine, Bishop of Hippo (modern Tunisia), 354–430

June 4 Receive the Holy Spirit

[Peter continued:] 'Let the entire house of Israel know with certainty that God has made him both Lord and Messiah, this Jesus whom you crucified.'

Now when they heard this, they were cut to the heart and said to Peter and to the other apostles, 'Brothers, what should we do?' Peter said to them, 'Repent, and be baptized every one of you in the name of Jesus Christ so that your sins may be forgiven; and you will receive the gift of the Holy Spirit. For the promise is for you, for your children, and for all who are far away, everyone whom the Lord our God calls to him.'

Acts 2.36–39

The crowd in Jerusalem was anguished by a new thought. There was a sense in which Jesus had died for them, but there was also a sense in which they had sided with those who drove the nails into his hands. They shared the guilt. For centuries, Christians have dwelt on the implications of this: it is our wrongdoing as a world which took Jesus to the cross.

The burden of a personal involvement in the death of an innocent man would be unbearable were it not for the fact that the cross is not only the scene of our crime, but the place of our forgiveness. The ironies are dazzling. The one we rejected is the one who welcomes us. The one we injured is the one who brings us healing. The one we nailed down is the one who brings us release. The one we left to die is the one who gives us life. In response Peter suggests three things:

- Repent (it means turn your life completely round).
- Be baptized (publicly 'come out' as a follower of Jesus).
- Receive the Holy Spirit (making God an integral part of your life).

Find an image of Jesus and take a close look. What has the artist done to make us feel involved in Jesus' life or death? It might be an icon, a great European painting, a complex modern interpretation, or a view of Jesus from the developing world. If there are no books at hand, visit
www.rejesus.co.uk/expressions/faces_jesus/index.html

You, crucifixion, are here!
You, resurrection, are here!
You, ascension, are here!
You, spirit-medicine of life, are here!
Hail, hail, hail! May happiness come!

An ancient African prayer

June 5   Three thousand converts

[Peter] testified with many other arguments and exhorted them, saying, 'Save yourselves from this corrupt generation.' So those who welcomed his message were baptized, and that day about three thousand persons were added. They devoted themselves to the apostles' teaching and fellowship, to the breaking of bread and the prayers.

Acts 2.40–42

A quiz! Three quotes from three decades – can you put a name to each?

- *From the eighties*: 'There is no such thing as society. There are individual men and women, and there are families.'
- *From the nineties*: 'Choose life. Choose mortgage payments; choose washing machines; choose cars; choose sittin' oan a couch watching mind-numbing and spirit-crushing game shows, stuffin' junk food intae yir mooth. Choose rotting away.'
- *From the noughties*: 'Because I'm worth it.'

It may be that every single decade of Christian history could be viewed as a 'corrupt generation' from which people needed to be saved – even the very first decade. But notice what it meant to the first congregation of Christians to be counter-culture. Learning together, caring together, honouring Jesus together, praying for each other. It meant living as community.

There are undoubtedly 3,000 people today who would gladly exchange an individualistic and self-serving life for one in which the same values that marked out the first Christians were evident. In fact, you probably know some of them.

Not only does every decade have quotations and advertising slogans; every week does! What are the soundbites of this week, and how do they compare with Margaret Thatcher, Irvine Welsh and L'Oreal in defining the spirit of the age? You'll find the quotes of the week in most Sunday newspapers, and this week's advertising slogans almost everywhere you look.

Lord Jesus, together in your name:
may we rejoice in what is good,
may we find alternatives to what is self-centred,
may we seek to change what is corrupt,
in this our generation. Amen.

June 6 No one in need

Awe came upon everyone, because many wonders and signs were being done by the apostles. All who believed were together and had all things in common; they would sell their possessions and goods and distribute the proceeds to all, as any had need. Day by day, as they spent much time together in the temple, they broke bread at home and ate their food with glad and generous hearts, praising God and having the goodwill of all the people. And day by day the Lord added to their number those who were being saved.

Acts 2.43–47

Four features of the first Christian community challenge us across the centuries:

- they were happy together;
- they were excited by what God was doing;
- everyone liked them;
- and others were joining them.

But the joys of the first church did not come automatically; they took effort:

- they worked at being a community which had a shared life;
- they focused on addressing the needs of poor people;
- they welcomed each other into their homes hospitably;
- and all this happened in the context of engaging worship of God.

Longing for the first four features won't change a church. However, setting out to put effort into the second set of objectives might be the secret of stumbling into the first.

Four questions that relate your own church to the one in Jerusalem:

- Does absolutely everyone in my church need their own lawn-mower, and are there other things we could share?
- Are the world's poorest communities better off right now because of my church?
- How many of my church know what colour my front door is?
- What would happen to our worship if I made a personal effort to be enthusiastic?

In thy house, O Lord, let us dwell in peace and concord. Give us all one heart, one mind, one purpose, so that all who believe in thee may together extol thy name, O Lord God, most glorious and excellent over all.

From the anonymous book Godly Prayers, *published in 1552*

June 7   Sharing everything

The whole group of those who believed were of one heart and soul, and no one claimed private ownership of any possessions, but everything they owned was held in common. With great power the apostles gave their testimony to the resurrection of the Lord Jesus, and great grace was upon them all. There was not a needy person among them, for as many as owned lands or houses sold them and brought the proceeds of what was sold. They laid it at the apostles' feet, and it was distributed to each as any had need. There was a Levite, a native of Cyprus, Joseph, to whom the apostles gave the name Barnabas (which means 'son of encouragement'). He sold a field that belonged to him, then brought the money, and laid it at the apostles' feet.

Acts 4.32–37

When a name gets changed, there is always a good reason. When the Windscale nuclear reprocessing plant in Cumbria changed its name to Sellafield, there must have been people who hoped that any negative associations it had would change with it. In March 2001 the Royal Mail changed its name to Consignia at a cost of half-a-million pounds. Fifteen months and £1 billion of losses later, they changed it back. In June 2002 the accountancy firm Price Waterhouse Cooper briefly changed its name to Monday – a failure that rather overestimated people's enthusiasm for the start of a working week.

It must be remarkable to have your name changed to 'the encourager'. And even more so to deserve it so much that people forget you were originally called something else. Barnabas was later to strengthen the work of churches, to build bridges between old enemies, and to train promising young people. But he first earned his name through an act of generosity on behalf of people in need.

In 1964 a twenty-year-old organization called the Department for the Inter-Church Aid and Refugee Service changed its name to Christian Aid. Snappy, huh!

It is interesting to reflect on how its work has subsequently echoed that of Barnabas.

Try to identify the names of someone who has encouraged you and someone who needs encouragement. Make a couple of phone calls this evening for some idle chatter!

Holy Spirit, the encourager:
give me grace to follow in the steps of Barnabas,
who followed in the steps of Jesus,
who gave everything on behalf of a needy world. Amen.

June 8   Distributing food

During those days, when the disciples were increasing in number, the Hellenists complained against the Hebrews because their widows were being neglected in the daily distribution of food. And the twelve called together the whole community of the disciples and said, 'It is not right that we should neglect the word of God in order to wait on tables. Therefore, friends, select from among yourselves seven men of good standing, full of the Spirit and of wisdom, whom we may appoint to this task, while we, for our part, will devote ourselves to prayer and to serving the word.' What they said pleased the whole community.

Acts 6.1–5

When the Holy Spirit came at Pentecost the result was a united, inspirational congregation of Christians. Right? Hmm! No! Church has never been that simple.

In its early days the Jews who spoke Greek thought that the Jews who spoke Aramaic were getting a better deal. This presented a problem to those who led the church. They realized that their skills were in teaching and leading worship. They knew that there were vital tasks to be done in pastoral and practical work, but that they had overlooked them because they were time-consuming.

Their decision about what to do was a model in resolving conflicts in church (or anywhere, for that matter). First, they admitted that they had got something wrong. Second, they involved the whole community in finding a satisfactory solution. Third, they opted to give away some of their power and delegate it to others. Fourth, they made it clear that they didn't see those whose role was to be a practical one as second-rank, because they too had to be evidently wise and godly. The picture at the end of this story is of genuine reconciliation – for a time, at least!

Christian Aid partners many organizations that work to resolve conflict, and to strengthen communities as peace is slowly built after the end of a war. In Angola thirty years of civil war are over, but it will be many years before their legacy has been dealt with.

Christian Aid supports COIEPA, the Angolan ecumenical peace initiative, to consolidate peace at grassroots level. Find out more at www.christianaid.org.uk/world/where/safrica/angolap.htm

May the Lord of peace himself give you peace at all times and in every way. The Lord be with all of you. And may the grace of our Lord Jesus Christ be with us all.

2 Thessalonians 3.16

June 9   Religious arguments

The word of God continued to spread; the number of the disciples increased greatly in Jerusalem, and a great many of the priests became obedient to the faith.

Stephen, full of grace and power, did great wonders and signs among the people. Then some of those who belonged to the synagogue of the Freedmen (as it was called), Cyrenians, Alexandrians, and others of those from Cilicia and Asia, stood up and argued with Stephen. But they could not withstand the wisdom and the Spirit with which he spoke.

Acts 6.7–10

The Church was growing. It was well-organized, it was popular and it was increasing in credibility. Many of the humble and pious Jewish priests (a different group from the wealthy and politically astute high priests who had been responsible for Jesus' arrest) were coming to faith. No wonder the Jewish authorities were unsettled – not only their synagogue members but now their staff as well were following the Way of Jesus (as it was known). On all previous occasions the death of the ringleader had led to revolutionary cells collapsing. But then, on all previous occasions, it was not God they had been trying to kill. This movement was stronger now than when Jesus had fed and preached to 5,000 people.

This threat to the authority of the Jewish leaders was taking place freely in the grounds of their own temple. So action was needed. There were sufficient articulate Jews living in Jerusalem to create an intelligent debate. Among them was an intellectual and craftsman from Cilicia called Saul, who was later to become very significant in the unfolding story of God at work in the world. And he joined others in something which has lost neither its appeal nor its danger in 2,000 years – a religious argument.

Make a point of chatting to someone from a different faith group today. And then pray for a better understanding and deeper tolerance between faiths.

O Jesus Christ, my Way
to the God of all salvation,
I lift to you all men and women of other faiths:
may they find their way to the mercy at the heart of God;
may they find the truth on the journey through life we take
*   together;*
may they find in me a friend who learns and teaches;
and so may humankind be at peace. Amen.

June 10 Stephen

[Members of one of the synagogues] secretly instigated some men to say, 'We have heard [Stephen] speak blasphemous words against Moses and God.' They stirred up the people as well as the elders and the scribes; then they suddenly confronted him, seized him, and brought him before the council. They set up false witnesses who said, 'This man never stops saying things against this holy place and the law; for we have heard him say that this Jesus of Nazareth will destroy this place and will change the customs that Moses handed on to us.' And all who sat in the council looked intently at him, and they saw that his face was like the face of an angel.

Acts 6.11–15

Stephen must have known he was in peril. The leaders of the Christian Church had already been flogged to scare them into silence. I wonder whether Stephen wondered how he managed to get into such danger – he was, after all, only one of the men who organized the distribution of food to old people.

Doing something on behalf of the poor in the name of Jesus may not seem subversive, but history has repeatedly shown the risks of obeying God's call to stand alongside the poor and oppressed.

A horribly recognizable cycle was in motion. It began with theological disagreement. It still seemed respectable when the debate accelerated into an argument. It got out of hand here when it descended into slander. Before the night was over it would degenerate into violence. I have no doubt that those who opposed the young man subsequently justified their actions as a defence of deeply held values. They always do! But actually, what did it for Stephen was that they didn't like the look of his face.

The Jubilee Campaign is a human rights pressure group, lobbying to protect children's rights and the persecuted Church. To stand alongside those who are experiencing today the things that Stephen went through, visit www.jubileecampaign.co.uk

Keep a-inchin' along, keep a-inchin' along, (Massa Jesus comin'
    by an' by);
Keep a-inchin' along like a po' inch worm, (Massa Jesus comin'
    by an' by);
I died one time, guine di no mo', (Massa Jesus comin' by an' by);
O you in de Word an' de Word in you, (Massa Jesus comin' by an' by);
How can I die when I'm in de Word? (Massa Jesus comin' by an' by).

Spiritual of enslaved Afro-American people

June 11   Martyrdom

[Stephen said, 'Your ancestors] killed those who foretold the coming of the Righteous One, and now you have become his betrayers and murderers.' . . . They became enraged and ground their teeth at Stephen. But filled with the Holy Spirit, he gazed into heaven and saw the glory of God and Jesus standing at the right hand of God. 'Look,' he said, 'I see the heavens opened and the Son of Man standing at the right hand of God!' But they covered their ears, and with a loud shout all rushed together against him. Then they dragged him out of the city and began to stone him; and the witnesses laid their coats at the feet of a young man named Saul. While they were stoning Stephen, he prayed, 'Lord Jesus, receive my spirit.' Then he knelt down and cried out in a loud voice, 'Lord, do not hold this sin against them.' When he had said this, he died.

Acts 7.52, 54–60

Stephen was the first person to die because of his belief that Jesus was the Messiah (the Righteous One). His execution took place outside the walls of Jerusalem, with serene confidence and with words of forgiveness. It is described in a way calculated to remind us of Jesus.

What is the difference between a martyr and a suicide bomber? There is no difference in the courage or commitment. However, there are other differences that make martyrdom a Christ-like death and suicide bombing a terrible wrong. In Stephen's death there is no trace of hatred for those around him. His are not the words of someone with nothing left to lose, but of someone for whom love is finding its costly conclusion. Archbishop Rowan Williams suggests in *Writing in the Dust: Reflections on 11th September*: 'The terrible self-abandonment of the suicidal killer is like a grotesque parody of the self-abandonment of love.'

Suicide killings make headlines. Bring to mind one that has been reported recently, and think of those who still grieve. Martyrdoms are rarely reported. Yet it is certain that, somewhere in the world, commitment to God will have cost people their lives this week. Try to imagine the sorrow of their families too, and be humbled.

When I survey the wondrous cross
Where the young Prince of Glory dies,
My richest gain I count but loss,
And pour contempt on all my pride.

Isaac Watts (1674–1748), from 'Crucifixion to the World by the Cross of Christ'

June 12 A scattered church

Saul approved of [the killing of Stephen]. That day a severe persecution began against the church in Jerusalem, and all except the apostles were scattered throughout the countryside of Judea and Samaria. Devout men buried Stephen and made loud lamentation over him. But Saul was ravaging the church by entering house after house; dragging off both men and women, he committed them to prison.

Now those who were scattered went from place to place, proclaiming the word.

Acts 8.1–4

Out of death comes resurrection. That is the nature of God.

Out of the execution of Jesus grew a Church convinced that he was alive and inspired by it. Out of the martyrdom of Stephen and the persecution that followed grew a Church which spread the good news of Jesus to places it had never reached before. Out of the fear of Christians running for their lives grew a religion not just for Jerusalem but for all the world. And Saul is mentioned in particular, because his ruthlessness was going to be resurrected into a faith that would shape the future of the planet. The Christians' greatest enemy was about to confront the reality of Jesus Christ, change his name to Paul, and become their greatest missionary.

Dennis Lennon, the Scottish theologian, writes: 'Like mice peering over the edge of a Persian carpet we are usually too near to events in a crisis to detect the divine design in them. We must take it on trust that God will always do what perfect wisdom suggests to infinite love.'

Be aware, everywhere you go on this summer's day, of life insisting on reproducing itself. Look for a dead dandelion displaying its seeds, waiting for the wind to scatter them (you might even help them on their way)! Look for brightly coloured flowers attracting insects to spread their pollen. Look for trees beginning to form the seeds that will bring new life in years to come. And be hopeful!

Above the level of the former years,
the mire of sin, the slough of guilty fears,
the mist of doubt, the blight of love's decay –
O Lord of light, lift all our hearts today!

H. M. Butler (1833–1918), from the hymn 'Lift up your hearts'

June 13   How to be wise

The proverbs of Solomon, son of David, king of Israel:
For learning about wisdom and instruction, for understanding words of insight, for gaining instruction in wise dealing, righteousness, justice, and equity; to teach shrewdness to the simple, knowledge and prudence to the young – let the wise also hear and gain in learning, and the discerning acquire skill, to understand a proverb and a figure, the words of the wise and their riddles.

The fear of the Lord is the beginning of knowledge; fools despise wisdom and instruction. Hear, my child, your father's instruction, and do not reject your mother's teaching; for they are a fair garland for your head, and pendants for your neck.

Proverbs 1.1–9

Israel's wise men and women were a special group who, together with priests and prophets, were trusted for advice about turning godliness into practical action. King Solomon was renowned for his wisdom, and seems to have had this anthology compiled.

Having reverence for God appears as the first priority for a successful life. But the Proverbs are resolutely practical. They stress that it is no good having an admirable spiritual life, but ending up lonely, socially inept, compassionless, in trouble with the law and, worst of all, broke!

In the first place, avoiding these will depend on whose voice catches your ear, particularly when you are young. Not everyone can listen to their parents as voices which lead them toward God or toward justice. So who are the mature Christians whose wise example has been 'a fair garland for your head'?

As names come to mind, scribble them in the margin. Spend time considering where you will meet most pressure this week to let your godly standards drop. Let the memory of the wise men and women who have influenced you help you prepare to resist.

May the Lord our God be with us, as he was with our ancestors; may he not leave us or abandon us, but incline our hearts to him, to walk in all his ways, and to keep his commandments . . . which he commanded our ancestors . . . and may he maintain the cause of his people, as each day requires.

Further words of Solomon, this time from 1 Kings 8.57–59

June 14   Love and faithfulness

My child, do not forget my teaching, but let your heart keep my commandments; for length of days and years of life and abundant welfare they will give you. Do not let loyalty and faithfulness forsake you; bind them around your neck, write them on the tablet of your heart. So you will find favour and good repute in the sight of God and of people.

Proverbs 3.1–4

I don't think I have a problem with love, nor with faithfulness, but I do have a problem with forgetfulness! The people I love most and to whom I am committed to be faithful become so close to me that I take their presence for granted. In these proverbs the wise man advises us to remind ourselves of the joy and responsibility of loving and being loved. We are to carry it around with us as if it were on display like a tie or a necklace. We are to jog our memories with it as if we had scribbled it on a post-it note.

What will the result of this be? These verses mention two things: God will be just as pleased as the people we love are, and we will develop a good reputation in the community. Both of those are dramatically underrated today – but perhaps they shouldn't be! These proverbs tell us that, in obedience to God, they are the secret of a long and fulfilled life.

Almost everyone has a tie, a necklace or something similar. Go and find one. At some point during today put it on, and as you do so make a point of thinking about the people you love. You may find yourself challenged about your forgetfulness or your faithfulness – or simply thankful. If you are in a position to buy a new tie or necklace, you could wear it as a secret sign between you and God of your commitment to those you love. If not, writing a post-it note to rediscover in time to come might be even more effective!

I can do nothing
for my family, for people, for the Lord.
For the abundant love
of the Lord, of people, of my family
I just give thanks,
just give thanks.

Misuno Genzo, paraplegic poet from Tokyo, written using a code based on the movement of his eyelids

June 15   Trusting God

Trust in the Lord with all your heart, and do not rely on your own insight. In all your ways acknowledge him, and he will make straight your paths. Do not be wise in your own eyes; fear the Lord, and turn away from evil. It will be a healing for your flesh and a refreshment for your body.

Proverbs 3.5–8

Banknotes in the USA contain the words 'In God we trust' as part of their design. A Wall Street bullion broker was devising a corporate mission statement as an exercise to build up his staff's motivation. The team's wittiest suggestion was 'Ingot we trust'.

Let's be honest, learning to trust God is not a straightforward matter as we walk life's paths. It can't be bought for banknotes like a pair of shoes. And a pair of shoes doesn't inexplicably let you down!

The writer urges us to see times when God takes us through hardship as part of our training to be disciples. Just as a crawling infant sees a stair-guard solely as an attempt to prevent her enjoying a rollercoaster ride, we cannot share the wisdom of God when he leads us through difficulty. Sometimes it is only in retrospect that we can begin to glimpse God's ways shaping us in love, rather than rebuking us in punishment. The wisdom that is found in the context of his eternal call upon us, rather than the ever-changing 'insight' of society, can only come with long-term trust.

Learn the first two sentence of today's Bible reading by heart along with their reference, Proverbs 3.5–6. If the principle is as important as the writer says it is, then who knows when the memory of it will influence a future decision for good!

There's a time for healing and a time for forgiving.
There's a time for building bridges, and that time is now.
O, take our hearts, Lord, and take our minds.
Take our hands, Lord, and make them one. Amen.

From a banner that hangs in St George's Cathedral, Jerusalem

June 16 Setting priorities

Honour the Lord with your substance and with the first fruits of all your produce; then your barns will be filled with plenty, and your vats will be bursting with wine ...

Happy are those who find wisdom, and those who get understanding, for her income is better than silver, and her revenue better than gold. She is more precious than jewels, and nothing you desire can compare with her. Long life is in her right hand; in her left hand are riches and honour. Her ways are ways of pleasantness, and all her paths are peace. She is a tree of life to those who lay hold of her; those who hold her fast are called happy.

Proverbs 3.9–10, 13–18

All my alarm bells are going off! For this society, in which accumulating money has become the measure of success, these words seem to give a dangerous comfort. They make honouring God sound like entering a tombola – give generously to him and you will be rewarded with prizes. But the thrust of the whole Bible does not tell us that following God will make us wealthy – in fact the reverse may be true.

There are priorities to work out by reflecting on these verses. They suggest the secret of getting life in proportion. A long life is more important than money. A pleasant life is more important than a long one. And wisdom is more important than anything.

Prosperity, long life, pleasant life, peace, wisdom – in what order do you put these as you plan for the future?

Try reading the verses again in a global context, rather than a personal one. The people of Israel were instructed to give away the 'first fruits' (the first and best part of their harvest). Before they did anything else with their income, they were to be selfless.

What would it mean in practice if the wealthy nations of the North were to 'honour the Lord' in their trade and their economics? Where and how might 'barns be filled'?

Yours, O Lord, are the greatness, the power, the glory, the victory, and the majesty; for all that is in the heavens and on the earth is yours ... All things come from you, and of your own have we given you.

1 Chronicles 29.11, 14

June 17   Generosity

Some give freely, yet grow all the richer; others withhold what is due, and only suffer want. A generous person will be enriched, and one who gives water will get water. The people curse those who hold back grain, but a blessing is on the head of those who sell it. Whoever diligently seeks good finds favour, but evil comes to the one who searches for it. Those who trust in their riches will wither, but the righteous will flourish like green leaves.

Proverbs 11.24–28

The person who wrote these ancient words of wisdom must have looked out at the harvest fields on a glorious summer day. He knew that farmers were hoarding grain knowing that, when shortages came during the winter months, they could bump up their prices and make a big profit. God's attitude was: 'That may be good business, but it is bad justice and bad compassion. Better to be generous and loved than rich and isolated.'

Over the next few years we will be hearing a great deal about multinational companies which are modifying seeds genetically. They create crops that give a fine harvest but don't generate any new seeds so that, rather than keeping back some of this year's crop to sow next year, the farmer in the developing world will have to go back to the powerful company again and again to buy new seeds.

Now what is that? A generous attempt to feed the rapidly growing population of the world, or selfishness by those who are rich that will be paid for by those who are poor?

Find out about genetically modified organisms from Christian Aid's report *Selling Suicide*. A short version can be read at www.christianaid.org.uk/indepth/0206gm/gmcrops.htm

Gracious God, who has given us more than we dream or deserve, make me a person whose generosity stands out – as green as a leaf.

June 18 Animals

Better to be despised and have a servant, than to be self-important and lack food. The righteous know the needs of their animals, but the mercy of the wicked is cruel. Those who till their land will have plenty of food, but those who follow worthless pursuits have no sense.

Proverbs 12.9–11

Whatever would Solomon have made of a battery hen coop?

These verses are about short-term gain and its long-term impact. The farmer who treats his or her animals oppressively needs to see that, although profits increase now, there will be a price to pay in the future in terms of the world's health and well-being. But God has a warning for others too. The luxuries that are sold to us on page after page of glossy magazines offer instant pleasure, but it is worthless to believe that it is possible to obtain a fulfilled life by purchasing them.

In the Philippines, Christian Aid supports the work of Muslim–Christian Action for Rural Development. They have credit schemes that help farmers improve their work by, for instance, sharing an animal for heavy farming tasks. A water buffalo can do the work of many humans, and MuCARD can also provide emergency veterinary welfare because those who work the land in the Philippines know that proper care for an animal is not just sentimentality, but vital for a secure supply of food. When a calf is born, it is given back to the MuCARD programme to be loaned to another group of farmers so that the benefits continue.

Be aware of every animal that crosses your path today – pets, farm animals, wildlife, spiders! Each time you see one, think of those in the developing world whose livelihood depends on the care they give to their animals.

Hear our humble prayer, O God, for our friends the animals, especially for animals who are suffering; for any that are hunted or lost or deserted or frightened or hungry; for all that must be put to death. We entreat for them all thy mercy and pity, and for those who deal with them we ask a heart of compassion, gentle hands and kindly words. Make us true friends to animals and so to share the blessing of the merciful.

Albert Schweitzer (1875–1965)

June 19 Little by little

Wealth hastily gained will dwindle, but those who gather little by little will increase it. Hope deferred makes the heart sick, but a desire fulfilled is a tree of life.

Proverbs 13.11, 12

Christian Aid has refused to look to the National Lottery for funding. The poorest people in the world do not need luck to improve their lot: they need justice. These verses give God's blessing to long-term, hardworking improvements – not to sudden gain either through corruption or fortune.

When Torina Begum's husband Abdul lost his arm in a train accident she became the main earner of the family. In Namoshankarbati village in Bangladesh she started off by saving five takas per month (about six pence – half a day's wage in the rice-husking mill where she worked). Christian Aid partners the Christian Commission for Development in Bangladesh, which supports community groups that run credit schemes. Torina needed to sign a document, but since she could not read or write she had to leave a thumbprint. She was determined to learn, so CCDB arranged for her to go on a literacy course. After six months of saving, Torina took out loans to buy a goat and a calf. A long time went by before her longing was fulfilled, but as months passed they bred, and selling the young meant she could repay the loan and take a new one. This time she bought a rickshaw and, with her new skills in literacy and numeracy, started a business. It is flourishing – she now has three rickshaws hired out to local villagers at thirty takas per day.

On a scrap of paper write one of the proverbs that has struck you particularly during the past week. Put it in your wallet, purse or cheque book so that you are reminded of it next time you spend or save.

O God, grant that always, at all times and in all places, in all things both great and small, we may ever do your most holy will and be Jesus Christ's faithful servants to our lives' end.

A Bangladeshi prayer used daily by the nuns of Christa Sevika Sangha (the Little Handmaids of Christ)

June 20   Needy neighbours

The poor are disliked even by their neighbours, but the rich have many friends. Those who despise their neighbours are sinners, but happy are those who are kind to the poor. Do they not err that plan evil? Those who plan good find loyalty and faithfulness.

Proverbs 14.20–22

Before you nod wisely at these proverbs and move on, stop for a moment and ask yourself – are they actually true? Some of the Bible's proverbs sum up how the world is, but shouldn't be. Some challenge us because they are wise about how the world could be, but isn't. And some exaggerate the truth into a quotable quote, then challenge us to react! Which is this?

There are two clichés which we ought not to accept without first allowing God to challenge them. One is that all those who live in poor countries are miserable, and that all would be well if only they could have lifestyles like those in the UK and Ireland. The other is that poor people are somehow compensated by being loving and joyful all the time.

The truth is more complex. Rich people and poor people the world over have neighbours. They fall in love with them, fall out with them, make friends with them, take advantage of them, help them out, or ignore them. In these verses, God is challenging us to relate to those in our community in a way that pleases him, not on the basis of whether or not we stand to gain from having them nearby. If we are going to change the way the nations of the world relate, we may need to begin by changing the relationships in our own street.

Write the names of your neighhbours in the margin. As you do so, reflect on your relationship with them and how clearly it demonstrates the values of God's kingdom. Take the opportunity to 'plan what is good' as the proverb puts it. If you don't know the names of some of them, then an obvious action for today presents itself!

I call God's love and faithfulness to bless my street;
I call God's love and faithfulness to bless my community;
I call God's love and faithfulness to bless my world;
And I hear God's call to me to make it happen.

June 21 Learning to work

Better is a dry morsel with quiet than a house full of feasting with strife. A slave who deals wisely will rule over a child who acts shamefully, and will share the inheritance as one of the family. The crucible is for silver, and the furnace is for gold, but the Lord tests the heart. An evildoer listens to wicked lips; and a liar gives heed to a mischievous tongue. Those who mock the poor insult their Maker; those who are glad at calamity will not go unpunished. Grandchildren are the crown of the aged, and the glory of children is their parents . . .

Discipline your children while there is hope; do not set your heart on their destruction. A violent-tempered person will pay the penalty; if you effect a rescue, you will only have to do it again. Listen to advice and accept instruction, that you may gain wisdom for the future.

Proverbs 17.1–6; 19.18–20

What do these verses teach you about work?

In Guatemala City a boy of fifteen squats on the steps leading to Sears department store. His job is selling newspapers from a makeshift stand, and these are his words: 'God, I have nothing to offer you. I don't know if this pleases you, but I only have these newspapers. Only with them do I earn my bread. You know, Lord, that I have no mother nor father. They have killed them, and now I have no one to teach me to work.'

What can a child from Guatemala teach you about work?

Buy a newspaper today. Notice the person you buy it from, who is known to and loved by God. As you flick through, look out for stories from the developing world, especially if they are from Central America. As you turn each page, spend a moment in prayer to God for the people and issues you read about in the articles.

Jesus, we believe that you are living.
The steps that you took before, we are taking now.
The resurrection is present in each sister and brother
*   who rises up.*
Help us so that all people may be resurrected in a
*   new Guatemala,*
where peace, justice and equality will reign,
so that nobody is hungry.

Prayer of a woman from the Guatemalan Committee for Justice and Peace

June 22   Shopping

*Diverse weights and diverse measures are both alike an abomi-
nation to the Lord. Even children make themselves known by
their acts, by whether what they do is pure and right . . . 'Bad,
bad,' says the buyer, then goes away and boasts.*

Proverbs 20.10–11, 14

Suppose one of the wise men and women who wrote these
sayings were transported forward 3,000 years. Who might they
condemn today?

Certain sellers perhaps? The car salesman who turns back a
milometer? The publican whose taps are fixed to provide more
froth than drink?

Or maybe certain buyers? The man who pretends that a shirt is badly made
in order to get the price reduced, then brags to his friends, 'Half price, and the
shop assistant didn't even notice she was being fooled!' Or the woman who
keeps quiet about being given too much change?

These things happen on a global scale too. Again and again it is the world's
poorest people who fall victim to unjust trade.

Here is a cause for rejoicing! Over recent years fairly traded
products have progressed from being something bought from a
table in a draughty church hall to something stocked by every
major supermarket. Goods with the Fairtrade logo have been
bought from a producer who has been guaranteed a minimum
price (and thus is not vulnerable to dramatic falls in the worldwide price of
commodities). He or she can be sure of covering the cost of production, but
there will also be an extra premium that is invested in the education or health
of the community. Read more about the power that shoppers have to influence
the world for good at the website of the Fairtrade Foundation,
www.fairtrade.org.uk

*Try to recall everything you have purchased during the last 48
hours. Thank God for what you have enjoyed. If you are aware
of having been wasteful or dishonest, confess it to God.*

June 23   Living on the land

Do not remove an ancient landmark or encroach on the fields of orphans, for their redeemer is strong; he will plead their cause against you.

Proverbs 23.10–11

Brazil is a wealthy country, but only a minority enjoys its riches. Three-quarters of the population of rural Brazil have no land at all, and most cannot feed their children adequately. Zaires Morais de Moura was like that ten years ago until he came into contact with the Movimento Sem Terra (the Landless Rural Workers' Movement, a partner of Christian Aid). It is an organization that helps Brazilian people claim what is legally theirs – the right to settle on the 40 percent of rural land that is idle.

Powerful landowners are not happy to see groups get the official title of dis-used land. They don't let it happen without a fight – often a violent one. But in the eyes of God the Defender ownership should not depend on strength, but on justice. When poor people face aggressors, God stands alongside them now just as he did in the days when poor Hebrews found that the landmarks which indicated the extent of their land had been interfered with by powerful opponents.

Movimento Sem Terra helped Zaires and his neighbours establish their rights on a piece of land by an airport, form an agricultural co-operative, learn good farming practices (they grow tea and cashew nuts), and develop a business. Ten years on he is building a house for his family which will allow them to have flowing water and a toilet of their own for the first time.

Go to a shop and buy some cashew nuts and tea (fairly traded if possible). Drink a toast to those in Brazil who seek justice. Turn back to 11 May to read more about Brazil.

When we first arrived there were just a few little huts. Then we were able to build new ones, and now [secure houses]. Each year people organize themselves better and improve their working methods. It has been a slow process, but we've got there . . .
Please keep praying, because Brazil needs your prayers. And please pray for our leaders, that they may be guided to adopt policies that will help us.

Zaires Morais de Moura

June 24 Justice for all

Partiality in judging is not good. Whoever says to the wicked, 'You are innocent', will be cursed by peoples, abhorred by nations; but those who rebuke the wicked will have delight, and a good blessing will come upon them. One who gives an honest answer gives a kiss on the lips.
Prepare your work outside, get everything ready for you in the field; and after that build your house. Do not be a witness against your neighbour without cause, and do not deceive with your lips. Do not say, 'I will do to others as they have done to me; I will pay them back for what they have done.'

Proverbs 24.23–29

It is 1000 BC. A rich farmer is trying to acquire the land of his Israelite neighbours. He is offering them a fraction of its true value. The land has been in their family for generations, but since their father died they have no near kinsman who will stand in court to be their defender, as the law requires. Is the family beyond hope? Not at all! God will be their Defender and Kinsman. No rich businessman, no biased judge, no revenge-seeker will ever share the special concern that God has for the poor. Even if it appears that the corrupt get away with it, the writer of the Proverbs insists that in the short term they will lose their good name (which should not be underestimated), and in the long term God will see justice done.

There is nothing new about a plaintiff losing a case because the defendant can afford a clever, expensive lawyer. On a global scale we are right to be anxious when the institutions that oversee the trading and financial relationships of nations meet with scores of lawyers and economists representing the richest countries, but the poorest countries sharing only one or two. God is standing alongside those who are innocent but not in a good position to defend themselves. Where are you standing?

If you have answered honestly, you deserve a kiss on the lips. The Proverb said it in black and white. Hmm! I wonder who!

Pray that the innocent will walk free from prison, that minorities will overcome discrimination, and that everyone who works in the justice system will be convicted of the need for honesty and integrity.

June 25   Hard work

I passed by the field of one who was lazy, by the vineyard of a stupid person; and see, it was all overgrown with thorns; the ground was covered with nettles, and its stone wall was broken down. Then I saw and considered it; I looked and received instruction. A little sleep, a little slumber, a little folding of the hands to rest, and poverty will come upon you like a robber, and want, like an armed warrior . . .

The lazy person says, 'There is a lion in the road! There is a lion in the streets!' As a door turns on its hinges, so does a lazy person in bed. The lazy person buries a hand in the dish, and is too tired to bring it back to the mouth. The lazy person is wiser in self-esteem than seven who can answer discreetly.

Proverbs 24.30–34; 26.13–16

Sometimes the Proverbs show what life is like, sometimes they show what life is not like but ought to be, and sometimes their point is made by exaggerating so much that we are shocked (or amused) into working out the truth for ourselves. It is usually easy to work out which is which, but it does mean that we have to read the Bible wisely.

For instance, look through these proverbs, trying to see them not through your own eyes but through someone else's. How might they aggrieve or give hope to:

- someone who is unable to find paid employment;
- someone whose hard work is rewarded with an unfairly low wage;
- someone who feels trapped in an unfulfilling job;
- someone whose main activity is unpaid hard work?

What would you say to someone who suggested that poor people get that way because they are lazy?

Tackle a chore today that you have been putting off for a long time – and then give yourself a reward!

God give me work till my life shall end,
And life till my work is done.

On the grave of the novelist Winifred Holtby (1898–1935)

June 26   Too rich or too poor?

*Two things I ask of you; do not deny them to me before I die:
Remove far from me falsehood and lying; give me neither poverty
nor riches; feed me with the food that I need, or I shall be full,
and deny you, and say, 'Who is the Lord?' or I shall be poor, and
steal, and profane the name of my God.*

Proverbs 30.7–9

Six tough questions today. Take your time!

- What are the dangers of being wealthy?
- What potential for good does it open up?
- What are the dangers of being poor?
- What potential for good does it open up?
- What are the dangers of having precisely the resources that you now have?
- What potential for good do they open up?

As you go through the next twenty-four hours, imagine yourself
in the position of someone who is at the opposite end of the
wealth/poverty scale from you. If you were this person, what
would you be doing at various stages of the day? What worries,
joys or temptations might occur? What emotions will arise?
What impact would all these things have on relationships with your loved ones
and family?

*At the end of the day, pray for those who experience in reality
what you have imagined.*

June 27 Responsible government

The words of King Lemuel. An oracle that his mother taught him:
No, my son! No, son of my womb! No, son of my vows! Do not give your strength to women, your ways to those who destroy kings. It is not for kings, O Lemuel, it is not for kings to drink wine, or for rulers to desire strong drink; or else they will drink and forget what has been decreed, and will pervert the rights of all the afflicted.

Proverbs 31.1–5

There is something touching about these verses. I picture a hung-over teenager realizing for the first time that a night on the razzle comes with a price tag. A queen, knowing that her son needs to learn the responsibilities into which he is growing, delivers a strict telling-off. But she is a mother as well, and she can't resist putting her arms around him and trying to love the headache away.

Whether or not this over-romanticizes the scene, it teaches something sober. Leadership brings responsibility for the oppressed. If money that has been given for medicines and teachers is stolen to create palaces and private armies, donors are outraged. None more so than God.

In recent years part of Christian Aid's work in developing countries has been to build up 'civil society' – the organizations within a country that stabilize it by encouraging democracy, fighting corruption and holding government to account. Churches are in the forefront of this work, and so are trade unions and community groups. The temptation for leaders to act selfishly will never go away – not in this country nor in the developing world. But the ability to oppose corruption is growing stronger.

In the margin, write the names of people over whom you have an influence. It may be that you are a mother, like Lemuel's, in which case your children's names will top the list. Or are you a teacher, church leader, godparent, politician, prefect, friend, employer or leader of a children's group? If it occurs to you that you have not spent enough time with someone recently, underline the name and take action.

Pray for the people whose names you have written, and for national leaders who are in today's newspaper for bad reasons or good.

June 28 Speaking up for the voiceless

Give strong drink to one who is perishing, and wine to those in bitter distress; let them drink and forget their poverty, and remember their misery no more. Speak out for those who cannot speak, for the rights of all the destitute. Speak out, judge righteously, defend the rights of the poor and needy.

Proverbs 31.6–9

Recommending alcohol as escapism from distress strikes us awkwardly in a culture that has moved on for 3,000 years. But of course, medicine has moved on too, and we now have pain relief that tackles the same issues in different ways.

Campaigners who work in partnership with poor people are concerned about the lack of access that they have to medicines which others take for granted. The huge transnational corporations that develop new medicines wield great power. It is possible to patent drugs so that they can only be sold expensively under a brand name, even though it would be possible for those in developing countries to produce medicines that have the same impact at a cheaper price. Changing the rules would be costly, decreasing the profits of the companies and making drugs more expensive in wealthier countries. But it would have a very positive impact on health in poorer nations.

In health care, as in every other area, the world's poor communities need those with influence to speak on their behalf. The problem today is not so much that they 'cannot speak' but that their articulate voices are not given space by the media. How can you and I speak up for them?

Go to the shelf where you keep medicines and do an audit. Throw away anything past its use-by date. Check that what you stock is secure against children. Be sure you are prepared for accidents that might require first aid. And be aware of the privilege of being able to access medicines with such ease.

Lord Christ, who has known pain, bring healing this day to those whose cries go unheard.

June 29   A working woman

A capable wife who can find? She is far more precious than jewels. The heart of her husband trusts in her, and he will have no lack of gain. She does him good, and not harm, all the days of her life. She seeks wool and flax, and works with willing hands. She is like the ships of the merchant, she brings her food from far away. She rises while it is still night and provides food for her household and tasks for her servant girls. She considers a field and buys it; with the fruit of her hands she plants a vineyard. She girds herself with strength, and makes her arms strong.

Proverbs 31.10–17

Am I alone in finding the last chapter of Proverbs hard to read? It seems to echo the media demand for every female to be Superwoman – to have a shining career, a stylish home and perfect children. To cook like Delia Smith, but be as thin as Kate Moss. To be endlessly creative in bed, to give hours of service to the community (church for instance), to clean the gutters so as not to stereotype men, and still to be up-to-date with the music that's playing in the clubs at 2 am.

Women make up one-third of the world's workforce. But they earn roughly one-tenth of the world's wages. They are entitled to about one-hundredth of the world's rights. Of the people who live in absolute poverty (earning less than seventy pence a day) over seventy percent are women. That's 1,200 million.

But Proverbs is not an instruction book for women. It's a poem! The reason the qualities mount up is that the poet thinks of one for every letter of the Hebrew alphabet. An A–Z of 'thank yous' by a man to the world's women. As Christian women and men let us work for the day when equality of the genders is a reality. Until then, 'thank you' is not a bad start.

To which women do you owe a debt of gratitude – a relative, a friend, a wife? Send an email, write a letter or make a phone call that subtly lets them know.

There are countless women in the developing world to whom you also owe a debt. Thank God for the lifestyle that you lead, and pray for the anonymous millions whose underpaid work allows you to live as you do.

June 30   A just reward

She perceives that her merchandise is profitable. Her lamp does not go out at night. She puts her hands to the distaff, and her hands hold the spindle. She opens her hand to the poor, and reaches out her hands to the needy . . . 'Many women have done excellently, but you surpass them all.' Charm is deceitful, and beauty is vain, but a woman who fears the Lord is to be praised. Give her a share in the fruit of her hands, and let her works praise her in the city gates.

Proverbs 31.18–20, 29–31

The A–Z of female qualities which began yesterday continues. But now it embraces responsibilities toward women that all the world must share – fair trading rules, just pay for work, concern for poverty, and full recognition.

BIDII is the Swahili word for 'effort'. It also stands for the Benevolent Institute of Development Initiatives, a partner of Christian Aid in Kenya. It is training women to cook foods that are not traditionally eaten, like the purple bud of a banana tree and cassava leaves. This is having a big impact on the lives of these women and their families as it provides them with alternative food sources in an area that has experienced drought and food shortages.

BIDII also works to increase clean water supplies, which are vital to prevent disease. And it supports women as they develop small-scale projects, such as silk-screen printing and soap-making, to help them to earn an income to help pay their children's school fees.

Not having a city gate at which to praise these African women, let's use the pages of this book to do what the proverb-writer asked!

Find out more about Christian Aid's work in Kenya at www.christianaid.org.uk/world/where/eagl/kenyap.htm

Mother and Father of all people,
For the women whose gender has denied them
promotion or dignity or human rights,
we bring our prayers;
For the women whose gender has enabled them
to create, to inspire and to provide,
we bring our praises.

July 1 Fishermen

As he walked by the Sea of Galilee, [Jesus] saw two brothers, Simon, who is called Peter, and Andrew his brother, casting a net into the lake – for they were fishermen. And he said to them, 'Follow me, and I will make you fish for people.' Immediately they left their nets and followed him. As he went from there, he saw two other brothers, James son of Zebedee and his brother John, in the boat with their father Zebedee, mending their nets, and he called them. Immediately they left the boat and their father, and followed him.

Matthew 4.18–22

This cannot, surely, have been the first time Jesus met these workmen. There is nothing unplanned or reckless about the way he calls them to follow him. It has all the marks of a plan that was careful and strategic. 'Come and follow me', was the next phase in God's plan for individual lives and for a needy world. It wasn't a five-year plan; it was plan for the next five minutes. It wasn't a five-year plan; it was a plan for the next 5,000 years. It was a plan for all eternity, but its start was (and always will be) here and now.

And the first disciples were obviously compelled and enthralled by this man. They committed themselves to his burning compassion, his loving mind, his technicolour imagination, his strong will, his shaping hands. How is it that when he is described today, Jesus comes across as worthy, saintly and bland? No wonder people who want to enjoy the exciting extremes of life don't see the appeal of the fireworks that must once have been part of following him! And still is now for those who take seriously Jesus' challenge to change the world!

If somebody asked you, 'What impresses you most about Jesus?', what would you reply? Write some words that come to mind in the margin. When you have done so, think about whether they generate the excitement in you that they could – or perhaps once did. What would a genuinely passionate response to Jesus look like?

Lord, let it not be that I follow you merely for the sake of following a leader, but let me respond to you as Lord and Master of every step I take. Amen.

From the prayer letter of Lahore Diocese, Church of Pakistan

July 2   The sick

Jesus went throughout Galilee, teaching in their synagogues and proclaiming the good news of the kingdom and curing every disease and every sickness among the people. So his fame spread throughout all Syria, and they brought to him all the sick, those who were afflicted with various diseases and pains, demoniacs, epileptics, and paralytics, and he cured them. And great crowds followed him.

Matthew 4.23–25

Why did Jesus gather around him fishermen, not scholars? Because scholars would have fallen at the first hurdle. The theology of the day taught that if you met a person who was disabled, blind or had leprosy it was your duty to murmur, 'Praised be the reliable Judge.' If Jesus had chosen conventionally religious people as disciples they would have protested at him involving himself with people who were sick, because suffering was the scourge of God. Wrong, said Jesus!

He trained his disciples to see what God was doing among those with physical and mental illnesses. They became God's collaborators in bringing the healing that announced that the King had arrived and his kingdom was breaking through. It heralded the day still to come when, in heaven, the cure will be total, trapped minds will be free, and all evil will be banished.

Every act of healing done in the name of Jesus becomes part of this cry of joy that permeates the Gospels – something irrefutably good is under way.

Christian Aid's partner Health Unlimited works in the places where it is most difficult for people to get medicine when they are ill. For example, in remote areas of Cambodia they are building health posts and then training local people to give treatment. Sam Ossophea's family were all killed during the Pol Pot era, but he escaped to a United Nations refugee camp, learned English, and became a Christian when a friend gave him a Bible. Later he trained in health care. Now, on his motorbike, he travels to isolated villages to train nurses how to immunize children against measles, and explain how a mosquito net can keep malaria away. Find out more about Health Unlimited at www.healthunlimited.org

O God, make the door of this house wide enough to receive all who need human love and fellowship, and a heavenly Father's care; and narrow enough to shut out all envy, pride and hate. Make it a gateway to thine eternal kingdom.

Prayer at the door of a Christian hospital, by Bishop Thomas Ken (1637–1711)

July 3   A man with leprosy

When Jesus had come down from the mountain, great crowds followed him; and there was a leper who came to him and knelt before him, saying, 'Lord, if you choose, you can make me clean.' He stretched out his hand and touched him, saying, 'I do choose. Be made clean!' Immediately his leprosy was cleansed. Then Jesus said to him, 'See that you say nothing to anyone; but go, show yourself to the priest, and offer the gift that Moses commanded.'

Matthew 8.1–4

Jesus' generation thought that leprosy was incurable; they were wrong. They believed that it was so contagious that sufferers should be exiled to remote colonies; they were wrong. They believed that leprosy was a punishment from God for sin, and that only God could heal it because doing so was as difficult as raising the dead. Wrong again! Understandably, there were far-fetched rumours of actions that might bring about a miracle.

The man who came to Jesus was almost certainly driven by desperation. He may have heard tales of other people being cured, which led him to believe that Jesus had the ability to heal if he chose. Jesus' reply was disarmingly simple, but it brought with it a healing that was not merely physical, but also social and spiritual.

Until his recent death, Patrick Chazika lived at Silvera House, a project in Zimbabwe that is funded by Christian Aid. While he was living with HIV, he was cared for by a pastoral worker who provided blankets, hospital fees and counselling. He told one of Christian Aid's staff, 'I feel very sad for my son Daniel. I'm so proud of him. He is doing so well at school, but I am worried what will happen to him. I know that I am almost through. Maybe I've just a few days left. If I had good food I might live a few more days, but there's really not enough to eat. Last night we all slept without eating.' Look at some photographs of work that Christian Aid supports to bring care in physical, social and spiritual ways to people who are living with HIV.

Visit www.christianaid.org.uk/hivaids/index.htm and click on the photo galleries. As you do so, ask yourself whether there are connections between the Bible story and what you are reading.

O Jesus Christ, who has known great anguish, be close to all who face death this day in loneliness or fear, and grant them peace. Amen.

July 4   A paralyzed man

Some people were carrying a paralyzed man lying on a bed. When Jesus saw their faith, he said to the paralytic, 'Take heart, son; your sins are forgiven.' Then some of the scribes said to themselves, 'This man is blaspheming.' But Jesus, perceiving their thoughts, said, 'Why do you think evil in your hearts? For which is easier, to say, "Your sins are forgiven", or to say, "Stand up and walk"? But so that you may know that the Son of Man has authority on earth to forgive sins' – he then said to the paralytic – 'Stand up, take your bed and go to your home.' And he stood up and went to his home. When the crowds saw it, they were filled with awe, and they glorified God.

Matthew 9.2–8

Claiming to forgive sins is really easy (it is an invisible process that nobody has to prove). Claiming to heal disabilities is really difficult (because everyone can see with their own eyes whether or not it has succeeded). However, to the scribes (Bible scholars) a claim to be able to forgive sins was really outrageous, because it was an assertion that only God could make. So Jesus was deliberately propelling himself into controversy.

But Jesus had a trick up his sleeve! He was willing to offer proof. In front of their eyes he did the really difficult bit (he healed a paralyzed man). They had to admit that he was someone who could do the impossible. So he left them with no choice but to believe that when he did the controversial bit (announcing that he was God by telling the man that he was forgiven) what seemed impossible might also be true.

When was the last time you saw something happen that, as far as you were concerned, was impossible? Turn it over in your mind and think what it might teach about God and his world.

In our anxiety, you Lord;
in our pain, you Lord;
in our hopes, you Lord.
For healing, you Lord;
for peace of mind, you Lord;
for recovery, you Lord.
Only you, always you, faithfully you.
Blessed are you who heals the sick,
blessed are you who binds up wounds,
blessed are you who forgives sins.
Humbly we look to you for healing, for safe keeping, and for salvation,
for there is no other in whom we can so confidently put our trust. Amen.

July 5   Matthew

As [Jesus] sat at dinner in the house, many tax-collectors and sinners came and were sitting with him and his disciples. When the Pharisees saw this, they said to his disciples, 'Why does your teacher eat with tax-collectors and sinners?' But when he heard this, he said, 'Those who are well have no need of a physician, but those who are sick. Go and learn what this means, "I desire mercy, not sacrifice." For I have come to call not the righteous but sinners.'

Matthew 9.10–13

This reads like Matthew's autobiography. As a tax-collector he would have been hated by the local population. He was a Jew who, by becoming a civil servant, had chosen to collaborate with the occupying Roman powers. Even worse, he would have been regarded as wicked by the religious authorities, the Pharisees, because tax-men were stereotyped as godless people who despised God's laws. The question is: Do life-choices such as those make people bad company for Christians, or make them the very people whom churches should seek to attract?

The slopes around the entrance to my church in South London are perfect for skateboards. Local teenagers hang out there for hours and hours. They smoke cannabis, swear at full volume, and have sex in the alley. This poses a real dilemma for my church: should they take measures to stop them littering the grounds, or should they welcome them to use the skateboarding facilities that the church has unwittingly provided? Who is our church for?

(Incidentally, their names are Tim, Dan, Dan, Stuart, Jon, Mel and Becca. They call me Petey-boy!)

Next time you are walking down a street past a church, stop and have a look at the building. Try and look through the eyes of an outsider at the style, the notice boards, the upkeep, the environment. What message is it giving to an outsider: 'Keep out' or 'This is for you'?

God of all people,
as Christians, give us open hearts,
as families, give us open hands,
as churches, give us open doors,
so that all in our communities may find in Jesus
welcome, hope and good news. Amen.

July 6 Mission workers

Jesus went about all the cities and villages, teaching in their synagogues, and proclaiming the good news of the kingdom, and curing every disease and every sickness. When he saw the crowds, he had compassion for them, because they were harassed and helpless, like sheep without a shepherd. Then he said to his disciples, 'The harvest is plentiful, but the labourers are few; therefore ask the Lord of the harvest to send out labourers into his harvest.'

Matthew 9.35–38

Sheep without a shepherd behave in a curious way. They follow a 'leader' from among themselves in what appears to be an orderly way. The only snag is that their leader doesn't know the way and is as likely to lead them to disaster as to security. I often think of Jesus' description of his society as 'harassed and helpless' when I look at our own. How did we get to a state where we take moral advice from a runner-up on *Big Brother*, or emotional advice from an astrologer in a TV guide? G. K. Chesterton, the twentieth-century novelist, wrote: 'When people stop believing in God, they do not come to believe in nothing; they start believing in anything.'

Meanwhile intractable problems – injustice, violence, pollution – continue to blight our world out of sight (or perhaps out of mind). No wonder Jesus urged us to pray for people to approach this world with God's priorities – as a labourer as well as a leader. That is what distinguishes the way a mission worker operates from the way a celebrity operates. And it applies whether you find yourself in a school, in an office, in the National Health Service, or in a developing world country.

Can you see yourself as a 'labourer in the harvest'? Christian Aid recruits people as volunteers in this country to work in the interests of the world's poorest people. Consider the opportunities by visiting www.christianaid.org.uk/aboutca/vol/vol.htm. The organization Christians Abroad matches needs in the developing world with those in the UK and Ireland who are looking for ways to volunteer overseas. Their website is www.cabroad.org.uk

O Lord, send people who are passionate enough
  to right what is unjust,
until your kingdom come;
send people who are caring enough
  to stand alongside those in pain,
until your will is done;
send people who are humble enough to make known the Saviour,
until the world is won. Amen.

July 7 Samaritan opponents

When the days drew near for [Jesus] to be taken up, he set his face to go to Jerusalem. And he sent messengers ahead of him. On their way they entered a village of the Samaritans to make ready for him; but they did not receive him, because his face was set towards Jerusalem. When his disciples James and John saw it, they said, 'Lord, do you want us to command fire to come down from heaven and consume them?' But he turned and rebuked them.

Luke 9.51–56

This was not the first time that there had been a tense stand-off on the hill outside this Samaritan village. Seven hundred years earlier troops of King Ahaziah had encountered the prophet Elijah there on their way to the shrine of the god Baal. The king had broken his hip and sent the delegation to Baal's soothsayers to find out whether he would recover. Elijah ferociously upbraided them for worshipping a meaningless god and, when they tried to arrest him, called down fire from the sky that incinerated them.

James and John must have recalled this from synagogue-school days. They were furious that the Samaritan villagers had insulted Jesus. ('Have that stupid, half-caste tribe no idea of the significance of this man?') Outraged, they demanded violence. Every eye fell on Jesus: 'How utterly wrong-spirited you are. The spirit within you must never be a spirit of revenge, for it is a Holy Spirit.' And he set his face toward another hill, on which he would submit to violence without a word for the peace of an entire needy world.

In Burundi, Christian Aid's partner JAMAA is working to reconcile Hutus and Tutsis over a decade after brutal violence broke out between the two African tribes. Working with young people who would find themselves on opposite sides if they were fighting, they use football to foster reconciliation. Michel is a Hutu; Abdul is a Tutsi. In other circumstances they would be enemies, but Michel is a defender and Abdul a goalkeeper in the same team. Michel says, 'Because of JAMAA what we believed was impossible has been made possible. We have friends on both sides.' Find out more about Christian Aid's work in Burundi at www.christianaid.org.uk/world/where/eagl/burundp.htm

God send that there may be an end at last. God send that there may be peace again. God in heaven send down peace.

July 1628 diary entry of Hartich Sierk, a peasant during the Hundred Years War

July 8 Mary and Martha

[Jesus] entered a certain village, where a woman named Martha welcomed him into her home. She had a sister named Mary, who sat at the Lord's feet and listened to what he was saying. But Martha was distracted by her many tasks; so she came to him and asked, 'Lord, do you not care that my sister has left me to do all the work by myself? Tell her then to help me.' But the Lord answered her, 'Martha, Martha, you are worried and distracted by many things; there is need of only one thing. Mary has chosen the better part, which will not be taken away from her.'

Luke 10.38–42

It seems as though this was the first meeting between Jesus and two sisters who were to become his close friends. No wonder Martha was so anxious to please! Jesus, however, wanted her to stop impressing him and to start enjoying him. Even though Jesus was present in that home, he did not bring much joy or peace with him – until he was allowed to!

People who support Christian Aid's work tend to be activists. And quite right too, because justice is not going to be achieved for the world's poorest people unless committed people take action! But people who work so hard that they have no time to stop and reflect on what they are doing are losing out as well. Time spent worshipping and appreciating the Saviour of the world is not wasted time: it strengthens and inspires us for the 'many tasks' he calls us to. And in that context we come to prioritize those tasks so that they cease to be a worry and start to be worthwhile achievements.

Make a list of the things you urgently need to do – around your home; for your family and work; as part of your church and campaigning life. Is there too much going on in your life or home to allow Jesus' presence to banish anxiety? Might a change of routine offer you time to enjoy Jesus, rather than busily do things for him?

Speak, Lord, for your servant is listening.

1 Samuel 3.9

July 9   Children

They came to Capernaum; and when [Jesus] was in the house he asked the disciples, 'What were you arguing about on the way?' But they were silent, for on the way they had argued with one another about who was the greatest. He sat down, called the twelve, and said to them, 'Whoever wants to be first must be last of all and servant of all.' Then he took a little child and put it among them; and taking it in his arms, he said to them, 'Whoever welcomes one such child in my name welcomes me, and whoever welcomes me welcomes not me but the one who sent me.'

Mark 9.33–37

As centuries go by, the stories about Jesus seem increasingly charming and less shocking. Today we honour children's rights. They have become consumers whose tastes shape our economy. But in Jesus' world a child was a financial drain that needed harsh discipline to turn it into a hardworking adult. So who does Jesus choose to represent greatness in his new kingdom? A nonentity! I should imagine the disciples found this unsettling.

Jesus was unmasking their greed for power. They may have imagined that the road Jesus was leading them on would end with them governing a country after a coup. They were heading in completely the opposite direction from him. The mark of greatness in Jesus' eyes is not what a person achieves for himself or herself; it is what can be achieved on behalf of someone who is defenceless, needy or despised.

In 1889, inspired by these verses and shocked that the neglect some children suffered at the hands of their parents in the poorest parts of East London was not illegal, the clergyman Benjamin Waugh founded the London Society for the Prevention of Cruelty to Children. He and his inspectors worked tirelessly to rescue children who were suffering abuse. From the first they campaigned for laws to protect vulnerable children. His organization is now the NSPCC, one of the UK's largest charities. Visit their website at www.nspcc.org.uk

We pray to you with folded hands:
    protect, O God, all your children.
May there be no sorrow or false laughter.
Grant to us wisdom; grant to us strength,
    As learners and teachers, show us the way.
May there be no shadows; may there always be light.
We pray to you with folded hands: protect O God all your children. Amen.

A prayer on the wall of the Anganwadi Centre, Kutubkeda Village, West India

July 10 Other faiths

John said to [Jesus], 'Teacher, we saw someone casting out demons in your name, and we tried to stop him, because he was not following us.' But Jesus said, 'Do not stop him; for no one who does a deed of power in my name will be able soon afterwards to speak evil of me. Whoever is not against us is for us. For truly I tell you, whoever gives you a cup of water to drink because you bear the name of Christ will by no means lose the reward.'

Mark 9.38–41

John does not come out of this very well. He was obviously zealous about making Jesus' name known. But he wanted to keep a monopoly on healing people within his own circle of friends. He was more interested in status than in service.

In response, Jesus said some things which challenge all who address the needs of the world. First, think positively – treat everyone who is in sympathy with the aim of eradicating poverty as an ally. Second, think creatively – look for ways to work collaboratively with others, even if they are not from the same faith. Third, think generously – rejoice at every sign of God's grace in action rather than rejecting the contributions of people who do not share every detail of your ideology.

Then Jesus goes further. This should not only affect the way we give, but also the way we receive. The outsider who shows compassion to a Christian (even with something as small as offering a drink) will be rewarded in God's kingdom as richly as the Christian who is doing large-scale good. There is no room for prejudice of any kind in the way God's healing is administered worldwide.

It is Christian Aid's belief that they are called by God to work for and alongside people of all faiths and none, wherever the need is greatest. As part of the Interfaith Humnitarian Group, it brings together people from the Jewish, Muslim and Christian communities. Look up 'places of worship' in the telephone directory and discover where these communities gather in your locality. How could you find out more?

Now may every living thing, young or old, weak or strong, living near or far, known or unknown, living or departed or yet to be born – may every living thing be full of bliss.

Words of the Buddha to use in prayer to God

July 11   Taxes

[The chief priests sent to Jesus] some Pharisees and some Herodians to trap him in what he said. And they came and said to him, 'Teacher, we know that you are sincere, and show deference to no one; for you do not regard people with partiality, but teach the way of God in accordance with truth. Is it lawful to pay taxes to the emperor, or not? Should we pay them, or should we not?' But knowing their hypocrisy, he said to them, 'Why are you putting me to the test? Bring me a denarius and let me see it.' And they brought one. Then he said to them, 'Whose head is this, and whose title?' They answered, 'The emperor's.' Jesus said to them, 'Give to the emperor the things that are the emperor's, and to God the things that are God's.' And they were utterly amazed at him.

Mark 12.13–17

Which side are you on? Mark's first readers were Jews who divided into two groups – those who thought it would be best for Israel to collaborate with Roman rule, and those who plotted to overthrow the occupying power. When his enemies tried to trap him into revealing his attitude to the despised poll tax, Jesus was trapped in three ways. Telling the Jews to pay taxes to their enemy would have made his popularity plummet. Inciting them not to pay would have meant arrest. And hesitating would have made the crowds doubt his sincerity.

But in a brilliant answer, Jesus says everything while appearing to say nothing. Pointing to the image on the coin (Caesar's head and the words 'august and divine son') settled the matter immediately, because Caesar's claim to be a god immediately made the coin itself an evil idol. Jesus had turned the question round to his interrogators: 'It is you who handle these coins, not me! Which side are *you* on?'

When did you last have a look at the coins in your wallet? Get them out now and remind yourself what appears on them. Any idea what the various Latin, Welsh or English quotations mean? Go to www.24carat.co.uk/coininscriptions.html and find out. Do they have anything helpful to say to Christians about how they should use their money?

May Jesus help me to choose sides carefully, to spend money wisely, to make decisions thoughtfully, and so may every use I make of money be done as if it were a gift to him. Amen.

July 12 A poor woman

[Jesus] sat down opposite the treasury, and watched the crowd putting money into the treasury. Many rich people put in large sums. A poor widow came and put in two small copper coins, which are worth a penny. Then he called his disciples and said to them, 'Truly I tell you, this poor widow has put in more than all those who are contributing to the treasury. For all of them have contributed out of their abundance; but she out of her poverty has put in everything she had, all she had to live on.'

Mark 12.41–44

Look at this incident through the eyes of a well-off community. It is about a widow who loved God. She had nothing in worldly terms. And yet she was prepared to give God everything she had. Through these eyes it is a charming story of devotion. We should have just such a love for God.

Now look at the same story through the eyes of a poor community. It is about a religious institution that had no qualms about how much suffering it caused. It increased its own wealth by charging the temple tax regardless of people's ability to pay. So heartless was it that a destitute woman was made to pay an entire penny – 'all she had to live on'. Through these eyes it is a challenging indictment of a church that no longer protects the poor. We should examine our own churches rigorously.

It is unsettling when you see a familiar Bible story from a new viewpoint, isn't it! To whom do these stories belong – rich communities or poor communities? Depending on how you answer, Jesus' words leave you either charmed or challenged.

Cut a piece of paper to the size of a credit card. On it write: 'Out of her poverty she gave everything she had.' Put it in your wallet so that you are reminded of this story from time to time when you are about to spend money.

In the midst of hunger and war
we celebrate the promise of plenty and peace.
In the midst of doubt and despair
we celebrate the promise of faith and hope.
In the midst of sin and decay
we celebrate the promise of salvation and renewal.
In the midst of death on every side
we celebrate the promise of the living Christ.

Words from the Asian Women's Resource Centre for Culture and Theology

July 13   Wealthy women

[Jesus] went on through cities and villages, proclaiming and bringing the good news of the kingdom of God. The twelve were with him, as well as some women who had been cured of evil spirits and infirmities: Mary, called Magdalene, from whom seven demons had gone out, and Joanna, the wife of Herod's steward Chuza, and Susanna, and many others, who provided for them out of their resources.

Luke 8.1–3

We tend to romanticize the circumstances in which Jesus' ministry took place. We imagine that he set off into the country-side like a mythological hero – penniless like Robin Hood, wandering like Hercules, under the open skies like Rob Roy. But that isn't what happened. The Jesus mission was organized, disciplined and (most important) paid for. By whom? Not nameless people who rustled together some onions to make hungry disciples an occasional pot roast, but women who generously did what it took to make Jesus' vision a reality.

We know who some of them were. Joanna was the wealthy wife of the manager of Herod's household. What an irony! The money that her husband earned by maintaining the king's centre of oppression was being redirected via his wife into good news for the poor, healing for the sick, and hope for those who had lost their way through life.

But they weren't all affluent. Mary Magdalene was herself one of the people who had lost their way through life. Rescued from a life of prostitution and calmed from a mental illness, she cannot have been rich. And yet she was following Jesus, and the Bible picks her out as someone who was contributing financially to his project, not just receiving from it.

And Susanna. Nobody knows anything about her. Was she rich or poor? No idea! Perhaps she represents you.

Take a moment to think about whether you could be added to the list of people who are still 'providing for Jesus' ministry out of their resources'. How would that be recognized in what you do and say?

I do not choose wealth; I do not choose poverty –
I choose liberty.
I do not choose merriment; I do not choose misery –
I choose life.
I do not choose success; I do not choose failure –
I choose Jesus.

July 14 Why do people suffer?

There were some present who told [Jesus] about the Galileans whose blood Pilate had mingled with their sacrifices. He asked them, 'Do you think that because these Galileans suffered in this way they were worse sinners than all other Galileans? No, I tell you; but unless you repent, you will all perish as they did. Or those eighteen who were killed when the tower of Siloam fell on them – do you think that they were worse offenders than all the others living in Jerusalem? No, I tell you; but unless you repent, you will all perish just as they did.'

Luke 13.1–5

Cruel speculations persist. People who are HIV-positive are suffering from something that is their own fault. A lie! Those who are poor have got into that state because they are lazy. A lie! These are some of the poisonous thoughts that stop people supporting the work of God's kingdom. There is nothing new about them.

Pilate (a vicious little sadist) had arranged for Jewish Passover pilgrims to be butchered in their own temple. The messengers who brought the news to Jesus were inviting him to say, 'Bad things happen to people who are sinful.' But he didn't. Collapsing towers do not kill people because they are wicked, but because they have the misfortune to be caught up in tragic events. Equally, people who have a disability are complete, wonderful men and women made in the image of God – nothing has happened before or since their birth to single them out as sinful.

But there is a sting in Jesus' tale! Just when you expect him to say, 'All humans, joyful or suffering, are good', he says the opposite. No one is perfect. Everyone needs God's forgiveness. The problem of suffering is not that occasionally we are all a bit like the suffering pilgrims; it is that occasionally we are all a bit like like the cruel Pilate.

Consider the price of medicines. Look up the World Health Organisation survey at www.who.int/en. A Tanzanian would have to work 500 hours to pay for tuberculosis treatment; a Swiss person just ninety minutes. The blatant injustice of that is one of the sins of which the world needs to repent.

No single teardrop lies hidden from you, my God, my Creator, my Deliverer. No, nor any part thereof. Alleluia!

Simeon of Emesa, who lived as a hermit in the deserts of Syria in the sixth century

July 15   Grudging do-gooders

On one occasion when Jesus was going to the house of a leader of the Pharisees to eat a meal on the sabbath, they were watching him closely. Just then, in front of him, there was a man who had dropsy. And Jesus asked the lawyers and Pharisees, 'Is it lawful to cure people on the sabbath, or not?' But they were silent. So Jesus took him and healed him, and sent him away. Then he said to them, 'If one of you has a child or an ox that has fallen into a well, will you not immediately pull it out on a sabbath day?' And they could not reply to this.

Luke 14.1–6

Even a Pharisee might have admitted that in an absolute emergency (such as your own child falling down a hole) a breach of the law was permissible to save a precious life. Jesus was persuading his critics that a correct understanding of the sabbath made it the most appropriate day of all on which to serve God by joyfully liberating the frustrated and eagerly healing the sick. Their problem was not just a wrong attitude to the sabbath; they had a grudging attitude to the whole business of doing good.

There are two attitudes to the work we undertake on behalf of the world's poor. We can see it as something we grit our teeth to do because, although it is a costly and tiring effort, the world is in a state of emergency. Or we can approach it as a liberation we bring joyfully and a healing we offer eagerly. What is it that motivates you to do good?

For Jesus, the sabbath lasted from Friday evening to Saturday evening. For Christians it is a Sunday, the day of Jesus' resurrection. Mark out next Sunday as a day in which to do something good with a happy heart. Choose something that can be done not because your religion requires it of you, but just because the world is better when good people do good things!

Lord Jesus, set my heart on doing good –
merrily and eagerly,
tenderly and carefully,
madly and passionately –
with all the gladness that flooded the great, green earth
with heart and healing
on that Sunday when life came leaping from the tomb. Amen.

July 16 A place of honour

When [Jesus] noticed how the guests chose the places of honour, he told them a parable. 'When you are invited by someone to a wedding banquet, do not sit down at the place of honour, in case someone more distinguished than you has been invited by your host; and the host who invited both of you may come and say to you, "Give this person your place", and then in disgrace you would start to take the lowest place. But when you are invited, go and sit down at the lowest place, so that when your host comes, he may say to you, "Friend, move up higher"; then you will be honoured in the presence of all who sit at the table with you. For all who exalt themselves will be humbled, and those who humble themselves will be exalted.'

Luke 14.7–11

The statue of a deposed tyrant crashes from its plinth and local people dance for joy. Words from the song of Jesus' mother come to mind: 'My soul glorifies the Lord and my spirit rejoices . . . He has brought down rulers from their thrones, but has lifted up the humble.'

I wonder whether Mary sang that song to her toddling child. It is a song of dramatic, world-changing events. But its themes are echoed here when Jesus gives quiet, domesticated advice. We have a God who is passionately concerned about international justice and power. Of course we do! But he is equally concerned about our personal values and the way they are revealed as we relate to people in church, at work, or just around the dinner table.

What you seek in the wide world, begin to model among your own friends.

Spend a while thinking about how important you are. Go to the kitchen. Pour water into a bowl. Stick your finger in the water. Then take it out and look at the hole you have made.

I believe in God, who is great and mighty beyond
*   all understanding;*
I believe in God, who knows the number of the stars;
I believe in God, who heals the broken-hearted and binds up
*   their wounds;*
I believe in God, who has a special place for the humble;
I believe in God, and therefore I sing with thanksgiving.
For he is he.
And I?
I am only I.

Inspired by Psalm 147.1–6

July 17   Welcome the poor

[Jesus said to his host,] 'When you give a luncheon or a dinner, do not invite your friends or your brothers or your relatives or rich neighbours, in case they may invite you in return, and you would be repaid. But when you give a banquet, invite the poor, the crippled, the lame, and the blind. And you will be blessed, because they cannot repay you, for you will be repaid at the resurrection of the righteous.'

Luke 14.12–14

I love almost everything about Christmas, but there is one aspect that I could do without. It involves guessing the value of what your friends might give you, making adjustments to account for whether they are single or a couple, buying a present that costs the same, then crossing your fingers that you will not be trapped into the embarrassment of being given a present by someone when you have nothing to give back. It's ridiculous, isn't it! And it could not possibly be further from the open-handed spirit of hospitality that Jesus recommends here.

In the Democratic Republic of Congo, Jacqueline Kakubi is bringing up her four orphaned grandchildren. The youngest is three and the oldest seventeen. Five years ago their parents became too ill with HIV to care for them. Jacqueline had no hesitation in opening her home to them, and they moved in. She is seventy-four. At an age when she might have expected to slow down and be taken care of herself, she is now the family's main breadwinner. She says, 'God has allowed me to live this long, so I have hope in him.' She collects and sells firewood to pay the rent, but gets the support she needs to care for the children from Amo-Congo, an organization that is funded by Christian Aid.

I cannot imagine what kind of spirit it takes to provide hospitality in such a selfless way. All I know is that some truly wonderful things happen in Africa and I urgently need to learn from them.

I should imagine that Jesus' straightforward advice gives you a sufficient motivation for action without me adding anything!

Make us worthy, Lord, to serve our fellow men and women throughout the world, who live and die in poverty and hunger. Give them, through our hands, their daily bread this day. And by our understanding and love, give them peace and joy. Amen.

Mother Teresa of Calcutta (1910–97)

July 18 How long, O Lord?

The oracle that the prophet Habakkuk saw:
O Lord, how long shall I cry for help, and you will not listen?
Or cry to you 'Violence!' and you will not save?
Why do you make me see wrongdoing and look at trouble?
Destruction and violence are before me;
strife and contention arise.
So the law becomes slack and justice never prevails.
The wicked surround the righteous –
therefore judgement comes forth perverted.

Habakkuk 1.1–4

My six-year-old godson is the world's worst travelling companion. When I took him to Alton Towers he asked, 'How much longer?' before the car had left the drive. But in the voice of Habakkuk, 600 years before Jesus, we recognize not just impatience, but true distress. The things he bewails are still familiar today: violence between nations; the injustice of one's own people; the perplexity of not seeing God act as the Bible promises he will; the agonizing silence of unanswered prayers.

Habakkuk battles with the great question that echoes down the centuries: why does the good and just God in whom we have put our faith allow things to happen which are neither good nor just? The book is a dialogue. Tomorrow's extract shows that God does reply, but the fact that the prophet keeps answering back suggests that they are not replies that fully satisfy him. How familiar!

By the time we reached the theme park my godson had asked, 'Are we there yet?' about twenty times. I don't think he ever lost faith that I knew where I was going and that the rollercoasters would be worth the journey – but it was a close thing.

Listen to a news broadcast or read a newspaper with extra concentration today. Count how many items leave you asking Habakkuk's question, 'How long, O Lord?'

I believe, I believe, I believe with a perfect faith
in the coming of the Messiah;
in the coming of the Messiah I believe.
And even though he tarry I nevertheless believe.
Even though he tarry, yet I believe in him.
I believe, I believe, I believe.

Written on a wall of the Warsaw ghetto by an unknown Jew

July 19   God's ways and our ways

Look at the nations, and see! Be astonished! Be astounded!
For a work is being done in your days that you would not believe
    if you were told.
For I am rousing the Chaldeans, that fierce and impetuous nation,
    who march through the breadth of the earth to seize dwellings
      not their own.
Dread and fearsome are they; their justice and dignity proceed from themselves.
Their horses are swifter than leopards, more menacing than wolves at dusk;
their horses charge.
Their horsemen come from far away; they fly like an eagle swift to devour.
They all come for violence.

Habakkuk 1.5–9

Habakkuk had asked, 'How much longer will violence and injustice persist before you act?' This is God's answer. But it cannot possibly be the one he hoped for. God is saying, 'I do plan to act, but when it happens you might not like what you see.' Sure enough, Habakkuk saw God's plan fulfilled – it was decisive, it was timely, and it was perplexing. The ruthless Babylonian empire was on the march. In 597 BC Jerusalem, the capital city of Judah, fell into enemy hands and ten years later it was destroyed.

It seemed a catastrophe. It is only now, hundreds of years later, that we can see how events that shaped God's people – triumphs and downfalls – fitted into God's perfect plan for the coming of Jesus, God's clearest communication and ultimate solution.

Christian Aid works in the land where Habakkuk once lived, and supports partner organizations that seek justice where wrong seems prevalent, and reconciliation where there has been hatred. They need continual support if they are to recognize their work as fitting into God's plan for the future of his world while a new eruption of violence is a daily fear.

There is a gallery of superb photographs of Christian Aid's work in Israel and the Occupied Palestinian Territories at
www.christianaid.org.uk/news/gallery/peace/image1.htm
    Pray about what you see.

We pray to the Lord Jesus,
great shepherd of the flocks,
for peace to surround Jerusalem,
for peace wherever men come bent on violence,
for peace in our homes and our families,
so that all may go their ways with justice and security,
and dance where soldiers marched.

July 20   Why does God tolerate evil?

Are you not from of old, O Lord my God, my Holy One?
You shall not die.
O Lord, you have marked them for judgement;
and you, O Rock, have established them for punishment.
Your eyes are too pure to behold evil,
and you cannot look on wrongdoing;
why do you look on the treacherous,
and are silent when the wicked swallow those more righteous than they? . . .
I will stand at my watchpost, and station myself on the rampart;
I will keep watch to see what he will say to me,
and what he will answer concerning my complaint.

Habakkuk 1.12–13; 2.1

Habakkuk is bewildered. The everlasting God will respond to injustice by allowing an even bigger catastrophe? Surely he must have misheard!

But there is a realism about what he reveals. There is no more peace or justice in the world today than there was 3,000 years ago. Politicians have to sound positive about international relations, but thoughtful Christians still watch the world, still look to God to be what we believe him to be, and still wrestle with the difficulties.

In and around Jenin, in what was Habukkuk's homeland, the Palestinian Agricultural Relief Committee supports small farmers and rural women, working with them to improve their ability to make a living from farming. It is doing vital work, and yet all this good and godly activity could not prevent its director, Dr Samer Al Ahmad, being injured by a tank shell when he ventured out to buy food at the end of a three-day curfew. Why does God tolerate wicked things disrupting righteous work? We stand at our watch and wait to see what he will say.

Christian Aid is a partner to the Palestinian Agricultural Relief Committee, supporting and funding them. Find out more about their work from their website www.pal-arc.org

O Lord my God, my Holy One, I pray for all the organizations that Christian Aid supports in the Occupied Palestinian Territories. Prosper their staff, strengthen their residents, and rebuild their hope. And so may the country of your birth once again become a place of hope and healing. Amen.

July 21 The glorious plan

Then the Lord answered me and said:
Write the vision; make it plain on tablets, so that a runner may
read it.
For there is still a vision for the appointed time; it speaks of the
end, and does not lie.
If it seems to tarry, wait for it; it will surely come, it will not delay . . .
'Alas for you who build a town by bloodshed, and found a city on iniquity!'
Is it not from the Lord of hosts that peoples labour only to feed the flames,
and nations weary themselves for nothing?
But the earth will be filled with the knowledge of the glory of the Lord,
as the waters cover the sea.

Habakkuk 2.2–3, 12–14

At last comes God's reassurance to Habakkuk: 'I am prepared to reveal some of my intentions, and you will be part of communicating them, so write this down. There is a definite plan and an appointed time for the end of these dreadful things. I am not going to reveal the timing to you, but you can trust me.'

This is true both for our personal troubles and for the global tragedies in which nations exhaust themselves with the sheer effort of oppressing others. God's intention is the inevitable emergence of good from hardship – maybe not with speed, but with certainty. His design is for a world as full of his glory as the sea is full of water – work on such a huge scale that we can barely glimpse his plan.

So be patient! Your work in tackling poverty now is building toward a time when God's justice will be made complete. Like Habakkuk, see yourself as a herald running with news of that certain future.

Look back on your life. Can you identify things that have happened (or failed to happen) which you now recognize as God preparing you for what you are currently doing? If the answer is yes, thank him; if the answer is no, ask him to help you trust.

March we forth in the strength of God
with the banner of Christ unfurled,
That the light of the glorious gospel of truth may shine
throughout the world,
Fight we the fight with sorrow and sin to set its captives free,
That the earth may be filled with the glory of God as the waters cover the sea.

Arthur Ainger (1841–1919), from the hymn 'God is working his purpose out'

July 22 Let all the earth be silent

What use is an idol once its maker has shaped it – a cast image,
  a teacher of lies?
For its maker trusts in what has been made,
though the product is only an idol that cannot speak!
Alas for you who say to the wood, 'Wake up!' to silent stone,
  'Rouse yourself!'
Can it teach? See, it is gold and silver plated, and there is no breath in it at all.
But the Lord is in his holy temple; let all the earth keep silence before him!

Habakkuk 2.18–20

How are we to behave during the long wait for God to act in response to the world's injustice? In different parts of his book, Habakkuk talks about those who try to seal themselves off from noticing the distress of the world by accumulating so much personal gain they they never need to come into contact with suffering. And of those for whom escapism is the only way of avoiding the issues (alcohol is the method he mentions). And of those who, having made a fortune at the expense of others, glorify the system that enables it (he compares them with fishermen who pillage the sea of every last fish and then worship their nets).

In today's verses Habakkuk warns that some will give up waiting for God and turn their worship to other things – inanimate things that shimmer with gold and silver (or bleep or speed or play music or flash lights, and gather dust in a hundred ways).

Objects that humans have created can be valuable in the quest to alleviate poverty. But in the end only a change of heart can bring lasting justice, not a change of technology. And it is an encounter with the holy God which changes hearts.

At some point during today, seek out silence. Try to find a place without the clatter of human voices or the buzz of machines. In the silence, remind yourself of the size and power of the holy God. Then tell him what your hopes, fears and priorities are at the moment.

Let all mortal flesh keep silence,
  and with fear and trembling stand;
Ponder nothing earthly-minded, for with blessing in his hand
Christ our God on earth descendeth, our full homage to demand.

Gerard Moultrie, translating the ancient 'Liturgy of St James'

July 23   Unexpected joy

I hear, and I tremble within; my lips quiver at the sound.
Rottenness enters into my bones,
   and my steps tremble beneath me.
I wait quietly for the day of calamity to come upon the people
   who attack us.
Though the fig tree does not blossom, and no fruit is on the vines;
though the produce of the olive fails and the fields yield no food;
though the flock is cut off from the fold and there is no herd in the stalls,
yet I will rejoice in the Lord; I will exult in the God of my salvation.
God, the Lord, is my strength; he makes my feet like the feet of a deer,
and makes me tread upon the heights.

Habakkuk 3.16–19

Here at the end of Habakkuk's book is one of the Bible's most unexpected passages. Knowing that he is surrounded by suffering, Habakkuk finds himself first in awe, then patiently trusting in God, then inexplicably overtaken by joy, so much so that he feels like skipping childishly across the hills.

It answers a question that anyone who understands the extent of the world's injustice asks from time to time – is it possible to be happy once one knows about the tragedy unfolding elsewhere on the planet? And Habbakuk's answer is 'Yes'. Life is full of potential for joy. But it hasn't been won easily. Looking back over the book, we can trace the attitudes that led Habbakuk to that position. First he reminded himself what God had done for his people in the past. Then he placed himself resolutely on the side of justice. Standing in a hushed wonder before God followed. And finally he prayed that the God of power would also be merciful.

This is a pattern for all Christians – true joy in the goodness of life, not taken lightly or selfishly, but nevertheless there to seize with all the strength God gives.

In the margin write your personal twenty-first-century equivalents of the barren fig tree, the bare fields, the empty sheep pen, and so on. Read the passage again in your own updated version and reflect on its challenge.

My Father, I thank you with all my heart
that though the human condition speaks to me
of hopes unfulfilled, of the mark missed,
the bloom fading, the chill of autumn, and beyond that the dark,
yet the Christian condition is joy.

Timothy Dudley Smith

July 24   Great is your faithfulness

[God] has made my teeth grind on gravel, and made me cower
*   in ashes;*
my soul is bereft of peace; I have forgotten what happiness is;
so I say, 'Gone is my glory, and all that I had hoped for from
*   the Lord.'*
The thought of my affliction and my homelessness is wormwood and gall!
My soul continually thinks of it and is bowed down within me.
But this I call to mind, and therefore I have hope:
The steadfast love of the Lord never ceases, his mercies never come to an end;
they are new every morning; great is your faithfulness.

Lamentations 3.16–23

Nobody knows who wrote the five poems known as Lamentations, but we can guess when they were composed. They lament the destruction of Jerusalem in 587 BC. All that Habakkuk anticipated had come to pass. The poems grieve over the suffering of loved ones and the destruction of a beloved homeland, but agonize over something worse – God seems to have rejected his people because of their sin. The poems are still read aloud in synagogues at this time of year to mark the anniversary of the catastrophe.

We have cheated the poet of his opportunity to show the depth of his desolation, because today's extract joins the poem at a turning point. At his low point the writer's complete loss of hope acts as trigger to bring him to his spiritual senses, as if despair at his own helplessness leaves him nowhere else to go but to God. To recall that God is still sustaining life and consciously to seek a daily reason to thank him does not spring easily from the human heart – it is an act of will that only the grace of God can uphold. And yet remarkably it is a sentiment heard from oppressed communities of the world again and again.

On the next seven pages of the book write the name of the day of the week. Each morning seek out a reason to be thankful to God, even if it requires an act of will, and write it in the margin.

Train us, Lord, to fling ourselves upon the impossible, for beyond the impossible is your grace and your presence.

A prayer of Luis Espinal (1932–79), a priest murdered while investigating activities of the military dictatorship of Bolivia

July 25   Hope in the face of despair

'The Lord is my portion,' says my soul,
    'therefore I will hope in him.'
The Lord is good to those who wait for him,
    to the soul that seeks him.
It is good that one should wait quietly
    for the salvation of the Lord.
It is good for one to bear the yoke in youth,
to sit alone in silence when the Lord has imposed it,
to put one's mouth to the dust (there may yet be hope),
to give one's cheek to the smiter, and be filled with insults.

Lamentations 3.24–30

These verses are very personal, and not everyone will be able to share the attitude that the poet adopted in the face of his sorrow. To be so positive in the face of such suffering is remarkable:

• He decides that if his relationship with God is intact, there must be hope worth waiting for.
• He searches the Bible for inspiration ('the Lord is good to those who wait for him' is a quotation from a psalm).
• He resolves to be patient, waiting quietly for God to save him from distress.
• There is a resignation that prompts him to sit in silence at the Lord's bidding.
• And yet there is a rebellion that leads him to stick his neck out in defiance of those who are persecuting him – who, after all, is the one who is filled with disgrace, the oppressor or the oppressed?

Listen prayerfully to a news broadcast today. If any of the items report distress or suffering, ask yourself – is this a case for quiet resignation or for active defiance?

O Lord, remember not only the men and women of goodwill, but also those of ill will. But do not only remember the suffering they have inflicted on us, remember the fruits we bought thanks to this suffering – our comradeship, our loyalty, our humility, the courage, the generosity, the greatness of heart which has grown out of all this. And when they come to judgement, let all the fruits that we have borne be their forgiveness. Amen, amen, amen.

Found written on a piece of wrapping paper near the body of a dead child in Ravensbrück concentration camp in 1945

July 26   Rights for prisoners

The Lord will not reject for ever.
Although he causes grief, he will have compassion
according to the abundance of his steadfast love;
for he does not willingly afflict or grieve anyone.
When all the prisoners of the land are crushed under foot,
when human rights are perverted in the presence of the Most High,
when one's case is subverted – does the Lord not see it?

Lamentations 3.31–36

Three things today give substance to a Christian's refusal to despair:

- Suffering is only a temporary experience.
- God is by nature merciful.
- His heart is resolutely set against abuse of the most vulnerable, even of prisoners.

Marie Yolene Gilles works for the National Coalition for Haitian Rights. She visits the scandalously overcrowded prisons of Haiti to insist that criminals (particularly political criminals who have not been accused of a crime) live in conditions that fulfil agreed minimum standards. It is controversial work. In 1989 her home was attacked by order of the then President, Prosper Avril. The house was ransacked. Her colleague was killed. Marie escaped by a back door and went into hiding. She emerged in 1990 after the President was overthrown, was reunited with her young daughters, and went back to her work monitoring human rights abuses in prisons. And one of the first people whose human rights she was called upon to defend was Prosper Avril, the politician who gave the orders to have her killed the year before.

Who will speak up for those unable to speak about the suffering in their lives? Wherever men, women and children are denied their rights to freedom, to justice, or to worship 'the Most High', God looks on with deep compassion.

Find out more about Christian Aid's partners in Haiti at www.christianaid.org.uk/world/where/lac/haitip.htm

O holy God,
your heart rejoices in light, in freedom and in joy,
and so does mine.
This world can be a place of darkness, of bondage and of pain,
and my heart grieves.
Give me courage to oppose all that is evil,
so that my voice speaks what my heart feels.

July 27   Return to the Lord

Who can command and have it done, if the Lord has not
*   ordained it?*
Is it not from the mouth of the Most High that
*   good and bad come?*
Why should any who draw breath complain about the
*   punishment of their sins?*
Let us test and examine our ways, and return to the Lord.
Let us lift up our hearts as well as our hands to God in heaven.

Lamentations 3.37–41

It is undeniable that God has set in motion a world in which both calamities and good things happen. Humans have a lamentable record of putting calamities for others out of their minds, if the result has been good things for themselves.

Confessing what we have done wrong to God will leave us at peace with him for ever. But actions, even when God has forgiven them, have consequences. We need to be realistic about the fact that it will not turn back the clock and make the impact of the sin disappear from the lives of those who have been harmed. There are people in the developing world whose lives have been impoverished by our reckless use of energy, our relentless drive to have cheaper goods in our shops, and our determination to have a comfortable life.

To 'return to the Lord' requires not only confession, but also commitment to a new way of life.

Take an action that begins, albeit in a small way, to compensate those in countries far away for the damage that has been done to their lives by sinful things in our lives.

We are people who are eager to do well, but slow to do good.
We are people who are eager to save time, but slow to give time.
We are people who are eager to improve our lives, but slow to
*   improve our world.*
And still the world's resources are enjoyed by few, not shared
*   by all.*
Let us test and examine our ways, and return to the Lord.
In your mercy, Lord, forgive us. Amen.

July 28　A living sacrifice

I appeal to you therefore, brothers and sisters, by the mercies of God, to present your bodies as a living sacrifice, holy and acceptable to God, which is your spiritual worship. Do not be conformed to this world, but be transformed by the renewing of your minds, so that you may discern what is the will of God – what is good and acceptable and perfect.

Romans 12.1–2

Somebody told me last week that he felt he was trapped in a 'spiral of wealth'. Its material effects are completely different from the spiral of poverty, but it stifles and entangles with the same inevitability. It sets us on a path through life on which we constantly need to seek a slightly larger salary, a slightly more comfortable home, slightly more complex gadgets, slightly more up-to-date possessions. We excuse ourselves in a hundred ways (saving time, providing for a family, needing space) but in many cases it happens simply because the world has squeezed us into its mould. It takes a strong will to decide, 'I believe that God is calling me to something less.' In fact, more than a strong will; it takes a 'renewed mind'.

This letter, which Paul wrote to the church in Rome, has page after page of explanation of how the life, death and resurrection of Jesus have brought all the glories of eternal life with God to his followers. We join it at the point where he begins to explain what practical difference this should make to Christians. Paul makes it clear that worship is not a matter of singing and praying; it is shown by what we do with our lives and 'bodies'. There seem to be three alternatives – adopting the standards by which the rest of society lives, inventing our own rules, or trying to work out the 'good, acceptable, perfect' ways of God.

Get rid of something you don't need! Take books and CDs to a charity shop, bottles to a recycling bank, duplicate kitchen equipment to a shelter. Cancel repayment of a loan, put a grudge out of your mind, forget about a disagreement. Revisit plans you have for the future and investigate whether there is a simpler option.

Lord God,
lead us away from the ways of the world,
and into the simplicity of the Saviour,
so that we may know what it means to be free. Amen.

July 29   Use your gifts

[Do not] think of yourself more highly than you ought to think, but think with sober judgement, each according to the measure of faith that God has assigned. For as in one body we have many members, and not all the members have the same function, so we, who are many, are one body in Christ, and individually we are members one of another. We have gifts that differ according to the grace given to us: prophecy, in proportion to faith; ministry, in ministering; the teacher, in teaching; the exhorter, in exhortation; the giver, in generosity; the leader, in diligence; the compassionate, in cheerfulness.

Romans 12.3–8

'God has created me to do some definite service; he has committed some work to me which he has not committed to another. I have my mission – I may never know it in this life, but I shall be told it in the next.

'I am a link in a chain, a bond of connection between persons. He has not created me for naught. I shall do good. I shall do his work. I shall be an angel of peace, a preacher of truth in my own place while not intending it, if I do but keep his commandments. Therefore I will trust him.

'Whatever, wherever I am, I can never be thrown away. If I am in sickness, my sickness may serve him; in perplexity, my perplexity may serve him; if I am in sorrow, my sorrow may serve him. He does nothing in vain. He knows what he is about. He may take away my friends. He may throw me among strangers. He may make me feel desolate, make my spirit sink, hide my future from me – still he knows what he is about.'

Cardinal John Henry Newman (1801–90)

There are two ways of using your gifts. One – wait until a church asks you to help and then do it grudgingly. Two – analyze whether you have space in your life to be generous with the things God has made you good at. Which makes more sense?

Dearest Lord, teach me to serve thee as thou deservest: to give and not to count the cost, to fight and not to heed the wounds, to toil and not to seek for rest, to labour and not to seek reward save that of knowing that I do thy will.

Ignatius of Loyola (1491–1556)

July 30 Sincere love

Let love be genuine; hate what is evil, hold fast to what is good; love one another with mutual affection; outdo one another in showing honour. Do not lag in zeal, be ardent in spirit, serve the Lord.

Romans 12.9–11

Diana Campbell is a nurse with Jamaica AIDS Support, an organization funded by Christian Aid, which provides care for people living with HIV and runs projects to educate young people how to protect themselves from the virus. Diana says this about her work:

'You cannot just preach love. You have to show love, to go down into the Valley of the Lepers and not scorn the people you find there. You have to go to the depths to be with the person who is rejected and forsaken. You have to pray and ask God for a heart to be able to do this. Good things on this earth are not generally easy.

'As Christians we need to share whatever God has blessed us with, be it money, time, food or love. If you see people with HIV you need to comfort them. If the Church does not show and do love, how can people know God?'

Find out more about Christian Aid's work in Jamaica at www.christianaid.org.uk/world/where/lac/jamaicap.htm

In the face of a tragedy we can barely comprehend,
we cry to you, O Lord, for:
protection for the healthy,
courage for the frightened,
a change of heart for the prejudiced,
consolation for the bereaved,
strength for the carers,
good news for the poor,
and, in the goodness of your mercy,
one day a cure. Amen.

July 31   Joyful, patient, faithful, sharing

Rejoice in hope, be patient in suffering, persevere in prayer. Contribute to the needs of the saints; extend hospitality to strangers.

Romans 12.12–13

Forty thousand people in Jamaica live with HIV, and thousands more are orphaned because of the virus. Jamaica AIDS Support, which has been partnered by Christian Aid since it was formed ten years ago, runs programmes of health care and education. Its nurses visit those who are HIV-positive in their homes, and JAS organizes support groups and a one-to-one 'buddy' system giving friendship to people who might be ostracized. Diana Campbell is one of the nurses:

'My hope is in Christ. God is my number one priority. Where he leads me I will follow. My other hope is that I can help children and travel. I want to help others and be an ambassador for people with HIV and AIDS. I want to live, be good and show love. And one day God will wipe away all our tears.

'[When people learn that they are HIV-positive] they are rejected by their families, so they need support. Many families placed their relatives in the JAS hospice and left. We became the only family they had. The patients would be upset by this and take it out on us – so we got sad. They need someone to say, "I love you". We are giving them the love they really need from their families.

'As a nurse I care for them, bathe and feed them. But as a Christian I know there is a Supernatural Person really in charge and people can choose to reach out to him for his comfort.'

Wear a red AIDS ribbon in support of the work of people like Diana Campbell, and in solidarity with those who suffer from the disease. For other ways in which you can side with those who combat HIV, visit www.stopaidscampaign.org.uk

All-powerful Lord, have compassion on all who live with HIV. Inspire the nurses who work to ease pain. Guide the scientists who seek a cure. Lead the pharmaceutical companies to be generous in making help available to the poor. And may your Creative Spirit bring about the end of AIDS, for which we long and pray. Amen.

Paul Waddell

August 1 Living in harmony

Bless those who persecute you; bless and do not curse them. Rejoice with those who rejoice, weep with those who weep. Live in harmony with one another; do not be haughty, but associate with the lowly; do not claim to be wiser than you are.

Romans 12.14–16

It is possible to read these words and be so familiar with the concepts that they don't have any impact on you. So take time to make them personal, one phrase at a time, to you, your family, your work, or your church:

- Someone makes your life complicated or drains you. What is his or her name? Are you able to register the good things about him or her as well as cursing the difficulties?
- Someone has had a joyful success. Who? Are you genuinely glad for them, or jealous?
- Someone is in crisis. Yes? An embarrassment to avoid or an opportunity to engage?
- A recent argument. Can you attach a name to this? What are you doing to restore harmony?
- Someone in financial or social need. Who do you know that fits the description? You help practically, of course, but do you help with real friendship or at a distance?

If, after thinking about these, you feel that you are not as wise as you claimed you were, that is a good starting point for making yourself useful to God.

All these instructions involve personal relationships with people at a point at which relating is not easy. Make a start! Focus on one person and take one action which will improve their life in a very small way.

Peace between neighbours, peace between kindred,
Peace between lovers, in the love of the King of life.
Peace between person and person,
*   peace between wife and husband,*
Peace between woman and children,
*   the peace of Christ above all peace.*
Bless O Christ my face – let my face bless every thing;
Bless O Christ mine eye – let mine eye bless all it sees.

Ancient Scottish Gaelic blessing

August 2 Overcome evil with good

Do not repay anyone evil for evil, but take thought for what is noble in the sight of all. If it is possible, so far as it depends on you, live peaceably with all. Beloved, never avenge yourselves, but leave room for the wrath of God; for it is written, 'Vengeance is mine, I will repay, says the Lord.' No, 'If your enemies are hungry, feed them; if they are thirsty, give them something to drink; for by doing this you will heap burning coals on their heads.' Do not be overcome by evil, but overcome evil with good.

Romans 12.17–21

The aim of the Sanayee Development Foundation is to contribute to reconciliation and peace-building in Afghanistan and neighbouring Pakistan. With the support and funding of Christian Aid, about 15,000 young people benefit from its programmes, which include peace education in refugee schools and English language courses. Thousands more read its publications.

One of the SDF projects is the *Rainbow* magazine, which is enormously popular among children. During the years when the Taliban governed Afghanistan, it gave them virtually their only access to entertainment. It is brightly coloured and full of uplifting stories. And now, with its emphasis on practical peacemaking, it is extremely influential in the development of young minds.

One of its keenest readers, and would-be contributors, is Yalda Shams. She is twelve, and goes to Lecy Mehri School in Herat, Afghanistan. She is one of the few girls who received an education during the years when the Taliban governed the country. That is because she cut her hair off, dressed in boys' clothes, and kept quiet. Now 6,000 girls are at Yalda's school. The challenge for all children of Yalda's generation will be to seek positive ways of addressing evil, where previous generations have repaid evil with violence.

Up-to-date information about the work which Christian Aid supports in Afghanistan can be found at
www.christianaid.org.uk/world/where/meeca/afghanip.htm

O Prince of Peace,
confound all those who seek
to change the world through violence;
prosper all those whose hearts are set upon reconciliation;
and teach us, when confronted by evil,
how to respond with both the strength and the sacrifice of Christ. Amen.

August 3   Authorities

Let every person be subject to the governing authorities; for there is no authority except from God, and those authorities that exist have been instituted by God. Therefore whoever resists authority resists what God has appointed, and those who resist will incur judgement. For rulers are not a terror to good conduct, but to bad. Do you wish to have no fear of the authority? Then do what is good, and you will receive its approval; for it is God's servant for your good. But if you do what is wrong, you should be afraid, for the authority does not bear the sword in vain!

Romans 13.1–4

The Bible repeatedly tells us that all who exercise authority do so only with God's permission. He has put them there to do good. God is sovereign, not presidents, generals or chief executives. These verses give us hope that the fallible humans who have power over us, whether we chose them or whether they took their positions by force, do not have the last word.

But this does not mean that all who exercise authority do so in the way God would wish. How should we respond to evil leaders? And what should we do when a responsible leader makes a decision that runs counter to our understanding of God's will for this world? Other parts of the Bible suggest that there are occasions on which 'we must obey God rather than human authorities' (Acts 5.29). Sometimes those who worship God are called upon to declare defiantly that those in authority are wrong.

The key is to determine before God what is 'good conduct'. In doing what we sincerely believe to be good, we can live without fear of disappointing God or compromising his values.

Make a mental list of all who are in a position of authority that impacts on your life. Start with those you know (a line manager or head teacher) and work your way up to national government. Don't forget directors of businesses or the media. For whom should you be praying today?

King of all kings, I pray for all whom you have called to exercise authority. To the leaders of the nations give honesty, and a desire to serve rather than be served. To the leaders of society give courage, and a voice to speak the truth. And to me, whenever I am able to influence someone for good, give a love like Jesus had. Amen.

August 4   Paying tax

One must be subject [to those in authority], not only because of wrath but also because of conscience. For the same reason you also pay taxes, for the authorities are God's servants, busy with this very thing. Pay to all what is due them – taxes to whom taxes are due, revenue to whom revenue is due, respect to whom respect is due, honour to whom honour is due.

Romans 13.5–7

Should we obey someone in authority if their actions seem to be contrary to the ways of God? Don't let fear of being punished (or 'wrath') dictate your decision what to do, but rather be guided by a determination to do what is righteous (according to your 'conscience').

As an example of what he means, Paul addresses the tempting possibility of deciding that the money we give in taxes to human authorities could be better used if it were given directly to churches, charities and anyone else who furthers the work of the kingdom of God. (Tempting, both because it seems a godly thing to suggest, and also because it might save a few quid!) But Paul is clear. God has chosen not to govern the world by his direct command, but to keep chosen human beings 'busy' making decisions on his behalf. They deserve our respect, there is a place for honouring the work they do, and we should not withhold the resources they need to organize society in a way that is good for it.

Christian Aid supports several organizations that hold those in authority to account for the way they deal with money. The Uganda Debt Network monitors what is happening to funds that have become available to the authorities in Uganda through the cancellation of debt, seeking to ensure that it is not wasted but used for projects from which the poorest people will benefit. Advocacy and lobbying against corruption is as vital to the development of poor countries as digging wells. Find out more at www.udn.or.ug

We lift before you, Lord God, our brothers and sisters who seek to serve you faithfully in countries where government is corrupt or chaotic. We ask that you will strengthen them, encourage them, and show them what is right. We pray that we may learn from them to do what is best, instead of what is easiest, and to do what is good even when we are fearful. Amen.

August 5 Let no debts remain

Owe no one anything, except to love one another; for the one who loves another has fulfilled the law. The commandments, 'You shall not commit adultery; You shall not murder; You shall not steal; You shall not covet'; and any other commandment, are summed up in this word, 'Love your neighbour as yourself.' Love does no wrong to a neighbour; therefore, love is the fulfilling of the law.

Romans 13.8–10

'Have I obeyed enough?' is an irrelevant question. The question God wants us to ask is, 'Have I loved enough?' To that we can never answer 'Yes'. When Jesus loved the world to the uttermost it went beyond rules and commandments, and it did not stop until it encompassed every human of all times and places. That is the extent of the love which we are called to copy. Daunting!

Many poor countries have become heavily indebted to the nations and banks of the rich third of the world. When Paul wrote 'Owe no one anything' he could not possibly have imagined such a world. But he would surely have insisted that poor countries were 'neighbours' to rich countries and that love, not legalism, should be a feature of the way international debt is handled.

Before the debts were incurred, rich countries reaped vast benefits from poor countries. They took their citizens away as slaves, they dug deep into their mineral resources, and their status as empire-builders was used to benefit the rich far more than the poor. When we stop discussing 'law' and instead discuss 'love' and 'neighbours' it ceases to be clear who owes what to whom.

The United Kingdom is a heavily indebted rich country.

The President of Tanzania wrote an extraordinary letter thanking those who have campaigned for poor countries to be relieved of their unpayable debts. The debt relief that Tanzania has received allowed President Benjamin Mkapa to double spending on fighting poverty, notably abolishing primary school fees. He wrote, 'Without doubt, thanks to your efforts Tanzania can attain universal basic education during 2006.' Today's action is to accept his thanks, and find out more at www.christianaid.org.uk/world/where/eagl/tanzanip.htm

Forgive us our debts, as we forgive those who are in debt to us. Amen.

From a literal translation of the Lord's Prayer

August 6   Behave decently

You know what time it is, how it is now the moment for you to wake from sleep. For salvation is nearer to us now than when we became believers; the night is far gone, the day is near. Let us then lay aside the works of darkness and put on the armour of light; let us live honourably as in the day, not in revelling and drunkenness, not in debauchery and licentiousness, not in quarrelling and jealousy. Instead, put on the Lord Jesus Christ, and make no provision for the flesh, to gratify its desires.

Romans 13.11–14

When Jesus told his followers that he would come to Earth again, this time in glory, they assumed that he meant it would happen very soon. In fact it has taken far longer than Paul imagined when he was writing this letter to the Christians in Rome. We do not tend to wake up every morning thinking, 'Maybe today!' So if the Christians Paul was writing to needed an alarm call, how much more do we!

The correct response to knowing that one day we will meet Jesus face to face is to live constantly in a way which is pleasing to him. Paul describes it as being daytime people, not night-time people. Daytime is when people tend to be sober, hardworking and reputable. Night-time is when emotions flare, excess causes its damage, and the temptation to be unfaithful sexually is highest.

Our world seems to be have been in a state of night for as long as it is possible to remember, but Paul declares that dawn is on its way and with the dawn will come the Saviour. 'Get up and get dressed!' he writes. 'Get dressed in the values and ways of Jesus, so that you are ready.' Consciously focusing on doing what is right achieves more than desperately trying to resist what is wrong.

Write the words 'Put on the Lord Jesus Christ' on a card and prop it by your alarm clock so that it is the first thing you read tomorrow morning. What would you put right before you go to bed if you knew that when the alarm goes off you would meet Jesus face to face?

Praise be to God, in whom there is no darkness, and who has sent upon us once again the light of heaven.

A prayer from India, spoken together by families at the evening lighting of the lamps

August 7 I will give bread

The whole congregation of the Israelites complained against Moses and Aaron in the wilderness. The Israelites said to them, 'If only we had died by the hand of the Lord in the land of Egypt, when we sat by the fleshpots and ate our fill of bread; for you have brought us out into this wilderness to kill this whole assembly with hunger.'

Then the Lord said to Moses, 'I am going to rain bread from heaven for you, and each day the people shall go out and gather enough for that day. In that way I will test them, whether they will follow my instruction or not.'

Exodus 16.2–4

The Hebrew people had escaped from slavery in Egypt and embarked upon a painful time of learning. Their destination was Canaan (the present-day site of Israel and the Occupied Palestinian Territories), a journey of some forty days. It was to take forty years. A miserable cycle of delay was established – rejoicing at their freedom, complaining at the hardship of nomadic life, rebellion, God's gracious intervention, and short-lived periods of contentment. The biggest test, as it still is for any refugee community, was to find enough food to secure their future until they could settle in a permanent home.

The Hebrews learnt that trust in God had to be renewed every day. Their selective memories looked back to Egypt and remembered the certainty, but not the misery. Yes, they had food. But they also had oppression, exploitation and no control over their destiny. The miracle that set them free had been spectacular, but one mighty experience of God is not enough for a lifetime. A fulfilled life is one in which every day reawakens our trust in God. By only ever having enough bread for the coming day the Hebrews were learning to rely on God one day, at a time.

'Give us this day our daily bread.'

The world in which we live gives us very different security needs. Sort out your insurance papers. Are there things which you should get around to insuring for your peace of mind? Are you paying for any insurance that you don't actually need?

Let the peoples praise you, O God;
let all the peoples praise you.
The Earth has yielded its harvest;
God, our God, has blessed us.
May God continue to bless us;
let all the ends of the Earth revere him.

Psalm 67.5–7

August 8   Manna

In the evening quails came up and covered the camp; and in the morning there was a layer of dew around the camp. When the layer of dew lifted, there on the surface of the wilderness was a fine flaky substance, as fine as frost on the ground. When the Israelites saw it, they said to one another, 'What is it?' For they did not know what it was. Moses said to them, 'It is the bread that the Lord has given you to eat. This is what the Lord has commanded: "Gather as much of it as each of you needs, an omer to a person according to the number of persons, all providing for those in their own tents."' The Israelites did so, some gathering more, some less. But when they measured it with an omer, those who gathered much had nothing over, and those who gathered little had no shortage.

Exodus 16.13–18

'Manna' is a Hebrew word and it means, 'What the Dickens is this?' Or something equally robust! That was the reaction of the Hebrews when they first caught sight of the food God had provided. Did he provide it because of their complaints or despite them?

The next thing the people had to learn about trusting God was that his provision was to be shared fairly. No one was to have less or hoard more than they needed. When it comes to the basic needs of life (and there is nothing more basic than the need for bread) God's intention is that all people should have enough, no matter what their circumstances.

One of Christian Aid's partners is the Young Women's Christian Association in Zimbabwe. As a result of their training courses there is now a bakery project called 'Bambamani' (it means 'working together'). It has allowed women to find a new source of income at a time when Zimbabwe's problems are acute. The cost of ingredients is rising steadily and the local market will not be able to withstand an increase in bread prices. However, the group has a vision for the future and wants to invest in a new storage cupboard (because bread does not keep fresh without one). To find out how Christian Aid is responding to the needs of Zimbabwe's poorest communities, visit www.christianaid.org.uk/world/where/safrica/zimbabp.htm

Blessed be thou, Lord God, who bringest forth bread from the Earth and makest glad the hearts of thy people.

An ancient Jewish prayer

August 9 Food that lasts

Some boats from Tiberias came near the place where [the people] had eaten the bread after the Lord had given thanks. So when the crowd saw that neither Jesus nor his disciples were there, they themselves got into the boats and went to Capernaum looking for Jesus.
When they found him on the other side of the sea, they said to him, 'Rabbi, when did you come here?' Jesus answered them, 'Very truly, I tell you, you are looking for me, not because you saw signs, but because you ate your fill of the loaves. Do not work for the food that perishes, but for the food that endures for eternal life, which the Son of Man will give you. For it is on him that God the Father has set his seal.'

John 6.23–27

A miracle had just taken place. From five loaves and two fish, Jesus had satisfied a crowd of 5,000. The creator of all things, who has been multiplying fish and bread unceasingly since life began, accelerated the process unforgettably. He left the crowd greedy for more. Greedy for more spectacle and (in a land where food security was a constant anxiety) greedy for more bread. So they tracked Jesus down.

Jesus had hoped that by discovering the bread they would be set free to glimpse the never-ending God. But in fact, one glimpse of God made them think they had discovered never-ending bread. Jesus sees through such carelessly disguised materialism. He acknowledges that people need food, but he insists that there is a spiritual nourishment which people need as well.

Millions in the well-fed world who have never gone to bed hungry would agree that having enough is never enough. Bread perishes, clothes wear out, possessions break – no wonder these things cannot fully satisfy. Genuinely Christian aid knows that people have an inner life which needs feeding as much as a physical body.

Make a point of 'saying grace' before your next meal. Acknowledge that God is the creator through whose goodness all our food comes to us, and we have spiritual needs that only he can fulfil.

I am weak but thou art mighty,
Hold me with thy powerful hand.
Bread of heaven, bread of heaven,
Feed me now and evermore.

William Williams, from the hymn 'Guide me O thou great Jehovah'

August 10   The true bread

[The crowd asked], 'What must we do to perform the works of God?' Jesus answered them, 'This is the work of God, that you believe in him whom he has sent.' So they said to him, 'What sign are you going to give us then, so that we may see it and believe you? What work are you performing? Our ancestors ate the manna in the wilderness; as it is written, "He gave them bread from heaven to eat."' Then Jesus said to them, 'Very truly, I tell you, it was not Moses who gave you the bread from heaven, but it is my Father who gives you the true bread from heaven. For the bread of God is that which comes down from heaven and gives life to the world.' They said to him, 'Sir, give us this bread always.'

John 6.28–34

Jesus had talked about pleasing God, so the people asked what hard work was required in order to earn God's approval. Jesus answered that they were on completely the wrong track. Their relationship with God did not depend on how hard they tried to be good, but on what they believed. God himself would do all it took for them to enjoy an eternal relationship with him. Their challenge was to believe that Jesus was truly God's own messenger.

So the crowd asked Jesus to prove his credentials. Understandable enough! The desire for proof has echoed down the centuries. They wanted him to equal Moses' feat of providing food when their ancestors were in the desert. But Jesus swatted their question away – it made Moses sound like a conjurer! In fact, only God himself could provide the proof they were looking for, and the 'bread' with which he was going to reveal himself was different from anything they had ever eaten. They didn't realize that Jesus was referring to himself.

Try a different kind of bread next time you go to a shop. Naan bread, pitta bread, chapatti, bagels, sourdough, rye bread, soda bread – we are spoilt for choice! As you eat, bring to mind the way the need for bread unites humans around the world.

As this bread, once dispersed over the hills, was brought together and became one loaf, so may thy Church be brought together from the ends of the Earth into thy kingdom. Amen.

Part of the Didache, an instruction book for the churches that dates from before 150

August 11   Believing in Jesus

Jesus said to them, 'I am the bread of life. Whoever comes to me will never be hungry, and whoever believes in me will never be thirsty. But I said to you that you have seen me and yet do not believe. Everything that the Father gives me will come to me, and anyone who comes to me I will never drive away; for I have come down from heaven, not to do my own will, but the will of him who sent me. And this is the will of him who sent me, that I should lose nothing of all that he has given me, but raise it up on the last day. This is indeed the will of my Father, that all who see the Son and believe in him may have eternal life; and I will raise them up on the last day.'

John 6.35–40

What kind of hunger was Jesus addressing? The yearning within humans that cannot be satisfied by being consumers. We hunger to know what is the real measure of our worth. We hunger to know the full truth about ourselves and the life that we never asked to be born into. We hunger to be reassured about the instinct deep inside us that we are destined for something more than the brief spell during which we inhabit this body.

And what does Jesus offer? A lasting satisfaction that those questions have been dealt with. An assurance that nothing more is needed for our spiritual well-being than what God has already given us. A resurrection that will put the triumphs and disasters of our experience on Earth into a context that makes sense of them.

The image of eating bread suggests the wonderful simplicity of receiving these things. Coming to Jesus is no more complicated than swallowing. Just believe, and it is done.

Be conscious of things that you normally do by reflex. Be aware of swallowing. Then think about blinking. Be mindful of the need to breathe out and in. Can you feel your pulse? Jesus is offering to be as instinctive a part of life as those things. Are you aware of him?

You called, you cried, you shattered my deafness. You sparkled, you blazed, you drove away my blindness. I tasted, and now I hunger and thirst. You shed your fragrance, and I drew in my breath, and I pant for you.

Augustine, Bishop of Hippo (modern Tunisia), 354–430

August 12   Eternal life

The Jews began to complain about [Jesus] because he said, 'I am the bread that came down from heaven.' They were saying, 'Is not this Jesus, the son of Joseph, whose father and mother we know? How can he now say, "I have come down from heaven"?' Jesus answered them, 'Do not complain among yourselves. No one can come to me unless drawn by the Father who sent me; and I will raise that person up on the last day. It is written in the prophets, "And they shall all be taught by God." Everyone who has heard and learned from the Father comes to me. Not that anyone has seen the Father except the one who is from God; he has seen the Father.'

John 6.41–46

Sometimes we read about the crowds who followed Jesus, and we are bemused that they could miss the point of what he said. But we have had the benefit of twenty centuries during which he has been worshipped as God. His followers must be forgiven for hesitating over acclaiming him as one who 'came down from heaven'. After all, some of them remembered him having his nappies changed!

'Stop arguing!' said Jesus, pointing out that since none of them had seen God they had no authority to be dogmatic.

'Start listening!' said Jesus, directing them to words that were written in the Bible.

Theological debate can have a vital role in helping us understand the ways of God. But it is only when we recognize in it God drawing us to himself that it has a genuine value – otherwise it is just the effort of humans who like the sound of their own words. Through the Bible, through Jesus, through the Spirit at work in the world around us, through 2,000 years of Christians attempting to understand, we try to become people who have 'heard and learned'. Seeing in person is for the future.

Think back to recent arguments. What impact have they had on your relationships? Do those relationships still have room for improvement? What can you do to mend them without reopening the arguments?

Glory to you, God of all my hopes! Lead me into understanding;
Glory to you, Jesus of human history! Raise me to eternal life;
Glory to you, Spirit of all that is divine! Guide me into truth;
Father, Mother, Lord and Saviour,
Glory to you in all the names by which you are known.

August 13 Bread of life

[Jesus said,] 'I am the bread of life. Your ancestors ate the manna in the wilderness, and they died. This is the bread that comes down from heaven, so that one may eat of it and not die. I am the living bread that came down from heaven. Whoever eats of this bread will live for ever; and the bread that I will give for the life of the world is my flesh.'

John 6.48–51

The Hebrews who ate bread in the desert were long dead. But Jesus was creating a community in which his followers would live for ever. For the first time he hints at the cost. It would take the death of Jesus (his flesh given for the world) to bring eternal life.

Shove 225g self-raising flour and a swoosh of salt through a sieve into a bowl. Before your fingers get greasy, set the oven to 220°C or gas 7. Break 50g of butter into pieces and throw them in the bowl. Squish the butter and flour between your fingers until it looks like breadcrumbs. Sprinkle in 25g of sugar and jiggle it around. Pour in 150ml of milk, a bit at a time, and mix until it is soft and even.

Shake some flour over a board (or straight on a table if it is clean and not an antique). Put the dough on the board and bash it round a bit. With a rolling pin (or a bottle) roll it until it is 1cm thick. Cut out circles (they sell special cutters for this, but if you press down with a glass you get the same result). You should get six, and if you squeeze the remains and roll it again you will get another two.

Smear a thin layer of butter over a metal baking tray. Put the circles on the tray, spaced out. Splash a bit of milk over the tops. By this time the oven should be really hot. Put them in for ten minutes. Peep in. If they have risen to twice their height and gone golden brown, take them out. If not, give them another minute. Leave them to go cold (a wire tray is good, because air gets underneath). Cut them in half and ladle jam and cream in.

Scones. Fantastic! Never fails. Trust me!

O Lord, who fed the multitudes with five loaves, bless the bread that we are about to eat.

A traditional grace from Egypt

August 14   Eating and drinking

The Jews then disputed among themselves, saying, 'How can this man give us his flesh to eat?' So Jesus said to them, 'Very truly, I tell you, unless you eat the flesh of the Son of Man and drink his blood, you have no life in you. Those who eat my flesh and drink my blood have eternal life, and I will raise them up on the last day; for my flesh is true food and my blood is true drink. Those who eat my flesh and drink my blood abide in me, and I in them.'

John 6.52–56

These words remind us of the bread and wine of a Communion service. Unlike the other Gospels, John does not record the events of Jesus' last supper, at which he asked his followers to eat and drink as the way of remembering that, in him, they had encountered God as flesh and blood. Instead he records these words that reflect on the significance of the ritual. By the time John was writing his Gospel (maybe seventy years after Jesus said these things) Communion had been celebrated, argued over, abused, reformed, turned from a meal into a service, and become a precious part of Christian experience. It's not surprising that John wanted his readers to get back to the heart of what it meant.

Jesus explains that it is not enough to be impressed by him, or to revere his teachings. That would be like admiring the loaves on display from outside a bakery window. If he is to be nourishing and sustaining to us, only complete incorporation will do. Jesus is asking to be taken so completely into the fabric of our lives that it is as if he is within us. What better metaphor of that than eating and drinking! And what better symbol of it than the bread and wine of Communion.

After your main meal today, put a piece of bread on the table and pour out a glass of wine. (It doesn't matter whether you do this alone or in company because it is not a Communion service, just a meditation.) Read Jesus' words again (aloud if there is more than one of you). Then eat and drink, asking for an ever-closer relationship with Jesus.

O Jesus, Bread of Life,
be before my eyes to inspire me,
be close to me to comfort me,
but more than that,
be within me to nourish me. Amen.

August 15   The Spirit gives life

When many of his disciples heard it, they said, 'This teaching is difficult; who can accept it?' But Jesus, being aware that his disciples were complaining about it, said to them, 'Does this offend you? Then what if you were to see the Son of Man ascending to where he was before? It is the spirit that gives life; the flesh is useless. The words that I have spoken to you are spirit and life. But among you there are some who do not believe.'

John 6.60–65

In the chapter of the Bible we have been reading for the last few days, the same words and ideas come back again and again. Each time, though, Jesus adds a new layer of meaning. It is like driving round and round a multi-storey car park. But as far as the crowd was concerned, this time he had gone too far. They had, after all, only come because they thought he was going to provide supper. Now he had turned cannibal on them! Eating flesh? Drinking blood? Time to pay for their ticket and drive to the exit.

You would expect Jesus at this point to make his message simpler. But he is uncompromising. There is more to life than eating and sleeping, and those who are to be disciples need to grapple with big, spiritual questions about existence. If they are not prepared to do some hard thinking about the meaning of life now, what chance will they have of doing it once he has ascended to heaven?

What have you started but not finished? A piece of DIY that hit complications; a book that required too much effort; a household task for which you ran out of energy; an eyesore that you have got used to rather than deal with; a relationship which has lacked effort for too long? Take some steps today to move a project forward.

O God our Father, by whose mercy and might the world turns safely into darkness and returns again to light: we give into thy hands our unfinished tasks, our unsolved problems, and our unfulfilled hopes, knowing that only that which thou dost bless will prosper. To thy great love and protection we commit all those we love, knowing that thou alone art our sure defender. Amen.

A prayer of the Church of South India

August 16   To whom else could we go?

Because of this many of his disciples turned back and no longer went about with him. So Jesus asked the twelve, 'Do you also wish to go away?' Simon Peter answered him, 'Lord, to whom can we go? You have the words of eternal life. We have come to believe and know that you are the Holy One of God.'

John 6.66–69

This is one of the most bitter-sweet moments of the Bible. It is the first time that Jesus experienced people turning their back on him. Understanding his teaching had become so demanding for the crowd that they gave up. You can hear the disappointment in Jesus' words as he turned to his closest friends: 'Do you want to go too? You are free to go if you want to.'

It was a desperately difficult moment for Peter. He must have looked back at the ropes of secuity he had severed in order to follow Jesus – the job he abandoned, the family he left, the roots from which he had cut himself. With words of sadness, resignation and determination he sighs, 'Well, where else can we go? It always was you or nothing. We have left ourselves with no choice but to keep following.' So, for the hundredth time, or the thousandth, he throws in his lot with Jesus.

What is it about Jesus that allows a person to stake everything on following him? A realization that Jesus is not just an inspirational human. The 'bread' that he offers feeds the hope that death is not the end. Peter had discovered that, in Jesus, God's unique holiness had touched the Earth.

People need bread and people need hope. They don't need one or the other: they need both. Malawi is a country that faces long-term agricultural problems. Failed harvests in recent years led to a million people needing emergency food aid. Christian Aid partners worked tirelessly to help. But their objective is to help farmers move on from being dependent to facing the future with hope. Churches Action in Relief and Development runs a land-husbandry project to help small farmers improve their crop yields. They train farmers to make compost, and teach them how to use trees to prevent soil being washed away from their land. Read more about Malawi at www.christianaid.org.uk/world/where/safrica/malawip.htm

God bless Africa: guard her children, guide her rulers, and give her peace. Amen.

Archbishop Trevor Huddleston (1913–98)

August 17 We are thirsty

The Israelites journeyed by stages, as the Lord commanded. They camped at Rephidim, but there was no water for the people to drink. The people quarrelled with Moses, and said, 'Give us water to drink.' Moses said to them, 'Why do you quarrel with me? Why do you test the Lord?' But the people thirsted there for water; and the people complained against Moses and said, 'Why did you bring us out of Egypt, to kill us and our children and livestock with thirst?'

Exodus 17.1–3

'Everybody in the world has the right to safe water.' Agreed! But what exactly does it mean? The right to safe water collected from a well a mile away? The right to safe water in a standpipe in your street? The right to safe water available from a tap in your own home? Which one would you settle for?

Mali is one of the poorest and driest countries in the world. Half the population lacks clean water, and regular droughts lead to food shortages. The Pel Catholic Mission, a Christian Aid partner, has built over 500 concrete wells in Mali, transforming the lives of 80,000 people. In Segué Plaine, which now has a well, Albertine Somboro recalls: 'Before it would take us an hour to get two litres of water. Now we don't have to go so far, we have been able to increase the vegetables that we grow. We can earn more money to look after our children.'

When clean water arrives in a village, the number of children who die from trivial diseases declines. And because they do not have to waste hours on the chore of carrying water in a bucket, children are able to go to school and (this must not be underestimated) play with their friends.

Christian Aid publishes a beautiful booklet for children that explains how clean water makes such a difference to a village. *Splash!* has pictures of wells in Mali, as well as puzzles, prayers and models to make. Free of charge from the addresses at the back of the book, it is ideal both for primary schools and for children in churches. And, of course, for your favourite nephew and niece!

Lord God, never let me take life-giving water for granted. In a tap, in a bottle, in a glass, in a shower, in a hose, in a saucepan, in a cistern, in a kettle, in a radiator, in a rainfall – thank you, thank you, thank you!

August 18   Water from the rock

Moses cried out to the Lord, 'What shall I do with this people? They are almost ready to stone me.' The Lord said to Moses, 'Go on ahead of the people, and take some of the elders of Israel with you; take in your hand the staff with which you struck the Nile, and go. I will be standing there in front of you on the rock at Horeb. Strike the rock, and water will come out of it, so that the people may drink.' Moses did so, in the sight of the elders of Israel. He called the place Massah and Meribah, because the Israelites quarrelled and tested the Lord, saying, 'Is the Lord among us or not?'

Exodus 17.4–7

Something happens here that is all too familiar in our own relationship with God. Within days of God dramatically revealing himself to be their provider and carer, the Hebrews find themselves going through another time of profound challenge. This time it is thirst – such a thirst that it has driven them to the point of violence. But need did not drive them to recall the times when God had intervened to sustain them; instead it led them to question whether he was there at all.

We have expectations of God that we are not prepared to reciprocate. We require him to make himself known to us day after day after day. And yet we are lazily reluctant to open ourselves to God in such a constant way. It is almost impossible to find a proper answer to the question, 'Is the Lord among us or not?' if the only times when we seek him are crises.

Go and pour yourself a tall glass of water. Stick it in the fridge so that in half an hour it will be perfect for an August day. Then come back later and treat yourself to a rest in an armchair with a cool drink and a chance to dwell on the question of whether or not God is in action in your life.

O God, you are my God, earnestly I seek you;
my soul thirsts for you, my body longs for you,
in a dry and weary land where there is no water.

Turn these words from Psalm 63.1 over in your mind. Let them lead you to reflect on how you might be able to seek out the presence of God as a more constant feature of your life.

August 19   A Samaritan woman

[Jesus] left Judea and started back to Galilee. But he had to go through Samaria. So he came to a Samaritan city called Sychar, near the plot of ground that Jacob had given to his son Joseph. Jacob's well was there, and Jesus, tired out by his journey, was sitting by the well. It was about noon.

A Samaritan woman came to draw water, and Jesus said to her, 'Give me a drink.' (His disciples had gone to the city to buy food.) The Samaritan woman said to him, 'How is it that you, a Jew, ask a drink of me, a woman of Samaria?' (Jews do not share things in common with Samaritans.)

John 4.3–9

'Jews do not share things in common with Samaritans' is an understatement. The extent of the conventions that Jesus was overturning is huge. As a respectable Jewish male he should not have approached a woman (on account of her gender); he should not have approached a Samaritan (on account of their religious differences); and he certainly should not have approached someone so socially unacceptable that she was collecting water alone at a ludicrously hot time of day (on account of its all-round weirdness). And yet Jesus seems completely at ease – as far as he was concerned it was a meeting of equals.

There are three things here to which Christian Aid aspires because they seem to be marks of genuine mission: it takes place between two equal partners; it starts with no preconceptions about religious differences; and it seeks to break down prejudices of all kinds. In those circumstances God can be set free to work not only in those who receive but also in those who give – and the distinction between the two ceases to be obvious.

With whom do you find conversation awkward? What causes this – age, class, gender, sexuality, race, beliefs, the fear of saying the wrong thing, or just the fact that some people seem boring? Make a plan to start a conversation with no agenda, and see whether Jesus' example inspires you.

God of every tribe and tongue, I ask you to bless my conversations. Let my words be rich with encouragement, and slow to anger; strong with compassion, and set against prejudice. Word of God, give me language that refreshes those I meet. Amen.

August 20 Living water

Jesus answered [the woman], 'If you knew the gift of God, and who it is that is saying to you, "Give me a drink", you would have asked him, and he would have given you living water.' The woman said to him, 'Sir, you have no bucket, and the well is deep. Where do you get that living water? Are you greater than our ancestor Jacob, who gave us the well, and with his sons and his flocks drank from it?' Jesus said to her, 'Everyone who drinks of this water will be thirsty again, but those who drink of the water that I will give them will never be thirsty. The water that I will give will become in them a spring of water gushing up to eternal life.' The woman said to him, 'Sir, give me this water, so that I may never be thirsty or have to keep coming here to draw water.'

John 4.10–15

The Jews of Jesus' day did not believe that water flowed the way it did for a scientific reason. They hadn't heard of gravity. They believed that water followed its path because God willed it that way. Cisterns were specially constructed so that the water in them still flowed in its natural direction. They called this water 'living water'. The Roman authorities built mighty aqueducts in order to bring the Jews clean water, and were bewildered that righteous Jews rejected it. They thought the water had been contaminated.

There are lessons to learn for people who have the needs of the world's poorest people at heart. There is a danger of imposing on people a solution to their problems which, because we don't understand the situation properly, is not appropriate. Can you imagine anything more dismaying than saying to people who live in poor countries, 'We can help you have a life just like ours'? They would surely look at our stress-filled, secular society and wonder why we want to burden them with a life like ours!

In order to avoid imposing inappropriate solutions on poor people, Christian Aid works through 'partners' – organizations in the developing world that are best positioned to understand the local needs. To find out more about it, visit www.christianaid.org.uk/world/how/how.htm

God of the waters, may all who call out to you in thirst find what they seek – living water to those in physical need; living water to those in spiritual need. Amen.

August 21   Spirit and truth

Jesus said to [the woman], 'Go, call your husband, and come back.' The woman answered him, 'I have no husband.' Jesus said to her, 'You are right in saying, "I have no husband"; for you have had five husbands, and the one you have now is not your husband. What you have said is true!' The woman said to him, 'Sir, I see that you are a prophet. Our ancestors worshipped on this mountain, but you say that the place where people must worship is in Jerusalem.' Jesus said to her, 'Woman, believe me, the hour is coming when you will worship the Father neither on this mountain nor in Jerusalem. You worship what you do not know; we worship what we know, for salvation is from the Jews. But the hour is coming, and is now here, when the true worshippers will worship the Father in spirit and truth, for the Father seeks such as these to worship him.

John 4.16–23

Some people assume that this woman was morally lax. However, at a time when men died young it was not impossible for a woman to have been widowed five times, and for her currently to be under the protection of her late husband's brother.

The woman asked a religious question: the Samaritans held Mount Gerizim to be the most sacred place, but the Jews worshipped in Jerusalem, so who was right? She reminds me of people today who are bewildered by the huge number of Christian denominations. Jesus did not get bogged down in controversy, but instead talked about something more important. God is not looking for a particular way of worshipping him. What matters is spirit (a deep and honest inner reality) and truth (an integrity that puts off all disguises).

Criticizing the way other people worship God occupies far more conversation than it should. We all know what we prefer, and we all imagine that God prefers it as well. Is there anything you could do to demonstrate a willingness to set differences aside?

Eternal God, whose image lies in the hearts of all people, we live among people whose ways are different from ours, whose faiths are foreign to us, whose tongues are unintelligible to us. Help us to remember that all religion is an attempt to respond to you, and that the yearnings of other hearts are much like our own, and are known to us. Amen.

A prayer of the World Council of Churches

August 22 Is this the Messiah?

[Jesus continued,] 'God is spirit, and those who worship him must worship in spirit and truth.' The woman said to him, 'I know that Messiah is coming' (who is called Christ). 'When he comes, he will proclaim all things to us.' Jesus said to her, 'I am he, the one who is speaking to you.'

Just then his disciples came. They were astonished that he was speaking with a woman, but no one said, 'What do you want?' or, 'Why are you speaking with her?' Then the woman left her water jar and went back to the city. She said to the people, 'Come and see a man who told me everything I have ever done! He cannot be the Messiah, can he?'

John 4.24–30

Today's reflection is by a guest contributor. Ephraem lived in Syria in the fourth century. A poet and church leader, he was passionately on the side of the poor. At a time of famine in the area that is now Turkey and Syria, there were moves to make resources go further by expelling refugees. Although the proposals were popular with the public, Ephraem mobilized the Church in protest and was successful in having money raised for bread to be distributed and an open-air hospital to be set up.

He wrote: 'Jesus came to the [well] as a hunter. He threw a grain before one pigeon in order that he might catch the whole flock. At the beginning of the conversation he did not make himself known to her. First she caught sight of a thirsty man, then a Jew, then a rabbi, afterwards a prophet, last of all the Messiah. She tried to get the better of the thirsty man, she showed her dislike of the Jew, she heckled the rabbi, she was swept off her feet by the prophet, and she adored the Christ.'

'Sunrise marks the hour for toil to begin, but in thy soul take time to prepare a dwelling for the day that will never end.'

O Lord and Master of my life, take from me the spirit of laziness, faint-heartedness, lust for power and idle talk. Give, rather, the spirit of chastity, humility, patience and love to your servant. Yes, my Lord and King, grant that I may see my own errors and not judge my brothers and sisters, for you are blessed from all ages to all ages. Amen.

Ephraem the Syrian (306–73)

August 23   The fields are ripe

The disciples were urging [Jesus], 'Rabbi, eat something.' But he said to them, 'I have food to eat that you do not know about.' So the disciples said to one another, 'Surely no one has brought him something to eat?' Jesus said to them, 'My food is to do the will of him who sent me and to complete his work. Do you not say, "Four months more, then comes the harvest"? But I tell you, look around you, and see how the fields are ripe for harvesting. The reaper is already receiving wages and is gathering fruit for eternal life, so that sower and reaper may rejoice together.'

John 4.31–36

Jesus' disciples arrive with their minds full of food. But Jesus has been awakening an awareness of the need for something more than bread and water. There is a vaccuum in each of us that can only be filled by God, just like there is a craving that can only be filled by food. Our world is 'ripe' with both needs. To address one without the other is fulfilling only half Jesus' challenge.

In Massachusetts, USA, in 1912 the government passed a law that women and under-eighteens could not work more than a fifty-four–hour week. The employers at the wool mill in Lawrence responded to the losses this would entail by reducing wages across the board. There was a historic strike, during which the women workers carried banners demanding that they needed not only a living wage, but also a life that was spiritually fulfilling. And they sang James Oppenheim and Martha Coleman's song 'Bread and Roses':

'Our lives shall not be sweated from birth until life closes;

Hearts starve as well as bodies; give us bread, but give us also roses!'

Look back on the last twenty-four hours. Make a mental list of what has fed your body (meals, drinks, snacks). Then make a mental list of what has fed your soul (music, prayer, beauty). Has one outweighed the other? If so, put it right before you sleep.

'No art and love and beauty their drudging spirits knew.
Yes, it is bread we fight for – but we fight for roses, too!'

Use the words of the song to remember those who have died for lack of food, but also those whose lives have withered for lack of living water and bread from heaven.

August 24   Remember God's works

O give thanks to the Lord, call on his name,
make known his deeds among the peoples.
Sing to him, sing praises to him; tell of all his wonderful works.
Glory in his holy name; let the hearts of those who seek the
    Lord rejoice.
Seek the Lord and his strength; seek his presence continually.
Remember the wonderful works he has done,
his miracles, and the judgements he uttered,
O offspring of his servant Abraham, children of Jacob, his chosen ones.
He is the Lord our God; his judgements are in all the earth.

Psalm 105.1–7

The psalm we are going to read this week tells the history of the Hebrew people. To us it is the ancient story of a remote people, but to the Jews who sang this song 3,000 years ago it was the chronicle of how they came to be who they were. As we read the history of the people of God over the coming days we would do well to reflect on what the world needs to learn from the triumphs and disasters of the story of the Jews. That is precisely what this introduction calls us to do. Look through it again to find these key words:

- Thank – because this is a story of God continually taking the initiative.
- Tell – because it is a story that all are called to share.
- Rejoice – because goodness has and will triumph.
- Seek – because there are times when it is not obvious that goodness has and will triumph.
- Remember – because if we forget we will be condemned to repeat past catastrophes again and again.

Look back on your own history. Where did you first meet God as your story unfolded? What are the key events that have delighted, dismayed and taught you since then? Use the pattern that the psalm suggests as you recall these things – thank, tell, rejoice, seek, remember.

My stories and memories in the timeless hands of God;
my regrets and sorrows in the healing hands of God;
my dreams and aspirations in the caring hands of God;
my wounds and anguish in the just hands of God;
my living and departed friends in the loving hands of God;
all my past and all my future,
for the hands of God are fully to be trusted. Amen.

August 25　Abraham

[God] is mindful of his covenant for ever,
of the word that he commanded, for a thousand generations,
the covenant that he made with Abraham, his sworn promise to
*　Isaac,*
which he confirmed to Jacob as a statute, to Israel as an
*　everlasting covenant,*
saying, 'To you I will give the land of Canaan as your portion for an inheritance.'
When they were few in number, of little account, and strangers in it,
wandering from nation to nation, from one kingdom to another people,
he allowed no one to oppress them; he rebuked kings on their account,
saying, 'Do not touch my anointed ones; do my prophets no harm.'

Psalm 105.8–15

Four thousand years ago in a city in present-day Iraq there was a curious disturbance. In this place of many gods, each with its own controllable idol, one wealthy man claimed to have had a remarkable revelation. It was that there is only one God, and that he is invisible. So convinced was he of this discovery that he was prepared to leave his comfortable home and set off on a journey to a land that the God he worshipped told him was to be the dwelling of his unborn descendants. This was the beginning of the Jewish faith, from which would subsequently emerge the Christian and Muslim faiths. The man's name was Abraham and with him and his descendants God made 'the old covenant' (or 'old testament' – it means the same). They would be his people and he would be their God. And these were the signs:

- They were protected even though they were 'few in number'.
- A home was found for landless and 'wandering' people.
- 'Oppressed' people were given protection.
- Powerful people who acted unjustly were 'rebuked'.

When God's blessing is given, these are the signs that accompany it. They were evident when the Hebrews were a weak and humble tribe; they need to be evident in every nation, humble or powerful, that claims to worship the same God today.

Listen with extra attention to a news bulletin today and bring to mind places in the world where a strong group appears to be oppressing a weak one. Use this psalm's criteria to help you work out God's attitude.

Lord God of history, may those who have known what it is to receive mercy be convicted of the need to show mercy, so that all who are weak may rejoice in your protection. Amen.

August 26   Joseph

When [God] summoned famine against the land,
    and broke every staff of bread,
he had sent a man ahead of them, Joseph,
    who was sold as a slave.
His feet were hurt with fetters,
    his neck was put in a collar of iron;
until what he had said came to pass, the word of the Lord kept testing him.
The king sent and released him; the ruler of the peoples set him free.
He made him lord of his house, and ruler of all his possessions,
to instruct his officials at his pleasure, and to teach his elders wisdom.

Psalm 105.16–22

Yesterday we heard how Abraham's family made their home in Canaan. It was a precarious place in which to live, and the people of God were not immune from catastrophes. One of Abraham's descendants, Joseph, was the victim of a plot that led to him being taken as a slave to Egypt. But the view the psalm takes is that this event, even though it involved terrible suffering, should be seen as part of God's long-term plan to bring good out of evil. Joseph prospered unexpectedly in Egypt and rose to political power. He was able to use that position to bring relief to his clan when famine struck. Joseph said, 'Though you intended to do harm to me, God intended it for good.' It is a model of both the risk and the reward of defying prejudices and doing what is right during a time of emergency.

Physicians for Human Rights is an Israeli organization committed to bringing health care to all, including those in the Occupied Palestinian Territories. Every week they take doctors and nurses, all of whom volunteer their time, into the West Bank to set up a mobile clinic in a village where Palestinians are denied access to medical care. Each week they go to a different village, selected with the help of the Union of Palestinian Medical Relief Committees. Although it is illegal for Israeli citizens to enter some areas of the West Bank, Physicians for Human Rights go without fail, risking two years in prison if they are arrested. Christian Aid is in partnership with both the Israeli and the Palestinian organization. Find out more at their websites, www.phr.org.il (click 'English') and www.upmrc.org

Light of the World, until the dawn comes when suffering is at an end, stand alongside all those whose witness shines in the darkness, giving them courage, safety and hope. Amen.

August 27   Slaves

Then Israel came to Egypt;
Jacob lived as an alien in the land of Ham.
And the Lord made his people very fruitful,
and made them stronger than their foes,
whose hearts he then turned to hate his people,
to deal craftily with his servants.
He sent his servant Moses, and Aaron whom he had chosen.
They performed his signs among them, and miracles in the land of Ham.

Psalm 105.23–27

The psalm we are reading is the history of how God led the Hebrews from the days when they were a single family to the days when they were established as a thriving nation in the Middle East. The lesson it repeats is that we cannot see the purpose of suffering and adversity at the time we are going through them, but in retrospect it is possible to discern that God has been at work even through the most intolerable circumstances. Yesterday we read how terrible misfortunes that fell upon Joseph led to him being in Egypt at just the right time to rescue the Hebrews from famine in their own land. Today we read how Jacob (Joseph's father) led the Hebrew people (Israel) to Egypt and thus escaped death.

However, as years went by, the people who were warmly welcomed into Egypt when they arrived seeking asylum fell out of favour with their hosts. The Pharaoh of Egypt, observing them grow in number and fearing they might ally themselves with a potential invader, incited his people first to hate the Hebrews and then to force them into slave labour. The story of how a nation can first offer a safe home to refugees and then turn against them has been repeated over and again through history. Today we need another Moses and another miracle.

The Refugee Council is the largest organization in the UK working with asylum seekers. Their website draws attention to developments in the circumstances of refugees and responds to myths that have grown up concerning those who seek asylum in the UK. Visit it at www.refugeecouncil.org.uk

Lord of the journey,
we ask for your protection on all who have fled their homes:
grant them strength on their journeys;
grant that they may find places of compassion at which to rest;
ease their fear as they throw in their lot with strangers;
and, God of all the world, keep alive their vision
of returning to a secure and welcoming home. Amen.

August 28   Moses

[God] sent darkness, and made the land dark; they rebelled
 against his words.
He turned their waters into blood, and caused their fish to die . . .
He gave them hail for rain, and lightning that flashed through
 their land.
He struck their vines and fig trees, and shattered the trees of their country.
He spoke, and the locusts came, and young locusts without number;
they devoured all the vegetation in their land, and ate up the fruit of their ground.
He struck down all the firstborn in their land, the first issue of all their strength.

Psalm 105.28–29, 32–36

Yesterday we read how the Hebrew people became enslaved.
Today we see God beginning their rescue. Plagues were sent to
demoralize the Egyptians to the point at which they let the
Hebrews go. But at the time, the events must have been terrifying
for the Hebrews too. I wonder whether Moses, their leader,
reassured them that these natural phenomena were part of God's plan, or
whether they could see only the terror!

The teaching of the Bible is that every living and inert thing in all creation has
been brought into existence to give glory to God. So it is a difficult but undeniable truth that all nature, whether we see it as positive or negative, is there for
good. The viruses praise God in their multiplying as surely as the roses praise
God with their perfume.

Day or night, look for seven things out of the window. Find something beneficial and something harmful. Pick out something
animal, vegetable and mineral. Identify something visible and
invisible. These are part of a good Creator's good creation.

Let all that is visible worship the Lord:
High mountain ranges and leaves on the tree;
microscopic creatures, sky-scraping towers;
cascading waters and stars in the sky;
colours of the rainbow, people of the nations;
lightning and landscape, sunset and shadow –
greatly give praise to the One who created you.

Let all that's invisible worship the Lord:
life-giving oxygen, cool of the breeze;
electrical current and radio waves;
scent of the flower and taste on the tongue;
burning emotion, mysterious sleep;
silence and gravity, music and laughter –
greatly give praise to the One who created you.

August 29　The exodus

[The Lord] brought Israel out of Egypt with silver and gold,
and there was no one among their tribes who stumbled.
Egypt was glad when they departed, for dread of them had
*　　fallen upon it.*
He spread a cloud for a covering, and fire to give light by night.
They asked, and he brought quails,
*　and gave them food from heaven in abundance.*
He opened the rock, and water gushed out;
*　it flowed through the desert like a river.*

Psalm 105.37–41

Many theologians of South and Central America draw inspiration from this part of the great unfolding story of the way God has dealt with humankind. The Hebrew people (here called Israel, although it describes a very different group of people from the nation we call by that name today) had been an oppressed tribe labouring as slaves in Egypt. Now they were liberated, and it was God's doing.

'Liberation theology' finds parallels between this and the aspirations of the world's poorest people, enduring their own kind of oppression in nations where they are governed with cruelty, and a world in which they are kept poor by systems devised in the interests of the rich. Those who work and pray for the end of injustice look to God with hope and trust to do what he has done before:

- leading his people into financial security ('silver and gold');
- creating a vigorous and active community in which no one 'stumbles';
- forming confident people, with no fear ('dread' is perhaps too strong a word);
- guiding people to live in ways pleasing to him (not with a literal 'cloud' and 'fire' to lead them through the desert, but with God's own Spirit);
- giving them a secure supply of food, so that hunger never blights life again.

'Liberation theology' looks at the Bible through the eyes of poor communities and discovers there social, political and economic meanings that make the word of God vividly relevant to daily life in the developing world. Its insights are sometimes startling to those who read the Bible from a comfortable and secure home.

There is a short history of liberation theology at www.landreform.org

So that the oppressed may be led out from their suffering;
so that the innocent may walk free from prison;
so that minorities may live without fear;
so that the whole Earth may worship in freedom;
your kingdom come, your will be done. Amen.

August 30   God's people rejoice

[God] remembered his holy promise, and Abraham, his servant.
So he brought his people out with joy, his chosen ones with
    singing.
He gave them the lands of the nations,
    and they took possession of the wealth of the peoples,
that they might keep his statutes and observe his laws. Praise the Lord!

Psalm 105.42–45

As far as this psalm is concerned, the climax of the story of God's dealings with the Hebrews ('his chosen ones') sees them settled in a land which it had been their destiny to occupy for hundreds of years. However, it is not clear from the psalm whether that was the end of the story. The question of whether God intends that today's descendants of Abraham (which is how the Jews see themselves) should be the sole occupants of this 'Promised Land' is one that has profound implications for the Middle East today.

Some hold that the descendants of those original tribes of Hebrews are the present-day state of Israel, and should 'take possession of the wealth of the peoples' who occupy the land just as they did centuries ago. Others hold that the coming of Jesus has changed our understanding once and for all, and that the promises of God to his chosen people should now be interpreted in a spiritual way. Disputing this has been the subject of many books. But, tragically, disputing this has also been the cause of many deaths. A peaceful Middle East will only be secured when its inhabitants 'keep God's statutes and observe his laws'. Scripture that was written with the intention that people cry out, 'Praise the Lord!' is frequently used as a weapon to fight a battle.

A general knowledge quiz! How many walls can you think of from the past and present that have been built to divide people from people? Two to start your list are the Berlin Wall and Hadrian's Wall. If you can make the list up to five, well done! If it reaches ten award yourself a treat. Does the list depress you, or are you living under the protection of one of them today?

Words from Isaiah 25.4 to dwell on until they lead you to say
'Praise the Lord!':
You have been a refuge for the poor, a refuge for the needy in his
distress, a shelter from the storm and a shade from the heat. For
the breath of the ruthless is like a storm driving against a wall.

August 31   The Promised Land

Great is the Lord and greatly to be praised in the city of our God.
His holy mountain, beautiful in elevation,
*   is the joy of all the earth,*
Mount Zion, in the far north, the city of the great King.
Within its citadels God has shown himself a sure defence.
Then the kings assembled, they came on together.
As soon as they saw it, they were astounded;
*   they were in panic, they took to flight;*
trembling took hold of them there, pains as of a woman in labour,
as when an east wind shatters the ships of Tarshish.

Psalm 48.1–7

As we read yesterday, the Hebrew people occupied their 'Promised Land'. At first they lived in tribal areas, governed by a succession of heroic women and men (the 'judges'). Fighting off attacks from outside and resistance from inside, they came to believe that the unique way in which they were governed had disadvantages, and demanded to become a monarchy like the surrounding nations. Under their second king, David, the tribes united for a golden age of prosperity. David chose Mount Zion as his home and there built Jerusalem as his capital city. The Hebrews came to believe that Mount Zion was the actual dwelling place of God, and that with his presence Jerusalem was inviolable. No wonder the writer of the psalm extols its beauty.

Succeeding kings never equalled the leadership of David. A civil war divided the nation into Israelites (in the north, eventually conquered by Assyria) and Jews (in the south). Under King Hezekiah the Jews flourished again briefly. Sennacherib, conqueror of the north, swept through the country and besieged Mount Zion. But for reasons that have never been clear (perhaps a plague) his troops capitulated without a blow being struck. The writer of this psalm explains it by suggesting that the sheer majesty of the glorious city 'astounded' them and 'in panic they took to flight'. This psalm celebrates the Jews' victory.

Because the news we hear from inner cities is often discouraging, it is refreshing to read the Bible when it is positive about city life. What is the name of your nearest city? Picture it. What do you find in it to be joyful about? Make a plan to visit so as to get and give something worthwhile from it.

May God bless the city. Peace be there in all its noise and speed.
Let every brick and breath of the city express God's beauty.
Amen.

September 1   Secure in Zion

As we have heard, so have we seen in the city of the Lord of hosts,
in the city of our God, which God establishes for ever.
We ponder your steadfast love, O God, in the midst of your temple.
Your name, O God, like your praise,
    reaches to the ends of the earth.
Your right hand is filled with victory.
Let Mount Zion be glad, let the towns of Judah rejoice
  because of your judgements.
Walk about Zion, go all around it, count its towers,
consider well its ramparts; go through its citadels,
that you may tell the next generation that this is God, our God for ever and ever.
He will be our guide for ever.

Psalm 48.8–14

The Jews ('the towns of Judah') had survived war, famine and disease. They believed it was because their capital city was built on the mountain that God had chosen as his dwelling place. On Mount Zion a magnificent temple was constructed – a home fit for the Lord. It was at once a tribute to God and a tourist attraction: 'Walk about Zion . . . tell the next generation'!

But something went wrong in the Jews' attitude to Jerusalem. At first they rejoiced to make their communities reflect the justice of God ('your judgements') but as time went by they began to assume that the blessing of God was theirs by right, and could never fail them. Complacent that their home was 'established for ever' by God, they made alliances with other nations, compromising their worship by sacrificing to foreign gods. Alongside this went a disregard of God's standards of justice, which left the poorest people of Judah dispossessed. Again and again they were warned by God's prophets that exploiting the poor and bowing to idols would be their downfall. It was!

Take a walk around your home. Go into every room. Look at souvenirs and decorations that have become familiar and recall the appeal they first had. Be glad!

Before us it is blessed, behind us it is blessed,
below us it is blessed, above us it is blessed,
around us it is blessed as we set out with Christ.
Our speech is blessed as we set out for God.
  With beauty before us, with beauty behind us,
with beauty below us, with beauty above us,
with beauty around us we set out for a holy place indeed.

Prayer of Christians of the North American Navajo tribe

September 2   Exile in Babylon

By the rivers of Babylon – there we sat down
and there we wept when we remembered Zion.
On the willows there we hung up our harps.
For there our captors asked us for songs,
and our tormentors asked for mirth, saying,
*   'Sing us one of the songs of Zion!'*
How could we sing the Lord's song in a foreign land?

Psalm 137.1–4

The unthinkable has happened! The story of the people of God, which has been unfolding over the past week, reaches its lowest point here. Secure in and around their capital city Jerusalem, on Mount Zion, the Jews had come to believe that they were invincible. Despite warnings from the prophets they stopped acknowledging their continual need for God. They presumed on his protection, flirted with pagan religions, and created areas of poverty in the pursuit of wealth.

All this time a vast empire had been increasing in military power to the north. Babylon swept through the country, Zion was overrun, the temple smashed, and Jerusalem's finest taken captive and exiled to a foreign land. This psalm was written in Babylon by a people desolate at the memory of what they had lost. And something made their despair even greater – they believed that not only had they lost their homeland, they had also lost their God.

God, however, is endlessly surprising. Babylon turned out to be a place where the people of God thrived. That was due to a stunning discovery. They had not lost God when his temple was destroyed. He had come with them to their new dwelling. In fact, wherever they went, he would go with them. He was and is everywhere.

Recall all the houses in which you have lived. In the margin, make a list stretching back as far as possible. Can you bring to mind signs in each of them that God was present? Where were you happiest? Is your current home a place for weeping or singing? Is God there?

God at my door to make it a place of help and welcome;
God at my table to make it a place of friendship and sharing;
God at my bed to make it a place of love and rest;
God at my bathroom to make it a place of refreshment and
*   privacy;*
God at my chair to make it a place of learning and joy;
God in my home; God in my life;
God in my past and future. Everywhere!

September 3　Revenge

If I forget you, O Jerusalem, let my right hand wither!
Let my tongue cling to the roof of my mouth, if I do not
　　remember you,
if I do not set Jerusalem above my highest joy.
Remember, O Lord, against the Edomites the day of
　　Jerusalem's fall,
how they said, 'Tear it down! Tear it down! Down to its foundations!'
O daughter Babylon, you devastator!
Happy shall they be who pay you back what you have done to us!
Happy shall they be who take your little ones and dash them against the rock!

Psalm 137.5–9

From the misery of defeat in battle and exile in Babylon the thoughts of the Jewish people turn to revenge. Easy to condemn, of course! But hear the grief-stricken tears of the last two lines. Surely no one alive could have a baby snatched from their arms and murdered without having to deal with thoughts that wish ill upon the perpetrator. We will never be able to offer an alternative to revenge unless we understand how readily it eats into all human hearts.

Angelica Mendoza, from Ayacucho, Peru, is sixty-two years old. She is president of the National Association of Families of the Kidnapped, Detained and Disappeared of Peru. Her son Arquimedes, a university student, was taken from his house on 12 July 1983 by soldiers. He is classified as 'disappeared'. Angelica says, 'We have been working for twenty years to find our relatives. The people who did it have to tell us what they did with them. Don't forget us. Pressurize our government to act.'

Christian Aid partner, the Legal Defence Institute, encourages Peruvians to remember those who died, and works with those who survived to seek justice. Find out more about Peru by visiting www.christianaid.org.uk/world/where/lac/perup.htm

God, our promised land,
our journey has become long and hard
because we wander about like nomads not knowing where to go.
We are strangers in our own land,
　　without bread, a roof, a future.
But you came to find us with your life-giving breath.
You, who are also displaced, have become an exile with us.
You offer us anew the promised land.
Your Spirit urges us toward that joyous homecoming.

A 'Psalm for Life and Peace' by displaced rural people (campesinos) from Lima, Peru

September 4   Returning to Jerusalem

When the Lord restored the fortunes of Zion, we were like
those who dream.
Then our mouth was filled with laughter, and our tongue with
shouts of joy;
then it was said among the nations, 'The Lord has done great
things for them.'
The Lord has done great things for us, and we rejoiced.
Restore our fortunes, O Lord, like the watercourses in the Negeb.
May those who sow in tears reap with shouts of joy.
Those who go out weeping, bearing the seed for sowing,
shall come home with shouts of joy, carrying their sheaves.

Psalm 126.1–6

The Old Testament tells the story of God's dealings with the Jewish people, who understood themselves to be uniquely chosen by God. Yesterday's passage described their broken and vengeful state, having been taken captive to Babylon. They were there for about eighty years but it was a time when, unexpectedly, good things happened.

Hundreds of miles from their temple, they needed to find new ways to worship, so the synagogue system was established. Exiled from their homeland they needed to keep track of their past, so much of the Old Testament was written down for the first time. Many of them thrived and achieved positions of influence in Babylonian politics (for instance, Daniel and Esther). And finally an enlightened emperor called Cyrus developed a repatriation programme.

The psalm we are reading today is the overjoyed song of the Jews as they return home. It has become an anthem for all whose road through life is long and hard. It speaks of inextinguishable hope.

What names and faces come to mind when you read of those who 'go out weeping' or 'sow in tears'? Write down their names. Is today a good day to make a phone call?

From the East to the West,
from the North to the South,
all nations and peoples,
bless the Creator of creatures with a new blessing,
for God has made the light of the sun rise today
over all the world.

From the Dawn Service of the Orthodox Church in Armenia

September 5   Living in unity

How very good and pleasant it is
*   when kindred live together in unity!*
It is like the precious oil on the head,
running down upon the beard, on the beard of Aaron,
running down over the collar of his robes.
It is like the dew of Hermon, which falls on the mountains of Zion.
For there the Lord ordained his blessing, life for evermore.

Psalm 133.1–3

This series has told the story of the Jewish people from Abraham to resettlement around Jerusalem – the point at which the Old Testament leaves them. Shifts of power over succeeding years left them paying taxes to Alexander the Great, then to the Ptolemies of Egypt, then to the Seleucids of Syria. The Seleucid emperor Antiochus was advised disastrously to rein in the Jews by installing a cult to worship Zeus in the rebuilt temple at Jerusalem. It incensed the Jews and many were martyred rather than renounce God.

Two groups emerged – pious Hasideans (later known as Pharisees) and nationalistic Hasmoneans. They united to take up arms and, under Judas Maccabeus, achieved military victories. For a golden age of a few decades the Jews had independence. But a murderous power struggle led to civil war. One of the fighting families struck a deal with the rapidly growing Roman empire, and in a virtually bloodless coup the Jews became subject to Rome. Herod was appointed a puppet 'king of the Jews'. The office of high priest was put up for auction, which scandalized everyone. And into this mess was born the Saviour of the world!

Choosing Psalm 133 to illustrate this was a little ironic. Unity between people is like 'anointing oil' that was used by a priest whose job was to reveal God. And unity is also like 'the dew of Hermon' that was a life-saver on a dry and dusty mountain. There are profound lessons to learn from the history of the eastern Mediterranean. As oil they point us to God, and as dew they point us to refreshed lives. But these things will only be learnt by people who are able to live in unity.

In the margin write a list of things that divide Christians from other Christians. When your list is complete, ask yourself what has been gained and lost by taking a principled stand on each one.

Lord Jesus Christ, who once wept over Jerusalem because its people did not know how to make peace, I add my tears to yours.

September 6   A sower

[Jesus] said in a parable: 'A sower went out to sow his seed; and as he sowed, some fell on the path and was trampled on, and the birds of the air ate it up. Some fell on the rock; and as it grew up, it withered for lack of moisture. Some fell among thorns, and the thorns grew with it and choked it. Some fell into good soil, and when it grew, it produced a hundredfold.' As he said this, he called out, 'Let anyone with ears to hear listen!'

Luke 8.4–8

Am I alone in thinking this? In the developed world we are now in a television age in which everyone – everyone! – knows how serious are the inequalities that debase the human race. So why doesn't everyone demand change? Jesus' parable about what prevents people responding to the call of God helps us understand.

- Sometimes the message about the appalling nature of poverty gets lost among all the other messages that television gives us during the course of an evening – pecked by birds.
- Sometimes people are genuinely concerned but, because they are not aware of any way in which to respond, their passion declines – withered for lack of moisture.
- Some have good intentions, but have other priorities in their lives (Jesus later names them as 'worries, riches and pleasures') that overtake them – choked by thorns.
- But there are others for whom seeing the injustice of the world changes their entire lives and prompts them into action. The good news, according to Jesus, is that just one of these people is worth a hundred of the people who did nothing.

Can you identify yourself among the four 'soils' in Jesus' story?

Commit yourself to doing one thing that 'scatters the seed' by informing someone of what can be achieved when people are given the opportunity to grow out of poverty. A particularly appropriate way of doing this today is by supporting Christian Aid's harvest-time appeal. If you would like (free of charge) a pack that offers churches a way to celebrate the goodness of the Creator God and respond to the needs of his world, telephone 08700 767766 or go to www.christianaid.org.uk/worship/resources/index.htm and click on the 'harvest' link.

God of the harvest,
give life to the seed that you have sown in me,
so that the Earth may be a better place
because you and I lived here together. Amen.

September 7   A mustard seed

[Jesus] put before them another parable: 'The kingdom of heaven is like a mustard seed that someone took and sowed in his field; it is the smallest of all the seeds, but when it has grown it is the greatest of shrubs and becomes a tree, so that the birds of the air come and make nests in its branches.'

Matthew 13.31–32

Does size matter?

No, says Jesus, what matters is potential. The God who could have brought salvation to Earth with armies of angels chose instead to be born in obscurity. Jesus' ambition for the kingdom of God, which started so small, knew no bounds. Localized and threatened by powerful enemies, Jesus' mission must have seemed to his followers as fragile as a seed. But that was before the resurrection. The power of new life to exceed anything that went before it is phenomenal. We live in a world where Jesus is worshipped by more people than even existed on the globe when he walked on it. The closing chapters of the Bible look forward to the kingdom made perfect, describing it as a full-grown tree whose leaves make 'the healing of the nations' complete.

Sometimes our vision of the kingdom of God is obscured by smallness. The small amount we give to poor communities, the couple of evenings we spend collecting for Christian Aid, the postcard we send as part of a campaign for justice – mere mustard seeds! But in the goodness of God, those seeds have grown over recent years to make a genuine difference to the world's poorest people. That is the work of the kingdom.

Eat an apple! Before you take a bite, guess how many seeds it contains. (There is no prize for getting it right except feeling smug all day.) Pick the seeds out of the core and have a look at them. Now try to imagine how many apples there are inside each seed. Take a moment or two to reflect on how powerful is the potential for life that God has sown into the fabric of the universe.

Seeds we bring to you,
Fields we bring to you,
Hoes we bring to you,
Knives we bring to you,
Hands we bring to you,
Ourselves we bring to you:
Will you bless us, O Lord!

A prayer from Kenya, from a seed consecration service

September 8 Yeast

[Jesus] told them another parable: 'The kingdom of heaven is like yeast that a woman took and mixed in with three measures of flour until all of it was leavened.'

Matthew 13.33

Sometimes our vision of what the kingdom of God could become is obscured because the sheer extent of the world's need can overwhelm us. But a few grains of yeast work their way through an entire batch of dough, transforming it in every way. So it is that our faith in God works its way through our lives, changing the way we shop, the way we set our priorities, the way we treat our neighbours, the way we think about the whole world. That is how our small actions come to impact on the lives of people in countries far away.

However, that may not be the whole of what Jesus intended us to learn from this parable. When he used yeast as a metaphor on other occasions he was talking about the evil that can subversively damage what is good in our world. This parable does not allow us any hint of complacency. The task of resisting the injustice of the world which traps the poor in poverty is a task that goes on and on. At large-scale campaigning events Christian commitment to the kingdom is evident, but it is through the things that we do out of sight that the world changes. That is how yeast works, and that is how God works.

Last month we spent several days thinking about bread as an image of what God wants to do in his world. Now it is time to think about the impact that yeast has on bread. Next time you buy bread (for breakfast or for a lunchtime sandwich) choose a different kind from your usual purchase. If you usually eat bread that has yeast in it, choose an unleavened loaf – or vice versa. Be aware of the countries where this kind of bread is usually eaten, and pray for its poorest people.

O God,
to those who have hunger,
give bread.
And to those who have bread,
give the hunger for justice. Amen.

A thanksgiving grace said at mealtimes in many Latin American countries

September 9   A hidden treasure

[Jesus said,] 'The kingdom of heaven is like treasure hidden in a field, which someone found and hid; then in his joy he goes and sells all that he has and buys that field.'

Matthew 13.44

My godson has asked for a metal detector for his birthday. He has asked for it over and over again since February, because he's convinced that there is something buried in the local woods, where there was a Roman settlement. But he is so single-minded that I don't see how I can get him anything else. And if he finds treasure and proves my scepticism wrong, I will be so happy!

I've got a hidden agenda to go with his hidden treasure. I'm praying that somewhere in the future of a wonderful little boy (and preferably after he's had an opportunity to fling a small handful of wild oats as far as they can decently go) he will stumble upon Jesus as a treasure of inestimable value. He knows the name; he knows the routine; he's been surrounded by the love of Christians all his life. But I'm waiting for the day when, unexpectedly I'm sure, Jesus reaches out and grabs hold of him. The same Jesus who has become so precious to me. The one who – brought up in the artisan middle-classes, educated, intelligent – turned his back on all of that and made his home among the poor, relied on others, defied convention, stayed single, trod a delicate line between friends in the brothel and friends in the synagogue, inspired people that a world of justice was not only desirable but possible, and died with words of love and forgiveness on his lips.

Because then my godson will find that everything else that was important to him, metal detector and all, can be traded in with much rejoicing as he makes his journey home.

What in or around your home – alive or inert – do you treasure more than anything else? Before you sleep tonight, spend some time enjoying it. As you do so, think of the treasure that Jesus talked of which puts the values of the world into their proper perspective.

Jesus, into thy hands I give the heart
Which left thee but to learn how good thou art.

George MacDonald (1824–1905)

September 10   A pearl

[Jesus said,] 'Again, the kingdom of heaven is like a merchant in search of fine pearls; on finding one pearl of great value, he went and sold all that he had and bought it.'

Matthew 13.45–46

God does not force anyone into his kingdom. The King wants people who want him. The kingdom of God – that place where justice is universal, peace is assured, suffering is at an end, and the human condition is complete fulfilment – is populated by people who want those things more than anything else in the world. In the hands of the God who has a habit of giving graciously, out of proportion to our hesitant desires and mixed motives, our investment is totally secure. No wonder this parable bursts with glee!

Here is a hundred pounds – sadly imaginary! You are going to an auction and you can spend it all. However, you have to decide in advance what you are going to bid for. Below are the ten valuable things that are in the sale. Your task is to divide up your hundred pounds according to how important they are to you. Which one is your personal 'pearl of great value'? And if it is not one of these, what else would you bid every last penny you have got for?

- Lasting good health
- Creative, artistic or musical talent
- Physical beauty
- Worry-free financial comfort
- Adventure and excitement
- A close and supportive family life
- Warm and happy friendships
- An active sporting life
- A career full of achievement
- Respect for what you are and do

I want my eyes opened to the reality of other people,
to hear what they are not able to articulate.
I want to see justice run like a river,
bringing healing and peace to the nations.
I want the eyes of my heart to see the grace of God
that is present in every child, woman and man I meet.
I want to be able to see differently, to think differently, to live kindly,
to walk humbly, to serve graciously and gratefully.
Come Lord Jesus! Come always and save me –
that I may want what you want,
that I may live in you,
that I may be completely holy.

Romeo L. del Rosario, the Malaysian theologian and poet

September 11   A net

[Jesus said,] 'The kingdom of heaven is like a net that was thrown into the sea and caught fish of every kind; when it was full, they drew it ashore, sat down, and put the good into baskets but threw out the bad. So it will be at the end of the age. The angels will come out and separate the evil from the righteous and throw them into the furnace of fire, where there will be weeping and gnashing of teeth.'

Matthew 13.47–50

Oh God, the world is chaotic! Why is it that, after all this time, evil persists on this planet? Are you to blame, God, for the fact that there is still suffering? You could so easily do something about it. A sudden heart attack to get rid of a tyrannical dictator – that would take negligible effort on your part! A medical breakthrough that would mean the end of AIDS – what is stopping you? An overnight decision by two tribes to stop a vicious war – you want it, so why not do it?

Jesus announced, 'The kingdom of God is here.' But that kingdom of goodness and justice exists alongside unyielding wickedness. This parable suggests that this is not God's failure, but his design. Wherever Christians and their allies are working to make peace or to end poverty, the kingdom of God has arrived as a model of and a signpost to the new order that is yet to come.

The net in the parable was a dragnet that swept across the floor of the sea between two boats collecting everything, absolutely everything, in its path. This is God's plan for the end of human time. The removal of evil will be total and final, not piecemeal. Today, the anniversary of a momentous evil deed, the Christian challenge is to demonstrate amid the chaos what the kingdom will one day be.

Get yourself sorted out! Go through your cupboards, shelves and attic. Separate what you want to keep and what is rubbish that should have been thrown away ages ago.

Eternal light, shine in our hearts,
eternal goodness, deliver us from evil,
eternal power, be our support,
eternal wisdom, scatter the darkness of our ignorance,
eternal pity, have mercy on us,
that with all our heart and mind and soul and strength
we may seek thy face and be brought by thine infinite mercy
to thy holy presence.

Alcuin of York (735–804)

September 12   Who is my neighbour?

A lawyer stood up to test Jesus. 'Teacher,' he said, 'what must I do to inherit eternal life?' He said to him, 'What is written in the law? What do you read there?' He answered, 'You shall love the Lord your God with all your heart, and with all your soul, and with all your strength, and with all your mind; and your neighbour as yourself.' And he said to him, 'You have given the right answer; do this, and you will live.'

Luke 10.25–29

I don't think that the lawyer who asked Jesus this question had any interest in finding out the answer! He actually wanted to know whether Jesus was 'sound' (in other words, whether he believed the same things that the lawyer did). The implication of it was, 'How little can I get away with and still scrape into God's approval?'

The man asked a question about religion; he went away with an answer about love. It is easier to be religious than to be loving. He approached Jesus to get knowledge; he went away challenged to a new attitude. It is easier to learn than to change. Jesus, of course, knew all this. So when the man set himself the ludicrously unobtainable target of perfection – total love of God and equal love of humanity – Jesus nodded sagely and agreed: 'Yes, that's all you need to do!' I don't know how he kept a straight face!

In fact there is nothing a human can do to earn eternal life. It is not ours to obtain; it is God's to give. The reason we can be completely sure that we will inherit eternal life is not that we have a perfect love for God; it is that God has a perfect love for us.

If you were going to give up something that is evidence of how religious you are, and instead take up something that is evidence of how loving you are, what would you stop and start as of today? How do you think Jesus would react?

Let my heart always think of him,
let my head always bow down to him,
let my lips always sing his praise,
let my hands always worship him,
let my body always serve him with love.
O Lord of grace, immense like a mountain peak full of goodness,
do thou forgive my sins!

A prayer by H. A. Krishna Pillai, (1827–1900), the Indian hymn-writer

September 13   A good Samaritan

Wanting to justify himself, [a lawyer] asked Jesus, 'And who is my neighbour?' Jesus replied, 'A man was going down from Jerusalem to Jericho, and fell into the hands of robbers, who stripped him, beat him, and went away, leaving him half dead. Now by chance a priest was going down that road; and when he saw him, he passed by on the other side. So likewise a Levite, when he came to the place and saw him, passed by on the other side. But a Samaritan while travelling came near him; and when he saw him, he was moved with pity. He went to him and bandaged his wounds, having poured oil and wine on them. Then he put him on his own animal, brought him to an inn, and took care of him. The next day he took out two denarii, gave them to the innkeeper, and said, "Take care of him; and when I come back, I will repay you whatever more you spend." Which of these three, do you think, was a neighbour to the man who fell into the hands of the robbers?' He said, 'The one who showed him mercy.' Jesus said to him, 'Go and do likewise.'

Luke 10.29–37

This is a shocking story, but it is so familiar that it has become comfortable. The hero, a Samaritan, is a heretical hate-figure. Jesus is not saying, 'Your love must extend as far as loving people like that.' Rather, he is saying, 'You must accept that people like that are capable of displaying God's love more genuinely than you are.'

You can clearly see the places in the world where God is honoured because that is where, quite unexpectedly, you are aware of mercy, generosity and compassion between an Israeli and a Palestinian, a Christian and a Muslim, an Indian and a Pakistani, a Tutsi and a Hutu, an atheist and a believer, you and . . .

A vicar and a nun walk by, but a drug addict stops to help. David Beckham and Prince William walk by, but a paedophile stops to help. Try finding three people to fill the roles in an updated parable of the good Samaritan, then stop and think what your choices reveal about your own prejudices.

Lord Jesus, I need your help to love those people whom I find unlovely. And if I could not bring to mind who those people are, I need your help even more. Amen.

September 14   A rich fool

[Jesus] told them a parable: 'The land of a rich man produced abundantly. And he thought to himself, "What should I do, for I have no place to store my crops?" Then he said, "I will do this: I will pull down my barns and build larger ones, and there I will store all my grain and my goods. And I will say to my soul, Soul, you have ample goods laid up for many years; relax, eat, drink, be merry." But God said to him, "You fool! This very night your life is being demanded of you. And the things you have prepared, whose will they be?" So it is with those who store up treasures for themselves but are not rich towards God.'

Luke 12.16–21

What they said about wealth:

- *Colonel Sanders, founder of the Kentucky Fried Chicken chain:* There's no reason to be the richest man in the cemetery. You can't do any business there.
- *Spike Milligan, comedian:* Money can't buy you friends – but you can get a better class of enemy.
- *Hugh Grant, actor:* They love me in Japan. But unfortunately I don't want their love. I want their money.
- *Katherine Mansfield, twentieth-century writer:* I must say I hate money, but it's the lack of it I hate most.
- *Madonna, actress and singer:* Do you really think I'm a material girl? I'm not. Take it! I don't need money; I need love.
- *Neil Simon, singer:* Money brings some happiness, but after a certain point it just brings more money.
- *Albert Schweitzer, doctor and missionary to Africa:* If there is something you own that you can't give away, you don't own it – it owns you.
- *The North American Cree Indian declaration:* Only when the last tree has died and the last river has been poisoned and the last fish has been caught will we realize that we cannot eat money.

Write something about money which is your own personal reaction to the parable that Jesus told. It doesn't have to be witty or wise, like the quotations above; it just has to be true.

Lord God, give me a chance to get rid of all this clutter – in my home, in my head, in my life. And when I have made space, give me instead the things that you know would be good for me. Amen.

September 15   Locusts

Hear this, O elders; give ear, all inhabitants of the land!
Has such a thing happened in your days,
    or in the days of your ancestors? . . .
What the cutting locust left, the swarming locust has eaten.
What the swarming locust left, the hopping locust has eaten,
and what the hopping locust left, the destroying locust has eaten . . .
The fields are devastated, the ground mourns;
for the grain is destroyed, the wine dries up, the oil fails.
Be dismayed, you farmers, wail, you vine-dressers,
over the wheat and the barley; for the crops of the field are ruined.
The vine withers, the fig tree droops.
Pomegranate, palm, and apple – all the trees of the field are dried up;
surely, joy withers away among the people.

Joel 1.2, 4, 10–12

Joel's prophecy makes grim reading! He describes a land stripped bare and exhausted. A plague of locusts decimated Palestine six centuries before Jesus. A catastrophe! But Joel saw what had happened as a sign, warning God's people that he was judging them. When we look at our world, stripped bare by over-production, exhausted by pesticides, should we too see it as a warning from God of what is to come unless we change our ways?

In Somaliland, Christian Aid's partner Candlelight for Health and Education is helping to reverse long-standing practices that have damaged the environment. They are doing so not with locusts, but with bees! Traditional bee-keeping involved setting light to the trees to create smoke and drive bees away from the honey so that it can be collected. The landscape is scarred with scorched, dead trees. Candlelight provides training and loans protective clothing so that farmers can both improve their yield and preserve their environment. 'I am producing fifty per cent more honey now and the quality is much better,' says farmer Abdullahi Mohammed. 'I have learnt how to care for the bees and use the by-products such as beeswax. And what's more, I no longer get stung all the time!'

Find out more about Christian Aid's work in war-weary Somalia and Somaliland at
www.christianaid.org.uk/world/where/eagl/somaliap.htm

To the bare earth that we have exhausted,
to the stark lands which we have stripped,
to the weary people whom we have dismayed,
return, O Lord, with blessed and refreshing joy. Amen.

September 16 Rend your hearts

Even now, says the Lord, return to me with all your heart,
with fasting, with weeping, and with mourning;
rend your hearts and not your clothing.
Return to the Lord, your God, for he is gracious and merciful,
slow to anger, and abounding in steadfast love,
and relents from punishing.
Who knows whether he will not turn and relent,
and leave a blessing behind him,
a grain offering and a drink offering for the Lord, your God?

Joel 2.12–14

Yesterday we read of an ecological catastrophe that engulfed Joel's homeland 600 years before Jesus – a warning to both his generation and ours that we cannot endlessly abuse the environment in which God has placed us without consequences. But God is a God whose nature is committed to recycling. The carbon dioxide that we breathe out is taken in by the world's trees, which thrive on it and emit the oxygen that we need to survive. The leaves that are getting ready to fall off the trees will break down into their elemental goodness and enrich the earth to produce an embarrassing abundance of beauty next spring. The word that the Bible uses to describe God's endless recycling is 'redemption'. It means buying back, restoring the original value, bringing good out of bad.

I can never get over the Earth's determination to undo the harm we do to it! Or for that matter our own bodies, in which cuts heal, bones mend and heartbreak eases on and on through our lives until, in the goodness of God, we are redeemed through the last and greatest healing and come into his presence made perfect for ever. This is the kind of 'gracious and merciful' God we worship.

Make an extra effort to recycle this week, then get into the habit. Retrieve paper from the basket so that you can write on both sides of it. Take plastic carrier bags out of the bin so that you can reuse them at the shops. Make a point of choosing food with minimal packaging. Check the labels of cleaning products to see whether they are doing more harm than good.

So that we may live more simply – make us like the bread;
So that we may see more clearly – make us like the water;
So that we may be more selfless – make us like the Christ. Amen.

A traditional Russian prayer before meals

September 17 Do not be afraid

Do not fear, O soil; be glad and rejoice, for the Lord has done
  great things!
Do not fear, you animals of the field, for the pastures of the
  wilderness are green;
the tree bears its fruit, the fig tree and vine give their full yield.
O children of Zion, be glad and rejoice in the Lord your God;
for he has given the early rain for your vindication,
he has poured down for you abundant rain,
  the early and the later rain, as before.
The threshing-floors shall be full of grain, the vats shall overflow with wine
  and oil.

Joel 2.21–24

The stark message of Joel is that all the prayers in the world for situations of poverty are a waste of breath if they are not matched by a change in the lifestyle we lead which is causing them. 'Rend your heart and not your clothing' was the demand in yesterday's reading, referring to the ancient Jews' habit of praying with such fervour that their clothes got ripped with the effort of it. Change your behaviour and not your style of worship! Then we will leave our descendants a world in which they need not fear.

Today, it as if Joel bursts with excitement when he thinks about what God is able to do to restore the land that a plague of locusts had destroyed. He virtually breaks into song when he pictures the land, the animals, the plants and the people coming together harmoniously to sustain the planet. Ecology is the vision God has laid before us for heaven; it is also the challenge God has laid before us for Earth.

Before the end of the day, make a point of looking for the four things that God liberates from fear in these verses – soil, animals, trees, humans. If you find yourself in a place where you can see all four together, so much the better. As you look at each one, mutter the age-old Jewish response to a sight of great beauty: 'Blessed art thou, O Lord our God, who hast such things as these in thy world.'

Lord, grant us eyes to see within the seed a tree,
Within the glowing egg a bird, within the shroud a butterfly:
Till, taught by such, we see beyond all such creatures – thee!
And hearken for thy tender word and hear it, 'Fear not: it is I.'

Christina Rossetti (1830–94)

September 18   Compensation

I will repay you for the years that the swarming locust has eaten,
the hopper, the destroyer, and the cutter, my great army, which I
*   sent against you.*
You shall eat in plenty and be satisfied, and praise the name of
*   the Lord your God,*
who has dealt wondrously with you. And my people shall never again be put
*   to shame.*
You shall know that I am in the midst of Israel,
and that I, the Lord, am your God and there is no other.
And my people shall never again be put to shame.

Joel 2.25–27

It is not only the natural world that God recycles; he recycles experiences as well. Nothing that happens in our lives need be wasted – there is always something that God wants us to learn. If we allow him to, he can recycle our mistakes to produce wisdom. He can recycle our sadness to generate sympathy for others. He can recycle good fortune to produce generosity. For the Christian nothing that happens, good nor bad, is wasted. And so, after the catastrophe that the Jewish people suffered when locusts destroyed their harvest, God declares, 'I will repay you.'

Some years ago a project into which I had tipped hours of work came to nothing, and I felt dismal about the waste. A friend sent me a card inside which he had written, 'God will compensate you for the years the locusts have eaten.' At the time I did not even recognize the allusion, let alone understand how it could be true! But with the benefit of hindsight I can see that I am smarter, more faithful and perhaps even grateful for what happened. And the fact that I am passing the story on to you is proof in itself that God recycles our life experiences.

Revisit some of the experiences of your past that seemed a waste of time – people who seemed important but with whom you have lost touch, projects in which you invested energy, but which came to nothing, experiences that left you confused and questioning. In retrospect can you see what God has taught you through them that might be valuable to others?

God of the echoing centuries of time,
grant me a glimpse beyond the darkness to the morning;
grant me a glimpse beyond the cold to the Spring;
grant me a glimpse beyond the tomb to the resurrection;
until experience of your faithfulness leads me into patient trust.

September 19   I will pour out my Spirit

I will pour out my Spirit on all flesh;
your sons and your daughters shall prophesy,
your old men shall dream dreams,
   and your young men shall see visions.
Even on the male and female slaves,
   in those days, I will pour out my spirit.
   I will show portents in the heavens and on the earth, blood and fire and columns of smoke. The sun shall be turned to darkness, and the moon to blood, before the great and terrible day of the Lord comes. Then everyone who calls on the name of the Lord shall be saved; for in Mount Zion and in Jerusalem there shall be those who escape, as the Lord has said, and among the survivors shall be those whom the Lord calls.

Joel 2.28–32

Joel looks ahead to 'the day of the Lord' – the time when, in the goodness of God, things come to a head and the Holy Spirit is cascaded upon the Earth to change the way God relates to his people.
   Joel thought this day would be dreadful. But our position in history helps us, because we now understand these verses in a way Joel never could. At Pentecost the Holy Spirit was poured out in a room in Jerusalem and the little, local mission of Jesus exploded worldwide. His followers looked back at today's verses and realized with enormous excitement that they had come true. Their fulfilment had far exceeded anyone's anticipation, and the results had shaken heaven and Earth.
   Many of us face the next few years of our lives with fear. But the message of Joel is that God transforms. At the moment we foresee fire and blood. But God is a redeeming God and, if we allow him to exceed our expectations, we will find the years to come to be tongues of flame, winds of change, and words such as we never heard before. The future will be, for us, Pentecost.

Go through your diary for the weeks ahead. Every time you see an event that you are not looking forward to, draw a flame beside it to remind you, when the day arrives, that the Holy Spirit is active throughout the world no matter what that day brings.

Come rushing wind; come refining fire;
cleanse us, enliven us and burn within us.
Set us on fire with love for our God
and for the poor of the Earth.

Janet Morley

September 20 A warning received

Samuel reported all the words of the Lord to the people who were asking him for a king. He said, 'These will be the ways of the king who will reign over you . . . He will take one-tenth of your grain and of your vineyards and give it to his officers and his courtiers. He will take your male and female slaves, and the best of your cattle and donkeys, and put them to his work. He will take one-tenth of your flocks, and you shall be his slaves. And in that day you will cry out because of your king, whom you have chosen for yourselves; but the Lord will not answer you in that day.'

But the people refused to listen to the voice of Samuel; they said, 'No! but we are determined to have a king over us, so that we also may be like other nations, and that our king may govern us and go out before us and fight our battles.'

1 *Samuel* 8.10–11, 14–20

In the Bible stories that we know best, God sends a message to a human and he obeys. But in this story, humans send a message to God and he obeys. Tomorrow we will find out whether it was a good idea!

Eleven centuries before Jesus, the tribes of Israel were governed by 'judges' who took their religious authority directly from God. Some were superb (such as Deborah); some were appalling (such as Samson); and the current one, Samuel, had been respected and loved but was now elderly. The difference between a judge and a king was that monarchs established dynasties.

The Israelites trusted their own political astuteness more than they trusted in God. Samuel told them it was not a good idea; God told them it was not a good idea. However, when humans make their mind up to do something it is the nature of God to give them freedom to do it. No matter what the consequences!

Tomorrow you are going to find out what happened after the Israelites ignored God's advice. Write down what you think happened so that you will be able to compare.

Save us, O Lord, from the snares of a double mind. Deliver us from all cowardly neutralities. Make us to go in the paths of your commandments, and to trust for our defence in your mighty arm alone, through Jesus Christ our Lord. Amen.

Richard Hurrell Froude (1803–36)

September 21   A warning ignored

*This is the account of the forced labour that King Solomon con-
scripted to build the house of the Lord and his own house . . . as
well as all of Solomon's storage cities, the cities for his chariots,
the cities for his cavalry, and whatever Solomon desired to build,
in Jerusalem, in Lebanon, and in all the land of his dominion. All
the people who were left of the Amorites, the Hittites, the Perizzites, the
Hivites, and the Jebusites, who were not of the people of Israel – their descendants who were still left in the land, whom the Israelites were unable to destroy
completely – these Solomon conscripted for slave labour, and so they are to this
day.*

1 Kings 9.15, 19–21

The most frank comment one can make in response to this dismal
episode in Israel's history is, 'Well, they were warned!' Today's
Bible passage shows clearly what happens when God's standards
of justice are defied. Humans act as if they own other humans.
And surely, then as now, God weeps.

The work of Anti-Slavery International draws attention to the fact that we
live in a world still capable of tolerating men, women and particularly children
working in conditions that defy God's desire for humans to live in freedom. At
its website (www.antislavery.org) there is information about bonded labour
(people who are tricked, many in India, into never-ending work for themselves
and their descendants as reimbursement for a loan they will never pay off),
trafficking of women or children who are forced into domestic work or prostitution (eastern Europe has become one of many centres), or the worst forms of
child labour (such as the children who work in mines in Colombia, or the forty
per cent of the New People's Army in the Philippines that are under eighteen).

This is the world we have chosen; this is the world God challenges us to
change.

Have you ever been convinced that something was right, but
done something different on the basis of your own judgement?
What do you feel you have learned from the experience?

O Lord, grant me freedom,
but hold me tight so that I may use it with wisdom.
O Lord, grant this nation freedom,
but hold us tight so that we may use it to make freedom universal.
O Lord, grant humankind freedom,
and let the enslaved people of the world step out
into the light and liberation of the kingdom of God. Amen.

September 22   Bless this house

Woe to him who builds his house by unrighteousness,
    and his upper rooms by injustice;
who makes his neighbours work for nothing,
    and does not give them their wages;
who says, 'I will build myself a spacious house
    with large upper rooms,'
and who cuts out windows for it,
panelling it with cedar, and painting it with vermilion.
Are you a king because you compete in cedar?
Did not your father eat and drink and do justice and righteousness?
Then it was well with him.
He judged the cause of the poor and needy; then it was well.
Is not this to know me? says the Lord.

Jeremiah 22.13–16

What does the house in which you live tell about the kind of person you are? Does it proclaim to the world, 'This person prizes comfort', or 'This person lives on behalf of others', or 'This person cares about the future of the planet'?

Jeremiah is eyeing the palace of a king called Jehoiakim. His father Josiah had acted as a guardian of his people; Jehoiakim exploited them for his personal gain. The father took on austerity and thus revealed his commitment to justice; the son displayed ostentation and thus revealed his lack of concern for the vulnerable. Jeremiah reminds us of what the Bible tells us again and again – that the evidence which displays our personal commitment to God is the concern we have for 'the cause of the poor and needy'. But he tells us something new as well – that the circumstances in which we choose (or are forced) to live reveal the truth about whether our claim to have God's priorities at heart is genuine or not.

Stand outside your home and take a look at it as if you are seeing it for the first time. Imagine someone from one of the world's poorest communities is coming to visit. In your imagination, explain to her how you come to be living in these circumstances.

Do you find this enriching or uncomfortable? In your imagination, offer generous hospitality. Then work out how you are going to make that generosity a reality.

God bless this house from site to stay,
from beam to wall, from end to end,
from ridge to basement, from balk to roof-tree,
from foundation to summit, foundation to summit.

An ancient Celtic blessing to be said standing outside a dwelling place

September 23   Pray unselfishly

The word of the Lord of hosts came to [Zechariah]: 'Say to all the people of the land and the priests: When you fasted and lamented in the fifth month and in the seventh, for these seventy years, was it for me that you fasted? And when you eat and when you drink, do you not eat and drink only for yourselves? . . . 'Render true judgements, show kindness and mercy to one another; do not oppress the widow, the orphan, the alien, or the poor; and do not devise evil in your hearts against one another.' But they refused to listen, and turned a stubborn shoulder . . . They made their hearts adamant in order not to hear the law and the words that the Lord of hosts had sent by his Spirit.

Zechariah 7.4–6, 9–12

It is the sixth century BC. For seventy years the Jews have held religious fasts in which they lament the destruction of the temple when their land was conquered. Seventy years! Get over it! The temple has been rebuilt, for goodness' sake! Is all this fasting still a genuine outpouring to God, or has it just become a ritual in which you persist because it makes you feel good to do all this breast-beating?

Hang on, though! You may actually be lamenting the wrong thing. The real problem is that the rich have become 'adamant' that the problems of the poor have nothing to do with them. Zechariah's message is that prayers which cry out, 'Why is this awful thing happening to me?' may eventually become just self-centred. Where are the people whose prayers cry out for those who are oppressed?

Over the coming days, be aware of who you are praying for. How long can you go without praying for yourself? A day, a weekend, a week? It may be that the Spirit will change your prayers. Or it may be that your prayers will change you.

The stones cry out, 'Mercy for those unjustly imprisoned.'
The plants cry out, 'Mercy for those who have no medicine to
*   heal them.'*
The stars cry out, 'Mercy for those whose minds are trapped in
*   darkness.'*
The fruits cry out, 'Mercy for those who have nothing to feed to their children.'
The rivers cry out, 'Mercy for those who have no water to drink.'
My heart should join this cry.
Give me words to say, O Lord of Hosts,
and give me deeds to match my words.

September 24   Wearying God

You have wearied the Lord with your words. Yet you say, 'How have we wearied him?' By saying, 'All who do evil are good in the sight of the Lord, and he delights in them.' Or by asking, 'Where is the God of justice?'

See, I am sending my messenger to prepare the way before me, and the Lord whom you seek will suddenly come to his temple. The messenger of the covenant in whom you delight – indeed, he is coming, says the Lord of hosts.

Malachi 2.17 – 3.1

Eighty years have gone by since yesterday's message. Initial excitement over the building of the temple has worn off. Economic prosperity that was promised has not materialized. The people feel that their God has proved a bit of a let-down. Worship starts to be a matter of going through the motions; for some it stops altogether.

Sounds familiar?

In those circumstances people start to throw accusations at God that simply are not true. Wicked people continue to thrive whether times are good or bad, but when circumstances are difficult, people start to blame God for it. Because God does not intervene to stop unjust people prospering, it is assumed that he cannot, or that he is cruel, or that he simply doesn't exist.

From his eternal viewpoint God bides his time. Graciously? Well, no! Fed up, actually! He knows that the day when he will intervene is coming steadily closer. In Malachi's time God was preparing to send Jesus, with John the Baptist as his messenger to announce God's call for justice. And in our time God is preparing for the return of Jesus on a climactic Day of Justice. And who is his messenger this time? You or me, I suppose!

Of all the emotions we (rightly or wrongly) attribute to God, the one we use least is the one Malachi talks about – being totally fed up. Is there anything in the way you think or pray or behave that you imagine neither angers nor pleases God, but just really wears him out? Is change possible?

Into a world where wicked people prosper, Jesus come;
into a world where careless people damage the planet,
   Jesus come;
into a world where lazy people have lost the desire to worship,
   Jesus come;
until all people live in a world without violence or need,
we join our voices to the millions who cry, 'Come Lord Jesus!'

September 25   Who can endure?

Who can endure the day of [God's] coming, and who can stand when he appears? For he is like a refiner's fire and like fullers' soap; he will sit as a refiner and purifier of silver, and he will purify the descendants of Levi and refine them like gold and silver, until they present offerings to the Lord in righteousness. Then the offering of Judah and Jerusalem will be pleasing to the Lord as in the days of old and as in former years.

Then I will draw near to you for judgement; I will be swift to bear witness against the sorcerers, against the adulterers, against those who swear falsely, against those who oppress the hired workers in their wages, the widow and the orphan, against those who thrust aside the alien, and do not fear me.

Malachi 3.2–5

Whenever I hear someone preach about Jesus returning to bring human time to a final climax, my first thought is to rejoice that all that is wrong in the world will be put right. My second thought is that I hope it doesn't happen before my holiday . . . or my retirement . . . or, in fact, the end of my life. My thrill at the prospect of meeting God is tempered by a nagging anxiety about what he might say. My life has not (and this won't come as a surprise to anyone) been perfect!

For whom is God's Day of Justice good news and for whom is it bad news? God will call those who have been defiantly unjust or immoral to account for the pain they have caused. But for their victims and for those who have stood alongside them, the coming of God can bring nothing but good.

Malachi tells us that God will purify his creation. The images he chooses are fierce but magnificent. A refining fire blazes, but produces glittering silver. A fuller's soap (a bit like a dry-cleaning fluid) scalds, but bleaches clothes into a pristine state. Making the world pure is not going to be pain-free.

Read a newspaper. Be aware of those who have been oppressed and wronged. These are the people for whom healing will come on the day of the Lord.

Sing to God, sing praise to his name and rejoice before him –
a father to the fatherless, a defender of widows, is God in his holy dwelling.

Psalm 68.4–5

September 26 Robbing God

I the Lord do not change; therefore you, O children of Jacob, have not perished. Ever since the days of your ancestors you have turned aside from my statutes and have not kept them. Return to me, and I will return to you, says the Lord of hosts. But you say, 'How shall we return?'

Will anyone rob God? Yet you are robbing me! But you say, 'How are we robbing you?' In your tithes and offerings! You are cursed with a curse, for you are robbing me – the whole nation of you!

Malachi 3.6–9

We all make promises to God: 'I will give a percentage of what I earn to his work. I will spend time in prayer every day. I will worship him every Sunday.'

The Jews of Malachi's day made promises as well: 'I will tithe all the produce I farm – the first tenth, the best tenth, to be used for the upkeep of the temple.' But if you are an ancient Jewish farmer, what do you do in a bad year? Or after two consecutive harvests fail? Are you tempted to think, 'The temple will have to look after itself this year; I have to feed my family'? And if the rains failed for the third time?

'Enough is enough,' says Malachi. 'This is robbing God.'

We have lean years too. What happens to our promises in hard times? 'I will give, but I will count the percentage after I've paid my tax, not before. I will pray, but if I oversleep and have to rush I will let myself off. I will worship, but if I am at a party until the early hours of Sunday morning I probably need the sleep more.' Two thousand years on, we too occasionally need someone to say, 'Enough is enough!'

Malachi's final accusation is that not only have individuals fallen short of their responsibilities to God, whole nations have as well. If a nation in today's world is 'robbing God', what form does it take? Which present-day prophets say, 'Enough!'?

Dearest Lord, teach me to be generous. Teach me to serve thee as thou deservest, to give and not to count the cost, to fight and not to heed the wounds, to toil and not to seek for rest, to labour and not to seek a reward save that of knowing that I do thy will.

Ignatius of Loyola (1491–1556)

September 27   Put God to the test

'Bring the full tithe into the storehouse, so that there may be food in my house, and thus put me to the test,' says the Lord of hosts; 'see if I will not open the windows of heaven for you and pour down for you an overflowing blessing. I will rebuke the locust for you, so that it will not destroy the produce of your soil; and your vine in the field shall not be barren,' says the Lord of hosts. 'Then all nations will count you happy, for you will be a land of delight,' says the Lord of hosts.

Malachi 3.10–12

How can I be sure that the energy I put into following God is not a waste? What assurance do I have that setting aside money for God's work is not effectively throwing it away? Is there any proof that when I come to pray I am not just talking to myself?

Good questions! In an age in which we can get a 100 per cent refund if we are not completely satisfied with the goods we buy, it is not unreasonable for people to expect God to offer some sort of guarantee . . . is it?

You expect an outraged Malachi to thunder that the Lord almighty will not tolerate such questioning. However, it is not Malachi's voice that we hear: it is God's. And his tone is altogether more compassionate. God says, 'If you are not sure, put me to the test. Try living as you would do if you knew beyond doubt that everything you have heard about me is true. Then see for yourself whether I can be trusted.'

Take a risk on trusting God! Pray about something you have never mentioned before. Give money or effort as a priority instead of seeing what can be spared. Make a decision to stop worrying about something and surrender it into God's care instead. Tell someone that you have been reading the Bible today. See what happens!

To you, O Lord, I lift up my soul; in you I trust, O my God. Do not let me be put to shame.

Psalm 25.1–2

September 28 Swords into ploughshares

In days to come
the mountain of the Lord's house shall be established as the
highest of the mountains,
and shall be raised up above the hills.
Peoples shall stream to it, and many nations shall come and say:
'*Come, let us go up to the mountain of the Lord,*
to the house of the God of Jacob;
that he may teach us his ways and that we may walk in his paths.'
For out of Zion shall go forth instruction,
and the word of the Lord from Jerusalem.
He shall judge between many peoples,
and shall arbitrate between strong nations far away;
they shall beat their swords into ploughshares,
and their spears into pruning hooks.

Micah 4.1–3

Perhaps seven million weapons are hidden in Mozambique. Although the civil war is over, poverty is still a reality, so it is no surprise that many soldiers have hidden their weapons in case they are ever needed again. But, inspired by the theme of 'swords into ploughshares', the Christian Council of Mozambique has developed a scheme in which weapons can be exchanged for tools.

'Anyone can bring a gun to us', says Bishop Dom Dinis Sengulane about the Transforming Arms into Tools project. 'We do not ask for people to give their name. If a child brings just three bullets we will give him exercise books and materials for school in exchange. A group of farmers brought us 500 guns and we gave them a tractor in return. A woman brought her husband's gun and we gave her a sewing machine.' The weapons are cut up, then handed to local artists who create sculptures out of them. In a country in which many struggle to earn enough to eat, a plough can make the difference between life and death. So can a gun. Now there is a choice.

Read more about Christian Aid's work in Mozambique at www.christianaid.org.uk/world/where/safrica/mozambp.htm, and click the 'swords into ploughshares' link to see photos of the sculptures.

Peace! How I long to hear you,
Come to our land, run, run, we are waiting for you,
Our children are crying for you; our mothers are praying for you.
Peace! How I long to see you,
Spread your light to my people, bright like the morning sun.
Let your rays fall on my people, my beautiful African people.

A prayer from the Adjumani district of Sudan

September 29   No one will be afraid

Nation shall not lift up sword against nation, neither shall they
    learn war any more;
but they shall all sit under their own vines and under their own
    fig trees,
and no one shall make them afraid; for the mouth of the Lord
    of hosts has spoken.
For all the peoples walk, each in the name of its god,
but we will walk in the name of the Lord our God for ever and ever.

Micah 4.3–5

War is unspeakably dreadful, and one of its hidden evils is that its legacy continues for years and years after the guns have stopped firing. To reach a state where people can 'sit under their own vines' and 'no one shall make them afraid' requires decades of painstaking work. It could be a dispiriting thought if it were not for the fact that all the Bible's prophets found the Lord in the end to be a God of salvation and life, not of destruction and death.

During the 1990s Rwanda experienced a civil war which culminated in the genocide of 1994. Since then, the country has been on a slow road to recovery. Thousands still live in makeshift homes, without enough water or food. Rape was one of the weapons used in the war, and consequently many survivors or orphans of the genocide are now living with HIV. Nearly all the 25,000 refugees who fled to Tanzania have returned to Rwanda voluntarily. Those suspected of taking part in the genocide will join the thousands currently being tried by Rwanda's traditional justice system *gacaca*, establishing the truth through testimony and public confessions.

Christian Aid has worked with partner organizations in Rwanda since the mid-1960s. Work focuses on agricultural rehabilitation, low-interest loans to help people start small businesses, health education (especially HIV), and promoting peace and *gacaca*. Don't forget Rwanda!

Read more about how Christian Aid works through its partners in Rwanda at
www.christianaid.org.uk/world/where/eagl/rwandap.htm

Lord Jesus, we ask you to bless and to accept the ministry of all of those who are widowed in Rwanda in these days, and called to take on responsibilities formerly undertaken by their menfolk. Give them friends and a community to cherish both them and their gifts, and a lively sense of the communion of saints to
encourage and support them. For your loving mercy's sake. Amen.

A prayer of the Association of Widows of the Genocide of April 1994, a Christian Aid partner

September 30   Act justly

'With what shall I come before the Lord,
   and bow myself before God on high?
Shall I come before him with burnt-offerings,
   with calves a year old? . . .
He has told you, O mortal, what is good;
and what does the Lord require of you
but to do justice, and to love kindness, and to walk humbly with your God?*

Micah 6.6, 8

As long as there have been humans on the planet, there have been attempts to earn God's favour by religious effort. Usually the thinking behind this striving is that the more unpleasant your action is, the more likely it is to please God. That is why in Micah's day people attempted to impress God by giving away their most valuable property to be burnt in a sacrifice, the smoke and smell of which ascended toward the skies from where they imagined God was watching.

Through the years, the means people have used to prove their devotion to God by self-affliction have changed. The days of being bricked up in a hermit's cell have passed. The days of flagellating oneself with whips have passed. Even the days of extended fasting are passing. But don't underestimate the pain of sitting through an excruciatingly boring service week after week under the impression that such feats of endurance earn God's approval.

And what is God's attitude to all this? According to Micah, God always had and always will have a different agenda. He is longing for Christians with lives that reflect his nature – taking action to bring about social justice, seeking out ways to be kind to people whose lives need it, having a day-by-day relationship with God not based on a need to impress him but on a desire to recognize his greatness. When it is expressed this way, the Christian faith, for all its sacrificial challenge, sounds like a matter of joy!

Based on the last line of the Bible passage, choose three actions that will bring equal amounts of pleasure to you and to God. Before the week is out, do one thing that will contribute to making the world fairer, do a simple kind thing for a friend, and set aside some time to relax and enjoy God's company.

Teach me, Lord God, to go through life doing good – not because it will win me favours from you, but because loving and serving you is a genuine pleasure. Amen.

October 1   Seventy-seven times

Peter came and said to [Jesus], 'Lord, if another member of the church sins against me, how often should I forgive? As many as seven times?' Jesus said to him, 'Not seven times, but, I tell you, seventy-seven times.'

Matthew 18.21–22

The most difficult thing about these words of Jesus is that it is blindingly obvious what they mean! He was recalling a story from the Old Testament of a man called Lamech, who trumpeted his intention to take vengeance seventy-seven times over for the wound someone had inflicted on him. When the laws of the Old Testament stipulated that punishment should be 'an eye for an eye and a tooth for a tooth' they sound brutal to our understanding of justice, but they were in fact designed to stop revenge escalating out of control for generations. But these words of Jesus do not just limit the desire for vengeance; they turn it on its head.

It is impossible to insist that someone forgives another person; it can only come from the heart. And it is very difficult to find the resources to forgive someone when the offence continues two, four, seven, seventy-seven times. It might be the repeated mocking of an accent, or the thoughtless noise of a neighbour, or the favouritism of a parent for another child. How much more difficult it must be when an entire nation has to look for the resources to forgive what has happened in its recent past.

The fragile peace in Sierra Leone after a decade of violence is being strengthened by a Truth and Reconciliation Commission that provides a forum for victims and perpetrators of violence to tell their story. A Special Court was established in 2002 to bring perpetrators of human rights abuses to justice. But Sierra Leone is still classed by the United Nations as the poorest country in the world. And violence in neighbouring countries swells the population with refugees. Read about Christian Aid's work in Sierra Leone by following the links at www.christianaid.org.uk/world/where/wca/sierrap.htm

Lord Jesus, I do not know how I will find the grace fully to forgive all that has wounded me in a lifetime of hurts – great and small, intentional and accidental. But I do know that if I am going to do so, the strength I need can only be found in you. Take my desire to get even and turn it into a desire to get even more like you. Amen.

October 2 A king forgives a debt

[Jesus said,] 'The kingdom of heaven may be compared to a king who wished to settle accounts with his slaves. When he began the reckoning, one who owed him ten thousand talents was brought to him; and, as he could not pay, his lord ordered him to be sold, together with his wife and children and all his possessions, and payment to be made. So the slave fell on his knees before him, saying, "Have patience with me, and I will pay you everything." And out of pity for him, the lord of that slave released him and forgave him the debt.'

Matthew 18.23–27

God is the king and each of us is the slave who owes him everything despite having absolutely no resources with which to pay. Ten thousand talents is a colossal debt. When the slave pleads, 'I will pay you everything', he is fooling himself. Equally self-deluding is any attempt by a human to do enough good to outweigh all that has grieved and angered God. Only God interveing to forgive will do.

And will God intervene? Goodness! God's forgiveness is total, free, and has no strings attached. It is limitless, unending, and asks nothing in return. Before the day you were born, God knew the whole dismal truth about how you would fail his standards. Did he hesitate about making you the subject of his ceaseless love? Not for a moment! He knew what he was taking on. And nothing that has happened since has made him change his opinion.

Is anything you have done wrong in the past holding back your future? As far as God is concerned it can be forgiven and forgotten. But it is human instinct to hang on to these things long after God has lost interest in them. On a card, write down embarrassments and failings that make you cringe when their memory ambushes you. Seal the card in an envelope and throw it in the dustbin.

The Lord is merciful and gracious, slow to anger and abounding in steadfast love . . . He does not deal with us according to our sins . . . As far as the east is from the west, so far he removes our transgressions from us.

Turn these words from Psalm 103.8, 12 over in your mind. Take in how liberating they are, thank God that they are true, and work out what difference they should make to the way you relate to others.

October 3   A servant fails to forgive

[Jesus continued his parable: 'A slave who had been forgiven a huge debt] came upon one of his fellow-slaves who owed him a hundred denarii; and seizing him by the throat, he said, "Pay what you owe." Then his fellow-slave fell down and pleaded with him, "Have patience with me, and I will pay you." But he refused; then he went and threw him into prison until he should pay the debt. When his fellow-slaves saw what had happened, they were greatly distressed, and they went and reported to their lord all that had taken place. Then his lord summoned him and said to him, "You wicked slave! I forgave you all that debt because you pleaded with me. Should you not have had mercy on your fellow-slave, as I had mercy on you?" And in anger his lord handed him over to be tortured until he should pay his entire debt. So my heavenly Father will also do to every one of you, if you do not forgive your brother or sister from your heart.'

Matthew 18.28–35

A vicar, at the end of his tether, wrote to the *Church Times*: 'My archdeacon comes into my parish and meets individuals without my knowledge. Recently he has asked someone to become churchwarden. Despite my requesting that I be kept informed of these activities, he continues to do so. Is this outrageous intervention into the business of my church allowed? What should I do?'

A week later came this wonderful reply: 'I would definitely invite this particular archdeacon to lunch every month. After he has politely refused twice, step up the invitation to every two weeks. At luncheon, do not even mention the matter in hand. Just feed him, listen to him, and pray together. Six months from now, all will be resolved. It's also quite possible that you will be asked to be the new archdeacon.'

After the Second World War, many nations had huge debts written off. These are the very same nations that are owed debts today by poor countries in the developing world. Does that remind you of anything in the story? If you would like to tell the UK Chancellor of the Exchequer what you think, his email address is ministers@hm-treasury.gsi.gov.uk

Give me, Lord God, a forgiving heart. A heart that is slow to blame, willing to try to understand, and quick to forget. O Lord God, give me a heart like your own. Amen.

October 4   Workers in the vineyard

[Jesus said,] 'The kingdom of heaven is like a landowner who went out early in the morning to hire labourers for his vineyard. After agreeing with the labourers for the usual daily wage, he sent them into his vineyard. When he went out about nine o'clock, he saw others standing idle in the market-place; and he said to them, "You also go into the vineyard, and I will pay you whatever is right." So they went. When he went out again about noon and about three o'clock, he did the same. And about five o'clock he went out and found others standing around; and he said to them, "Why are you standing here idle all day?" They said to him, "Because no one has hired us." He said to them, "You also go into the vineyard." When evening came, the owner of the vineyard said to his manager, "Call the labourers and give them their pay, beginning with the last and then going to the first."'*

Matthew 20.1–8

If I had been working since dawn I would undoubtedly expect there to be an extra reward for sweltering through the whole day. Surely I would deserve more than the latecomers! In the same way it is human nature to hope that heaven will be more enjoyable for people who have been faithful, chaste and sacrificial for their entire lives than for those who sneak in on their deathbed. That suffering martyrs should get a better cloud or a bigger harp than portly bishops!

But in this parable Jesus insists that God is equally generous to all without exception. He is perfectly generous. He can't be more perfect than perfect! His generosity is incomprehensible in human terms. Awesome! No one has more than God's best. But absolutely no one has less than his best. Should we be thrilled that we are equal in his eyes, or disgruntled that God loves people who deserve it less? That is the quandary that faces the workers in tomorrow's concluding part of the story.

When did you first become aware of God's love becoming real to you? Early in the morning of your life? At noon? Or quite recently? What is there to be learnt from people whose experience is the opposite?

In the morning of my life, energy!
At the noon of my life, service!
Toward the twilight of my life, perseverance!
And, Lord God, with every breath of my life, gratitude. Amen.

October 5   The last will be first

[Jesus continued his parable:] 'When those hired about five o'clock came, each of them received the usual daily wage. Now when the first came, they thought they would receive more; but each of them also received the usual daily wage. And when they received it, they grumbled against the landowner, saying, "These last worked only one hour, and you have made them equal to us who have borne the burden of the day and the scorching heat." But he replied to one of them, "Friend, I am doing you no wrong; did you not agree with me for the usual daily wage? Take what belongs to you and go; I choose to give to this last the same as I give to you. Am I not allowed to do what I choose with what belongs to me? Or are you envious because I am generous?" So the last will be first, and the first will be last.'

Matthew 20.9–16

Jesus teaches that God will be equally generous in saving everyone who turns to him. He must have originally had in mind the Gentiles who had been hearing the good news from him for a matter of months. They had the same rights in God as the Jews who had been 'the chosen people' for thousands of years. That might have seemed unreasonable, but God's vineyard is no place for competitiveness, or pride, or limiting God through our human notions of fairness.

It is typical of the generosity of God that paedophiles and suicide bombers encounter the same mercy and grace as missionaries and trade justice campaigners. Rich or poor, committed or apathetic, hard-working or idle, pure or sinful – there is nothing we can do to earn God's favour. He has been gracious to us not because of the way we have served him, but because of the way Jesus has served us.

Who is at the bottom of your list of people with whom you would enjoy spending time? Put the last sentence of the Bible passage into action.

O God, enlarge my heart, that it may be big enough to receive the greatness of your love. Stretch my heart, that it may take into it all those around the world who believe in Jesus. Swell my heart, that it may take in all those who are not lovely in my eyes, and whose hands I do not want to touch. Amen.

A prayer from South Africa

October 6   Sorting sheep

[Jesus said,] 'When the Son of Man comes in his glory, and all the angels with him, then he will sit on the throne of his glory. All the nations will be gathered before him, and he will separate people one from another as a shepherd separates the sheep from the goats, and he will put the sheep at his right hand and the goats at the left. Then the king will say to those at his right hand, "Come, you that are blessed by my Father, inherit the kingdom prepared for you from the foundation of the world; for I was hungry and you gave me food, I was thirsty and you gave me something to drink, I was a stranger and you welcomed me, I was naked and you gave me clothing, I was sick and you took care of me, I was in prison and you visited me . . . Truly I tell you, just as you did it to one of the least of these who are members of my family, you did it to me."'

Matthew 25.31–36, 40

This story puzzles people. The Bible tells us repeatedly that we are forgiven people, and that our place in heaven is assured because of the resurrection of Jesus. But there is a suggestion in this parable that Jesus will turn to the people he loves and say, 'Have you done enough good things to be acceptable to me?'

Don't worry!

Look more closely. This is not a story about individuals; it is about 'all the nations' of the globe. The message is that our entire world should be one in which vulnerable people have their needs addressed. As individuals we can look forward to a future in which we will know the salvation of God for ever. But as a world, God demands that we create a present generation in which eradicating suffering is a priority.

Worry!

All the categories of people in Jesus' story refer to actual men, women and children who have needs about which Christian Aid is passionate. People who are hungry, thirsty, alienated, unprotected, ill, imprisoned – can you think of a community for whom each of those six needs is a real issue?

Buy half a dozen eggs and write one of the categories on each. As you do so, tell God about the needs of people the world over. And when you come to crack each one, tell him again!

October 7   Goats

[Jesus continued his parable:] 'The Son of Man will say to those at his left hand, "You that are accursed, depart from me into the eternal fire prepared for the devil and his angels; for I was hungry and you gave me no food, I was thirsty and you gave me nothing to drink, I was a stranger and you did not welcome me, naked and you did not give me clothing, sick and in prison and you did not visit me . . . Truly I tell you, just as you did not do it to one of the least of these, you did not do it to me." And these will go away into eternal punishment, but the righteous into eternal life.'

Matthew 25.41–43, 45–46

Jesus asked me, 'How much do you love me?'

I replied, 'More than ever! I am praying more than before and when I sing songs of worship I really mean them.'

'All that is fine,' said Jesus. 'But where is the evidence that you love me?'

Suddenly I was confused: 'Is there something else you want me to do?'

'There is only one test of how much you love me. How have you treated vulnerable or despised people?'

I needed to be reassured: 'And how much do you love me?' I asked.

He smiled. 'This much!' he said. And he spread wide his arms, and died. And knowing that such a perfect love guarantees my place in God's company for all eternity, I found that my desire to serve vulnerable and despised people was transformed.

Goats get such a bad reputation in this story that we should remind ourselves how vital they are to thousands in the developing world. Many of Christian Aid's partners help families rear a goat because it is a source of milk, manure (and therefore plants), and offspring. At Global Gang, Christian Aid's website for children, youngsters learn about African goats through a game that involves moving farmers around the screen in a race against time as night falls. You are far too adult to play that, aren't you! (If I am wrong, it is at www.globalgang.org.uk/goats/launch5.htm. Go on – be a kid!)

Lord Jesus, don't let me treat the message of this parable so gravely that I worry wrongly that you will not welcome me into eternal life. But Lord Jesus, don't let me treat its message so lightly that there is no evidence of my love for you. Amen.

October 8 A lost sheep

All the tax-collectors and sinners were coming near to listen to [Jesus]. And the Pharisees and the scribes were grumbling and saying, 'This fellow welcomes sinners and eats with them.'

So he told them this parable: 'Which one of you, having a hundred sheep and losing one of them, does not leave the ninety-nine in the wilderness and go after the one that is lost until he finds it? When he has found it, he lays it on his shoulders and rejoices. And when he comes home, he calls together his friends and neighbours, saying to them, "Rejoice with me, for I have found my sheep that was lost." Just so, I tell you, there will be more joy in heaven over one sinner who repents than over ninety-nine righteous people who need no repentance.'

Luke 15.1–7

The Pharisees were protecting their uncorrupted lives by setting themselves apart from anything (or anyone) that might stain it. Jesus, in contrast, was out in the middle of life's mess – and enjoying it! He was accused of being morally lax because he chose the company of people who had been rejected by polite society. But Jesus found worth in people when others could not see it.

There is no shortage of 'tax-collectors and sinners' in today's society. What are they like? Lost and searching for something more satisfying, as in Jesus' day. Where are they found? Not usually in churches! At parties, in nightclubs, in front of television sets, bringing up children, in shopping malls, working long hours to fund an exciting lifestyle. So there is a choice before us. Our faith can either take us to a place where we only meet Christians and do religious activities. Or it can take us to a place where people have chaotic lives and the decisions are complicated. It takes courage to go down the route that Jesus went.

Who in your circle of acquaintances is least likely to accompany you to church? Make an arrangement to go with them to a place they would enjoy instead. Jesus will go with you!

Christ, do not remain here at Corcovado surrounded by divine glory. But go down there into the favelas. Come with me into the favelas and live with us down there. Don't stay away from us; live among us, and give us new faith in you and in the Father. Amen.

A prayer from Rio de Janeiro, Brazil

October 9   A lost coin

[Jesus said,] 'What woman having ten silver coins, if she loses one of them, does not light a lamp, sweep the house, and search carefully until she finds it? When she has found it, she calls together her friends and neighbours, saying, "Rejoice with me, for I have found the coin that I had lost." Just so, I tell you, there is joy in the presence of the angels of God over one sinner who repents.'

Luke 15.8–10

God is a seeking God. We do not have a God who stays in a remote heaven waiting for people to do something religious. Rather, we have one who is passionately at work in the world to retrieve something precious – humankind. If that is the message of this parable of Jesus, then he chose to include three surprising elements.

- First, Jesus pictures God as a woman. If that causes mild surprise today, ask yourself how Jesus' original hearers must have reacted!
- Second, he pictures God as poor. The silver coin that the woman lost was a drachma (an entire day's wages), and we know from the fact that she had to light a lamp that she lived in a meagre, dark house, not a wealthy one with windows.
- Third, he tells us of a hardworking God. There were no slaves to be ordered about to find this coin; the woman rolled up her sleeves and swept.

God is good. Humans are precious. Life is best when humans are close to God. We're all heading for a party.

(I'm typing this with a smile as broad as the Pacific Ocean. I can't help it!)

Work out roughly what a day's wages is for you. Write it on a piece of paper. What would you do if you lost that much money today? If you unexpectedly found that much money today, what would you spend it on?

There are 1.6 billion people in the world who have a daily wage of less than seventy pence per day. There are 3.1 billion people (just over half the world's population) who have a daily wage of less that £1.40 per day.

Yours, O Lord, is the greatness and the power and the glory and the majesty and the splendour, for everything in heaven and earth is yours . . . Everything comes from you, and we give you only what comes from your hand.

1 Chronicles 29.11, 14

October 10   A lost son

Jesus said, 'There was a man who had two sons. The younger of them said to his father, "Father, give me the share of the property that will belong to me." So he divided his property between them. A few days later the younger son gathered all he had and travelled to a distant country, and there he squandered his property in dissolute living. When he had spent everything, a severe famine took place throughout that country, and he began to be in need. So he went and hired himself out to one of the citizens of that country, who sent him to his fields to feed the pigs. He would gladly have filled himself with the pods that the pigs were eating; and no one gave him anything.'

Luke 15.11–16

What happens when you put things before people? It is almost always a recipe for trouble. And that is true whether the question is addressed to a person whose life is unbalanced, or to a world whose wealth is unequal.

'Lost' is an enduring word to describe the feeling of being unsatisfied or alienated by what life offers. Young people sometimes announce that they intend to explore the developing world in order 'to find themselves'. The young man in the story did so in the most destructive way – certainly for himself and probably for those among whom he lived. He was reduced to poverty by his own recklessness ('dissolute living') and by circumstances beyond his control ('famine'). Imagine the misery of a Jew being forced to work among the pigs that he had been taught to despise as vermin since birth.

What difference would it make if we read the story as being not just about an individual who has put himself out of touch with God, but of a wealthy nation or an entire world that has lost its desire to recognize the kingdom of God as its home?

The developing world is not a playground. It is possible to travel there in a way that takes advantage of its sunshine and beauty, but damages its economy or culture. If you have never thought about the negative impact of tourism, visit the website www.tourismconcern.org.uk

Lord, I am a countryman coming from my country to yours. Teach me the laws of your country – its way of life, its spirit – so that I may feel at home there.

William of St Thierry (1085–1148)

October 11 A son comes to his senses

[The young man] said, 'How many of my father's hired hands have bread enough and to spare, but here I am dying of hunger! I will get up and go to my father, and I will say to him, "Father, I have sinned against heaven and before you; I am no longer worthy to be called your son; treat me like one of your hired hands."' So he set off and went to his father. But while he was still far off, his father saw him and was filled with compassion; he ran and put his arms around him and kissed him. Then the son said to him, 'Father, I have sinned against heaven and before you; I am no longer worthy to be called your son.' But the father said to his slaves, 'Quickly, bring out a robe – the best one – and put it on him; put a ring on his finger and sandals on his feet. And get the fatted calf and kill it, and let us eat and celebrate; for this son of mine was dead and is alive again; he was lost and is found!'

Luke 15.17–24

It is four o'clock in the morning. You are a mother with a deep love for your teenage daughter, but you are exhausted. She said she would be in by midnight, but here you are, still awake at the window. What will you do this time? Wrench her heartstrings with tears? Rip into her with anger? Ban her from leaving the house for the rest of her life?

The way Jesus describes the love of God is extraordinary. God is out in the street running toward us. The prepared speech of remorse is brushed aside. No expense is spared to celebrate. Punishment is not even mentioned. To call this a second chance underestimates it; this is grace.

Do you share the inclusive love of the Father? Is there anyone whom you keep at arms' length, not realizing that God has that person enveloped in an embrace?

O God, my Mother, you carried me from conception. You delivered me from darkness. You nourished and sustained me. You let me crawl and taught me to walk. You put the first word in my mouth. You encouraged and guided me. You agonized in my hurts and my hurtfulness. O Mother, you let me go, but you never stopped loving.

Anonymous, based on themes from Hosea 11

October 12   A resentful brother

[After telling his story about a young man who had returned home and been reunited with his father, Jesus continued:] 'Now his elder son was in the field; and when he came and approached the house, he heard music and dancing. He called one of the slaves and asked what was going on. He replied, "Your brother has come, and your father has killed the fatted calf, because he has got him back safe and sound." Then he became angry and refused to go in. His father came out and began to plead with him. But he answered his father, "Listen! For all these years I have been working like a slave for you, and I have never disobeyed your command; yet you have never given me even a young goat so that I might celebrate with my friends. But when this son of yours came back, who has devoured your property with prostitutes, you killed the fatted calf for him!" Then the father said to him, "Son, you are always with me, and all that is mine is yours. But we had to celebrate and rejoice, because this brother of yours was dead and has come to life; he was lost and has been found."'

Luke 15.25–32

Things my father gave me: male pattern baldness, an outrageous sense of humour, a complete inability to dance, and a Christian upbringing!

I have been a Christian every single day of my life. There have been times when I treated my Father appallingly (whole stretches of my life when, like the lost son, I ignored him). At other times I acknowledged my Father reluctantly (like the elder son in today's story who begrudged the joy experienced by those who did not seem to deserve it). But right now it seems like the most sensible thing I have ever done – sharing God's passion for the poor, for a just world, for lives lived to the full.

I think I am starting to take after my Father.

Who were the key influences for good during the years when you were growing up? What have they taught you about God? What could you do today to show your appreciation or to honour their memory?

May the love of God draw forth from me gratitude for all that shaped me during my growing years, and forgiveness for all that damaged me. Amen.

October 13   A persistent widow

Jesus told them a parable about their need to pray always and not to lose heart. He said, 'In a certain city there was a judge who neither feared God nor had respect for people. In that city there was a widow who kept coming to him and saying, "Grant me justice against my opponent." For a while he refused; but later he said to himself, "Though I have no fear of God and no respect for anyone, yet because this widow keeps bothering me, I will grant her justice, so that she may not wear me out by continually coming."' And the Lord said, 'Listen to what the unjust judge says. And will not God grant justice to his chosen ones who cry to him day and night? Will he delay long in helping them? I tell you, he will quickly grant justice to them. And yet, when the Son of Man comes, will he find faith on earth?'

Luke 18.1–8

This is a story to encourage us that no huge, terrible evil that stains our world is too big to pray about. But it should also warn us against having unrealistic expectations that God will grant us whatever self-centred trivia we nag him about because we can't find a parking space, or because it's so important that the opposition misses a penalty, or because we need the teacher to forget to collect in the homework we haven't done.

God may be silent, but he is not indifferent. Those who have absolutely nowhere else to go for justice except to God know this to be true. In the UK the number of people who go to church is dwindling by about a hundred a day. In the developing world the Church is growing at a phenomenal rate – about ten times the rate at which Christianity is declining in Europe. Where will Jesus find faith on Earth when he returns? Faith grows wherever people know what it means to throw themselves on the mercy of the Judge of judges.

The Bible tells us, 'Nothing is impossible for God.' Five times, in fact! Write it on a card to put by the radio, television, or wherever you hear the news.

My hands are small, but God is working through me;
my heart is fickle, but Jesus is loving alongside me;
my sentences are hesitant, but the Spirit is praying for me –
evil will not have the last word.

October 14   A pharisee and a tax collector

[Jesus] told this parable to some who trusted in themselves that they were righteous and regarded others with contempt: 'Two men went up to the temple to pray, one a Pharisee and the other a tax-collector. The Pharisee, standing by himself, was praying thus, "God, I thank you that I am not like other people: thieves, rogues, adulterers, or even like this tax-collector. I fast twice a week; I give a tenth of all my income." But the tax-collector, standing far off, would not even look up to heaven, but was beating his breast and saying, "God, be merciful to me, a sinner!" I tell you, this man went down to his home justified rather than the other; for all who exalt themselves will be humbled, but all who humble themselves will be exalted.'

Luke 18.9–14

The problem with this story is that as soon as we hear that it is about a Pharisee we know that he is going to come out of it badly. Pharisees always do in Bible stories. Take a moment to appreciate the shock that Jesus' original audience must have felt on being told that a tax-collector, treacherously collaborating with the occupying Roman government, was more acceptable to God than a religious celebrity. And then spare a thought for the Pharisee, going without water in the dust of Jerusalem twice a week while praying for the nation. To pray, 'God, I thank you that I am not like that proud Pharisee' would be as bad as the original story.

The fact is that the truth about us comes out when we are praying. Not when we are praying aloud for others to hear, but when we are alone with God. He listens to urgent, sincere prayer with a compasssionate ear. But he will listen to proud, hypocritical prayer with a forgiving ear as well – that is the extent of how gracious God is.

Like the tax-collector, go and stand in a place where you are quite alone, bow your head, put your hands on your chest, and tell God the truth about how you are feeling.

Give me, good Lord, an humble, lowly, quiet, peaceable, patient, charitable, kind and tender mind – every shade, in fact, of charity, with all my words and all my works and all my thoughts to have a taste of thy holy blessed Spirit.

St Thomas More (1478–1535)

October 15   John's mission

Zechariah was filled with the Holy Spirit and spoke this prophecy [about his new-born son]:

'You, child, will be called the prophet of the Most High;
for you will go before the Lord to prepare his ways,
to give knowledge of salvation to his people
by the forgiveness of their sins.
By the tender mercy of our God, the dawn from on high will break upon us,
to give light to those who sit in darkness and in the shadow of death,
to guide our feet into the way of peace.'

The child grew and became strong in spirit, and he was in the wilderness until the day he appeared publicly to Israel.

Luke 1.67, 76–80

It is four years before the death of Jesus. At this wretched time of occupation by the Roman army a resurgence of hope is desperately needed. There is an expectation among the Jews of a dramatic revival of the tradition of prophecy. The ancient prophets had anticipated that the prophet Elijah would reappear to herald the leader who would overthrow the enemies of the Jews.

Into this setting strides a firebrand. He dresses himself as Elijah. He lives in the same primitive fashion. He roars and curses like Elijah. His name is John.

The words we have read today were spoken at his birth. His father Zechariah foresaw the excitement ahead, anticipating a radical mission and a message of forgiveness, mercy and peace. The long night was coming to an end, not with a death but with a dawn. Surely there is no better prayer for a new-born child than that he or she should grow up to lead a life that brings hope to oppressed people who live 'in darkness'.

Call to mind the names of children you have known since they were very young – your own or those of friends. Remember the hopes you had at their birth. Are there any for whom you promised to pray? Are there any with whom you expected to keep more closely in touch? What could you do this week to help that child grow into a bringer of good news?

Lord of the dawn, I lift to you this child whose future is known to you but hidden from me. Make of me an example worth following, a protector worth trusting, and a friend who points to the light, as we walk together in the tender mercy of our God. Amen.

October 16 Prepare the way

The word of God came to John son of Zechariah in the wilderness. He went into all the region around the Jordan, proclaiming a baptism of repentance for the forgiveness of sins, as it is written in the book of the words of the prophet Isaiah:

The voice of one crying out in the wilderness:
'Prepare the way of the Lord, make his paths straight.
Every valley shall be filled, and every mountain and hill shall be made low,
and the crooked shall be made straight, and the rough ways made smooth;
and all flesh shall see the salvation of God.'

Luke 3.2–6

John was quoting from writings that were six centuries old, and Isaiah himself was referring back to events in ancient history. For the Hebrew people the first great escape (or exodus) had been headed by Moses, when God's people were led out from slavery in Egypt into freedom. The second exodus (to which Isaiah referred) brought the Jews back from exile in Babylon to a homeland around Jerusalem, and its leaders were a new set of heroes – Zerubbabel, Nehemiah, Ezra. Now, said John, a third exodus was at hand. But this time nothing less than the salvation of the world was at stake.

John pictured the Messiah (the leader anointed to release the oppressed people) riding out to victory in his chariot. Just ahead of him the engineers are building the road on which he travels, frantically trying to keep pace with his progress.

But John will go on to explain that this different kind of leader was travelling a different kind of road – across the treacherous terrain of the chaos of the human heart. The engineering required was forgiveness of what had gone before. And the personal sign of seeking forgiveness and setting out on a new and smoother road was baptism.

Hence the surprising nickname – John the Baptist.

Make today a 'straightening out' day. Clear rubbish out of the path. Iron clothes. Tidy rooms. Will it make a difference in the great eternal scheme of things? No. Will it make you feel good? Yes!

O thou great Chief, light a candle in my heart, that I may see what is therein and sweep the rubbish from thy dwelling place.

The prayer of a schoolgirl from Ghana

October 17   What must we do?

John said to the crowds that came out to be baptized by him, 'You brood of vipers! Who warned you to flee from the wrath to come? Bear fruits worthy of repentance . . . The crowds asked him, 'What then should we do?' In reply he said to them, 'Whoever has two coats must share with anyone who has none; and whoever has food must do likewise.' Even tax-collectors came to be baptized, and they asked him, 'Teacher, what should we do?' He said to them, 'Collect no more than the amount prescribed for you.' Soldiers also asked him, 'And we, what should we do?' He said to them, 'Do not extort money from anyone by threats or false accusation, and be satisfied with your wages.'

Luke 3.7–8, 10–14

The Messiah is coming, announced John the Baptist, and you have two choices. You slither away like a snake and hope you get away with it. Or you admit that things must change and turn right round in your behaviour ('repent' means turn around – not just a matter of saying sorry, but of completely reforming).

Sounds costly? You bet it is! A genuine encounter with the reality of the God who created the universe is such a profound experience that it is not going to leave you thinking, 'Oh, I really must sing another hymn!' Rather it is going to leave you determined to take on God's characteristics.

- Out goes vanity (two coats); in comes generosity.
- Out goes indulgence (too much food); in comes action for the poor.
- Out goes dishonesty (especially in the finances connected with your work); in comes integrity.
- Out goes a restless desire for more (no matter your rank); in comes contentment.

The astonishing thing is that people flocked to John wanting to make those changes. Is it possible that people in rich countries today are turning their backs on organized religion because it asks too little of them?

Three things to look at – your wardrobe, your food cupboard, your payslip. John couldn't possibly have expected people to take him at his word, could he?

Turn me round, Lord God, so that I come to you not with a new set of words, but with a new state of mind. Amen.

October 18   Jesus will come

As the people were filled with expectation, and all were questioning in their hearts concerning John, whether he might be the Messiah, John answered all of them by saying, 'I baptize you with water; but one who is more powerful than I is coming; I am not worthy to untie the thong of his sandals. He will baptize you with the Holy Spirit and fire. His winnowing fork is in his hand, to clear his threshing floor and to gather the wheat into his granary; but the chaff he will burn with unquenchable fire.'

Luke 3.15–17

It is easy to understand why the Jewish crowds thought that John might be their Messiah. His life displayed everything that was finest about the religion of the Old Testament Jews – passionate, zealous for justice, stretching up to God. That way of life could be deeply inspiring for a local crowd – but it could never allow all humankind to see God's salvation. God was working on an infinitely bigger plan.

When Jesus came (the one whom Christians recognize to have been the Messiah), it was not to baptize individuals with water, but to baptize the whole world with the Holy Spirit. Baptism with the Holy Spirit is invisible; it imparts the life of God to us. It drenches our inner selves with divine life. It incites our love; it inspires our desire to be like Jesus; it divides what is good in us from what is wicked; it begins all our beginnings.

I have heard some people say that when they are deeply aware of the Holy Spirit within them their nerve-ends burn as if they are close to a fire. Fair enough! But a surer sign is a true delight in God, and the same concern for others that Jesus had.

Baptism with water is something you choose for yourself or for your children. Baptism with the Holy Spirit is something that God chooses for you – and for every Christian. It means having God spiritually active within you. For some, that starts at a specific moment, like an alarm clock waking up their faith. For others it is something they have been faithfully aware of all through their lives. Look at your own life and ask whether the evidence shows God the Holy Spirit to be dormant or ablaze.

Holy Spirit,
think through me
until your ideas
are my ideas.

Amy Carmichael (1867–1951)

October 19   The baptism of Jesus

Herod the ruler, who had been rebuked by [John] because of Herodias, his brother's wife, and because of all the evil things that Herod had done, added to them all by shutting up John in prison.

    Now when all the people were baptized, and when Jesus also had been baptized and was praying, the heaven was opened, and the Holy Spirit descended upon him in bodily form like a dove. And a voice came from heaven, 'You are my Son, the Beloved; with you I am well pleased.'

Luke 3.19–22

Why did John baptize his cousin Jesus? Why not the other way round?

    That's a good question! Christians believe that Jesus was without sin of any kind, meaning that he of all people did not need to repent – let alone be baptized as a sign of that. But the significance of Jesus' baptism is rooted in another core Christian belief – that in Jesus God himself was walking on the Earth as a human being. Totally human! No infinite powers; no absolute knowledge! Instead God identified with every one of the bruises, weaknesses and needs of human life – including the need to be baptized. From this moment on, Jesus had to accept that his ministry would take him through all the suffering that a radical mission for the kingdom of God can bring. And the fact that it cost John his freedom so soon after the jubilant events of the baptism must have made him shudder.

  It's an extraordinary thought! God looks at his own Earth, ruined by injustice, and says, 'What can be done?' But from the depths of time eternal he already knows what has to be done. So he slips on a pair of Levis, he reaches for a sweater, he slaps on some aftershave, and he says, 'OK. I'll go!' And there he is, walking down Oxford Street among us.

Joan Osborne's wonderful song 'What If God Was One of Us?' pictured God in every way human – a stranger on a bus heading homewards. That is what 'incarnation' means. Try to imagine God walking the Earth today as one of us. Where do you picture him? Or her? Among the people of what country? Or religion?

Lord Jesus,
who shared with me the cuts and strokes of a human body,
understand my pain,
be part of my pleasure,
and make of me a person with whom God is well pleased. Amen.

October 20   Is he the one?

When Jesus had finished instructing his twelve disciples, he went on from there to teach and proclaim his message in their cities.

When John heard in prison what the Messiah was doing, he sent word by his disciples and said to him, 'Are you the one who is to come, or are we to wait for another?' Jesus answered them, 'Go and tell John what you hear and see: the blind receive their sight, the lame walk, the lepers are cleansed, the deaf hear, the dead are raised, and the poor have good news brought to them. And blessed is anyone who takes no offence at me.'

Matthew 11.1–6

John, locked in prison with endless time to worry, was dismayed and beginning to doubt. It must have been extremely hard for John to maintain faith that Jesus was the Messiah when he himself had become one of the captives that the Messiah was expected to liberate.

Dark times – when we are facing illness, loss or loneliness – are sometimes occasions when the beliefs which seemed secure in happier times offer little comfort.

So what did John do about it? He did not allow his doubts to wither his spirit into apathy. Instead he took his search to the place where he hoped to find answers. Jesus (in a frustrating way that will seem familiar to everyone who has doubted what they previously believed) would not give a straight answer to the question, 'Are you the Messiah?' Instead he replied, 'Look at the evidence, then work it out.'

This much is still true – when we see that sick people no longer die before they should, outsiders are no longer left to waste in solitude, and poor people start to thrive, we have a context in which the hard road we walk with Jesus seems the best route to find answers to our questions.

If you could send a messenger to Jesus in order to ask a question, what would it be? Write it in the margin. Over the coming days, keep the question in your mind – not expecting an unambiguous answer, but looking for evidence.

O great God, who art thou? Where art thou? Show thyself to me.

The prayer of Venkayya, the first dalit ('untouchable') convert in the Church of South India – a prayer offered every day for three years

October 21   John in prison

At that time Herod the ruler heard reports about Jesus; and he said to his servants, 'This is John the Baptist; he has been raised from the dead, and for this reason these powers are at work in him.' For Herod had arrested John, bound him, and put him in prison on account of Herodias, his brother Philip's wife, because John had been telling him, 'It is not lawful for you to have her.' Though Herod wanted to put him to death, he feared the crowd, because they regarded him as a prophet.

Matthew 14.1–5

In order to fulfil the ministry that God has called him to, Nader Abu Amsha has kept going at his job despite his office being shelled, his home being destroyed, and having been imprisoned. Nader heads the Young Men's Christian Association in Beit Sahour, just outside Bethlehem. Their work is to help young people who have either been born disabled or sustained injuries, particularly during the violence of recent years in Israel and the Occupied Palestinian Territories.

Running the YMCA would be extremely demanding under any circumstances, but accepting imprisonment by an occupying force as part of your work to improve the lives of the young people shows just how costly devotion to the values of the kingdom of God can be. But Nader keeps going back to the task of rehabilitating damaged people with great Christian faith and compassion.

John was neither the first nor the last person whose loyalty to the Christ was profoundly costly. But such sacrifice does not go unnoticed, even by those who are intent on evil. It drove Herod to seek out Jesus. Do not underestimate how attractive (or how challenging) goodness can be.

The Beit Sahour YMCA is a partner organization of Christian Aid. The prayer below is available as a beautifully designed bookmark to remind you to pray regularly for the lands of Jesus' birth. If you would like one, telephone 08700 787788 or contact one of the addresses at the back of the book.

Pray not for Arab or Jew, for Palestinian or Israeli, but pray rather for ourselves, that we might not divide them in our prayers but keep them both together in our hearts.

The prayer of a Palestinian Christian

October 22 John's death

 When Herod's birthday came, the daughter of Herodias danced before the company, and she pleased Herod so much that he promised on oath to grant her whatever she might ask. Prompted by her mother, she said, 'Give me the head of John the Baptist here on a platter.' The king was grieved, yet out of regard for his oaths and for the guests, he commanded it to be given; he sent and had John beheaded in the prison. The head was brought on a platter and given to the girl, who brought it to her mother. His disciples came and took the body and buried it; then they went and told Jesus.

Matthew 14.6–12

 Herod was both fascinated and frightened by John. He may have 'grieved', but he was too weak to risk his reputation by going back on a promise to a party guest. Nightmares must have followed, because the message of John would not let the king go. When Herod heard that Jesus was preaching with the same authority, he preferred to assume something bizarre (that John had come back from the dead) than something real (that godly truth survives human death).

Herod was the man from the palace; John was the man from the desert. In the palace, life is pampered and your understanding of what has true worth gets fat and fuddled. In the desert, life is stripped bare and you see the real issues clearly. The value of life becomes absolutely plain when you live close to death.

We need aid from the world's poorest communities in order to understand what matters and what is godly. We need Christian aid from the world's poorest people.

 All this overlooks something obvious about the story of John's death – it was absolutely disgusting and no one should die in these circumstances. Take a moment to recall those whose lives have been cut short because of their insistence on telling the truth or criticizing what is unjust. What names come to mind? For every name you know, there are a thousand whose names you do not know. But their names are known to God and to those who still love them. Acknowledge our debt to them.

 Pray for men and women who speak out for the values of the kingdom of God in circumstances that put their lives at risk. Ask God to give them courage, protection and an unwavering conviction that evil should not be allowed to flourish.

October 23   God is our refuge

God is our refuge and strength, a very present help in trouble.
Therefore we will not fear, though the earth should change,
though the mountains shake in the heart of the sea;
though its waters roar and foam, though the mountains tremble
*   with its tumult.*
There is a river whose streams make glad the city of God,
the holy habitation of the Most High.
God is in the midst of the city; it shall not be moved;
God will help it when the morning dawns.
The nations are in an uproar, the kingdoms totter; he utters his voice, the
*   earth melts.*

Psalm 46.1–6

I love this psalm. There have been several occasions when remembering it has sustained me at moments when the difficulties of life have threatened to overpower me. However, what if the earthquakes that threaten are not metaphorical but real (as they seem to have been for the composer)? Where is God at those times? He seems to have disappeared.

The writer knows this too, but he never suggests that God has deserted the needy. He writes of a river flowing through his city. There was no such river in Jerusalem! It is an invisible river, and only eyes with faith and imagination can see it. That river stands for God himself, offering life-saving sustenance to those who have experienced the most terrible circumstances. Invisibly, through the compassion and aid of those who help in his name, God sustains in desperate situations. And that is why those who recognize it need not fear.

There have been many times in recent years when the Earth has shaken and brought terrible suffering to people who were already in need. But we forget so quickly! Many people recall the shock and even the date of the tsunami that struck the Indian Ocean in 2004. But can you name other countries that are still rebuilding years after natural disasters? Remind yourself by reading www.christianaid. org.uk/world/emerresp/response.htm and try to recapture the same passion and generosity as you had when you first heard about these events.

O God our refuge and strength, our help in times of trouble,
have mercy, we pray, on the lands where the Earth has given way.
Protect the homeless; comfort the bereaved;
uphold the frightened; prosper those who rebuild.
O God our refuge and strength,
may those who live where the Earth trembles know no fear.
Amen.

October 24   The end of war

Come, behold the works of the Lord;
see what desolations he has brought on the earth.
He makes wars cease to the end of the earth;
he breaks the bow, and shatters the spear; he burns the shields
*   with fire.*
'*Be still, and know that I am God!*
I am exalted among the nations, I am exalted in the earth.'
The Lord of hosts is with us; the God of Jacob is our refuge.

Psalm 46.8–11

This is a psalm to return to day after day, season after season, so that we can see all that God has done in retrospect through years passing, empires rising and falling, world crises threatening and becoming history. And the cumulative experience of our lives is that God can be trusted.

We've flooded the bathroom, and the world didn't come to an end, and our faith didn't come to an end either. We've fallen in and out of love with all the wrong people in all the wrong ways, and we're still alive, and Jesus is still alive in us. We've lost our jobs and our car keys and our health and our tempers, and we're still bearing up, and it's still God who is bearing us up. We've been through, 'Why, why me?', and we've been through, 'Never, never again', and we've been through, 'Please, please no'. Our doubts and fears are not at an end. But that repeated determination of the Lord of hosts to be there and not to let us go is the reason we can overcome the world. And with that in mind, I suggest that we all . . .

Be still and know that God is God.

God of all times and seasons:
I come to you, the God of spring –
*   the new leaf God, the new life God, rejoicing in your creation;*
I come to you, the God of summer –
*   the colour God, the growing God, rejoicing in your sustenance;*
I come to you, the God of autumn –
*   the harvest God, the richness God, rejoicing in your fruitfulness;*
I come to you, the God of winter –
*   the waiting God, the still and secret God, rejoicing in your mystery.*
And so I surrender my time into your eternity;
I open my life to the edges of your timelessness;
And when I come to that place of stillness and silence,
There let me adore you.

October 25   Just government

Give the king your justice, O God, and your righteousness to a
   king's son.
May he judge your people with righteousness, and your poor
   with justice.
May the mountains yield prosperity for the people, and the hills,
   in righteousness.
May he defend the cause of the poor of the people,
give deliverance to the needy, and crush the oppressor.

Psalm 72.1–4

This psalm was written as a prayer for (or maybe by) King Solomon. It plays with his name, which sounds a bit like *shalom*, the Hebrew word that means prosperity or peace. It spells out the qualities that a national leader should have. The first thing to pray is that the leader and his or her deputies should be just – in creating the country's legal policies (as a 'judge'), its social policies (defending 'the cause of the poor'), its economic policies (and whatever 'yields prosperity'), its health policies (the present-day equivalent of helping 'the needy'), and its defence policies (when the time comes to decide how to confront 'the oppressor').

Within four verses, this psalm has set the agenda for virtually our entire Cabinet. The songwriter's prayer is that the justice of God himself will shape the decisions made by our political leaders. Prayers like these do not guarantee the emergence of a particular person, party or ideology in leadership, but they teach us how to pray, and they challenge those for whom we are praying.

If you have read this psalm seriously then you have already been praying for the political leaders of your country whether you like it or not. Are you confident enough in the work of God in the world to write to our leaders and tell them that you have been praying that they will 'defend the cause of the poor of the people' in their decisions? In the UK the addresses of the ministers whose work relates to the themes of this psalm are all in London: The Secretary of State for Constitutional Affairs, 54–60 Victoria Street, London SW1E 6QW; the Home Secretary, 50 Queen Anne's Gate, London SW1H 9AT; the Chancellor of the Exchequer, 1 Horse Guards' Road, London SW1A 2HQ; the Secretary of State for Health, 79 Whitehall, London SW1A 2NL; the Secretary of State for Defence, Old War Office, London SW1A 2EU.

Read the psalm again as a prayer, this time substituting the names of actual government ministers in the place where the psalm refers to Solomon 'the king'.

October 26　Let righteousness flourish

May [the king] live while the sun endures,
and as long as the moon, throughout all generations.
May he be like rain that falls on the mown grass, like showers
*　　that water the earth.*
In his days may righteousness flourish and peace abound, until
*　　the moon is no more.*
May he have dominion from sea to sea,
*　and from the River to the ends of the earth.*
May his foes bow down before him, and his enemies lick the dust.
May the kings of Tarshish and of the isles render him tribute,
May the kings of Sheba and Seba bring gifts.
May all kings fall down before him, all nations give him service.

Psalm 72.5–11

Three thousand years ago, this was a coronation anthem for King Solomon. To read it now with our own nation in mind is slightly embarrassing. Praying for power that stretches to the end of the Earth smacks of the days when Europe dominated the world through its empires, bringing harm as well as good.

However, I am convinced that some of Solomon's subjects were embarrassed by the way he used his power as well. His reign was characterized by wisdom – he gave the poor access to law courts, built the temple, established trade deals, and (comparatively) maintained peace. But he also accumulated vast wealth, used slave labour to build himself a palace, and turned from God to worship idols. Unsurprisingly, he did not live for ever! His actions set the scene for his country to divide and fight in the years after he died.

Soon after the psalm was written it came to be treated as a vision of the anticipated Messiah. From our perspective it is easy to see Jesus in these verses. In a way that no human leader could ever be, he is victorious, eternal, and committed to righteousness. Thank God for a leader in whose power we can rejoice without embarrassment.

Look up the words of the National Anthem. How do they compare with Solomon's anthem? If you were to write a new anthem as a prayer for the nation, what would it say?

Jesus Messiah, both the rulers and the ruled of this Earth are your family. May rich and poor alike find their value in you. May powerful and powerless find their dignity in you. May sinners and sinned-against find their salvation in you. With great joy and confidence we cry out, 'May the King live for ever!'

October 27   A king who rescues the poor

[The king] delivers the needy when they call,
the poor and those who have no helper.
He has pity on the weak and the needy, and saves the lives of
    the needy.
From oppression and violence he redeems their life;
and precious is their blood in his sight.

Psalm 72.12–14

Here are standards against which the government of any country can be measured. Are its leaders governing in the interests of those who have risen to power, or in the interests of 'those who have no helper'? Are its actions characterized by 'taking pity' and 'saving lives' when it is confronted by the needs of its people, or does it maintain its hold on power by 'oppression and violence'? At its heart this depends on whether every human life is valued for its intrinsic worth – what a Christian would describe as being in the image of God. Human blood is either 'precious' or merely useful in making a nation thrive.

Christian Aid began working in the north of Iraq in 1991. Since the fall of Saddam Hussein's regime it has been able to support work in the south and centre of the country as well. It supports projects to improve livelihoods, strengthen communities, promote human rights, and address the need for better water and sanitation. The new circumstances may pave the way for freedom, but the lack of security is hampering the reconstruction effort and many Iraqis still do not have access to basic services. Christian Aid's partners explain that what is needed is a genuine democracy, the end of discrimination and persecution, and reconstruction – not only from war, but from the social and economic effects of decades of authoritarian rule. Read more about Christian Aid's work in Iraq at www.christianaid.org.uk/world/where/meeca/iraqp.htm

Hail to the Lord's Anointed, great David's greater Son!
Hail in the time appointed, his reign on earth begun!
He comes to break oppression, to set the captive free;
to take away transgression, and rule in equity.
He comes with succour speedy to those who suffer wrong;
to help the poor and needy, and bid the weak be strong.
Before him on the mountains, shall peace, the herald, go,
and righteousness, in fountains, from hill to valley flow.

James Montgomery (1771–1854), from a hymn based on this psalm

October 28   Long live the king

Long [live the king!] May gold of Sheba be given to him.
May prayer be made for him continually, and blessings invoked
    for him all day long.
May there be abundance of grain in the land,
    may it wave on the tops of the mountains;
        may its fruit be like Lebanon,
and may people blossom in the cities like the grass of the field.
May his name endure for ever, his fame continue as long as the sun.
May all nations be blessed in him; may they pronounce him happy.
Blessed be the Lord, the God of Israel, who alone does wondrous things.
Blessed be his glorious name for ever; may his glory fill the whole earth.
Amen and Amen.

Psalm 72.15–19

This psalm has shown us the priorities that a nation's rulers should have – justice for its poorest, support for its weakest, and peace within its boundaries. Today's climax adds the realistic aims of generating sufficient wealth for its people to have enough to eat (in the rural communities around Jerusalem this meant successful farming, with an 'abundance of grain') and of creating a society in which people can better themselves and 'blossom'.

Even 3,000 years ago the writer recognized an international dimension. Not only would the whole world envy Israel, but every other nation would also 'be blessed'. It is the stability of a country that makes these things happen – as true today as it was then.

Stability is vital if a country is to emerge from poverty. That is why Christian Aid supports trade unions, human rights organizations and cultural associations that make communities strong in the face of natural or manmade assaults. To an outsider, giving to such organizations is not so appealing as putting food in the hands of hungry children. But in the long term it is the work of such groups (building up 'civil society') that allows a hungry community to be changed permanently. Read the report of the projects that Christian Aid supported last year at www.christianaid.org.uk/aboutca/annrev/index.htm or by contacting one of the addresses at the back of the book and asking to be sent the latest 'Annual Review'.

Eternal God, give wisdom to all who make decisions about where money given to charities should go. May there be no waste, no dishonesty, and no loss. And so may generous sharing be a blessing both to those who give and to those who receive.
Amen.

October 29   The house of the Lord

I was glad when they said to me,
  'Let us go to the house of the Lord!'
Our feet are standing within your gates, O Jerusalem.
Jerusalem – built as a city that is bound firmly together.
To it the tribes go up, the tribes of the Lord,
  as was decreed for Israel,
to give thanks to the name of the Lord.
For there the thrones for judgement were set up,
  the thrones of the house of David.

Psalm 122.1–5

Jerusalem was the site of the temple, and for the Jews of 3,000 years ago that was the place where they gathered as a community to worship God. To understand this psalm you have to imagine a pilgrim, footsore from a walk of many miles to reach his capital, finally entering the city, staring in awe at the glittering walls of the temple, and realizing that the rumours he had heard about its beauty were true.

Let's be honest! For most churchgoers today going to a service on a Sunday morning is not such a breathtaking experience. In fact, sometimes we need a lot of persuasion that there is anything at all to be gained from going to church, rather than practising the Christian faith privately. So it is just as well that this psalm gives us some reminders of why public worship can help us:

- At its best it nourishes our inner life, making us 'glad'.
- It strengthens our sense of community as people 'bound firmly together'.
- It gives shape to our lives – to have a regular event to which we 'go up' and 'give thanks' creates a rhythm in the calendar of our lives.
- It is a place where we can come together to work for justice – as individuals we will always be weak when we try to change the world, but when we come together to put into practice 'God's judgements' we can be strong.

On a card, write down the words 'gladness', 'community', 'shape' and 'justice'. Next time you go to church (either joyfully or with a heavy heart) take the card with you. As the service begins, remind yourself of those four words.

Holy Spirit of God, sweep through your churches, we pray. Blow away all that is dull, hypocritical and unworthy. Instead refresh our worship with joy, friendship, purpose and a determination to do good. It is with great urgency that we offer this humble prayer. Amen.

October 30   Pray for the peace of Jerusalem

Pray for the peace of Jerusalem:
'May they prosper who love you.
Peace be within your walls, and security within your towers.'
For the sake of my relatives and friends I will say, 'Peace be
   within you.'
For the sake of the house of the Lord our God, I will seek your good.

Psalm 122.6–9

It has been a long time since I visited Jerusalem. It was 1989, and a time of tension. The friends I was with read these words as we stood on the Mount of Olives and looked across at the shining domes of the city. The signs of a city that longed for a peace that it could not enjoy were already evident. I remember burnt-out shops, children throwing stones, and all the petty incoveniences of tightened security. Now on television I watch with dismay as the intensity of those scenes is multiplied many times over, and I very often find myself recalling my visit and praying for the peace of Jerusalem. It is a site that is precious to three of the world's largest religions – Christianity, Judaism and Islam. My reaction to seeing Jerusalem for myself was that it felt as if God put an intolerable strain on the city 2,000 years ago by choosing it as the very spot where he would be made human, and that the city has been tearing itself apart under the pressure of trying to bear the responsibility ever since.

The fact is that what happens to Jerusalem, and to the Israelis and Palestinians who seek to make a living in the land around it, has become the focus for even bigger political issues that will have an impact on everyone in the world. It is more pertinent than ever that we should pray for peace 'for the sake of my relatives and friends', because we may all be affected by the outcome. At a time when many are seeking to do harm in the region, this psalm forces us to choose whether we are people who say, 'I will seek your good.'

Find the latest news about Christian Aid's work in Israel and the Occupied Palestinian Territories at
www.christianaid.org.uk/world/where/meeca/isrpalp.htm

On those who weep in Israel,
trapped by fear, victims of violence,
Lord have compassion.
On those who weep in Palestine,
trapped by force, victims of injustice,
Lord have compassion.
We pray for the peace of Jerusalem. Amen.

October 31   Have mercy

To you I lift up my eyes,
   O you who are enthroned in the heavens!
As the eyes of servants look to the hand of their master,
as the eyes of a maid to the hand of her mistress,
   so our eyes look to the Lord our God until he has mercy upon us.
Have mercy upon us, O Lord, have mercy upon us,
for we have had more than enough of contempt.
Our soul has had more than its fill of the scorn of those who are at ease,
of the contempt of the proud.

Psalm 123.1–4

There are two kinds of slavery, and both of them feature in this psalm.

The first kind is a gladly accepted humility. This kind of 'servant' looks to the hand of a master with pleasure because that hand is open with generosity or affection. The first half of the psalm is a picture of how God and humans might relate to each other.

The second kind is an enforced humiliation. This kind of 'servant' looks at the hand of a master with fear because that hand is clenched in threat. That is the relationship in the second half of the psalm. It is a picture of how rich and poor humans relate to each other when powerful people lose touch with the values of God's kingdom.

When people who live in rich communities read this psalm, the first half reminds them of all the good things that can happen to the world when Christians willingly take on the role of a servant. When people in poor communities read it, they identify with the second half, and cry out in pain to God because they too have had 'more than their fill' of the cynical behaviour of the rich.

Read the psalm again. What do you make of it? Does the song strike you as a meek one or an angry one? Is the Bible different when you see it through the eyes of someone in completely different circumstances?

And though I behold a man hate me,
may I love him.
O God, Father, help me Father!
O God, Creator, help me Lord!
And even though I behold a man hate me,
I will love him.

The prayer of an old man from the Dinka tribe of Sudan

November 1   Humble content

O Lord, my heart is not lifted up, my eyes are not raised too high;
I do not occupy myself with things too great and too marvellous
    for me.
But I have calmed and quieted my soul, like a weaned child with
    its mother;
my soul is like the weaned child that is with me.
O Israel, hope in the Lord from this time on and for evermore.

Psalm 131.1–3

This psalm is wonderfully encouraging for people who find that the complex theology about what God is like goes completely over their head. It is full of reassurance for anyone who has sat through a talk or sermon and thought, 'I've got no idea what you're talking about!' Obviously we need people to do some hard thinking about the complicated issues of the Christian faith. But there is also a place for quietly coming to God and saying to her, as the psalm writer does, 'Mother God, I'm completely bewildered, but I love you and I know you care for me.' A small, simple thought about God is in every way as significant as a deep, bewildering one.

And that is my small, simple thought about God for today!

Imagine that you are talking to a child – a weaned child of about three. Think of three things that you would want to tell them about God, in a way which they can begin to understand. Write down the three things you chose in the margin of this book. Then spend some time enjoying the fact that they are true for you as well as for a child.

'Tis the gift to be simple, 'tis the gift to be free,
'tis the gift to come down where we ought to be;
and when we find ourselves in the place just right,
'twill be in the valley of love and delight.
    When true simplicity is gained,
to bow and to bend we shan't be ashamed,
to turn, turn, will be our delight
until by turning, turning we come round right.

These are the words of an eighteenth-century Amish hymn. The Amish are a North American Mennonite group committed to a simple lifestyle, high standards of work and following the teachings of Jesus. Use their song to lead you into prayer about your own life and work.

November 2 Trust in the Lord

Praise the Lord! Praise the Lord, O my soul!
I will praise the Lord as long as I live; I will sing praises to my
God all my life long.
Do not put your trust in princes, in mortals, in whom there is
no help.
When their breath departs, they return to the earth;
on that very day their plans perish.
Happy are those whose help is the God of Jacob,
whose hope is in the Lord their God,
who made heaven and earth, the sea, and all that is in them;
who keeps faith for ever.

Psalm 146.1–6

Christians walk the same paths and stumble into the same emergencies as everyone else. Of course they do! But there is a big difference. Christians know that they are not at the mercy of a random fate. Nor ultimately subject to the power of other humans, who share their failing bodies and fear of death. Christians know that they are under the watchful concern of the Creator of all things, visible and invisible. So when a crisis arises, they know the first place to go for help.

So what does God protect us from? Obviously he doesn't protect us from misfortune in itself. Christians do their share of failing exams, succumbing to illnesses and breaking their hearts. We are not people of faith because we want to magic these away. What God can protect us from is the harm that these things can do to our inmost beings.

God can deal completely and thoroughly with the paralyzing worry inside us that destroys our courage and confidence. And because God is addressing the worry inside us, we find the resilience we need to deal with the trouble outside us. Secure in God eternally, Christians need not fall apart in a crisis. And that is indeed a reason to give praise.

If you can do so without distress, revisit some of the troubled times of your life. Ask yourself what it is that has made you strong enough to survive them and still be here reading these words. What have you learned about trust along the way – both trust in God and trust in humans?

Now I love you alone. You alone do I follow. You alone do I seek. You alone am I ready to serve. For you alone are almighty in justice. Under your sway I long to be.

Augustine, Bishop of Hippo (modern Tunisia), 354–430

November 3 Upholding the oppressed

[The Lord] executes justice for the oppressed;
  [he] gives food to the hungry.
The Lord sets the prisoners free;
  the Lord opens the eyes of the blind.
The Lord lifts up those who are bowed down;
  the Lord loves the righteous.
The Lord watches over the strangers; he upholds the orphan and the widow,
but the way of the wicked he brings to ruin.
The Lord will reign for ever, your God, O Zion, for all generations.
Praise the Lord!

Psalm 146.7–10

Human leaders are limited by their own mortality. At their worst they betray the trust that is placed in them. In contrast to leaders who maintain their hold on power by locking up the opposition, God can be recognized at work when prisoners are set free. In contrast to leaders who make political capital out of the hostility people have toward 'strangers' (be they refugees, street kids, destitute people, or anyone else who is perceived as receiving from society without contributing to it) God can be recognized at work when they are 'watched over' and 'upheld'.

There are some cases where the fact that earthly leaders are mortal is a blessing. Even if they cannot be voted out, they will one day be buried! The rule that counts is the Lord's, and it will endure for ever. When the news of abuses of human rights is dismaying it is to God's throne we look for reasons to shout, 'Alleluia!'

Many who work for Christian Aid's partners take personal risks when they pursue justice for oppressed people. In Bolivia, the poorest country in South America, the Centre for Research and Training of Peasant Farmers gives communities legal assistance to stay on their land in the face of intimidation by rich landowners. Members of staff have been attacked or forced to flee. However, their work goes on to achieve respect for basic rights in a country that was rich in minerals, but where the gap between the wealthy few and the impoverished majority is growing. Read about Christian Aid's work in Bolivia at www.christianaid.org.uk/world/where/lac/boliviap.htm

Long live justice! Long live the courage of all who pursue it! Long live those who seek freedoms that are theirs by right! Long live those who are determined that their children should grow in a better world than they did! Long live this beautiful planet! Long live hope! Enough is enough! Long, long, long live God!

November 4   Praise the Lord!

*Praise the Lord! Praise God in his sanctuary; praise him in his
     mighty firmament!
Praise him for his mighty deeds; praise him according to his
     surpassing greatness!
Praise him with trumpet sound; praise him with lute and harp!
Praise him with tambourine and dance; praise him with strings and pipe!
Praise him with clanging cymbals; praise him with loud clashing cymbals!
Let everything that breathes praise the Lord! Praise the Lord!*

Psalm 150.1–6

Our series ends with a bellow, reminding us why God is worthy
of our praise:

* 'In his sanctuary' – because God is at work in every strong and
  struggling church.
* 'In his mighty firmament' – because God's creation is an endless marvel.
* 'For his mighty deeds' – because good is stronger than evil, and that changes
  lives.
* 'According to his surpassing greatness' – all that he is, and all that we are not!
* With every kind of music – because all the country and western, drum 'n'
  bass, opera, trance, folk, symphonies, jazz, chamber music, garage, reggae,
  bhangra, roots and gospel belong to him.

Go and get the CD of your current favourite piece of music – it
doesn't matter whether it is a secular or sacred piece (or does it?).
On a slip of paper write: 'Let everything that breathes praise the
Lord!' Tuck it inside the cover, where it will be a reminder to you
every time you get it out to play that you can use this piece of
music to point you toward God. Alleluia!

*All you big things, bless the Lord!
Mount Kilimanjaro and Lake Victoria,
The Rift Valley and the Serengeti Plain,
Fat baobabs and shady mango trees,
All eucalyptus and tamarind trees:
Bless the Lord! Praise and extol him for ever and ever!
All you tiny things, bless the Lord!
Busy black ants and hopping fleas,
Wriggling tadpoles and mosquito larvae,
Flying locusts and water drops,
Pollen dust and tsetse flies,
Millet seeds and dried dagaa:
Bless the Lord! Praise and extol him for ever and ever!*

A psalm of praise from Africa

November 5   Perseverence

James, a servant of God and of the Lord Jesus Christ. To the twelve tribes in the Dispersion: Greetings.

My brothers and sisters, whenever you face trials of any kind, consider it nothing but joy, because you know that the testing of your faith produces endurance; and let endurance have its full effect, so that you may be mature and complete, lacking in nothing.

James 1.1–4

Over the next few weeks we are going to read an entire book of the Bible from beginning to end. It is a letter written by James and sent as a circular to Jews throughout the known world who had converted to Christianity.

Some people think the writer was the same James who was brother of Jesus and leader of the church in Jerusalem. If so, it was written from a context of persecution and poverty to people who were relatively prosperous. (The situation in Jerusalem grew so bad that Paul organized an appeal for aid in the churches he had founded.) It is as if the director of one of the partner organizations with which Christian Aid works in the developing world addressed a letter to us.

Knowing that, I am inclined to take what he says about facing difficulty more seriously. If he says that even in great hardship there is a reason to be joyful, it has come from experience, not from easy piety. Those who work their way through testing times emerge stronger, more mature, and in some way 'complete'. It is a challenge to our society's priorities to hear a poor person suggest that, having found those underrated qualities, he is 'lacking in nothing'.

There is no more appropriate day than 5 November to begin a letter from a community undergoing religious persecution. The festivities of Guy Fawkes' Night are rooted in the violent inability of communities five centuries ago to come to terms with each other's beliefs.

The good news is that the day which was once celebrated with venom and abuse is now celebrated with fireworks and cheerfulness. Go to the window tonight and look for some fireworks. As you see each one, think of a place in the world where one group persecutes another because of their religion.

Pray for the day when fireworks replace guns in the conflicts that you have brought to mind. You could let off one of your own as a bright symbol of hope for a dark and divided world.

November 6   Ask for wisdom

If any of you is lacking in wisdom, ask God, who gives to all generously and ungrudgingly, and it will be given you. But ask in faith, never doubting, for the one who doubts is like a wave of the sea, driven and tossed by the wind; for the doubter, being double-minded and unstable in every way, must not expect to receive anything from the Lord.

James 1.5–8

Writing from a context of poverty it would be understandable if James advocated praying for money. But he doesn't; instead he urges people to pray that they will become wise. Wisdom is spiritual and consists of us knowing the ways of God. But it is also practical and relates to the day-to-day business of living as a Christian. And of course, wealth cannot help us do either of those, which is why God is prepared to give us wisdom with such generosity and despite our failings.

So if God is prepared to be so open-handed in making his followers wise, why do Christians so often make asses of themselves? Because we are not always single-minded in wanting everything we do to be infused with God's wisdom. If half our mind is filled with God's values and the other half with the world's values, we will be as restless as a storm at sea.

Do you ever find yourself wavering between a passion that the world should be better for the world's poorest people and a reluctance to let go of the luxuries which make life comfortable?

Me too! Hmm! At least now we know what to pray for.

Bring to mind some specific decisions that need to be made in the near future. What help do you require in order to make them? Ask God to equip you to decide wisely.

Generous God, I ask for wisdom:
to know when to speak and when to stay silent;
to know when to oppose and when to tolerate;
to know when to spend and when to refrain;
so that my thoughts may become your thoughts
and my ways your ways. Amen.

November 7   Humble circumstances

Let the believer who is lowly boast in being raised up, and the rich in being brought low, because the rich will disappear like a flower in the field. For the sun rises with its scorching heat and withers the field; its flower falls, and its beauty perishes. It is the same way with the rich; in the midst of a busy life, they will wither away.

James 1.9–11

Like an open-air preacher, James shouts out his points – short, sharp and full of paradox. He says, 'The poor are rich because God loves them.' That kind of talk makes friends easily. He goes on, 'The rich are poor because they are relying on such a transitory route to satisfaction.' That is more likely to make enemies!

But is either statement really something that people should 'boast in'? It is certainly true that the rich can join the poor in boasting that a lively relationship with God brings more than the poor person lacks or the rich person possesses. Only an understanding of Jesus' willingness to be completely humbled can make sense of the contradictions.

On a visit to Santiago, Chile, one of Christian Aid's staff explained how the organization worked. 'Do you mean', a surprised voice asked, 'that during Christian Aid Week respectable church people in your country go out on to the streets to beg on behalf of the world's poor?' Well, in a sense they do! Could you take pride in being a beggar?

It is too early to consider being a Christian Aid Week beggar next May. But it is precisely the right time to consider fundraising for the Christmas appeal. What could you do that is humble but not humiliating? Carol singing? Collecting? Running a stall at a Christmas fair? Contact one of the phone numbers at the back of this book, or visit www.christianaid.org.uk/worship/resources/index.htm and Christian Aid can provide you with everything you need to collect money for a project that will not 'wither away'.

Lord God, I have heard so many times that the poor and weak need the rich and strong. Help me to realize that, in your kingdom, the opposite is also true. Amen.

November 8   Enduring hardship

Blessed is anyone who endures temptation. Such a one has stood the test and will receive the crown of life that the Lord has promised to those who love him. No one, when tempted, should say, 'I am being tempted by God', for God cannot be tempted by evil and he himself tempts no one. But one is tempted by one's own desire, being lured and enticed by it; then, when that desire has conceived, it gives birth to sin, and that sin, when it is fully grown, gives birth to death. Do not be deceived, my beloved.

Every generous act of giving, with every perfect gift, is from above, coming down from the Father of lights, with whom there is no variation or shadow due to change. In fulfilment of his own purpose he gave us birth by the word of truth, so that we would become a kind of first fruits of his creatures.

James 1.12–18

'Why is God putting me through this intolerable hardship?' Familiar question? A test pilot pushes a plane to extremes as well, not to break it up, but to make its reliability complete. Life's difficulties give us a reason to cling closer to God; they should not be a reason to give up on God.

However, don't find yourself thinking that difficulties are sent by God specifically to trick us into giving in to evil. Only what is good comes to us from God; evil comes when the greedy, proud or angry desires that are inert in every human are given a chance to come alive. The wonder is that, knowing what human inclinations would be, God still chose to bring humanity into existence. His intention was that we should be 'first fruits' (the finest and freshest of the harvest) of the world. How heartening to know that God had such high hopes for us, and still hasn't changed his mind.

If there is a cloudless sky, look up at the heavenly 'lights' of which God is described as the Father. Dwell for a minute or two on the age and distance of the sun or stars. How do they speak of the God who does not change?

O Lord my God, you are always more ready to give than I am to receive. Help me to recognize that every good thing in my life has been your gift, even when I am struggling through times of hardship. Amen.

November 9   Doers, not just hearers

You must understand this, my beloved: let everyone be quick to listen, slow to speak, slow to anger; for your anger does not produce God's righteousness. Therefore rid yourselves of all sordidness and rank growth of wickedness, and welcome with meekness the implanted word that has the power to save your souls.
But be doers of the word, and not merely hearers who deceive themselves. For if any are hearers of the word and not doers, they are like those who look at themselves in a mirror; for they look at themselves and, on going away, immediately forget what they were like. But those who look into the perfect law, the law of liberty, and persevere, being not hearers who forget but doers who act – they will be blessed in their doing.

James 1.19–25

A first-century mirror was not the silvered glass one in your bathroom. It was beaten bronze and gave a fuzzy image. If you wanted to be sure your face was not dirty, a quick glance was not sufficient. You would need to peer intently, work out what was required, then go and find some clean water. The same is true of the way we react to encoutering God. The real blessing of the Christian faith does not lie in listening to sermons, but in dwelling on what is true until it transforms what we do.

A genuine encounter with Jesus provokes action. James particularly looks for:

- a desire to listen and understand, instead of an urgency to make your point heard;
- a new focus to your anger, so that it is used in the cause of what God would consider just;
- an end to sordid habits – James uses the Greek word you would use if you hadn't changed your underwear for a week.

Think back through the last week of Bible readings, and pick out a phrase that has struck you. Write it on a post-it note and stick it on the mirror that you use most often. Turn it over in your mind when you come to shave or put on make-up over the next few days.

Speak Lord, for your servant hears. Grant me ears to hear, eyes to see, a will to obey, a heart to love. Then declare what you will, reveal what you will, command what you will, demand what you will.

Christina Rossetti (1830–94)

November 10   Orphans and widows

If any think they are religious, and do not bridle their tongues but deceive their hearts, their religion is worthless. Religion that is pure and undefiled before God, the Father, is this: to care for orphans and widows in their distress, and to keep oneself unstained by the world.

James 1.26–27

We tend to use the word 'religious' to describe people who faithfully say their prayers. But James points out that genuine religion is not so much displayed by what we say as by who we care for. And because some things do not change, he reminds us of the vulnerable groups that the Old Testament singled out for care – widows, orphans and refugees.

Wherever men go to war the burden will be carried for years after the conflict ends by widows, orphans and refugees. In Rwanda the Association des Veuves du Genocide d'Avril 1994 (AVEGA) was set up by the widows of the horrific genocide of which the country still bears the scars a decade or so later.

Women are now seventy per cent of Rwanda's population, their husbands and sons killed or dispersed when ethnic hatred turned even friends and neighbours against each other. Destroyed houses still need to be reconstructed and village communities re-established. Christian Aid supports AVEGA's work in building houses, building trust, and building plans for the future through agricultural projects.

It is almost impossible to understand how a person who has the same loves and aspirations and emotions as me could cope with such trauma and muster the strength to endure. The measure of my religion is how, and how much, I care.

James mentions two other aspects to practising our religion with integrity: speaking wisely, and refusing to collaborate with all that is evil in the world. Take the opportunity to talk to someone (a friend or neighbour whom you happen to meet) about your concern for the world's most needy people.

Lord Jesus, who has known grief, join this day in the tears of those for whom the struggle to endure bereft of love is almost too much to bear.

November 11   Favouritism

My brothers and sisters, do you with your acts of favouritism really believe in our glorious Lord Jesus Christ? For if a person with gold rings and in fine clothes comes into your assembly, and if a poor person in dirty clothes also comes in, and if you take notice of the one wearing the fine clothes and say, 'Have a seat here, please', while to the one who is poor you say, 'Stand there', or, 'Sit at my feet', have you not made distinctions among yourselves, and become judges with evil thoughts?

James 2.1–4

Discrimination comes in its ugly, obvious form, but also in a subtle form. In the church that James led, the arrival of a rich person was a surprise that left the Christians unsure how to react. They could be forgiven for wanting to make a special fuss and make a new member feel welcome in the style to which he was accustomed. But in today's churches it is the arrival of someone poor that commands attention. Well-dressed people blend into the pewscape! Your attitude is revealed by which of them you invite into your home.

A past director of Christian Aid tells of the first grant that she made. It was to a partner in India that intended to spend the money on brass musical instruments. Not surprisingly, she queried the value of tackling global poverty by investing in trombones.

Some time later she was able to visit the dalit community that received the instruments. An overjoyed man thanked her repeatedly. Owning an instrument had enabled him to earn a living in a band. But more than that, it had enabled him for the first time to enter the house of a person of higher caste (out of the question for 'untouchable' dalits) and to sit there on a chair.

Good news for poor people is not only a matter of money; it is a matter of dignity.

Bring to mind specific people to whom this Bible passage seems relevant. Regardless of whether they are rich or poor, what can you offer by way of friendship? With six weekends to go before Christmas, make a plan to do something hospitable by then.

Traditionally eleven o'clock today is marked by two minutes of silence to remember those who have died in war. Pray also for people who live in fear of violence and discrimination today, for in war it is always poor communities that suffer most.

November 12 Do not insult the poor

Listen, my beloved brothers and sisters. Has not God chosen the poor in the world to be rich in faith and to be heirs of the kingdom that he has promised to those who love him? But you have dishonoured the poor. Is it not the rich who oppress you? Is it not they who drag you into court? Is it not they who blaspheme the excellent name that was invoked over you?

James 2.5–7

Three hundred years after James wrote this letter the Roman emperor Julian the Apostate was trying to establish a sun-worshipping paganism as the national religion. Even though he despised Christianity he wanted to incorporate into his new religion elements that impressed him. He confessed to being inspired that Christians cared 'not only for their own poor, but ours as well'. Maybe the early Christians had responded to James' plea that their goodness should be indiscriminate. Why?

- Because putting your energy into eradicating poverty is an echo of God's 'choice' of the poor as examples of how we should depend on him in faith.
- Because using the strength that wealth brings in order to make gains 'in court' at the expense of poor people is an evil.
- Because abusing economic power is a 'blasphemy' for someone who claims to follow Christ, who made himself poor on behalf of humankind.

The Trade Justice Movement is dedicated to eradicating poverty by changing the rules under which international trade operates. It seeks to address the abuse of economic power which means that rich nations can call the shots when it comes to trading with poor nations. Christians and their friends are campaigning for governments to change the mandate of the World Trade Organization so that alleviating poverty becomes the most important objective of international trade. That way the world's richest nations could care 'not only for their own poor, but for the world's as well'. Frequently asked questions about this complicated subject get some straightforward answers at www.christianaid.org.uk/campaign/trade/tradeq.htm

Holy Spirit of God,
light a flame within me,
burning for justice,
glowing with kindness,
shining with hope
for the end of poverty
and the peace of all people
in this ever-turning world. Amen.

November 13 Mercy triumphs

You do well if you really fulfil the royal law according to the scripture, 'You shall love your neighbour as yourself.' But if you show partiality, you commit sin and are convicted by the law as transgressors. For whoever keeps the whole law but fails in one point has become accountable for all of it. For the one who said, 'You shall not commit adultery', also said, 'You shall not murder.' Now if you do not commit adultery but if you murder, you have become a transgressor of the law. So speak and so act as those who are to be judged by the law of liberty. For judgement will be without mercy to anyone who has shown no mercy; mercy triumphs over judgement.*

James 2.8–13

Jesus did not invent the saying, 'Love your neighbour as yourself.' He was quoting from the law that had governed the Hebrew people for many centuries. To live a life pleasing to God under the terms of that law was and is impossible – to break one part of it was to break every part of it.

Those of us who feel we have a better-than-average morality because we are neither murderers nor adulterers are cut down to size by discovering that something as everyday as showing favouritism has placed us under the judgement of God.

In the face of such judgement is there hope for any of us? The gospel of Jesus is not only good news for the poor; it is also good news for those who struggle to help the poor. The resurrection of Jesus ushered in a new phase in the relationship humankind has with the Lord. God will not condemn us for failing to be perfect, for Jesus succeeded in being perfect. Mercy has triumphed over judgement. But being recipients of God's mercy brings responsibilities with it. We are freely to show mercy to others, just as we have been shown mercy.

Work out who in your community, workplace, or even church, might feel themselves undervalued because of partiality. What would it take for them to be treated as a neighbour?

Blessed be the God and Father of our Lord Jesus Christ, the Father of mercies and the God of all consolation, who consoles us in all our affliction, so that we may be able to console those who are in any affliction with the consolation we ourselves have received from God.

2 Corinthians 1.3–4

November 14 Faith and actions

What good is it, my brothers and sisters, if you say you have faith but do not have works? Can faith save you? If a brother or sister is naked and lacks daily food, and one of you says to them, 'Go in peace; keep warm and eat your fill', and yet you do not supply their bodily needs, what is the good of that? So faith by itself, if it has no works, is dead.

But someone will say, 'You have faith and I have works.' Show me your faith apart from your works, and I by my works will show you my faith. You believe that God is one; you do well. Even the demons believe – and shudder.

James 2.14–19

Martin Luther, the sixteenth-century theologian, hated this part of James' letter! He knew that nothing a human could do, not even a lifetime of doing good, would earn him or her God's favour. Quoting the Bible, he insisted that only faith in God could open a place in heaven for someone. So these verses, which insist that faith is a waste of time unless it leads to action, led him to dismiss the letter as 'an epistle full of straw'.

Great man though Luther was, this seems harsh on James. He is making a different point – that a person who is doing nothing on behalf of the needy, but says he has faith in God, is inconsistent. After all, the devil believes in God, but you would hardly call him a champion of social justice! Our worship and our action for the poor are not alternatives – they are equally vital.

The irony is that Martin Luther was himself a man of action. He wrote 'Ninety-Five Theses' and nailed them to the door of the church in Wittenberg, Germany. Among other things they attacked the church for being concerned with its own wealth instead of the gospel of Christ.

If you were to deliver a message to those in power, what would you want them to change in the light of the teaching of Jesus and James? You probably cannot run to ninety-five, but you might manage five. Instead of posting them on a door, you could post them with a stamp!

Lord God, renew your Church and begin with me. Heal our land, tend our wounds, make us one, and use us in your service, for Jesus Christ's sake. Amen.

A prayer from Kenya

November 15   Abraham's example

Do you want to be shown, you senseless person, that faith apart from works is barren? Was not our ancestor Abraham justified by works when he offered his son Isaac on the altar? You see that faith was active along with his works, and faith was brought to completion by the works. Thus the scripture was fulfilled that says, 'Abraham believed God, and it was reckoned to him as righteousness', and he was called the friend of God. You see that a person is justified by works and not by faith alone. Likewise, was not Rahab the prostitute also justified by works when she welcomed the messengers and sent them out by another road? For just as the body without the spirit is dead, so faith without works is also dead.

James 2.20–26

James turns a bit rude here. It is unusual for a Bible writer to address his reader as 'dimwit'. So pay attention!

A person on a life-support machine is technically alive, but is not able to engage with the world in any meaningful way. Similarly a person who believes in God, but is not actively following Jesus' example, is technically a Christian. However, she is not enjoying the fullness of what it means to have faith.

Rahab is the most unlikely person to be held up as an example of faith – she was neither a worshipper of God nor virtuous. But when the Canaanite army came to arrest Jewish spies who were using her brothel, she hid them. Protecting vulnerable people regardless of their race is an act of faith. Abraham became known as a 'friend of God' because he trusted that God would not take away his only son. He was correct.

Abraham trusted God on the basis of years of following his call; Rahab had only heard rumours of what God had done. But both took a risk. When did your faith in God last lead you into action outside your safety zone?

Have you promised to pray for someone recently? A phone call today to find out whether there is anything practical you can do would not go amiss.

I ask the God of Rahab, the God of Abraham, my God:
for courage to protect vulnerable people, regardless of their race;
for trust to go where I would rather not go,
*   in answer to your call;*
for faith that is recognizable in everything I do. Amen.

November 16   Mind your tongue

Not many of you should become teachers, my brothers and sisters, for you know that we who teach will be judged with greater strictness. For all of us make many mistakes. Anyone who makes no mistakes in speaking is perfect, able to keep the whole body in check with a bridle. If we put bits into the mouths of horses to make them obey us, we guide their whole bodies. Or look at ships: though they are so large that it takes strong winds to drive them, yet they are guided by a very small rudder wherever the will of the pilot directs. So also the tongue is a small member, yet it boasts of great exploits.

How great a forest is set ablaze by a small fire! And the tongue is a fire. The tongue is placed among our members as a world of iniquity; it stains the whole body, sets on fire the cycle of nature, and is itself set on fire by hell.

James 3.1–6

Three things that wield power: teachers, tongues and training. Teachers, because they shape peoples' lives. (Don't rush to be a Christian leader, says James, unless you are sure your life measures up to what you preach.) Tongues, because words wound deeply. (Maybe James had personal experience.) Training, because a teacher is like a rudder and the tongue is like a bridle (small, but very influential).

In Malawi, the voices of the poorest people are often lost in the political process – they need teachers, they need to know how to use words effectively, and they need training to take part in democracy. The Public Affairs Committee (which Christian Aid funds) does all those things. It works with religious leaders and local politicians to help them take up their responsibilities. It lobbies the government so that the needs of ordinary people are not overlooked. The Public Affairs Committee has a small staff. But it only takes a small fire to ignite a whole forest!

Who was your favourite teacher? What has he or she added to your life? Whose life do you influence (as a parent, friend or leader)? What will be the very next thing you say to them? Make it count!

May I speak out for those who have no voices,
May I speak up for those unjustly blamed,
May I defend the rights of all the needy,
May every word be said in Jesus' name.

November 17 Praising and cursing

Every species of beast and bird, of reptile and sea creature, can be tamed and has been tamed by the human species, but no one can tame the tongue – a restless evil, full of deadly poison. With it we bless the Lord and Father, and with it we curse those who are made in the likeness of God. From the same mouth come blessing and cursing. My brothers and sisters, this ought not to be so. Does a spring pour forth from the same opening both fresh and brackish water? Can a fig tree, my brothers and sisters, yield olives, or a grapevine figs? No more can salt water yield fresh.

James 3.7–12

The minister had been invited to Sunday lunch by a family in the congregation. Dad asked him to say grace, but the minister replied, 'Why don't we let your young son Jackie say grace?'

Jack froze, 'I don't know what to say.'

'That's all right,' said Mum. 'Just say exactly what Daddy said to God at breakfast this morning.'

'Oh that's easy,' said the boy, shutting his eyes tight. 'O God, is it today that boring old man's coming to lunch?'

Hmm! Today I think James and jokes speak for themselves!

Technology has vastly improved the ease with which words get to people, but for some reason the speed with which we communicate brings with it a carelessness about how we use the words. It's not the technology's fault – it's the user who doesn't stop to think about the impact of blessing and cursing.

If you have to send a sensitive email today, consider writing a letter instead. If you are going to write a letter, think about making a telephone call instead. If you must make a phone call, would it be possible to speak face-to-face instead? Defy James and tame your tongue – for today at least.

Forgive, O Lord, the words which have wounded. Give me instead a language that is life-giving. Amen.

November 18   Ambition

Who is wise and understanding among you? Show by your good life that your works are done with gentleness born of wisdom. But if you have bitter envy and selfish ambition in your hearts, do not be boastful and false to the truth. Such wisdom does not come down from above, but is earthly, unspiritual, devilish. For where there is envy and selfish ambition, there will also be disorder and wickedness of every kind.

James 3.13–16

James must have known the old proverb of the Roman world: 'Divide and rule'. That strategy has characterized the actions of ambitious leaders for centuries. Set one group against another – the black against the white, the rich against the poor, the resident against the stranger – and you can have effective control over both. Do you recognize it in world politics? In corporate business? In advertising? It is the world's wisdom, indeed, but James describes it as 'devilish' and predicts that it will lead to 'disorder'. Recent years have shown disorder to be too moderate a word for what can follow when divisions of wealth, race or religion broaden.

When a leader's decisions are created from personal ambition, be it in a nation, at work, or even in a church, they will never be in tune with God's wisdom. So how can we recognize God's way? It will be distinguished by 'gentleness'. As well as a 'divide and rule' ambition, there is a 'unite and serve' ambition. This is why peacemaking is one of the strategies for reducing poverty in the work of so many Christian Aid projects.

In the margin, scribble the names of places and people whom you know not to be at peace – countries, specific groups, a workplace, even perhaps a family. For each one, think about what it is that lies behind the conflict. Is there an economic cause as well as a tribal one? Are there personal ambitions that obscure the desire to reach a settlement? If you don't know, how could you make yourself better informed?

In the presence of God, mention each situation that you have jotted down. In each case pray first for the leaders, next for those who are vulnerable to the decisions they make, then for those who actively seek peace in that place, and finally (if you can) for those whose ambitions are served by maintaining the turmoil.

November 19   Peacemakers

The wisdom from above is first pure, then peaceable, gentle, willing to yield, full of mercy and good fruits, without a trace of partiality or hypocrisy. And a harvest of righteousness is sown in peace for those who make peace.

James 3.17–18

James seems to provide nine 'sieves' through which every action and decision should be sifted in order to see whether they are wise. Can you pick them out? They are all worth dwelling on for a few moments.

Nine! Heaven help us!

James narrows in on one which will make it easier for heaven to help us. Those who seek to make peace are sowing in the earth from which justice will grow. So if you can't keep nine sieves in mind, one is a start.

The Diakonia Council of Churches is situated in part of South Africa where there is great deprivation. KwaZulu-Natal is, in some ways, as turbulent now as before there were democratic elections. Building peace is DCC's priority. It facilitates dialogue between groups that are in conflict, and works with churches to establish structures that give a real alternative to violence.

Bible study and prayer are at the heart of the process of helping churches to reflect theologically on how peace can be made. Those helped by its programmes include traumatized survivors of violence, and those who seek reconciliation and change on the long road to justice in a country bearing the scars of poverty and HIV. Christian Aid has worked closely with the Diakonia Council of Churches for many years.

Find out more about Christian Aids's work in South Africa at www.christianaid.org.uk/world/where/safrica/safrip.htm

We come to you, our only help and refuge. Help us, O God, to refuse to be embittered against those who handle us with harshness. We are grateful to you for the gift of laughter at all times. Save us from the hatred of those who oppress us. May we follow the spirit of your Son Jesus Christ. Amen.

The prayer of a Bantu pastor from South Africa

November 20   Quarrels

Those conflicts and disputes among you, where do they come from? Do they not come from your cravings that are at war within you? You want something and do not have it; so you commit murder. And you covet something and cannot obtain it; so you engage in disputes and conflicts. You do not have, because you do not ask. You ask and do not receive, because you ask wrongly, in order to spend what you get on your pleasures.

James 4.1–3

There are two ways of looking at these verses. They have a world-wide dimension, because it is true that nations go to war almost always because they want something they cannot obtain in any other way. It may be a territorial war over a fertile or mineral-rich area; it may be a tribal war about a benefit which it seems that one group has at the expense of another; it may be a centuries-old struggle for power. At the heart of it are ancient human needs – to feel secure; to be able to feed your children; to know your worth. The instinct to become angry seems to be built into the human survival kit.

But James won't allow us to distance ourselves from the violence of the world. He uses the same words that we use about guerillas and terrorists to describe the quarrels which disrupt churches, families and neighbours week after week. They happen, he says, because we accept in ourselves, in petty ways, things that we deplore in the world. The world's standards of self-interest can even infiltrate our prayers. We are more inclined to take action than to pray. And when we do pray, it is more likely to be about what we want God to do *for* us than what we want God to do *with* us.

Buy a local paper, or read one of the free papers that drops through your door. Is it true that the local stories of tragedy and triumph are small-scale versions of what is happening globally? Pray for the people whose names and photos appear in the paper, especially where the stories feature anger or distress.

O God who is known by many names,
we ask you to grant us peace:
deep in our hearts,
strong in our communities,
long in our nation,
wide in our world.
Do with us what it takes to make peace real. Amen.

November 21 A friend of the Earth

Adulterers! Do you not know that friendship with the world is enmity with God? Therefore whoever wishes to be a friend of the world becomes an enemy of God. Or do you suppose that it is for nothing that the scripture says, 'God yearns jealously for the spirit that he has made to dwell in us'? But he gives all the more grace; therefore it says, 'God opposes the proud, but gives grace to the humble.'

James 4.4–6

Sorry if the first word made you jump! No other book does 'rude' quite like the Bible. Very often it uses adultery as an image of being unfaithful to God. It hasn't lost its currency – virtually everyone then and now has seen with their own eyes what adultery does to a couple who made vows of permanent commitment. Being a 'friend of the world' brings into our relationship with God the same betrayal, evasiveness and deep hurt that adultery leaves in its wake.

'The world' is almost always used in a negative sense in the New Testament – something which we need to resist and from which we need to be saved. When we buy into the system of greed, power-mongering and pride that causes damage and division on a global scale it is effectively allying ourselves to the world. Curiously, a 'friend of the world' is precisely the opposite of what we now call a 'friend of the Earth', for it is greed and power that have brought our planet to its current environmental peril.

What can friends of God's Earth do? Recognize the strong desires which 'dwell in us'. Yes, even us! Humbly look to God for his grace and his help.

The website for the environmental charity Friends of the Earth is www.foe.co.uk. Look it up (or contact them at 26 Underwood Street, London N1 7JQ) and see whether you can find in it the 'spirit for which God yearns'.

God of the humble,
when I hear the world say that I need more,
remind me that I need sufficient;
and so may I become a friend to the Earth. Amen.

November 22   Submit to God

Submit yourselves therefore to God. Resist the devil, and he will flee from you. Draw near to God, and he will draw near to you. Cleanse your hands, you sinners, and purify your hearts, you double-minded. Lament and mourn and weep. Let your laughter be turned into mourning and your joy into dejection. Humble yourselves before the Lord, and he will exalt you.

James 4.7–10

I have a perverse dislike of being told what to do! As a teenager I can remember making up my mind to tidy my bedroom (in fact getting as far as gathering an armful of underwear from the floor), when the very sound of my father's voice from the foot of the stairs demanding that I make the room respectable before lunchtime made me drop the clothes and listen to a T-Rex LP instead. (I'm quite sure nobody told Marc Bolan he had to have a haircut!)

So I still react quite badly to James firing off commands: submit, resist, repent, lament. I suspect I am not the only one for whom it is difficult to 'humble yourself'.

However, in the unexpected economy of God, the humble are not losers. Those who are so aware of their weaknesses that it leads them to the verge of tears find that to be the point at which they are aware of God drawing near to them. The Christian life is not a once-for-all choice, but a daily series of choices: for God and against evil, for forgiveness and against taking joy in wrongdoing. To 'mourn and weep' begins the process in which God draws close, sins are forgiven, and your spirits rise as high as heaven.

A serious action today, because this part of the Bible gives us some serious instructions! Take time to think about whether there are areas of your life in which you are aware of fighting God. What would it take to be humble in those circumstances? You might be able to use tidying up your house as a symbol of tidying up your inner life.

Be thou my guardian and my guide, and hear me when I call;
let not my slippery footstep slide, and hold me lest I fall.
Still let me ever watch and pray, and feel that I am frail;
that if the tempter cross my way he may not yet prevail.

Isaac Williams (1802–65)

November 23   Do not judge others

Do not speak evil against one another, brothers and sisters. Whoever speaks evil against another or judges another, speaks evil against the law and judges the law; but if you judge the law, you are not a doer of the law but a judge. There is one lawgiver and judge who is able to save and to destroy. So who, then, are you to judge your neighbour?

James 4.11–12

The water cooler moment, when words are said about a colleague who is safely out of earshot. The playground moment, when teenage misdemeanours are recounted more for revenge than for justice. The church door moment, when gossip is spread about a fellow-Christian under the guise of wanting the issue to be prayed about. The doorstep moment, when someone refuses to give to Christian Aid because 'it goes to lazy people in countries run by dictators'. We know all about 'speaking evil against one another'!

Those who assume the role of a judge need to be aware that one day they too will be in the dock. And when the truth is made clear in the presence of a perfect God there will be very little to choose between any of us. Our supreme consolation is that the Lord is endlessly merciful and (although he would be justified in doing either) has chosen to save rather than to destroy. What is there to stop us emulating him?

Go out of your way today to say things that build people up – at work, at school, in church or on the doorstep. Count how many times you say something positive to someone so that you can feel good about it at the end of the day!

May the words of my mouth and the meditation of my heart be pleasing in your sight, O Lord, my Rock and my Redeemer.

Psalm 19.14

November 24   Plans for tomorrow

Come now, you who say, 'Today or tomorrow we will go to such and such a town and spend a year there, doing business and making money.' Yet you do not even know what tomorrow will bring. What is your life? For you are a mist that appears for a little while and then vanishes. Instead you ought to say, 'If the Lord wishes, we will live and do this or that.' As it is, you boast in your arrogance; all such boasting is evil. Anyone, then, who knows the right thing to do and fails to do it, commits sin.

James 4.13–17

I am a British supermarket. Everybody wants to buy my prawns because what was once a restaurant luxury is now the filling for an everyday sandwich. I want to offer a bargain price for them. The Bangladeshi coastline is an ideal place in which to create prawn farms. Vast farms produce seafood much cheaper than traditional methods, so those are the companies I want to do business with. So today or tomorrow swathes of mangrove swamp will be cleared and replaced with the salt lakes in which tiger prawns thrive. A huge investment!

I am a Bangladeshi farmer. Every few years a cyclone hits the coast and floods miles of it. In the natural order of things, this has been a positive event, replenishing the fish stocks and enriching the swamps with nutrients. But that was while the mangroves were standing. Without their protection, there is no shelter from the power of the weather, and the flood comes in across agricultural land, not as a blessing, but as a devastating killer that destroys houses, wipes out crops, and salinates the ground for years to come. A lost investment!

Supermarket managers and Bangladeshi farmers both need to plan for tomorrow. What would need to happen for each of them to plan 'as the Lord wishes'?

You can read more about Bangladesh, and the work Christian Aid has been supporting there, at
www.christianaid.org.uk/world/where/asia/banglap.htm

God of the flood-tides,
grant to those who live on treacherous coasts
and make their living in unpredictable waters
peace in the heart
and justice in the hand,
to deal with every circumstance that tomorrow may bring.
Amen.

November 25   Warning the rich

You rich people, weep and wail for the miseries that are coming to you. Your riches have rotted, and your clothes are moth-eaten. Your gold and silver have rusted, and their rust will be evidence against you, and it will eat your flesh like fire. You have laid up treasure for the last days. Listen! The wages of the labourers who mowed your fields, which you kept back by fraud, cry out, and the cries of the harvesters have reached the ears of the Lord of hosts. You have lived on the earth in luxury and in pleasure; you have fattened your hearts in a day of slaughter. You have condemned and murdered the righteous one, who does not resist you.

James 5.1–6

During Paris fashion week it was possible to buy a new top. It was white, short-sleeved, and made to measure. It was immaculate, with gold trimming on the sleeves, patterned with heart-shaped studs and little enamelled Coca Cola bottles. It cost £50,000. It was, when all is said and done, a T-shirt!

Who is James getting at when he speaks of 'you rich people'? I'm not a 'gold trimmings' dresser. I'm more of a Gap man myself! The label makes me feel good, I can afford it, and I'm a sucker for the adverts. Surely James isn't looking at my clothes when he delivers his curse! And yet something about the underpaid labourers whose plight has 'reached the ears of the Lord' is making me mightily uncomfortable.

When a BBC documentary scandalized Gap by revealing low wages and child labour in some overseas workshops with which they were associated, they immediately withdrew from those factories. Fine! But of course, if factories are forced to close, workers' livelihoods suffer. A much better solution is for retailers to work alongside factories to improve conditions. So let's tell them!

With winter coming you will be needing more layers of clothing. Go to the cupboard and see whether there are any old clothes that you have not worn for a couple of seasons. Could you wear these instead of buying new ones this year? If they have become a tight fit, that might deliver another challenge!

Lord of hosts, forgive me for tolerating the suffering of others in order to be fashionable. Change the practices of those who persuade me to change my clothes. And teach me to shop in a way that pleases you. Amen.

November 26   Await God's coming

Be patient therefore, beloved, until the coming of the Lord. The farmer waits for the precious crop from the earth, being patient with it until it receives the early and the late rains. You also must be patient. Strengthen your hearts, for the coming of the Lord is near. Beloved, do not grumble against one another, so that you may not be judged. See, the Judge is standing at the doors!

James 5.7–9

Next Sunday will mark the beginning of Advent, the season in the Church's year which Christians use to remind themselves that Jesus asked his followers to be prepared for him to return to this planet in glory. The concept of Jesus coming as 'judge' is disconcerting to those of us who are aware of our shortcomings. But for those in the world who are hungry because trade is unfair, or whose children have died from curable diseases, or whose farms have flooded because industrial nations have changed the climate, the ultimate restoration of justice will usher in rejoicing.

The Greek word that James uses for 'be patient' means 'have self-restraint'. It is a message to those who feel themselves to be poor, defrauded, condemned. He is pleading with them not to take the law into their own hands. Poverty never excuses violence. Rather they are to take strength from the prospect of justice when God makes all things perfect. And that puts the onus on Christians to be opening the doors to justice in preparation.

With Jesus Christ the Judge 'standing at the door', Advent is a valuable time for examining your life and being ready to meet Jesus. Put a pencil and paper next to your front door and make a note of who comes to it or through it between now and the end of Sunday. Be conscious of how you treat visitors, and what they reveal about your lifestyle.

At Advent we should try the key to our heart's door. It may have gathered rust. If so, this is the time to oil it, in order that our heart's door may open more easily when the Lord Jesus wants to enter at Christmas time! Lord, oil the hinges of our hearts' doors so that they may swing gently and easily to welcome your coming. Amen.

A prayer from Papua New Guinea

November 27 Job's example

As an example of suffering and patience, beloved, take the prophets who spoke in the name of the Lord. Indeed we call blessed those who showed endurance. You have heard of the endurance of Job, and you have seen the purpose of the Lord, how the Lord is compassionate and merciful.

Above all, my beloved, do not swear, either by heaven or by earth or by any other oath, but let your 'Yes' be yes and your 'No' be no, so that you may not fall under condemnation.

James 5.10–12

In the Old Testament Job, bereaved and in great pain, refused to give in to cynicism and kept alive his relationship with a God whose actions he could not understand.

The animated television series *God, the Devil and Bob* recasts the story in Detroit. Halted at a level-crossing Bob, suffering all the petty agonies of a twenty-first-century family, rounds on God, who is sitting in the passenger seat of his car: 'How could you let this happen? What is wrong with you? I just don't understand. There's cancer and war and random violence. Why? You're supposed to be good; you're supposed to love us. Why do you allow evil in the world?'

With a deep sigh God replies, 'Oh boy, that's the big one isn't it! That's what everyone wants to know. Look! You're not supposed to find this out until later, but the reason is . . .' God proceeds to explain, accompanied by expressive hand gestures. Unfortunately for us, every word of the explanation is drowned out by the noise of a passing train. But Bob's face is radiant: 'Wow! When you lay it out like that it just makes so much sense. I'm sorry I swore at you like that.'

'Oh that's OK' smiles God. 'People are passionate about this issue.'

What would you most like to say to God? Or shout at God? It might be personal or it might be about the nature of the world. Write it down. And then ask God for patience until the answers are clear.

Strike that thick cloud of unknowing with the sharp dart of longing love, and on no account whatever think of giving up.

Words to lead us into prayer from the anonymous fourteenth-century devotional book The Cloud of Unknowing

November 28   Pray for the sick

Are any among you suffering? They should pray. Are any cheer-
ful? They should sing songs of praise. Are any among you sick?
They should call for the elders of the church and have them pray
over them, anointing them with oil in the name of the Lord. The
prayer of faith will save the sick, and the Lord will raise them up;
and anyone who has committed sins will be forgiven. Therefore confess your
sins to one another, and pray for one another, so that you may be healed. The
prayer of the righteous is powerful and effective.

James 5.13–16

James comes toward the end of his letter, written from a context
of persecution and poverty to others who were prosperous in
comparison. He urges people, no matter what their situation, to
get their perspective right by sharing their feelings about it with
God. Prayer is not only for emergencies or for church services, it
is for all circumstances. Is there room in your life for prayer for those who
suffer; for unabashed praise; for expectant prayers for those who are ill; for
confessing sins; for praying alongside others as well as alone?

There is a hint here that we should expect God fully to heal any prayerful
person. Experience tells us that the truth is more complex than that. Jesus
himself said that physical healing would not be universal. But repeatedly the
Bible encourages us to bring our sick friends into God's presence requesting,
but not demanding, recovery. The testimony of those who pray sincerely is that
there is the possibility of full healing; that healing may be withheld until death
cures us perfectly; or that God powerfully restores us with his love, joy and
peace despite continuing illness.

Can you fit a name to every kind of person to whom James has
referred: someone who is suffering, a person with occasion to
rejoice, somebody who is sick, someone who knows their need of
forgiveness. Write down some names. Perhaps your own name is
among them. Take time to think about their needs. Would any of
them appreciate a phone call from you?

Wherever I go – only you! Wherever I stand – only you!
Just you, again you, always you!
You, you, you!
When things are good – you! When things are bad – you!
You, you, you!

An ancient hymn of the Hasidic Jewish people

November 29 Elijah's example

Elijah was a human being like us, and he prayed fervently that it might not rain, and for three years and six months it did not rain on the earth. Then he prayed again, and the heaven gave rain and the earth yielded its harvest.

My brothers and sisters, if anyone among you wanders from the truth and is brought back by another, you should know that whoever brings back a sinner from wandering will save the sinner's soul from death and will cover a multitude of sins.

James 5.17–20

Elijah was a prophet in Israel during the godless and ruthless reign of Ahab. He is significant for having defied the attempts of the king to eliminate the worship of God and replace it with the cult of the nature-god Baal. Elijah championed the poor and destitute, and stood alongside those whose land had been wrenched from them with no recourse to justice. His zealous stance took a personal toll, however, and left him susceptible to depression and fear. But what James commends him for is the prayer that consistently accompanied his every statement and action for God.

Does that persistence in praying and conviction that prayer makes a difference to the world feature among those who campaign for justice for the poor today? Of the three things that Christian Aid asks of its supporters – to pray, to act and to give – the first sounds easiest, but is actually the most likely to be taken for granted.

A large index of prayers that relate to the work Christian Aid does can be found at
www.christianaid.org.uk/worship/prayer/index.htm.

Visit it, and find something that it had not occurred to you to pray for.

The most direct way to others is always through prayer.

Dietrich Bonhoeffer (1906–45)

Go directly this very moment, through prayer, to a part of the world that needs God's intervention.

November 30   Light in darkness

There will be no gloom for those who were in anguish. In the former time [God] brought into contempt the land . . . but in the latter time he will make glorious the way of the sea, the land beyond the Jordan, Galilee of the nations.
The people who walked in darkness have seen a great light; those who lived in a land of deep darkness – on them light has shined. You have multiplied the nation, you have increased its joy; they rejoice before you as with joy at the harvest, as people exult when dividing plunder.

Isaiah 9.1–3

Out of all the learned books that have been written about the Old Testament prophets, no theologian has yet adopted my preferred scholarly approach – the Doctor Who method. Strange that! The Doctor Who method involves travelling between four time zones and holding them together in order to find out what the Time Lord reveals to us through Isaiah.

The first zone is the time at which Isaiah was actually writing – about 735 BC. King Ahaz was leading the Jews into a time of darkness and distress. Compromised by worship of false gods, he even sacrificed his own baby sons. Isaiah's message was one of light at the end of the tunnel. God would restore the fortunes of his people.

The second time-zone is one that we can see, but Isaiah could not. We know that Jesus' ministry far exceeded anything Isaiah could have anticipated. Galilee was the home of Jesus and the place where his life first enlightened God's world.

The third zone is the distant future. It is a point in time for which we still wait, at which God will step back into the world to end all injustice.

But there is a fourth time – right now. God still calls us away from a compromised faith to trust him alone. That is the way of light and hope in this and every century.

During the coming week, Christmas lights will be turned on in the streets of most towns. Each time you pass them during December, turn your mind to a place of darkness and distress in the world, and ask God to shine light into that situation.

God of all, keep before me the bright hope of light in the darkness – in the lessons of history, in the person of Jesus, in the uncertainty of the future, in the needs of my life today. Amen.

December 1 To us a child is born

A child has been born for us, a son given to us;
authority rests upon his shoulders; and he is named
Wonderful Counsellor, Mighty God,
     Everlasting Father, Prince of Peace.
His authority shall grow continually,
     and there shall be endless peace
for the throne of David and his kingdom.
He will establish and uphold it with justice and with righteousness
from this time onward and for evermore.
The zeal of the Lord of hosts will do this.

Isaiah 9.6–7

Once again the words of Isaiah inhabit four time-zones at the same moment.

In relation to his own day, Isaiah hoped for a monarch who would govern skilfully and champion the oppressed. The current king Ahaz was not such a ruler, but his child Hezekiah trusted God, and under him the people rallied.

However, we also recognize in Isaiah's words a description of Jesus: wonderful (in the Bible it means supernatural), divine and eternal (newborn and yet ancient), and the one who brings peace (which in Hebrew means thriving as well as being calm).

The third time-zone is the one to which believers look forward, when justice will be established for evermore in the final intervention of God in human affairs, the destiny for which he created the world.

And what of the present day? Let us pray for a government in this country that upholds the values Isaiah preached. Let us recognize in Jesus an authority against whom all the world's leaders can be judged. And let us not lose sight of God's plan for a kingdom of perfect peace and justice, even in today's messy and mundane realities.

Today is World AIDS Day. Look back at the Bible passage that speaks of the promise that a newborn child brings and weep for the children living with HIV. Read the words about government and pray for those whose decisions impact upon those who live with the virus. Read the words about peace and stand alongside those who bear the burden. Then wear a red ribbon today defiantly and with hope.

King of kings, we pray for those upon whose shoulders rests the government of this country. Give them the courage to do what is right, not merely what is popular. And restore in them a passion for doing good, not merely for looking good. Amen.

December 2   A descendant of David

A shoot shall come out from the stump of Jesse,
and a branch shall grow out of his roots.
The spirit of the Lord shall rest on him,
*   the spirit of wisdom and understanding,*
the spirit of counsel and might,
*   the spirit of knowledge and the fear of the Lord.*
His delight shall be in the fear of the Lord.

Isaiah 11.1–3

Advent means coming. Of all the seasons, this one inspires hope. In a month of dark nights, light will come. In a landscape of dead leaves, new growth will come. This is the promise of God. Previously, Isaiah pictured war as acres of felled trees. Now he introduces his advent. Out of a tree that looked lifeless a shoot has grown. And similarly, although the Jewish people seemed all-but-annihilated, something fragile and new was growing. This new hope for God's people was the promise of a Messiah. The new leader would be so significant that he was comparable with the great King David (indeed, David's father Jesse would be his ancestor).

In Sierra Leone, a ten-year civil war is over. President Ahmad Tejan Kabbah says, 'The war has ended, but a new war has started – a war on poverty.' Christian Aid works with partners in what the United Nations Development Programme identifies as the poorest nation on Earth so that something fragile and new can grow in Sierra Leone.

The Methodist Church of Sierra Leone is helping children who were scarred by the war to develop a new spirit. Boys as young as ten were captured and brutalized into becoming soldiers. Young girls were used as sex slaves. Through workshops, Bible studies, music and sport MCSL helps them settle back into their communities. Christian Aid's work in Sierra Leone includes peace-building, reviving the economy, and supporting marginalized people.

Life relentlessly insists on taking hold, even with winter almost upon us. Go outside and find life beginning in the most unlikely places. Look at the rubber surrounds to the windows of a car and find green signs of moss developing. Look at the cracks between paving stones and find weeds forcing their way up despite all resistance. Do something to help life on its way. (The possibilities are endless – and fun!)

O Christ Jesus, we know that you are alive and present in all of us. You strengthen us by your own journey to Calvary. We shall not give up!

A prayer from Sierra Leone

December 3   A righteous judge

He shall not judge by what his eyes see,
or decide by what his ears hear;
but with righteousness he shall judge the poor,
and decide with equity for the meek of the earth;
he shall strike the earth with the rod of his mouth,
and with the breath of his lips he shall kill the wicked.
Righteousness shall be the belt around his waist,
and faithfulness the belt around his loins.

Isaiah 11.3–5

Isaiah tells us more about the anticipated Messiah. He focuses on the quality of life he will bring to his people – stability, uncorrupted judgements, improvements to the conditions of poor people. He will not achieve this by military power or wealth – it will be the sheer goodness of what he says ('the breath of his lips') that achieves it. It is no surprise that many who met Jesus were convinced that he was the one.

This description of leadership is a profound challenge to the women and men who lead the world today. It is for these standards of integrity, compassion and commitment to the most vulnerable that we should be praying, voting, campaigning, or perhaps even standing for election. But it is not only the leaders of government who are required to live by such standards; it is also the leaders of business. Decisions that pamper to the logos that 'eyes see' or the music that 'ears hear', but do not give justice to the poor people whose labour creates the products that consumers want, are lamentably short of the standards God demands.

Play a trivial game with a serious point. Quiz yourself or a friend on how many of the world's political leaders you can name. Can you name one from each continent? Two? Three? You can find answers to this quiz at www.cia.gov/cia/publications/chiefs or in *Whitaker's Almanac*. Can you go on to name any chief executives of transnational corporations, some of whom wield as much power as national leaders?

In a wordless prayer, come into God's presence and picture the faces of world leaders who come to mind. Then see in your mind's eye the names of countries whose leaders you cannot (but perhaps should be able to) identify. And lastly picture the logos and labels of corporations the leaders of which are faceless to millions of people whose lives are touched by them. God grant them righteousness and faithfulness.

December 4   Beautiful feet

How beautiful upon the mountains
are the feet of the messenger who announces peace,
who brings good news, who announces salvation,
who says to Zion, 'Your God reigns.'
Listen! Your sentinels lift up their voices,
*   together they sing for joy;*
for in plain sight they see the return of the Lord to Zion.
Break forth together into singing, you ruins of Jerusalem;
for the Lord has comforted his people, he has redeemed Jerusalem.
The Lord has bared his holy arm before the eyes of all the nations;
and all the ends of the earth shall see the salvation of our God.

Isaiah 52.7–10

It has been four days since we first visited Isaiah, warning the government of Judah, eight centuries before Jesus, that if they pursued policies which compromised faith in God, catastrophe would follow. Today we leap forward 200 years and the disaster has happened. A new writer adopting the name and style of Isaiah picks up the same themes of judgement and hope.

The disaster? Judah has been overrun by a superpower and an entire generation of its citizens exiled to become a captive workforce in Babylon. The temple in Jerusalem has been ransacked and God seems lost in the rubble of the temple.

However, Isaiah speaks words of restoration. Not only has God survived the collapse of the temple, he has come with them to Babylon. In fact, so powerful is he that he is reigning everywhere to 'the ends of the earth'. We are so used to this idea that it doesn't surprise us. But to the Jews it was unexpected and longed-for news. They greeted it like the watchmen on a city wall greet a messenger on the mountainous horizon running from the battlefield, desperate and breathless, with the news that the war is over: 'Peace has come. We are on the winning side!'

Every year hundreds of feet run to bring good news to the poor in marathons and fun runs. To find out more about 'Running Water', Christian Aid's fundraising scheme for water projects, visit www.christianaid.org.uk/give/otherway/running.htm or order a pack from one of the addresses at the back of the book.

Lord God, who walked this Earth in Jesus, bless the feet of all who bring good news for the poor – those who journey in dangerous places, those who run the streets to raise money, and those who travel to spread the message. Step alongside them every pace of the way. Amen.

December 5   Come, all you thirsty!

Ho, everyone who thirsts, come to the waters;
and you that have no money, come, buy and eat!
Come, buy wine and milk without money and without price.
Why do you spend your money for that which is not bread,
and your labour for that which does not satisfy?
Listen carefully to me, and eat what is good,
and delight yourselves in rich food.
Incline your ear, and come to me; listen, so that you may live.
I will make with you an everlasting covenant, my steadfast, sure love for David.
See, I made him a witness to the peoples,
a leader and commander for the peoples.

Isaiah 55.1–4

Isaiah is in a marketplace: 'Roll up! Roll up! Come buy and eat!' But it is a bizarre market! Tangible things like bread and water are being given away free, but abstract things cost enormous amounts of money. Isaiah asks a question that he could equally ask of this generation as Christmas shopping gathers pace: 'Why on earth are you spending so much money in a quest for something that will never satisfy you?' He directs us to what is genuinely important – the 'steadfast, sure love' that God first had for King David, and now offers to 'all the peoples'.

These are the true values of God's kingdom: bread and water freely available to those who need it; priceless love for those who are disappointed by what money can buy.

Hawa Amadu has to walk a mile to fetch water for her family in the slum districts of Accra, Ghana. It costs her about forty pence per day. That is about the same as a London family, but of course her income is a fraction of what people earn in England. 'Sometimes I will go without food so my grandchildren can have water' she says. 'Soon we will have to drink air.'

The World Bank has made it a condition of receiving aid that Ghana allows foreign companies to bid for the right to supply water. But what will happen to the profits? Will they be invested in bringing water to poor areas? Or will they go to shareholders in rich countries?

Find out how changes to the rules of international trade could benefit Ghana's poorest people at www.christianaid.org.uk/world/where/wca/ghanap.htm

Lord God, let those who are thirsty come to the waters and find there refreshment – not people who are seeking to profit from their need. Amen.

December 6   Seek the Lord!

See, you shall call nations that you do not know,
and nations that do not know you shall run to you,
because of the Lord your God, the Holy One of Israel,
for he has glorified you.
Seek the Lord while he may be found,
     call upon him while he is near;
let the wicked forsake their way, and the unrighteous their thoughts;
let them return to the Lord, that he may have mercy on them,
and to our God, for he will abundantly pardon.

Isaiah 55.5–7

Isaiah sends his call out. Not just to the forlorn generation that is captive at the time in Babylon. Not just to the Jewish people. The call of God goes beyond that to the people of all nations. He has a plan so glorious that it will attract not only those who have historically worshipped him, but people from all times and places.

The plan of God is to draw near to humanity. To make his presence so obvious that he can easily be found. No wickedness is so great that it will block the path to God. His heart is set on forgiving. No thought is so evil that it will disqualify a person. God has made a decision to have mercy. Seize the opportunity while it is there. Return to the Lord – confessing, receiving, changing.

For a Christian the picture of God drawing near, making himself plain, calling people away from wrongdoing, and offering endless forgiveness is familiar. It is in the person of Jesus that we see him doing all these things.

Learn one of the phrases of today's Bible reading by heart, along with its reference: 'Seek the Lord while he may be found, call upon him while he is near. Isaiah 55:6'. Who knows when the memory of it will direct you to do the right thing at a crucial moment!

O Lord our God, grant us grace to desire you with a whole heart,
so that desiring we may seek and find you;
and so finding you, may love you;
and so loving you may hate those sins which separate us from
     you,
for the sake of Jesus Christ. Amen.

Anselm, Archbishop of Canterbury (1033–1109)

December 7   My ways are higher than yours

As the heavens are higher than the earth,
so are my ways higher than your ways and my thoughts than
    your thoughts.
For as the rain and the snow come down from heaven,
    and do not return there until they have watered the earth,
making it bring forth and sprout,
    giving seed to the sower and bread to the eater,
so shall my word be that goes out from my mouth;
it shall not return to me empty, but it shall accomplish that which I purpose,
and succeed in the thing for which I sent it.

Isaiah 55.9–11

Isaiah writes about God drawing near to humankind. How on Earth is this possible? Come to that, how in heaven is this possible? God is surely unreachably distant from human beings – vast beyond our understanding, holy beyond our imagination.

Isaiah used a metaphor from nature to help his original readers understand. The sky was, for the ancient Jews, so high above them that stretching up to it seemed impossible. And yet the rain tumbled from those unimaginable heights all the way to the ground at their feet. When it arrived it did them great good. Because of it crops could grow and mouths could be fed. In the same way, even though humans could not possibly reach up to God, he was willing to stretch down from an impossible height to bless the Earth. And that too would bring great good.

Well, years have passed and aeroplanes can take us above the clouds, so the power of the metaphor has relaxed. But the grace of God still comes to undeserving people who could do nothing by themselves to attain it. Silent as snow, slow as growth, nourishing as bread, the impossible is still being accomplished – God and human beings are being reconciled.

Look out of the window at the rain. (This is north-west Europe in December – it *must* be raining!) Dwell on what the rain, which we have found no way to control, can do. Bring to mind the hot countries that are desperate for a rainfall such as the one we are blessed with.

Until the rain is gentle to the dried-up land,
Until the people work their farms with dignity,
Until the hungry feed with no fear,
Until, in your kingdom, you accomplish everything
    that you purpose:
My heart cries out to you, Lord God,
for the people of the hot countries. Amen.

December 8   You shall go out with joy

You shall go out in joy, and be led back in peace;
the mountains and the hills before you shall burst into song,
and all the trees of the field shall clap their hands.
Instead of the thorn shall come up the cypress;
instead of the brier shall come up the myrtle;
and it shall be to the Lord for a memorial,
for an everlasting sign that shall not be cut off.

Isaiah 55.12–13

This is the jubilant climax of a song that we have been looking at for four days. It began with an invitation to come (to a marketplace where everything on which life depends is free of charge). It ends with an encouragement to go (into a renewed world, rejoicing in what God has done). Between the two have come a search for God, a discovery of forgiveness, and a change of life to a way of justice. This is the transforming nature of the kingdom of God, and its value is too good to keep to yourself. It is a gift to go out and share.

For whom is this gift? Not just for individuals, nor just for the Jews of the sixth century before Jesus. It is for the whole of creation itself, renewed, with evergreen trees replacing dried-up weeds. In the kingdom of God, people rejoice because they are treated with justice, the Earth is productive because it is tended with care, and the whole created order responds unforgettably to God. Next time you are in a draughty church faithfully praying with just three other people, remember that this is the magnificent vision which you are actually caught up in. And smile!

Seize this enthusiastic moment to revive the living things in and around your home. Tend the pot plants; sweep up the last of the fallen leaves; snip the dead wood out of the garden if you have one; tidy the road outside your door if you haven't. Remember that spring will follow winter, and get ready to enjoy the new life that is to come.

Go forth into the world in peace, looking up to Jesus, who was wounded for your transgressions, and bearing about in your lives the love and joy and peace which are the marks of Jesus on his disciples; and so may the blessing of God, Father, Son and Holy Spirit, be upon you.

A prayer from Northern Uganda, attributed to Canon Alipayo of Acholiland

December 9 Maintain justice

Thus says the Lord:
Maintain justice, and do what is right,
for soon my salvation will come, and my deliverance be revealed.
Happy is the mortal who does this, the one who holds it fast,
who keeps the Sabbath, not profaning it,
    and refrains from doing any evil.

Isaiah 56.1–2

Once again Isaiah looks ahead to the time when God will intervene in human affairs decisively to complete our 'deliverance'. But Isaiah asks the question to which we all want to know the answer: how can we live a happy life in the meantime?

His answer is radical. Happiness is to be found in doing good. Live out now the values that will be established for ever in heaven. Recognize the need for rest and happiness in the middle of work by keeping a 'sabbath', when the needs of humans are seen to be more important than the need for profitable business. Its religious significance and its practical value as a time of refreshment were and are equal.

In Honduras, Christian Aid seeks to work out Isaiah's radical challenge by partnering COMAL (the Alternative Community Marketing Network). Part of their work involves buying goods from farmers at a fair price and distributing them to isolated areas through 500 community shops, where the cost at which they are sold is also fair. They train poor farmers to process their produce (which then attracts a better price) and to improve their technology. Trinidad Sánchez, the director, says: 'COMAL believes that together we can construct an economic alternative for people if we respect the rights of people and practise justice. We need to read and interpret the Bible according to our lives and ask what God wants from people nowadays. Look, judge and act! People need to have hope, and we want to offer them the means to have hope.'

There are now over 350 products in British shops that are certified as fairly traded – from roses to marmalade, from footballs to Christmas puddings. Make a point of buying a new one this month.

Visit www.fairtrade.org.uk/products.htm to get ideas.

During a Bible study by the women's group La Esperanza ('Hope') in Honduras, one of the participants said, 'In the Bible it is written that what God gave us is for us all. I often think how beautiful it would be if everyone understood this.' Dwell on her words for a while, and then pray alongside her for such a world.

December 10   A memorial and a name

Do not let the foreigner joined to the Lord say,
'The Lord will surely separate me from his people';
and do not let the eunuch say, 'I am just a dry tree.'
For thus says the Lord: To the eunuchs who keep my sabbaths,
who choose the things that please me and hold fast my covenant,
I will give, in my house and within my walls,
a monument and a name better than sons and daughters;
I will give them an everlasting name that shall not be cut off . . .
For my house shall be called a house of prayer for all peoples.
Thus says the Lord God, who gathers the outcasts of Israel:
I will gather others to them besides those already gathered.

Isaiah 56.3–5, 7–8

In God's eyes, who is an insider, welcomed and loved? Under the Law of the Hebrew people two groups were specifically excluded – foreigners and eunuchs. To be a member of the community was based on family and land, so a person with no children and a person with no stake in the land were considered to be outside the scope of God's blessing. Isaiah demolishes that exclusive attitude. God is gathering to himself a people so diverse that insiders will continually be taken by surprise and need to make space for newcomers.

I wonder which 'people who cannot have children' today recognize the Church's insiders trying to keep them out, while God is longing to draw them to himself. Is it too provocative to suggest that homosexuals might see themselves in this way?

I wonder which 'foreigners' today experience no welcome from Christian people, while God is longing to create a 'house of prayer for all peoples'. Is it too provocative to find here an umbrella under which different religions and races could shelter while they talk about how to 'choose the things that please God'?

Think of groups across the world who are in some sense 'outcasts' of their communities. Give them your own personal 'monument and name' by writing their names in the margin.

'A memorial and a name' (in Hebrew, Yad Vashem) is what the museum of the holocaust, near Jerusalem, is called. Pray for the government and people of the present-day state of Israel, as they wrestle with their need for their home to be a place of safety but also their need to maintain justice for all who are gathered as their neighbours.

December 11   When the righteous die

The righteous perish, and no one takes it to heart;
the devout are taken away, while no one understands.
For the righteous are taken away from calamity, and they enter
* into peace;*
those who walk uprightly will rest on their couches.

Isaiah 57.1–2

Isaiah's prophecy has been dominated by two great themes – human injustice, and God's perfect plan for the future. These themes run all through the Bible, and occasionally crash into each other in huge questions that echo down the centuries. Here is one of them: Why do good people die young?

Isaiah's answer helps Christians grapple with the question in the light of their belief that life is eternal. Righteous people die unfairly – that is a fact of living in a world where people are oppressive to others. But see their deaths in the context of the glorious plan God has for the world. From the perspective of heaven it will look as if death simply sped their promotion from a place of suffering to a place of peace.

Oscar Romero was born in El Salvador in 1917. It was a country he loved and served as a priest and then a bishop. When he became archbishop in 1977 he used the position to speak out about the conditions of the poor and persecuted. He was prompted by the murder of his friend, the priest Rutilo Grande who had campaigned for better conditions for sugar cane workers, to call the Christians of El Salvador to unite against wrong. He documented abuses of human rights, presented files of information to the pope, and tried to establish the truth in a country where those who drew attention to the gross inequalities simply disappeared. Increasingly at odds with the government and attacked in the press, he was assassinated in March 1980 while celebrating Mass in the chapel of the hospital where he lived. Among his final words were: 'I must tell you, as a Christian, I do not believe in death without resurrection. If I am killed, I shall arise in the Salvadoran people.' If you live near London, visit Westminster Abbey, where his statue is on the west front of the building. If not, see it and read his story at www.westminster-abbey.org/tour/martyrs/6_or.htm

God's reign is already present on our earth in mystery. When the Lord comes, it will be brought to perfection.

Oscar Romero (1917–80)

Pray to glimpse the mystery. Look forward to the perfection.

December 12　Fasting is not enough

Shout out, do not hold back!
Lift up your voice like a trumpet!
Announce to my people their rebellion, to the house of Jacob
　　their sins.
　Yet day after day they seek me and delight to know my ways,
as if they were a nation that practised righteousness
and did not forsake the ordinance of their God;
they ask of me righteous judgements, they delight to draw near to God.
'Why do we fast, but you do not see?
Why humble ourselves, but you do not notice?'

Isaiah 58.1–3

What would happen if we all stopped singing hymns, then all stopped going to church, then all stopped praying altogether? Would the world be any different? Would we notice a difference to our lives? Would God notice? The people who originally heard Isaiah's words had not quite reached that point, but they were muttering something similar. They were fasting religiously, but God did not seem to be doing anything in response. Was God aware that they were seeking him, but deliberately turning a deaf ear? Or was it wrong to assume that worship would bring a reward for those who bothered to do it?

Isaiah attempts to look at the issue from the Lord's point of view. God sees his people ignoring the needs of the poor and allowing injustice to go unchallenged. And his attitude is, what is the point of all their prayer if they haven't yet addressed the basic need of human existence? In a world in which we are all compromised by growing inequality, it shouldn't be the times when we feel God is not listening that take us by surprise. Rather, it is on those occasions on which we are aware of God answering our prayers that his generosity should astonish us.

Pray inwardly, even if you do not enjoy it. It does good, though you feel nothing, see nothing, yes, even though you think you are doing nothing. For when you are dry, empty, sick or weak, at such time is your prayer most pleasing, though you find little enough to enjoy in it. This is true of all believing prayer.

Julian of Norwich, reclusive nun and writer (1342–1413)

Try doing what she suggests.

Look back on times when you have been aware of God answering prayer, or coming close, or inspiring hope, and thank God for such an undeserved blessing.

December 13   Humility

Look, you serve your own interest on your fast-day,
  and oppress all your workers.
Look, you fast only to quarrel and to fight and to strike
  with a wicked fist.
Such fasting as you do today will not make your voice
  heard on high.
Is such the fast that I choose, a day to humble oneself?
Is it to bow down the head like a bulrush, and to lie in sackcloth and ashes?
Will you call this a fast, a day acceptable to the Lord?

Isaiah 58.3–5

The Jews of Isaiah's day felt that God was taking no notice of their worship. But as far as the Lord was concerned, it was just a matter of pleasing themselves. It gave the appearance of religious discipline, but in fact it just produced irritability.

In every generation of worshippers there have been people who have managed to hold together excellence in religious activity and cruelty in attitude. Examples? The church choir that sings 'O praise ye the Lord' with spine-tingling perfection but seethes with dislike of the minister. The person leading prayers who is principally concerned to be better spoken, dressed and appreciated than last week's rival. Anyone whose work on Monday morning falls short of the justice and compassion of the God whom they have worshipped the day before. 'I do not respond for a good reason,' says the Lord. 'You are not talking to me; you are talking to yourselves.'

Look up next Sunday in your diary, or turn ahead in this book to the next day when you expect to go to a church. In the margin write, 'Why am I doing this?' When the day comes, let the reminder prompt you to have a different attitude to worshipping God that day. Put aside the things that annoy you about the building, the people, the choice of music or the style. Instead ask God to accept your praises, however imperfect, and make a better person of you. At the end of the day make another note in your diary of anything that lifted your spirits.

Gracious God, accept our worship:
May the men and women praise you,
May the babes and children praise you,
May the fields and cities praise you,
May the dark and daytime praise you,
May the noise and silence praise you,
May the joy and sorrow praise you.
Let our prayers bring you pleasure,
Gracious God, accept our worship.

December 14   The chains of injustice

Is not this the fast that I choose:
to loose the bonds of injustice, to undo the thongs of the yoke,
to let the oppressed go free, and to break every yoke?
Is it not to share your bread with the hungry,
and bring the homeless poor into your house;
when you see the naked, to cover them,
and not to hide yourself from your own kin?
Then your light shall break forth like the dawn,
and your healing shall spring up quickly;
your vindicator shall go before you,
the glory of the Lord shall be your rearguard.
Then you shall call, and the Lord will answer;
you shall cry for help, and he will say, Here I am.

Isaiah 58.6–9

Isaiah continues to explain what it means to worship God or 'fast' in ways which please him, instead of being self-serving. Today's worshippers have to find appropriate ways to approach something that his original readers could not have imagined – twenty-first-century Christmas. What was once a holy day prepared for by four weeks of fasting and repentance during Advent would be unrecognizable by our Christian ancestors. But Isaiah would have recognized it! Yesterday we read of people who 'serve their own interest on fast days, and oppress their workers'. So perhaps he would have understood the advertising, the greed, and the trinkets and baubles made by workers in the developing world for poor wages and under burdensome conditions – all done in the name of God's festival. Today we see his positive alternative – using the time to tackle injustice, to share with those who are in need, and to seek God.

Christian Aid supports a scheme that allows people to take control of the way they experience Christmas, and enjoy it in a way which makes sense of their faith and their concern for the developing world. 'Alternativity' is an initiative from Scotland. Its subscription newsletter has ideas for decorations that have Christian meaning, feasting without gluttony, and preparations that create space for spiritual reflection. Visit www.alternativity.org.uk to find out more, email alter@christian-aid.org, or write to the Edinburgh office at the address near the back of this book.

In my preparations for Christmas, may light shine forth. In relating to those with whom I celebrate, may healing spring up. In making room for Jesus in the middle of the festivity, may the glory of the Lord go before me and behind me. Amen.

December 15 Away with oppression

If you remove the yoke from among you,
the pointing of the finger, the speaking of evil,
if you offer your food to the hungry
* and satisfy the needs of the afflicted,*
then your light shall rise in the darkness
* and your gloom be like the noonday.*
The Lord will guide you continually, and satisfy your needs in parched places,
and make your bones strong;
and you shall be like a watered garden, like a spring of water, whose waters
  never fail.

Isaiah 58.9–11

How is it possible to make 'light shine in darkness' this Christmas
in a world in which the 'yoke' of oppressive injustice still weighs
heavy on such a large proportion of the world?

In Indian villages the dalit communities sing a song called 'We
are the shadows of the world'. Dalits (sometimes called 'untouch-
ables') are part of a caste system, which means that if you are born in poverty
it is difficult to escape it. So dalit people get the hardest jobs, like cleaning
sewers by hand, are paid the least money, and are scorned.

Thangamani and her husband Chinnakannu were nearly ruined six years ago
when he lost his job for refusing to break the law – a typical example of how
dalit people are treated. The legal costs could have led them into poverty and
hunger. A Christian Aid partner called Activists for Social Alternatives helps
dalit people through training, making them aware of their rights to counter
injustice, and giving small loans to help them begin work so as to restore their
dignity and make their way out of poverty. They have given Thangamani loans
to buy a gem-polishing machine and to have electricty connected to her house
for the first time so that she can operate it.

Dalit Christians understand the message of Christmas to be one
of hope – light to break into darkness and liberation to end
oppression through the birth of Jesus in humble circumstances.
Find out more about dalits at
www.christianaid.org.uk/world/where/asia/dalits/index.htm

God of all, it is so hard to live on the margins –
lonely and forgotten, despised and dependent.
Remember me.
Put back my confidence, restore my dignity, and walk down the
* edges with me.*
Then, knowing you Lord, my light shall rise, rise in hope.

A dalit prayer from the Church of South India

December 16   The light has come

Arise, shine; for your light has come,
and the glory of the Lord has risen upon you.
For darkness shall cover the earth,
*   and thick darkness the peoples;*
but the Lord will arise upon you,
*   and his glory will appear over you.*
Nations shall come to your light, and kings to the brightness of your dawn . . .
Violence shall no more be heard in your land,
devastation or destruction within your borders;
you shall call your walls Salvation, and your gates Praise.
The sun shall no longer be your light by day,
nor for brightness shall the moon give light to you by night;
but the Lord will be your everlasting light, and your God will be your glory.

Isaiah 60.1–3, 18–19

This chapter of Isaiah is flooded with light. Considering the darkness into which the Jews had sunk during exile in Babylon, these are words of remarkable hope. Salvation would come to God's people, but this salvation would embrace all other nations as well. People would be drawn to the God of the Jews not because they were conquered by violence, but because of the attractiveness of his kingdom.

This is a missionary call, but not a chauvinistic vision of Israelite or Christian supremacy in any political sense. The nations come to God gladly because they have seen his light. They see the peace with which God's followers live, and want to share it. They see the justice with which his followers treat the poor, and want to copy it. They see that the presence of God transforms lives, and want to experience it. Darkness is still in the world but the light has been switched on. God's people are called to show how compelling that light is.

Write 'Arise! Shine!' on a piece of card. Put it next to your bed-side light so it catches your attention when you wake up on the dark mornings between now and Christmas. Let it be a challenge to pray that your actions will make you a missionary to the attractiveness of God among the people you meet that day. (And also let it persuade you to get out of bed!)

O Lord Jesus, stretch forth thy wounded hands in blessing over thy people, to heal and to restore, and to draw them to thyself and to one another in love. Amen.

A prayer of the Church Mission Society for the peoples of the Middle East

December 17   The Spirit has anointed me

The spirit of the Lord God is upon me,
because the Lord has anointed me;
he has sent me to bring good news to the oppressed,
to bind up the brokenhearted,
to proclaim liberty to the captives, and release to the prisoners;
to proclaim the year of the Lord's favour, and the day of vengeance of our God.

Isaiah 61.1–2

Here's a puzzle! Who is the 'me' speaking in these verses? He or she is a character who appears many times in Isaiah, and often given the name 'the Servant'.

In one sense it is Isaiah himself, with a message to the captive Jews that the time would come when Jerusalem would be rebuilt and the prisoners go home.

At another level it is the whole historical nation of Israel, commissioned to proclaim that the blessings which were once bestowed on her were now to be extended to all the nations of the world.

Christians have no difficulty identifying these characteristics with Jesus, who quoted Isaiah's words many centuries later in a synagogue in Nazareth and claimed that they referred to him. (He left out the phrase about God's vengeance, as if he knew that the task of seeing justice done would not be completed in him.)

But it is possible that 'me' refers to me! Each Christian has a call to be a servant to the world in all the ways mentioned, filled with the Spirit of God just as Jesus was. Can you recognize yourself in any of those phrases?

Somewhere among your Christmas decorations, place a symbol that you intend to be a servant to the neediest people of the world, just as Jesus was. Perhaps a photograph, a candle, a plant, a verse from the Bible, or an image of Jesus born in humility. Let it remind you between now and Christmas of the true context in which we celebrate.

Brother, let me be your servant, let me be as Christ to you;
Pray that I may have the grace to let you be my servant too.
I will hold the Christ-light for you in the night-time of your fear;
I will hold my hand out to you, speak the peace you long to hear.

Richard Gillard, from the hymn 'Brother, let me be your servant'

December 18   Beauty instead of ashes

[The spirit of the Lord God is upon me,]
to comfort all who mourn;
to provide for those who mourn in Zion –
to give them a garland instead of ashes,
the oil of gladness instead of mourning,
the mantle of praise instead of a faint spirit.
They will be called oaks of righteousness,
the planting of the Lord, to display his glory.
They shall build up the ancient ruins,
they shall raise up the former devastations.

Isaiah 61.2–4

'I read in a book that a man called Christ went about doing good. It is very disconcerting that I am so easily satisfied with just going about.' This is a meditation of Toyohiko Kagawa, the twentieth-century Japanese reformer whose experience of being comforted when bereaved at an early age led him first to convert to Christianity, then to work among poor shipbuilders, and then to campaign passionately against the waste of life that came with war. His ministry took him from poverty (he lived for twelve years in a shed two metres square in the slums of Kobe) to high-ranking government approval, arrest, and finally international recognition.

To go about doing good among the poor and those who mourn requires more than just being a cheery companion. In these circumstances change does not come about quickly, but it can come steadily. It is like the slow maturing of an oak tree or the reconstruction of a ruined city. Are you prepared to be that kind of lifelong servant?

Christmas is often a difficult time for people who mourn. Loneliness can be a heavy burden, but so can company! Think about people you know who will be alone this Christmas. Try to be creative about what would give them gladness instead of mourning – a letter, a visit, an invitation, company for a visit to church, or being left alone. In the spirit of the Bible verses, use your imagination to offer them what they would prefer, not merely what you would like in the circumstances.

God's blessing upon all who enter the world this day,
and upon all who depart it.
God's peace upon all who begin to celebrate tonight,
and upon all who begin to grieve.
God prosper all who bring laughter in his name this Christmas,
and all who bring comfort. Amen.

December 19   Heaven and earth renewed

I am about to create new heavens and a new earth;
the former things shall not be remembered or come to mind.
But be glad and rejoice for ever in what I am creating;
for I am about to create Jerusalem as a joy,
    and its people as a delight.
I will rejoice in Jerusalem, and delight in my people;
no more shall the sound of weeping be heard in it, or the cry of distress.

Isaiah 65.17–19

Forgetting is not easy. In the theological college of Sri Lanka I met students training to lead churches in a country recovering from two decades of civil war. Tamils and Sinhalese had been fighting for the whole of their lives. Gnanarajah Manozuban said to me, 'We are separated by language and divisions. But every one of us is human, so I want to see God's image in your face.'

He told me his story: 'When I was thirteen I was hit by a shell. May I show you?' He lifted his shirt. There was a hole three centimetres deep in his hip. 'My mother was weeping. Our neighbours said, "Where is your God now?" The Red Cross took me to hospital. The doctor said I would not be able to walk for a year. But I was determined. I walked again after twenty-two days. Then I knew where my God was. That is what leads me to be training for ordination. It is not enough for me to say thank you to God with my prayers and thoughts; I need to say thank you with my whole life.

'I want to say to the man who did this to me, "You must never do this again. I want to be a Christian who forgives and forgets. I know that I have forgiven you. If you never do it again I will forget too, but I find forgetting harder."'

Christian Aid works in Sri Lanka building peace in the areas most painfully affected by the war, and strengthening the rights of poorly paid workers on the tea plantations. Find out more at www.christianaid.org.uk/world/where/asia/srilankp.htm

It is possible that today's Bible reading has stirred in your mind old disappointments or hurts that you would rather not have recalled. Dwelling on them today will not do you any good! Instead, positively thank God that they have a strict 'Use by' date, and that in heaven their hold over you will be gone for good.

December 20   The young and the old

No more shall there be in it an infant that lives but a few days,
or an old person who does not live out a lifetime;
for one who dies at a hundred years will be considered a youth,
and one who falls short of a hundred will be considered accursed.
They shall build houses and inhabit them;
they shall plant vineyards and eat their fruit.
They shall not build and another inhabit; they shall not plant and another eat;
for like the days of a tree shall the days of my people be,
and my chosen shall long enjoy the work of their hands.

Isaiah 65.20–22

Isaiah's vision of the future continues. The blessings of God's kingdom involve complete fulfilment:

* Human life is fulfilled, with children safely surviving childbirth and thriving in infancy.
* Human potential is fulfilled, with all people living healthily to a good age.
* Human work is fulfilled, with a society stable and free from the catastrophes that demotivate people from building permanent houses or planting crops – war, drought and other calamities that force people to leave their homes.

In Ghana, ninety-seven children out of every thousand die before they reach their fifth birthday; in the UK it is seven. In Ghana the average life expectancy is sixty years; in the UK it is seventy-seven. Why the difference? Among other things it is related to the fact that in the UK there are 167 doctors for every 100,000 people; in Ghana there are four. Our generation, which has the capability of making Isaiah's vision a present reality, is fulfilling it in a very unequal way.

UNICEF statistics that give a comparison of how children thrive country by country and decade by decade can be found at www.childinfo.org/cmr/revis/db2.htm. Look them up so that you can rejoice in what is being achieved as well as praying for the huge challenge that remains.

Lord God, forgive this world,
which has allowed its children to die of curable diseases;
to experience their growing years as a time of burden instead of
*   joy;*
to bear the weight of the wickedness of adults.
And in your mercy, grant us a will to change it. Amen.

December 21   The wolf and the lamb

They shall not labour in vain, or bear children for calamity;
for they shall be offspring blessed by the Lord –
and their descendants as well.
Before they call I will answer,
*   while they are yet speaking I will hear.*
The wolf and the lamb shall feed together,
the lion shall eat straw like the ox; but the serpent – its food shall be dust!
They shall not hurt or destroy on all my holy mountain, says the Lord.

Isaiah 65.23–25

Isaiah's vision for the kingdom that God is building – past, present and future – comes to a climax. He continues to spell out what it means to be completely fulfilled in God:

- Human family is fulfilled – an end to the fear that nags at every mother about what the future will hold for the child she has borne.
- Human intimacy with God will be fulfilled – a closeness to God that allows him to hear every whisper.
- Human oneness with the created order will be fulfilled – the environment will never again be a threat, nor will humans be a threat to the environment.

These are features of the intervention of our gracious God into the life of the planet. While we wait for the advent of this great day, Christians are called to be beacons – shining in today's world by demonstrating that these things are possible, illuminating the path to the world to come where God will establish these things once and for all.

With only a few days to go before Christmas, Christian symbols have appeared all over the country. Among the Christmas lights showing holly and snowmen you will catch sight of an occasional angel (if you look hard enough). Between the Santas and the fairy tales in shop windows you will see an occasional manger (if you are not moving too fast). This year, treat these as blessings that have dropped on to our streets to point the way to the great truths of Christmas. Try to enjoy the whole lot – even the cheesy parts!

For the sake of the past, make me a listener who learns;
For the sake of the present, make me a doer who helps;
For the sake of the future, make me a guide who points the way;
Until, in the fullness of time, all human souls come to the Light.
Amen.

December 22   Gabriel

The angel Gabriel was sent by God to a town in Galilee called Nazareth, to a virgin engaged to a man whose name was Joseph, of the house of David. The virgin's name was Mary. And he came to her and said, 'Greetings, favoured one! The Lord is with you.' But she was much perplexed by his words and pondered what sort of greeting this might be. The angel said to her, 'Do not be afraid, Mary, for you have found favour with God. And now, you will conceive in your womb and bear a son, and you will name him Jesus. He will be great, and will be called the Son of the Most High, and the Lord God will give to him the throne of his ancestor David. He will reign over the house of Jacob for ever, and of his kingdom there will be no end.'

Luke 1.26–33

The salvation of humankind begins with a girl of about twelve. She lives in a town that is the butt of jokes in a country that is occupied by an enemy force. She is in the process of moving from the control of her father to the control of a husband. And she is scared stiff.

The salvation of humankind ends with a great king taking control of a perfect kingdom that will never end, under the glorious control of God.

We identify with the beginning of salvation very closely, because we see many vulnerable people like Mary in the world today. We find it harder to recognize the triumphant end. However, it is Mary who unexpectedly found affirmation of her value in God's sight. When we treat those in the world who are like her with the conviction that they too are 'favoured by God', our confidence in the kingdom to come grows because we catch sight of the possibilities that it brings.

Every time you see the image of an angel today (unavoidable on cards and Christmas trees) recall the message brought to Mary. Don't forget that whenever angels arrived in the Bible their appearance was scary, not charming! But their message of the coming kingdom is not charming either – it is a gritty reality that involves eradicating poverty and bringing war to an end.

Angels from the realms of glory,
*   wing your flight o'er all the earth,*
Ye who sang creation's story
*   now proclaim Messiah's birth:*
Come and worship Christ, the newborn King.

James Montgomery (1771–1854)

December 23   The servant of the Lord

Mary said to the angel, 'How can this be, since I am a virgin?' The angel said to her, 'The Holy Spirit will come upon you, and the power of the Most High will overshadow you; therefore the child to be born will be holy; he will be called Son of God. And now, your relative Elizabeth in her old age has also conceived a son; and this is the sixth month for her who was said to be barren. For nothing will be impossible with God.' Then Mary said, 'Here am I, the servant of the Lord; let it be with me according to your word.'

Luke 1.34–38

Here is a message for dark evenings when the news is full of atrocities, and peace seems an impossible dream: 'Nothing will be impossible with God'.

And a message for those who have committed themselves to bring good news for poor people, but feel overwhelmed by the scale of the task: 'Nothing will be impossible with God'.

And a message for those who look ahead to Christmas celebrations that will be overshadowed by anxiety or sadness: 'Nothing will be impossible with God'.

Mary had everything to lose. Bearing an illegitimate child meant she was confronted with the certainty of losing her reputation and her future husband, the likelihood of being put out into beggary, the possibility of being executed if the religious authorities were so inclined. Under those circumstances it is staggering that someone should have the reckless faith to say, 'Here I am, the servant of the Lord.' But if we wish to open ourselves to the discovery that nothing will be impossible with God, that is the only possible starting place.

It is possible that over the next few days you will be called on to be a servant to many people – willingly or not. Take a moment to think through the days ahead and how you will make the most of them. Where will you make time to be a servant to God? And a servant to the wider world? And a servant to yourself?

Come close to me, Most High God, this Christmas. How dare I ask something so impossible? Because in Jesus you have been born into all the hurts and joys of human life. To a God who has graced the human form with such undeserved dignity what can I say? Here I am, the servant of the Lord.

December 24   Magnificat!

*Mary said, 'My soul magnifies the Lord, and my spirit rejoices
     in God my Saviour,
for he has looked with favour on the lowliness of his servant.
Surely, from now on all generations will call me blessed;
for the Mighty One has done great things for me,
     and holy is his name.
His mercy is for those who fear him from generation to generation.
He has shown strength with his arm;
he has scattered the proud in the thoughts of their hearts.
He has brought down the powerful from their thrones, and lifted up the lowly;
he has filled the hungry with good things, and sent the rich away empty.
He has helped his servant Israel, in remembrance of his mercy,
according to the promise he made to our ancestors,
to Abraham and to his descendants forever.'*

Luke 1.46–55

Mary, well acquainted with songs of praise from the Old
Testament, bursts out singing because suddenly the words have
changed from abstract theories to realities. She has discovered
that:

- God is merciful – perhaps this sprang from the fact that her cousin Elizabeth
  believed her story and did not turn her back on a pregnant, but unmarried,
  relative.
- God has a special concern for the humble and poor – he had bypassed the
  aristocracy and chosen her.
- God keeps his promises – no matter what past unfaithfulness has marked a
  person's life, God remains loyal year after year.

May the experience of a little girl who bubbled up with joy at the realization
that God was at work – personally, globally, eternally – allow you to greet
tomorrow morning with an excitement that you had forgotten was possible.

Find a candle and put it now in the quietest room in the house,
wherever you happen to be spending Christmas. At some point
during tomorrow, sneak away from the noise, go to the room and
light the candle. Make this a moment that counts between you
and Jesus. There is no need for words, but be thankful that there
is a glorious meaning to Christmas that much of the world is unaware of. Then
blow out the candle, go back and eat another mince pie, and don't tell anyone
what you have done!

*Light of the World, who in the secret of the night came down
from heaven to shine among the poor, kindle a flame of compassion in my heart that can never be extinguished. Amen.*

December 25   The birth of Jesus

A decree went out from Emperor Augustus that all the world should be registered. This was the first registration and was taken while Quirinius was governor of Syria. All went to their own towns to be registered. Joseph also went from the town of Nazareth in Galilee to Judea, to the city of David called Bethlehem, because he was descended from the house and family of David. He went to be registered with Mary, to whom he was engaged and who was expecting a child. While they were there, the time came for her to deliver her child. And she gave birth to her firstborn son and wrapped him in bands of cloth, and laid him in a manger, because there was no place for them in the inn.

Luke 2.1–7

- So here it is, merry Christmas, everybody's having fun!
- So this is Christmas, and what have you done? Another year over and a new one begun.
- Feed the world! Let them know it's Christmas time.
- Oh I wish it could be Christmas every day.
- Until then we'll have to muddle through somehow, so have yourself a merry little Christmas now.
- Joy to the world, the Lord has come; let Earth receive her king.
- A beautiful sight, I'm happy tonight, walking in a winter wonderland.
- Although it's been said many times, many ways: merry Christmas to you!

Listen to every Christmas song and carol as if you had never heard it before!

I lift my grateful heart to the Christ child,
who set aside the riches of heaven
to be born in a stable, helpless and among strangers.
I lift my heartfelt prayers to the Christ child,
from the comfort of my home this Christmas,
for the children growing up in poverty,
    without the education and care they need.
I lift my celebrating voice to the Christ child,
thankful for the food and the colour and excitement,
and wanting the good things I enjoy to be shared fairly throughout the world.
I lift my hopes and fears to the Christ child,
longing for a world in which violence is at an end,
and pleading for those who have known nothing but brutality all their lives.
To the Christ child of Bethlehem I pray:
out of injustice, out of warfare, out of fear,
    lift every human heart this Christmas.

December 26   Shepherds and angels

There were shepherds living in the fields, keeping watch over their flock by night. Then an angel of the Lord stood before them, and the glory of the Lord shone around them, and they were terrified. But the angel said to them, 'Do not be afraid; for see – I am bringing you good news of great joy for all the people: to you is born this day in the city of David a Saviour, who is the Messiah, the Lord. This will be a sign for you: you will find a child wrapped in bands of cloth and lying in a manger.' And suddenly there was with the angel a multitude of the heavenly host, praising God and saying,

'Glory to God in the highest heaven,
and on earth peace among those whom he favours!'

Luke 2.8–14

The Messiah's coming was not announced in the palace, nor the temple. It was made known to . . . well . . . to riff-raff! That was the reputation of hireling shepherds. Into the night of their tired-ness, loneliness and struggle, an angel comes and speaks joy.

We are so unaccustomed to joy! The truth is that most of life is lacklustre – we have more Boxing Days than Christmas Days. Joy breaks through from time to time in music, in sex, in success, in love. Or, as here, in new birth.

Surely God was giving a 'sign' that points us to the secret of joy. He had emptied himself in complete self-giving, an act so extraordinary that its glory sparked out to anyone awake enough to see it. The subsequent testimony of millions of Christians is that there is lasting joy to be found in living for others. It is something that cannot be deduced by logic; it can only be discovered by experience.

Extend your Christmas celebrations outside the group with whom you expected to spend the day – make a phone call, pre-pare a gift, send an invitation, devise a plan, take someone by surprise. Find a simple way to bring momentary joy into someone's life!

O Lord Christ, help us to maintain ourselves in simplicity and in joy – the joy of the merciful, the joy of brotherly love. Grant that, renouncing henceforth all thought of looking back, and joyful with infinite gratitude, we may never fear to precede the dawn, to praise and bless and sing to Christ our Lord.

From the Rule of Taizé, the Christian community in France

December 27   In the presence of Jesus

When the angels had left them and gone into heaven, the shepherds said to one another, 'Let us go now to Bethlehem and see this thing that has taken place, which the Lord has made known to us.' So they went with haste and found Mary and Joseph, and the child lying in the manger. When they saw this, they made known what had been told them about this child; and all who heard it were amazed at what the shepherds told them. But Mary treasured all these words and pondered them in her heart. The shepherds returned, glorifying and praising God for all they had heard and seen, as it had been told them.

Luke 2.15–20

The meeting between the shepherds and Jesus may have been over in minutes, but three powerful and enduring things remained:

- The shepherds went back to their humdrum job, but glorifying and praising – the truths of Christmas are so rich because they remind us of the possibility of glory in this sometimes dispiriting world.
- Everyone who heard the shepherds' account of what had happened was amazed – it encourages us to create a neighbourhood that is alive with the rumour of God at work.
- Mary turned the memories over in her heart – it was too much to take in overnight, and the significance of Christmas is something for us to dwell on too. And treasure!

Take a small piece of tinsel or and put it somewhere that you will see it every day throughout the coming year – in your purse, by the fridge, attached to the television remote control. As you see it from day to day let it remind you that the frivolous parts of Christmas are coming to an end, but the truth of what God has done for us by visiting the planet is enduring and able to transform mundane experiences.

He is little and weak that you may be great and strong. He is bound in swaddling clothes that you may be unbound from the fetters of death. He is on earth that you may be in heaven.

Words of Ambrose (340–97), Bishop of Milan. Dwell on them, like Mary. Praise God for them, like the shepherds. Perhaps let them prompt you to talk to others about the child in the manger.

December 28 Simeon

There was a man in Jerusalem whose name was Simeon; this man was righteous and devout, looking forward to the consolation of Israel, and the Holy Spirit rested on him. It had been revealed to him by the Holy Spirit that he would not see death before he had seen the Lord's Messiah. Guided by the Spirit, Simeon came into the temple; and when the parents brought in the child Jesus, to do for him what was customary under the law, Simeon took him in his arms and praised God, saying,

'Master, now you are dismissing your servant in peace,
according to your word;
for my eyes have seen your salvation,
which you have prepared in the presence of all peoples,
a light for revelation to the Gentiles and for glory to your people Israel.'

And the child's father and mother were amazed at what was being said about him.

Luke 2.25–33

The insight of Simeon was remarkable. He saw that the glory of God had returned to the temple, and it was named Jesus. He recognized the uniqueness of Jesus among all the boys brought to the temple for circumcision. But he also saw past the nationalistic blinkers of his day to foresee that Jesus would fulfil Isaiah's vision for a world with no religious divisions, where the salvation of God was revealed to Jews and Gentiles alike. With that knowledge, his thoughts were settled on consolation and on peace.

At this time of year, we recall the fact that, at the end of 2004, a tsunami in the Indian Ocean robbed many thousands of people of their lives, families and livelihoods. Its devastation gave us a glimpse of how small the globe now seems, bringing misery to the lives of both wealthy people and poor people. But the unity of purpose with which people responded, bringing together people of different religions and nationalities, also gives us a glimpse of the potential for goodness in a world in which every part connects with every other part. Take an appropriate action to remember those who work to bring consolation and peace where the scars remain – visible or invisible.

May the Lord bless you with all good and keep you from all evil;
may he give light to your heart with loving wisdom,
and be gracious to you with eternal knowledge;
may he lift up his loving countenance upon you for eternal
peace. Amen.

From the Dead Sea Scrolls

December 29　Magi

In the time of King Herod, after Jesus was born in Bethlehem of Judea, wise men from the East came to Jerusalem, asking, 'Where is the child who has been born king of the Jews? For we observed his star at its rising, and have come to pay him homage.' When King Herod heard this, he was frightened, and all Jerusalem with him; and calling together all the chief priests and scribes of the people, he inquired of them where the Messiah was to be born. They told him, 'In Bethlehem of Judea; for so it has been written by the prophet:
"And you, Bethlehem, in the land of Judah,
are by no means least among the rulers of Judah;
for from you shall come a ruler who is to shepherd my people Israel."'

Matthew 2.1–6

So here it is, the legend of the five kings!

Three of them who weren't! The magi were probably astrologers from Iran. The tradition that they were kings started six centuries later and came from a phrase of Isaiah's (the passage we read on 16 December), and the tradition that there were three came from . . . who knows! All of which distracts from the real significance – that they were Gentiles, not Jews. Salvation was dawning for the entire world.

The one who was but shouldn't have been! Herod had been put on the throne as nominal 'king of the Jews' by the Roman authorities because he came from a family that had been loyal to whoever happened to be in charge. No wonder he was scared when someone else claimed the title.

And an infant growing up out of the public gaze seven miles from Jerusalem. In the kingdom of God power does not depend on who holds high office, or who the public has decided to make great. It takes a wise man (or woman) to notice that!

Newspapers are about to honour the men or women of the year, and knighthoods will be announced tomorrow. Decide who, regardless of the hype, you think actually deserves to be acclaimed for their unrecognized work.

O God, who by a star guided the wise men to the worship of your Son, we pray that you will lead to yourself the wise and great of every land, that unto you every knee may bow, and every thought be brought into captivity; through Jesus Christ our Lord.

From the Book of Common Worship of the Church of South India

December 30   Gold, frankincense and myrrh

Herod secretly called for the wise men and learned from them the exact time when the star had appeared. Then he sent them to Bethlehem, saying, 'Go and search diligently for the child; and when you have found him, bring me word so that I may also go and pay him homage.' When they had heard the king, they set out; and there, ahead of them, went the star that they had seen at its rising, until it stopped over the place where the child was. When they saw that the star had stopped, they were overwhelmed with joy. On entering the house, they saw the child with Mary his mother; and they knelt down and paid him homage. Then, opening their treasure chests, they offered him gifts of gold, frankincense, and myrrh.

Matthew 2.7–11

Many gifts have changed hands in the past few days: a gift that speaks of deep love, a gift that eases a guilty conscience, a gift that stops a child nagging, a gift that allows a teenager some self-respect among his friends, a gift that is actually what you wanted yourself, a gift that says a heartfelt 'Thank you'. What were the 'invisible labels' on the gifts you gave and received?

Christian tradition sees the magi's gifts as symbolic – royalty, religion, death. Highly likely! But it is also possible that the wise men just made a huge blunder. Anticipating greeting the King of the Jews in a palace, they had brought presents appropriate for a state occasion. They may have fumbled with embarrassment in front of a family who patently had more basic needs: 'If only we had brought something more suitable – a loaf of bread perhaps, or a flask of wine.'

If you would like to make a gift to the world's poorest people to mark the turning of another year, send a cheque to the address at the back of this book, or use a credit card at www.christianaid.org.uk/give/secure/general.htm. But before you do so, think about the 'invisible label'. Guilt or ostentation are not the best motives. But if it is to honour Jesus' presence among the poor, it would be most welcome.

What can I give him, poor as I am?
If I were a shepherd I would bring a lamb;
If I were a wise man I would do my part –
Yet what I can I give him, give my heart.

Christina Rossetti (1830–94)

December 31 Young Jesus

The child [Jesus] grew and became strong, filled with wisdom; and the favour of God was upon him. Now every year his parents went to Jerusalem for the festival of the Passover. And when he was twelve years old, they went up as usual for the festival. When the festival was ended and they started to return, the boy Jesus stayed behind in Jerusalem, but his parents did not know it . . . When they did not find him, they returned to Jerusalem to search for him. After three days they found him in the temple, sitting among the teachers, listening to them and asking them questions. And all who heard him were amazed at his understanding and his answers. When his parents saw him they were astonished; and his mother said to him, 'Child, why have you treated us like this? Look, your father and I have been searching for you in great anxiety.' He said to them, 'Why were you searching for me? Did you not know that I must be in my Father's house?' But they did not understand what he said to them. Then he went down with them and came to Nazareth, and was obedient to them. His mother treasured all these things in her heart.

Luke 2.41–43, 45–51

This sole episode from Jesus' youth shows him exploring what it means to call God 'Father'. He was discovering that sometimes it would lead him into obedience and sometimes into defiance. With a typical adolescent's desire to be independent beyond his years, he was divided between a quiet life of conformity and the high-risk life to which God was calling him. He was also discovering that it would be expressed in religious activity, but also in the workaday experience of living, learning and growing. It was not just in the temple that people found his personality charming and his behaviour compelling; it was in the local streets.

At the end of a year during which you have supported Christian Aid, take a moment to think about what it will mean to call God 'Father' next year. Christian Aid will be there all year to help you pray, act and give in a way which makes sense of the priorities of the kingdom of God.

God bless the rich; God bless the poor;
God bless human life in all its glorious diversity;
God bless all who believe in life before death,
now and for every joyous moment of eternity.

About Christian Aid

The essential purpose of Christian Aid is to expose the scandal of poverty, to help in practical ways to root it out from the world, and to challenge and change the systems which favour the rich and powerful over the poor and marginalized.

We contribute our passion and experience to the broad movement of people who use their faith, talents and energies to fight for a better life for all.

In supporting this movement, we serve the churches in Britain and Ireland. We are driven by the gospel of good news to the poor, and inspired by the vision of a new Earth where all people can live in justice, peace and plenty.

Christian Aid's work is founded on Christian faith, inspired by hope, and acts to change an unjust world through charity – a practical love and care for our neighbours across five continents.

Some of the ways to contact Christian Aid

England

PO Box 100,
London,
SE1 7RT.
020 7620 4444

Scotland

PO Box 11,
Edinburgh,
EH1 1EL.
0131 220 1254

Northern Ireland

PO Box 150,
Belfast,
BT9 6AE.
028 9038 1204

Wales

P O Box 6055,
Cardiff,
CF15 5AA.
029 2084 4646

Republic of Ireland

17 Clanwilliam Terrace,
Dublin 2,
01 611 0 801

Websites

www.christianaid.org.uk
www.christian-aid.ie

Acknowledgments

The author and publisher are grateful to the following for permission to reproduce material under copyright. Every effort has been made to trace copyright ownership, and the publisher would be grateful to be informed of any omissions.

Brother Roger of Taizé, for 'Lord Christ you remain', © Ateliers et Presses de Taizé, 71250 Taizé Community, France.

John Carden, 'Jesus of the deep forest', in *A Procession of Prayers*, Cassell, 1998, permission sought.

Churches Together in England, for 'Thank you Almighty Lord', from *Friends Again*, CTE, 2003.

CLC Publications, for 'It is not far' and 'Holy Spirit, think through me', from *Mountain Breezes: The Collected Poems of Amy Carmichael*, Fort Washington PA, CLC Publications, 1999.

Margaret Cropper, 'Jesus Christ, God', in *Draw Near*, SPCK, permission sought.

Darton, Longman and Todd, for 'May your bounty' from *The Desert Is Fertile* and 'No sound as yet' from *A Thousand Reasons for Living*, Helder Camara, Darton, Longman and Todd, 1987.

Richard Gillard, 'Brother let me be your servant', in *Hymns Ancient & Modern*, Hymns Ancient & Modern, 2000.

Frank Houghton, 'Thou who was rich beyond all splendour', in *Hymns Ancient & Modern*, Hymns Ancient & Modern, 2000.

Martin John Nicholls, for 'More than land', and 'Hunger for Justice' from the album *Out of the Blue*, 2004.

H. A. Krishna Pillai, 'Let my heart', *Iratcaniya Yattirikam*, The Institute of Asian Studies.

Timothy Dudley Smith, for 'My Father I thank you', in *Someone Who Beckons*, Inter-Varsity Press, 1978.

Index of Bible References

1 September	Psalm 48.8–14	Secure in Zion
25 October	Psalm 72.1–4	Just government
26 October	Psalm 72.5–11	Let righteousness flourish
27 October	Psalm 72.12–14	A king who rescues the poor
28 October	Psalm 72.15–19	Long live the king
9 January	Psalm 104.1, 10–15	A delicate balance
10 January	Psalm 104.24–31	Circle of life
24 August	Psalm 105.1–7	Remember God's works
25 August	Psalm 105.8–15	Abraham
26 August	Psalm 105.16–22	Joseph
27 August	Psalm 105.23–27	Slaves
28 August	Psalm 105.28–29, 32–36	Moses
29 August	Psalm 105.37–41	The exodus
30 August	Psalm 105.42–45	God's people rejoice
29 October	Psalm 122.1–5	The house of the Lord
30 October	Psalm 122.6–9	Pray for the peace of Jerusalem
31 October	Psalm 123.1–4	Have mercy
4 September	Psalm 126.1–6	Returning to Jerusalem
1 November	Psalm 131.1–3	Humble content
5 September	Psalm 133.1–3	Living in unity
2 September	Psalm 137.1–4	Exile in Babylon
3 September	Psalm 137.5–9	Revenge
2 November	Psalm 146.1–6	Trust in the Lord
3 November	Psalm 146.7–10	Upholding the oppressed
4 November	Psalm 150.1–6	Praise the Lord!

Proverbs

13 June	Proverbs 1.1–9	How to be wise
14 June	Proverbs 3.1–4	Love and faithfulness
15 June	Proverbs 3.5–8	Trusting God
16 June	Proverbs 3.9, 10, 13–18	Setting priorities
17 June	Proverbs 11.24–28	Generosity
18 June	Proverbs 12.9–11	Animals
19 June	Proverbs 13.11–12	Little by little
20 June	Proverbs 14.20–22	Needy neighbours
21 June	Proverbs 17.1–6; 19.18–20	Learning to work
22 June	Proverbs 20.10–11, 14	Shopping
23 June	Proverbs 23.10–11	Living on the land
24 June	Proverbs 24.23–29	Justice for all
25 June	Proverbs 24.30–34; 26.13–16	Hard work
26 June	Proverbs 30.7–9	Too rich or too poor?
27 June	Proverbs 31.1–5	Responsible government
28 June	Proverbs 31.6–9	Speaking up for the voiceless
29 June	Proverbs 31.10–17	A working woman
30 June	Proverbs 31.18–20, 29–31	A just reward

Isaiah

| 30 November | Isaiah 9.1–3 | Light in darkness (Advent Sunday 08) |